HOUSEHOLD GODS

HOUSEHOLD GODS

THE BRITISH AND THEIR POSSESSIONS

DEBORAH COHEN

YALE UNIVERSITY PRESS
NEW HAVEN AND LONDON

For information about this and other Yale University Press publications, please contact:
U.S. Office:sales.press@yale.edu   yalebooks.com
Europe Office:sales@yaleup.co.uk   www.yaleup.co.uk

Set in Minion by J&L Composition, Filey, North Yorkshire
Printed in China through Worldprint

Library of Congress Cataloging-in-Publication Data
Cohen, Deborah, 1968–
    Household gods : the British and their possessions / Deborah Cohen.
       p. cm.
    Includes bibliographical references and index.
    ISBN 0–300–11213–0 (alk. paper)
    1. Great Britain—Social life and customs—19th century. 2. Great Britain—Social life and customs—1918–1945. 3. Decorative arts—Great Britain—History—19th century. 4. Decorative arts—Great Britain—History—20th century. 5. Social values—Great Britain. 6. Materialism—Great Britain. 7. Great Britain—Commerce—Social aspects. 8. Retail trade—Great Britain. I. Title.
DA533.C64 2006
941.081—dc22
                                                                          2006012782

A catalogue record for this book is available from the British Library

10 9 8 7 6 5 4 3 2 1

CONTENTS

ACKNOWLEDGEMENTS

I am very grateful to the institutions that have funded my research. A summer grant from the National Endowment for the Humanities supported exploratory research for the project. At a crucial stage in my work, a year at the National Humanities Center made all of the difference. I would like to thank Kent Mullikin, Eliza Robertson, Jean Houston, and Lois Whittington for their encouragement and assistance. My fellow fellows, especially the members of the 'Thinking Things' discussion group – Nick Frankel, Michael Kwass, Mark Parker, and John Plotz – demonstrated the virtues of interdisciplinarity in action; Tom and Kathy Brady made North Carolina feel like home. A grant from the Salomon research fund at Brown allowed me to finish archival research; a fellowship from the Howard Foundation helped me to complete the manuscript.

Archivists, curators and librarians in Britain, Canada, and the United States smoothed the path of my research. Many thanks to the curatorial staff of the Geffrye Museum (particularly Katharine Haslam and Eleanor John) and to Susan Edwards of the Glamorgan Record Office. David and Jane Coke-Steel gave me access to valuable family papers, and extended very welcome hospitality. Audiences at the North American Conference on British Studies, the North American Victorian Studies Association, Birmingham University, Cambridge University, the University of Cincinnati, the National Humanities Center, Rice University, the Royal College of Art, Stanford, and the University of Southern California have improved my work through their trenchant criticism. I would like especially to thank Leora Auslander, Francesca Carnevali, Becky Conekin, Margot Finn, Matthew Hilton, Lawrence Klein, Lara Kriegel, Thad Logan, Sharon Marcus, Frank Mort, Stefan Muthesius, Maura O'Connor, Michael Saler, Peter Stansky, John Styles, Adam Tooze, Martin Wiener, and Emma Winter for their helpful comments on papers. Jeremy Aynsley and the AHRB Centre for the Study of the Domestic Interior provided a scholarly home for this project. The German Historical Institute (Washington, DC) funded a workshop on 'Art and Society in the Long Nineteenth Century' that Peter Mandler and I organized. The chance to teach a summer DuPont seminar at the National Humanities Center allowed me to rethink the field of material culture with faculty colleagues.

A number of friends and colleagues have read work in progress: Jordanna Bailkin, Sarah Gleason, Jane Hamlett, Eleanor John, Tom Laqueur, Maud Mandel, Tara Nummedal, Cara Robertson, Anne Rush, Vanessa Schwartz (who first suggested that I turn my flea-market habit into a book), Julia Stephens and Karin Wulf; I thank them heartily for their perceptive comments. Colleagues at Brown have entered willingly into many a discussion about aesthetic matters; I am especially grateful to Tom Gleason and Amy Remensnyder, whose meticulous reading of the entire manuscript spurred me to finish it. Peter Mandler has encouraged this project from its earliest days. His critiques have strengthened the book's arguments; his insights have opened up new subjects. I am deeply indebted to his generous intellect.

Yale University Press' anonymous readers provided important direction at a critical stage. Robert Baldock and Adam Freudenheim, my two editors at Yale, have been all that an author could wish for. Heartfelt thanks, too, to Yale's expert production team: Candida Brazil, Beth Humphries and Stephen Kent. Clare Alexander, my agent, has cheered this book on with her keen eye for narrative and unstinting kindness. Four research assistants have contributed valuable insights: Christopher Brick, Alexis Goodin, Jessica Kremen, and Abigail Newman; I thank the UTRA program at Brown for funds to hire Kremen and Newman. To Louis Cohen, I owe an early acquaintance with the delights of the flea market. Every page of this book has profited from Tom Silfen's critical acumen and unflagging enthusiasm. His partnership has made this work a pleasure.

INTRODUCTION
THE BRITISH AT HOME

The Reverend Mark Rylands looked around Britain's Sunday landscape and concluded that his fellow citizens had lost their way. Everywhere he turned in the spring of 2002 it seemed that church pews were empty, while DIY superstores hummed with activity. The cult of home improvement had 'tempted' people away from traditional religion: 'Travelling around the parishes you see more people worshipping at car-boot sales and DIY stores than anywhere else.'[1] To the forty-year-old Somerset vicar, the nation seemed at a turning-point. For the majority of Britons, Sunday no longer meant church and worship, but leisure time to devote to house and garden.[2] What, he wondered, did the penchant for redecoration say about his fellow citizens? 'People want to build their homes, not a relationship with God.'[3] For the sake of the nation's soul, a new initiative was needed. In late March, Rylands launched the 'Get a Life' campaign to take the word of God to an increasingly irreligious population. As he told reporters: 'It's nice to have a smart home and a tidy garden, but it leaves a God-shaped hole in people.'[4]

Rylands had joined a time-honoured battle. Since the days of the Puritans, pious Britons had worried about the corrupting influence of luxury.[5] But if the contest between materialism and godliness was more than four centuries old, never before had the scales tipped so far in favour of guilt-free acquisitiveness. Amid a consumer boom of unprecedented proportions, the sums spent on home improvement soared to new heights.[6] Television programmes about homes monopolized the peak-time viewing hours, and interior design magazines crowded the news-stand shelves. The Ikea catalogue, quipped one reporter, now 'had a wider readership than the Bible'.[7] In the papers, Rylands' campaign was played for humour. The *Western Daily Press* urged the Reverend Rylands to take heart. 'The Bible is full of examples of what can be done with a little religious zeal.' After all, Noah's Ark was 'an incredible feat of carpentry'.[8]

Television and Ikea may have opened a new chapter, but infatuation with the home is an old story. From the early nineteenth century, house-pride came to define what it meant to be British.[9] According to the Edwardian nursery rhyme: 'The

Germans live in Germany; the Romans live in Rome; the Turkeys live in Turkey, but the English live at home.'[10] Travellers to Britain marvelled at the attention that all ranks of society, from dockers to dukes, lavished upon their dwellings. 'No nation,' wrote the architect Hermann Muthesius, a German attaché in the early twentieth century, 'has identified itself more with the house.'[11] In life, the British adorned even the most unassuming brick terraces with elegant names. In death, they embellished tombstones with the deceased's last earthly address. Beginning in the 1860s, glazed blue ceramic plaques honoured London's most illustrious residents by associating them in perpetuity with their dwellings.[12] Where you lived was all-important. The famed adage – the Englishman's home is his castle – verged, or so foreign visitors often observed, on understatement.

Household Gods is a history of the British love-affair with the domestic interior from the age of mass manufacture to modernism. In no other country was domesticity so celebrated and studiously cultivated. From the late eighteenth century, prosperous merchants and their wives had bolstered their claim to gentility with Wedgwood china, mahogany furnishings, and Turkey carpets.[13] By the 1860s and 1870s, rising incomes, combined with the bounty of industrial manufacture, carried the tide of consumption to new heights. Money fed house-pride: between the mid-nineteenth century and the Second World War, Britons enjoyed the highest average standard of living in Europe.[14] In many ways, we have inherited the materialistic world the Victorians made. And yet, we know surprisingly little about how they responded to their unprecedented prosperity. How, for instance, did the legendarily strait-laced Victorian middle classes reconcile moral good with material abundance? How can we explain their apparently insatiable, and to our eyes quixotic, demand for things? Why, put simply, did they stuff their houses full of objects? When and why did people first begin to believe, as many of us do, that our homes reflect our personalities?

This is a book about a century – from the 1830s to the 1930s – in which the competing claims of God and Mammon were put most urgently. The long road that led to today's home extravaganza began from an unlikely terminus: the evangelical revival that swept the country in the late eighteenth and early nineteenth centuries. For evangelicals, avarice, especially at home, counted among the most grievous of failings; their own dwellings were, above all, austere. But in an age of increasing affluence, the virtues of self-denial became considerably harder to maintain. The Victorians, caught between the commands of religious restraint and the lure of their newfound wealth, came up with an ingenious solution. Things had moral qualities. Urged on by clergymen who preached that beauty was holy, Victorians evaluated the merits of sideboards and chintzes according to a new standard of godliness. A correct purchase could elevate a household's moral tone; the wrong choice could exert a malevolent influence.

A new cast of advice-givers lined up to tell the British how to navigate the perilous waters of moral decoration. When, in 1871, the noted art critic Philip Gilbert Hamerton penned a dialogue on furniture, his dramatis personae included not only a clergyman, but a would-be home decorator, a philistine London merchant – and an artist.[15] For the Victorians, art was itself a moral enterprise. It bridged the gap between material and spiritual beauty, while loosening still further evangelical restraints on acquisitiveness. As artists decorated houses, and the nation's furniture stores proclaimed themselves museums, furnishing staked a claim as the pre-eminent British art form. The premium was on creativity and self-expression. To meet this demand luxurious emporia were born, dedicated to the premise that their customers deserved the widest selection of goods imaginable. A staggering variety of choices in bedsteads and fire irons, in tea tables and decorative gewgaws confronted shoppers at the turn of the twentieth century. Today's consumers have never seen anything like it.

Endowed with moral and artistic qualities, possessions – or so the Victorians came to believe – made the man. They were the first people to be so closely identified with their belongings. When the writer E.F. Benson went in search of the Victorian period, he chose neither J.S. Mill's essays nor Stanley's encounter with Livingstone to conjure up the spirit of the time, but a red velvet, opalescent beaded, tasselled pincushion in the shape of a blancmange, topped with a royal crown.[16] Queen Victoria herself, as Lytton Strachey gleefully noted, ordered all of her millions of possessions photographed from several angles.[17] No less an eminent Victorian than William Gladstone testified to this profound attachment. Facing retirement and short of money, in 1875 Gladstone was forced to sell the art and china collections he had assembled over a lifetime, as well as the house at 11 Carlton House Terrace where he had lived for nearly twenty years. By contrast to the matter-of-fact way in which he recorded for posterity the birth of his children, the sale of his house caused him anguish. 'The process as a whole has been like a *little death*,' he confided to his diary.[18] The regrets that haunted Gladstone were not reserved for the rich and famous. Memories of carpets and curtains, reported one country parson, were 'among the things which come up in the strange, confused remembrance of the dying man in the last days of his life'.[19]

The Victorian preoccupation with possessions reflected an age in which once-rigid distinctions of class and rank seemed to be rapidly eroding. The question, as late nineteenth-century observers noted, was no longer merely who you were, but what you had. For aristocrats, of course, land and title still guaranteed a privileged status. Among the middle classes, whose numbers more than tripled in the second half of the nineteenth century, possessions became a way of defining oneself in a society where it was increasingly difficult to tell people apart.[20] Homes – in this period nearly always rented, rarely bought – became flexible indicators of status, which could be exchanged for better accommodation as fortunes allowed.[21] Taste, viewed in the eighteenth century as a largely innate quality reserved for the well-born, was now a trait to be cultivated, available to all. It could reveal as much about a person as family background, occupation, religious sect, or political affiliation. A flair for the draping of a mantelpiece established a lady's artistic credentials. A man who found the right old Persian rug, wrote the poet Rosamund Marriott Watson, could count that part of his ascent of the social ladder secure: 'In such case you may possibly change your faiths, your friends, but not – most assuredly not – your carpet.'[22] The most sought-after of all possessions was a ghost-ridden house: 'To be the owner of a haunted house is, as all the world knows, the high ambition of everyone who has at last succeeded in establishing a name.'[23] Where flesh-and-blood forefathers were undistinguished, other-worldly relatives proved a handy acquisition.

But possessions did not just speak to the outside world. They offered a lifeline for coming to terms with one's own identity in a society so much in flux. From its origins in the 1890s, the idea of 'personality' was fundamentally intertwined with the domestic interior. Character, an older conception of the self, connoted a moral state. Personality, by contrast, was about earned distinctiveness, performance, and display. No place was more of a stage for the turn-of-the-century British than their homes – even if no one else was watching. Vincent Sheean, the dashing American war correspondent, identified this characteristic as 'interiority'. When one thought of Paris, he wrote, the first image that flashed into mind was that of a street scene, a *quai*, a café. The mention of London, by contrast, evoked the inside of a comfortable house. 'This interiority, so to speak, is not only a trick of my memory or a mere sense impression. It is a general characteristic of such English life as I have seen. Even the most social of Englishmen seemed most at ease in his own house – felt better, thought better, and talked better there; liked to take his psychological shoes off . . . .'[24]

By the First World War, evangelical inhibition had long since given way to guilt-less consumption in most British middle-class households. Individuality was the mantra of the moment, as Edwardians competed to formulate the most eccentric designs. Yet, in another two decades, that moment had passed as well. The idea of distinctiveness was in full retreat. The political slogan adopted by Stanley Baldwin and his inter-war Conservative Party, 'Safety First', could have applied just as aptly to the middle-class homes of the time.

The catastrophic effects of the war – more than 875,000 dead, another 1.6 million wounded – did much to discourage lavish display and promote a new simplicity in British décor. But the change was rooted in a more profound transformation of the British middle class. From the 1930s, the middle class was increasingly composed of salaried employees: managerial, conservative, and, above all, home-owners. The new homes that they occupied, often in suburban enclaves, brought with them a new social strategy, calculated to ease tensions between not-always-comfortable next door neighbours. Caution was the watchword and caution bred uniformity. The home was to be, above all, quiet, reserved, and neutral. As taste homogenized, the vast array of furnishing choices once available to the Victorians slowly disappeared. Grand one-of-a-kind emporia had been replaced by ubiquitous multiple shops, where what consumers encountered differed little from store to store and eventually from home to home.

As the tide of modernism swept through Europe, Britain remained behind, fixed comfortably and immovably in its design past. Blonde wood and tubular steel, the rage in Sweden and Germany, had little place here. Yet if the British were looking backward, they had lost something along the way that nostalgia could not recapture. The unruly Victorians had broken free of religious restraints, and then defied the best efforts of nineteenth-century design gurus to impose uniform standards of good taste on their beloved interiors. Now, the demands of social belonging had proved a more potent and ultimately irresistible force. The promise of personality had been absorbed into a more restrictive form of class expression.

* * *

The story of British taste has most often been told from the perspective of those who wished to improve it. In the aftermath of the Great Exhibition of 1851, the populace's purportedly bad taste became a *cause célèbre*. Some of the nineteenth century's most eloquent and energetic figures occupied themselves with the problem. At the South Kensington Museum, the indomitable Henry Cole launched a design reform movement that sought to educate consumers to prefer more tasteful objects. In a series of best-selling books and well-attended lectures, John Ruskin impressed upon his fellow Britons the moral and political consequences of their choices in manufacture. The socialist William Morris took direct action: in 1861, he opened a decorating business with the architect Philip Webb and the Pre-Raphaelite painters Ford Madox Brown, Dante Gabriel Rossetti and Edward Burne-Jones. The time had come, they noted in their prospectus, for 'artists of reputation' to devote their attention to decorative art.[25]

These men, movements, and institutions have attracted an army of scholars – and rightly so.[26] It would be difficult to exaggerate their importance; nearly everyone who wrote on the subject of design claimed a lineage from Ruskin and Morris. At the same time, however, their fame should not be read as evidence of the inevitable triumph of their principles. As they themselves often lamented, many people, if not most, misread their works, and consequently failed to comprehend their ideas – or if they understood them, chose not to implement them faithfully.[27] William Morris repudiated much of what was promoted under the popular label of art for the home, but his disapproval had no discernible effect upon sales.[28] Meanwhile, aesthetes such as Oscar Wilde, often credited with popularizing 'artistic' home decoration among the middle classes, probably did the cause more harm than good with their blasphemous pronouncements and infamous lifestyles.

Household Gods moves beyond these canonical figures of design reform to

1 Decoration as William Morris prescribed it. A show house in Bournville Village in the early twentieth century. The Quaker chocolate manufacturer George Cadbury intended that his Bournville settlement promote healthy and moral living – values that the arts-and-crafts décor of this model cottage ostensibly communicated.

2 Divergence from the ideal. An unidentified house in Bournville Village, early twentieth century. Arts-and-Crafts simplicity has been forsaken for such Victorian touches as dried flowers, statuary, and artfully draped fabrics.

explore the much broader set of forces that shaped consumer demand. Religious and moral qualms figure in this story, as too do anxieties about the opinions of neighbours and friends. The temptations of shopping vie with the constraints of the pocketbook; the urge to differentiate oneself confronts, time and again, the desire to fit in. Widening our lens allows the period of mass manufacturing to come into sharper focus. It was a much more dynamic arena than we have recognized – full of debate, tantalizing choices, and new, if fraught, means of self-realization. In actuality, as in Philip Gilbert Hamerton's fictive dialogue, preachers argued with artists about what colour to paint a room. A pioneering coterie of women journalists, meanwhile, wrestled with Henry Cole's disciples for control over female consumers. They counselled their readers to ignore design reform's fixed notions of 'right and wrong', and to express instead their own individual sensibilities. Their advice ran in violent contradiction to Ruskin's ideals. Now forgotten, the 'lady art advisors' led the way to self-expression in the home.

By focusing upon middle-class self-fashioning, *Household Gods* delves into the realm of what critics have often disdained as bad taste. Readers will encounter in these pages much more about the ugly and the ephemeral than about the beautiful and the transcendent.[29] A bamboo plant stand, dripping with fern pots, is more redolent of the late Victorian period than an elegantly streamlined tea service designed by Christopher Dresser, though it is the latter that is invariably displayed. A waste-paper basket fashioned from an elephant's foot betrays the aspirations of its Edwardian owners; a decorous C.F.A. Voysey wallpaper pattern that never went into production, by contrast, tells us chiefly about what museums have considered worthy design. The trend-setting purveyors of urban style, such as Liberty & Co., feature in this story, but so, too, do small-town furnishing shops, disorderly bazaars, and out-of-the-way antique stores. Flea markets and car-boot sales are as important as museums in reminding us of the richness of the material culture of the past.[30]

Uncovering the tracks of middle-class buyers required an investigation that reached beyond the invaluable storehouses of the Victoria & Albert Museum and its Archive of Art and Design. This quest launched an archival journey that eventually encompassed forty collections in England, Scotland, and Wales. In seeking to expand my inquiry beyond London's avant-garde, I looked for materials, especially unpublished diaries and family photograph albums, which could attest to life lived outside the tyranny of good design.[31] Throughout my research, I paid particular attention to the different parts that men and women played in the furnishing of houses. Though we tend to assume that home decoration is (and always has been) an affair for women, there was a time when married men occupied themselves with the details of furnishing, fretting about the appearance of their mantelpieces and seeking out appropriate cushions. How men relinquished that role – and why women took it up – is a crucial episode in the making of modern gender stereotypes.

My interest in the lived experiences – rather than just the ideals – of consumer behaviour led me, as well, to business records and the periodical press. The archives of manufacturers, design studios, and provincial retailers are rarely exploited sources for the history of consumer desire. Yet grimy stockbooks help us to understand what types of items sold, while correspondence with customers can tell us why. Trade papers provide a glimpse of the strategic considerations that governed the realms of distribution and supply. The voluminous output of the women's press, even as it taxes the historian's patience with its hundreds of thousands of pages, repays the attention with the sorts of insights rarely preserved in the historical record. Readers' letters, quoted in the lady art advisors' 'Answers to Correspondents' provide rare first-hand accounts of disputes between husbands and wives over home decoration.

In pursuing middle-class taste, this book breaches the conventional dividing lines between Victorianism and modernism. Taking a century as my subject has made it possible to trace a longer trajectory in which consumption shed the burdens of sin to take on the mantle of self-expression, and eventually class conformity. The focus throughout is on the middle classes, by some estimates a quarter of the population at the turn of the century, who constituted the largest and most important market for household furnishings.[32] I conclude with the decade that witnessed the single biggest home-building boom in British history: in 1939, more than a quarter of the population – and nearly 60 per cent of middle-class people – owned their own homes. Extending my inquiry to the period after 1945 would have illuminated the effect of a still greater mass market, but the story that I set out to tell about the struggle between older fixed canons of taste, new religious impulses, and novel consuming desires had largely run its course by the time of the Second World War. In the epilogue, I do, however, return to the Reverend Rylands' lament in order to place today's extravagant consumer boom within the long arc of the British love-affair with their houses.

As the first industrialized society, Great Britain offers a paradigmatic case study of the origins of consumer demand and the construction of the self in a period of mass manufacture and democratization. Many of the developments this book explores, of course, are not exclusively British. Before the First World War, the bourgeoisie of Western Europe and the United States had much in common. From Oslo to Boston, Marseilles to Hamburg, late nineteenth-century interiors were crammed full of objects. The parallels with American culture are probably the most striking; both Britain and the United States had to contend with the dilemmas of affluent Puritanism.[33] For the French, the legacy of radical republicanism was a politicization of styles, and a suspicion about the market, which Germans also shared.[34] For the remorselessly capitalist British, by contrast, the operation of the market provided a model of virtue. 'Political' furnishing was typified by the socialist William Morris, whose designs – as he acknowledged – ministered 'to the swinish luxury of the rich'.[35]

Consumerism has been lauded for its democratizing influences, and vilified as an agent of unbridled materialism. Both are true, and this book makes no attempt to weigh them in the balance. Still, I am perhaps less sceptical than some about the ways in which taste serves to confound class distinctions. In 1925, my grandmother arrived in the United States, a refugee from Russia's pogroms. At the age of sixteen she married, and with her husband set up a small grocery in Louisville, Kentucky. Each year, they divided the profits from the store. With his half, he went to the racetracks. She spent her half on the very best object she could afford. She had started – no one knows why – to collect late eighteenth- and early nineteenth-century furniture. In some years, she would purchase a Georgian sideboard from one of the plantation houses that lined the Ohio river; in others, a single teaspoon was all she could manage. She frequented auction houses, and despite the fact that she had never finished high school, assembled a specialist library in old silver, porcelain, and chinoiserie. She began, in her son's description, to 'talk like an Episcopalian'. Before her family counted as middle class by virtue either of education or income, they had become middle-class Americans through her things.[36]

Because my grandmother died when I was eight, I largely came to know her through her objects. Since I can remember, I have wondered about the stories that material things can tell us about the people who bought, sold, prized, and despised them. That way of putting the question is perhaps itself a late Victorian artefact – the legacy of an era in which the boundaries between a person's inner self and her belongings came to seem surprisingly indistinct. Those who vested their identity in their things discovered, on occasion, that possessions could even take on a life of their own. In his dialogue on furnishing, the art critic Philip Gilbert Hamerton permitted his clergyman the last word: 'We get so attached to some pieces of furniture that they become to us as if endowed with a kind of affection themselves, and we half believe not only that we love them, but that they love us.'[37] Home promised a passion that would always be requited. It would prove, like any other love-affair, far more troublesome. It was 1871, and the long reign of household gods had already begun.

CHAPTER 1

MATERIAL GOOD
MORALITY AND THE WELL-TO-DO

The woman who would become one of the early twentieth century's most celebrated interior designers was born into a strict evangelical household convinced of her own sin. Syrie Maugham – that dazzling hostess on the Riviera, celebrated for her 'white-on-white' schemes, proprietor of the international decorating concern called simply 'Syrie Inc.' – was the third of Dr Thomas Barnardo's seven children. Barnardo was a legendary Victorian philanthropist, who founded the homes for destitute children that still bear his name.[1] Well-built, with close-set eyes and moustaches waxed to a point, Barnardo was the model of evangelical correctness, as severe and unrelenting with his own offspring as with the destitute children who filled his notorious orphanages. Young Syrie was brought up in a household that was, even by the stringent standards of the day, unusually harsh. Entertainment was limited; theatre-going was strictly forbidden. At the family's twice-daily prayers, Dr Barnardo reviewed the transgressions committed by members of his household, and offered prayers for the sinner.[2] Syrie's parents taught her to aspire to a life of piety and self-scrutiny, consecrated to the performance of good works.

Eager to break free of the puritanical life at home, young Syrie made two disastrous marriages: first to the American Henry Wellcome, twenty-seven years her senior, and then to the writer Somerset Maugham, who notoriously preferred men.[3] Her private life a shambles, Syrie Maugham found her calling in the new field of interior decoration. After the First World War, she opened her own store in Baker Street with £400 of borrowed money. At the age of forty-four, Syrie reminded those who knew her of Queen Mary, and was known to inspire dread in her employees and some clients with her steely wit and quick temper.[4] Her methods were madcap – she pickled furniture by dipping it into a bath of lye – but her success was undeniable.[5] She greeted the Roaring Twenties with a villa in Le Touquet that made her an international name. Decorated in shades of white, it boasted carpets of sheepskin, luxurious white leather sofas, and bowls filled with white peonies. In addition to her shop in Baker Street, she founded stores in Chicago and New York.

3 Syrie Maugham, photographed by Cecil Beaton.

Militant Christianity and interior design: at first glance such a pairing seems incongruous, to say the least. But if her final destination was more splendid than most, Syrie Maugham's voyage from sombre black crepe to the glamorous splendour of an all-white villa in Le Touquet was not a solitary journey. Many other middle-class Britons accompanied her. Punished as a boy for catching butterflies on the Sabbath, the Cardiff apothecary, Robert Drane (son of the Congregationalist minister of the same name) spent the rest of his life, and especially Sundays, assembling collections of porcelain, silver, and religious icons. Sick with a failing liver, he wished only to complete his *catalogue raisonné* of Worcesterware before he died – a fine ambition, he confessed ruefully to a friend, for 'a christen man'.[6] It is tempting to understand the path followed by Maugham and Drane as a reaction – to interpret the embrace of material goods as a renunciation of evangelical asceticism. For some people it undoubtedly was. But a simple hypothesis of reaction cannot explain why, for two generations of Victorians, morality became *the* lingua franca for evaluating furnishings. Newspaper articles entitled 'The Moral Influence of Furnishing', religious folk running shops, dining-rooms decorated with quotes from the Book of Job: powering the locomotive of Victorian acquisitiveness was an engine that ran on the unlikely fuel of spiritual striving.

Every issue in Victorian Britain was subjected to moral analysis, but perhaps none is so puzzling to our sensibilities today as that of domestic décor. In an era in which

4 Drawing room of the Villa Eliza, Le Touquet, 1927.

middle-class standards of living were rapidly rising, emphasizing the moral virtues of possessions served to reconcile spiritual good with material abundance. Affluence did not mean that moral concerns were left behind.[7] This chapter explores the pentimento effect of vital religion, the shadowy imprint that remained even after eternal punishment was no longer preached from the pulpits. After the Second World War, religious leaders in Britain blamed materialism for the tide of impiety that had swept across a formerly God-fearing nation.[8] They were not entirely wrong, for mass consumerism – with its emphasis upon individual self-fulfilment and the instant gratification of pleasure – has undoubtedly abetted the forces of secularization in Britain, as in other countries.[9] But, for an important mid-Victorian moment, morality and materialism coexisted as mutually re-inforcing propositions before breaking decisively apart in the twentieth century. How Syrie Maugham and other middle-class Victorians came to travel the road from sin to self-expression is the necessary first step in understanding modern Britain's long-standing and guilt-free love-affair with the house.

Consumerism in the Age of Atonement

Among the most powerful forces in the making of the British middle classes was the evangelical revival.[10] By 1862, the year that Thomas Barnardo converted to vital religion, evangelicalism was already more than eighty years old. Its origins lay in the late eighteenth century, in a movement to reform the Church of England. Though neither as corrupt nor as degenerate as its Victorian critics later portrayed it, the eighteenth-century Church was nonetheless thoroughly enmeshed in the social hierarchies and politics of its day.[11] Appointment to a bishopric reflected strategic interests rather than religious fervour. Such positions came only to those who supported the government, and were often distributed as favours to the younger sons of the aristocracy. The best-endowed livings, with incomes in the thousands of pounds, went to the well connected, who in turn delegated their duties to badly paid and often complacent curates. To make ends meet, clergymen were forced to take on multiple parishes, with the consequence that regular services were limited in many areas, and sermons as likely to be pilfered from manuals as spoken from the heart.

Measured by Victorian standards, the atmosphere in the eighteenth-century Church was far from pious. Sermons preached from the pulpit tended to emphasize the rational qualities of religion; they were rarely fiery or even fervent. Given the prevailing belief that humans naturally tended to embrace virtue over vice, faith was not viewed as a burden. Most importantly for our purposes, godliness did not require that the pleasures of a worldly life be forsaken. Among the many entertainments pursued by the Georgian parson James Woodforde, of Weston in Norfolk, were card-playing (for stakes), betting on the horses, dancing, theatre-going, shopping, and above all else, eating and drinking. The five volumes of Woodforde's diaries (1758–1803) tell us little about the content of his sermons, but abound in details of the sumptuous meals he consumed, accompanied by wines, beers, and smuggled rum and gin. 'We had for Dinner,' he records one day in 1791, 'stewed Eels with Onions, a Saddle Mutton rosted, boiled Chicken and a Tongue, Veal-Cutlets, Beef-Stake Tarts in Turretts of Paste, Piggs Ears, &c. . .. Second course, a brace of fine Pheasants a rosted Rabbit, Amulet, Spinage and Eggs, Tartlets, &c. No kind of Desert whatever.'[12]

The religious revival that swept Britain in the later eighteenth century transformed not only the Church, but ultimately also the character of belief and morality in all aspects of public and private life. Revivalism ignited from below, as the dynamic preachers John Wesley and George Whitefield brought their brand of enthusiastic, or 'vital', religion to the country's labouring poor. Methodism was chiefly a religion of the lower orders, but its influence was felt among the middle and upper classes through the evangelical movement that took hold within the Church of England. Evangelicalism drew much of its force from the extraordinary turmoil of a revolutionary era. The British élite had followed events in France with horror. They had good reason to fear, for even as the French Revolution struck the European Continent, plunging Britain into decades of war, the quickening pace of industrialization had begun to transform the domestic landscape. The British were painfully conscious that theirs was the first country to industrialize, and opinions divided on whether this was a beneficial or even a lasting state of affairs. With labourers rioting over the introduction of machines and high bread prices, and famine always on the horizon, it seemed that Jacobinism could take root at home as well as abroad. And if the parlous political situation was not bad enough, a series of spectacular bank failures beginning in the 1820s shook the edifice of the country's financial system and devastated small investors.

Beyond the spectre of revolution was another, more disturbing development. As a consequence of industrialization and urbanization, the traditional, face-to-face hierarchical mechanisms of authority that had once regulated social interactions in villages and towns were disintegrating. It was unclear what new arrangements, if any, would replace them. In Britain's booming cities, rising rates of illegitimacy, crime, brawling, and drunkenness put observers in mind of a latter-day Sodom and Gomorrah.[13] Although new rules for personal conduct – promulgated in the torrent of manners manuals published from the 1770s onwards – offered guidance to those who recognized the significance of proper behaviour and comportment, they did little to civilize the populace at large.[14] An etiquette manual would not be sufficient to restrain a perfect stranger from imposing himself upon you in a coffee-house. Nor would it effect the wholesale improvement of character that some commentators increasingly suspected was needed. Human nature itself required reforming.

To the insecurities of middle-class life in the early nineteenth century, evangelicalism offered, if not comfort, then rules for living and the possibility of salvation through faith. Evangelicals shared with Methodists an overwhelming sense of the power of sin. In contrast to those eighteenth-century churchmen such as Woodforde who had subscribed to the reassuring belief in man's essential goodness, evangelicals believed that humanity was utterly depraved. Man was, as the Reverend Thomas Haweis put it, 'a fallen, corrupted creature, wholly defiled in his nature, and in consequence loathsome and hateful in the eyes of the Divine purity'.[15] In an act of atonement, God had sacrificed his own son to pay for mankind's sins. By faith in that atonement, ordinary mortals – charged from birth with the stain of original sin – could obtain forgiveness and prepare their way to heaven. Remember, the evangelicals told their children, you are mere worms of earth; every talent that has been given you is the creation of God.[16]

The omnipresence of sin required a radically different role for religion. Religious practice could not be sequestered to Sunday observances, but had to permeate every dimension of life. Evangelical enthusiasm, which had begun in the Church of England, soon spread through the dissenting faiths as well.[17] Practitioners of vital religion demanded of themselves a relentless self-scrutiny, a spiritual record-keeping that has left to posterity tens of thousands of closely written diaries, filled with anguished reflections upon the author's failings and exhortations for improvement.[18] All activities had to be judged according to the scale of righteousness. Religion, the evangelical Baptist reformer Joseph Hughes wrote to his cousin in

1790, 'ought to be our constant companion, or rather it ought to be incorporated and rendered, so to speak, a part of ourselves. Thus may trivial occurrences be sanctified, and we may promote the interest of our souls when we eat, when we drink, or whatever else we employ ourselves in'.[19]

With the fate of souls on the line at mealtimes, even the most ordinary acts provided an opportunity for conscience and trial. Self-denial was the evangelical watchword, evidence that the will had mastered the weakness of the flesh. The redoubtable Mrs Anne Grant, wife of a clergyman in the Scottish Highlands, herself the author of moral tracts and the mother of twelve, sought to impress upon her children a lesson common in evangelical households: 'there is no high attainment, moral or religious, no excellence, no felicity to be acquired, without habitual practice of self-command and self-denial'.[20] Indeed, temptation was part of God's plan for distinguishing the righteous from the sinners. 'It is a fearful thing, in this fluctuating state to possess much,' Mrs Grant mused, for 'in proportion to what we enjoy we must suffer under the privation of these enjoyments.'[21] Avoiding earthly pleasures prepared men to recognize divine grace, while vanity and avarice threatened to dislodge the godly from a virtuous path. The conceits of the passionate flesh could not be underestimated. Writing in 1804 amidst the Napoleonic Wars, Mrs Grant judged the lure of luxury a more fearsome foe than even the godless French, for 'the French we may hope to repel, if not overcome; but luxury will assuredly overcome us . . .'[22]

For those who possessed it, wealth could present an extreme form of moral tribulation. Bible-reading offered little comfort to the anxious. Hadn't Jesus said that it was easier for a camel to go through the eye of a needle than for a rich man to enter the kingdom of God? The oft-quoted teachings of Matthew offered a way forward: 'Lay not up for yourselves treasure upon earth, where moth and rust doth corrupt . . . but lay up for yourself treasures in Heaven.' The evangelical Quaker banker, Joseph John Gurney, fretted constantly about the fortune he amassed in a successful career, though he – like other evangelicals – donated a sizeable proportion of his income to charity. To his journal Gurney confided his fears about the moral jeopardy that money introduced. 'It calls for real watchfulness against avarice, against a careful spirit, and against worldliness in various forms.'[23] When Gurney's wife died of pleurisy only four years after their marriage, he consoled himself with the thought that God's 'awful dispensation' would not be in vain: 'My dependence on earthly things required to be shaken. I was in need of something to dislocate me from things visible; and to bring me to a nearer and more satisfactory apprehension of the heavenly inheritance.'[24]

At stake in the charge of worldliness was not only the fate of one's own soul, but the regard of the community. In religious circles, any display of wealth opened its bearers to harsh scrutiny, all the worse if it was at home, the haven where evangelicals sought to shield their families from the perversions of the world.[25] Gurney's cousin, John Barclay, renounced the family business, choosing to cast his lot with the 'poorer brethren and sisters'. Barclay judged the domestic décor of his fellow Quakers harshly. To excuse their indulgences, they protest 'that this or the other new or fashionable vanity is an improvement on the old article, – that this gay and gaudy trumpery will wear and keep its colour better than a plainer one, – that this precious bauble was given them by their relations'.[26] Small wonder that the wealthy and pious took care to hide their fortunes. On a tour to London in the 1850s, the French man of letters, Francis Wey, observed that there was a hypocritical inverse relationship between display and wealth in Britain. 'While in France prosperity has to be advertised to be credited, here it hides its head as though wishing to pass unnoticed.'[27]

Nowhere was the spirit of austerity reflected more clearly than in the homes of religious folk. The writer Augustus Hare's mother, an evangelically minded gentry-woman, condemned novel-reading as wicked; her house in Sussex was simple, with few things of any value and little colour. Her décor betrayed, as her avowedly mater-ialistic, late Victorian son judged, an 'almost spiritualised aspect'.[28] Dissenters,

5 Plaque of Sunderland lustre ware, 1800–20. Plaques such as these became common after John Wesley's tours of Sunderland and Staffordshire.

rightful heirs to the Puritan legacy, condemned luxuries and useless appurtenances, and sought to live in a fashion that accorded with their spiritual quest. Even when the anti-Corn Law reformer John Bright became a rich man, his house at One Ash bore the impress of his Quaker faith. On a tour abroad, he abstained from buying souvenirs, 'as our house is full of things'. According to Trevelyan, Bright's bio-grapher, 'Many people would have thought it bare'.[29] The only expensive furniture in One Ash was a present from Bright's admirers: carved bookcases containing 1,200 well-bound volumes.

6 John Bright's library.

One of the most vivid depictions of the evangelical home is Samuel Butler's painting, *Family Prayers* (1864). Butler is today best known as the author of the utopian fantasy *Erewhon* and the searing, posthumously published indictment of evangelical family life, *The Way of All Flesh*. But for the thirty-five-odd years that he lived in bachelor rooms in Clifford's Inn, his crusade against Victorian pieties was conducted in oil as well as on paper. Butler was the son of a Church of England clergyman and the grandson of the fearsome headmaster of Shrewsbury public school, Samuel Butler, Bishop of Lichfield; it was intended that he would follow in the family line. However, sent to work among London's poor as a lay assistant, he found himself unable to subscribe to the notion of infant baptism. The young man wanted to become an artist rather than a clergyman, but his father, the 'human Sunday' in Butler's memorable phrase, was adamantly opposed.[30] In 1859, he set sail for New Zealand to try his hand at sheep-farming. His first night at sea, he failed to say his evening prayers: 'the sense of change was so great that it shook them quietly off. I was not then a sceptic; I had got as far as disbelief in infant baptism, but no further. I felt no compunction of conscience, however, about leaving off my morning and evening prayers – simply I could no longer say them.'[31] Five years later, his fortune made, Butler returned to London. His first artistic act was to paint *Family Prayers*.

7 Samuel Butler, *Family Prayers*, 1864.

8 Samuel Butler at home, 15 Clifford's Inn.

Like *The Way of All Flesh*, Butler's painting is a semi-autobiographical work. While the custom of family prayers had been widespread only since the 1790s, in Butler's family, as in other devout households, it was a twice-daily affair that was woven deeply within the fabric of domestic life. Painted in the family dining-room at Langar Rectory, *Family Prayers* depicts a family (probably Butler's own) with suffocating intensity; the figures portrayed are inert, atavistic, sunk into their own private worlds.[32] What is striking about the room, especially as compared with Butler's own adult rooms, is the sparseness of its appointments. Grey walls are leavened only by pictures of landscapes. There are no gas lamps, no fireplace, no bric-à-brac. The furnishings are functional: the round table at which the father reads the Bible, chairs for the assembled members of the household. The most commanding object in the room is the glass-covered clock mounted high on the wall. The clock is both practical and deeply symbolic, for the injunction to employ one's time prudently was a leitmotif of evangelical teachings.[33] The hours in one's day were precious, a gift from God who expected them to be put to productive use. For those who, like Butler, had grown up chronicling with great precision in their journals how they had spent the minutes of their day (and excoriating themselves – or being excoriated – for the inevitably wasted time), the clock's ascendancy in the homely scene was only fitting.

It would be a mistake, however, to depict unrelieved sobriety as the hallmark of evangelical homes.[34] Some differentiation is necessary between the attitudes of those moderate evangelicals, like the famed Clapham Sect, and the more rigorous. Robert Louis Stevenson's strictly Calvinist father announced the family's piety with a bas-relief of the Massacre of the Innocents, set above the doorway to the inner hall.[35] The evangelicals who gathered in the late eighteenth century in Clapham, the suburb south-west of London that would become associated with the campaign against the slave trade, permitted themselves more comfort.[36] When it came to meals, the wealthy businessman John Thornton, the first to move to Clapham, believed – or so wrote his descendant, E.M. Forster – in the principle of 'Prayers before plenty. But plenty!'[37] While Thornton criticized the luxury-seeking tendencies of his day, he, like his more famous son, the MP Henry Thornton, sought to steer a measured course between 'austerity and ostentation'.[38] At the heart of the Thornton house, Battersea Rise, was an oval library, designed for Henry Thornton by William Pitt – a quintessentially elegant if spare eighteenth-century room with an Adam fireplace and ceiling, and a high-backed settee upholstered in green with red trim.[39]

Yet if life in the Thornton household was not lived only in shades of grey, too much attention to worldly matters nonetheless bespoke a worrying devotion to riches. Guilt about the modest entertainments they had allowed themselves, E.M. Forster tells us, tormented the Thorntons when they were ill or otherwise tried.[40] Henry Thornton's daughter Laura – like all of the Thorntons – adored the

house at Battersea Rise.[41] Betrothed at the age of twenty-three, she asked her fiancé to allow her a few final months at her Clapham home. 'I know full well,' she wrote to her suitor, 'that I love this home too much. I fear that I idolise it, and I doubt not that infinite Wisdom has for this reason ordered that I should not spend the rest of my life in it.'[42] Just as affliction could be welcomed as a 'blessing in disguise', a divine intervention to right a capsized vessel, so, too could comfort be regarded as morally suspect, potentially even as ruinous.[43] In their writings and speeches, evangelicals re-tooled the word 'luxury' to designate godly purposes. They spoke of the luxury of hearing someone preach, or the luxury of doing good.[44]

Not even moderate evangelicalism, then, could be regarded as a promising ground for the seeds of modern consumer society. Besieged by guilt about his book-buying, the Reverend Edward Bickersteth, secretary of the Church Missionary Society, vowed to perform an act of charity before he allowed himself to indulge in a purchase; it was not the books themselves that tormented him, but the fact that he had succumbed to material desires.[45] The activity of shopping, when it was discussed at all in the improving literature, was a stage setting for temptation and moral trial. One children's story, entitled 'The Last Shop', made the point for its young readers. Rosy, the daughter of a rich woman, behaved herself so well one day that her mamma told her they could go shopping. Her mother imposed only one condition: Rosy had to buy something out of each shop. So the little girl picked out lollipops at the confectioner's, a pair of crimson slippers at the tailor's, notepaper at the stationer's – and finally declared that she was ready to return home to enjoy her purchases. Not yet, said her mamma. 'I fear, my child, that there is one shop that you have omitted.' With this reminder, she led Rosy to the undertaker's, and had her measured for a coffin.[46] Through the unlikely vehicle of a shopping trip, a favourite evangelical lesson was conveyed. Death and the moment of judgment were inevitable, perhaps just around the corner, and those who wished to be saved had to overcome their natural propensity to vice.

But at the apparent apogee of evangelicalism's influence in the 1840s, there were signs that its hold was beginning to wane. Suffering, rather than a necessary corrective to humanity's sinfulness, was increasingly viewed as a state to be mitigated. The introduction of surgical anaesthesia in 1847 and the limited liability legislation of the mid-1850s bespoke new attitudes.[47] By the mid-nineteenth century, the 'age of atonement', as Boyd Hilton has termed it, had receded in favour of a religious doctrine that viewed every human being as the incarnation of a little bit of Jesus. 'Incarnationalism' was a moral standard both more forgiving and better suited to the times – for in the 1860s and 1870s Britons were accumulating wealth and possessions as never before. Incomes had remained obdurately low through the first half of the nineteenth century. The middle classes of the late eighteenth and early nineteenth centuries, whatever their religious convictions, had relatively little to spend on household consumption; objects such as a set of knives and a pair of candlesticks counted as luxuries, purchases to be made only rarely.[48] In Scottish middling-rank households, for instance, sofas, sideboards, and musical instruments only became customary from the 1820s and 1830s.[49]

10 Miss Margaret Bonar, *William Bonar's Dining Room at East Warriston House, Edinburgh*, c. 1850. The Bonars were a well-to-do banking family. This room – an example of refined simplicity, notably restrained by comparison to interiors of the later nineteenth century – was furnished in the 1830s and 1840s.

By the middle of the century, however, incomes took off. Measured in real terms, average income per head doubled between 1851 and 1901.[50] At the same time, the cost of necessaries, especially food, plunged, with the consequence that more people had more money to spend on luxuries previously unimaginable. The middle-class share of the population expanded spectacularly, from 12.5 per cent in 1851 (a number that had not budged since 1801) to 25 per cent by 1901.[51] Because the vast majority of people rented their houses, their capital was not tied up in buildings; on average, middle-class families paid 10 per cent of their income in rent.[52] For prosperous Victorians, possessions, especially portable property, provided an important outlet for extra disposable income.[53] What most struck the young French philosopher, Hippolyte Taine, as he toured England in the 1860s was the sheer wealth accumulated by the middle classes in their houses, so different in his mind from France. The people he met belonged, he wrote, to an 'opulent, free-spending middle-class very different from our own, financially straitened and looking twice at every penny spent'. Taine continued: 'To earn a lot consume a lot – such is the rule'.[54]

Whether or not rising incomes ended the 'age of atonement', there could be no doubt that sensibilities had, by the 1860s and 1870s, in some marked fashion changed. This was of course not true of every family, as the example of the Barnardos indicates.[55] Yet even Syrie Maugham's formidable father had to give some ground to changing times. Starting in the 1860s, Dr Barnardo organized a national 'Self-Denial' week each year to raise money for his orphanages. With its implicit assumption that self-denial could be contained within a week rather than pursued as a lifelong practice, Dr Barnardo's fund-raising mechanism offered testimony to the new order.[56] Wealth, no longer something to be hidden or given away, had become a sign of just rewards for a productive life.

But if the accumulation of worldly goods no longer raised most eyebrows, Victorians still remained preoccupied by questions of morality. The evangelicals were, as the historian Ford K. Brown famously put it, the fathers of the Victorians.[57] As the tide of severe religion ebbed, what was left in its wake was morality; all sorts of activities, including furnishing, offered a venue for moral improvement.[58] In an era which viewed humans as uniquely susceptible to their environments, furniture offered the chance to mould the man. According to the journalist Percy Russell, writing in 1874 after a trip to the furnishing emporium, Maple's, 'furniture, after all, must exercise a very important influence upon the character . . . it is ever possible so to order the interior of our abodes, supposing only the necessary means and the necessary taste are at command, as to produce a very satisfactory moral effect upon those inhabiting them'.[59] If the greater part of the world was not simply to be abandoned to the devil, secular things had to be made sacred.[60]

THE COMMANDMENTS OF TASTE

By the time that the Great Exhibition opened its doors on 1 May 1851, the hand-wringing over the state of British manufacture was already more than two decades old. And yet, what would eventually become a moral question implicating manufacturers, retailers, and consumers was, in the early nineteenth century, principally a matter of practical concern.[61] After two decades of war against the French, trade had, once again, begun on the Continent. Forced to compete, British manufacturers (or so their critics claimed) seemed to be losing ground not only in foreign markets, where their designs were rejected as tasteless, but at home as well, where those who could preferred to buy French. To assess how British design might be improved, Parliament had in the 1830s convened a Select Committee on Arts and Manufactures. Its witnesses were striking in their unanimity. While the British led the world in machine production, they trailed far behind their competitors, especially the French, in the crucial matter of design. Unless the government acted swiftly, Great Britain would forfeit its export markets. The country's industrial pre-eminence was at stake.

Among the Britons who rallied to the budding cause of design reform was Henry Cole. Cole began his career with the invention of a cataloguing system for

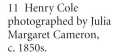

11 Henry Cole photographed by Julia Margaret Cameron, c. 1850s.

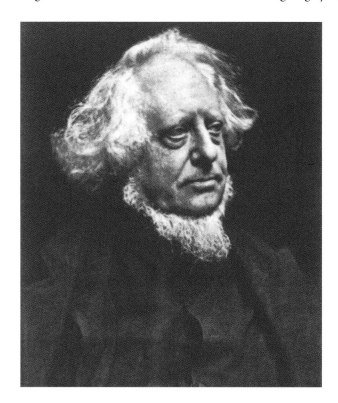

the Public Record Office and ended it at the helm of the South Kensington (later the Victoria & Albert) Museum. In between, he had a finger in every pie.[62] While still a junior civil servant, he contributed articles to the organs of enlightened liberal opinion, such as the *Westminster Review*, and studied art, exhibiting his sketches at the Royal Academy. In the 1840s, he worked on the introduction of penny postage, lobbied for a uniform railway gauge, and, along the way, published the first Christmas card, as well as popular guidebooks to the National Gallery and Hampton Court. After observing Cole's efforts on behalf of the railway gauge and penny postage, Richard Cobden offered to make him secretary of the Anti-Corn Law League, a position that Cole regretfully declined. His real mission was the reform of everyday life, and increasingly the degraded state of British design. Under the pseudonym 'Felix Summerly', Cole exhibited at the 1846 meeting of the Society of Arts a simple white tea set he had designed while visiting his friend Herbert Minton, of china-making fame. So successful was this enterprise – Prince Albert purchased one for breakfasts at Balmoral – that Cole launched a line of 'Art Manufactures' intended to demonstrate what could be accomplished when fine art joined with industry.

12 Furniture on display at the Great Exhibition, 1851.

13 The 'Gladiatorial Table', displayed at the Great Exhibition, was produced by the manufactory of Mr J. Fletcher, Cork.

In one sense, the Great Exhibition of 1851 represented the culmination of Cole's efforts. The glass-domed palace that opened its doors on May Day brought together the riches of industrial manufacture and resplendent finished goods, alongside raw materials harvested from all corners of the empire.[63] On its first day, 25,000 people crowded into the exhibition building meant to accommodate half that number. They strolled past the chunks of iron ore and blocks of stone displayed outside the palace's west entrance, meandered through aisle upon aisle of machinery (some in motion, rumbling and clanging), wandered around booths stacked high with a bewildering variety of objects. Taken together, there were more than 100,000 separate exhibits comprising everything from the utterly ridiculous artificial silver nose to the utilitarian portable water-closet. In the palace grounds visitors could inspect Prince Albert's model working-class flats, which demonstrated how Victoria's husband believed the lower orders should live. The exhibition was magnificent, if overwhelming in its scale and scope. According to one visitor, the artist Henrietta Ward: 'I can remember how people were so carried away by the extreme novelty of the whole thing that they lost themselves in an ecstasy of delight and walked and walked until they made themselves quite ill in their efforts to see all the wonders of the Palace of Industry.'[64] Nearly one-fifth of all Britons had visited the Crystal Palace by the time that the exhibition closed in October; many had come more than once to inspect its wonders.

But for Cole and other design reformers (especially the painter Richard Redgrave and the architect and designer Owen Jones), the Great Exhibition also made manifest the crisis of British industry – indeed, of British society.[65] Cole had long condemned the undisciplined, tasteless products churned out by British manufacturers. Called upon to testify before the 1849 Select Committee on the Schools of Design, Cole insisted that there existed fixed and absolute canons of taste; 'to act upon the principle of "every one to his taste", would be as mischievous as "every one to his morals"'.[66] Above all, then, the exhibition demonstrated the calamitous result of the notion of 'de gustibus': unchecked by principles, British manufacture had sunk to execrable levels of taste. The special targets of the design reformers' venom were domestic possessions tarted up to look like finer goods: pine grained to resemble mahogany, cotton dyed to fool the viewer into believing that it was silk, carpets ornamented to imitate clematis vines or jungle scenes or railroad stations. The public's desire for objects that it could not afford had led to 'universal infidelity' to the principles of design.[67] An avalanche of materialism threatened to bury correct taste altogether.

14 Wallpaper, 'Perspective Views of a Railway Station', c. 1853. Manufactured by Potters of Darwen, this paper was likely used to decorate public venues, such as hotels and bars.

In the aftermath of the Great Exhibition, what began as an issue of industrial competitiveness became entangled, in some cases even superseded, by moral concerns. Although the idea that design could be moral was not new – for two decades, the eccentric architect and Catholic convert A.W.N. Pugin had railed against deceptive decoration – Cole and his fellow reformers turned Pugin's diatribe into a fully fledged movement.[68] Objects, and particularly domestic possessions, became the subject of extraordinary scrutiny, criticized not only for how they looked, or how well they sold, but for the influence they might exercise over the house's inhabitants. Bad design, argued the reformers, had to be stamped out not because it failed to sell – indeed, the evidence abounded that the ugliest objects found a ready market. Rather, poor design posed a threat to the decency of a household. A tin bath painted to imitate marble, commented the author of *Our Homes and How to Make Them Healthy*, was to be avoided because 'All such shams and pretentious deceits should be repugnant to morality . . .'.[69] An object designed upon right-minded principles could elevate the moral tone, just as one that

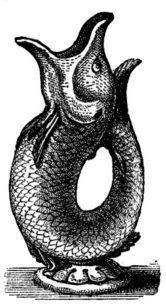

15 Fish Vase, depicted in G. L.'s *The Science of Taste*, 1879. Contorted into a posture that no fish could assume, and forced to hold water rather than swim in it, the fish vase violates the laws of nature and thus the laws of good taste as well.

betrayed false construction threatened it. By buying a wine-cooler in the form of a sarcophagus or a vase shaped like a fish, the consumer exposed himself (and his family) to a lie: 'If you are content to teach a lie in your belongings, you can hardly wonder at petty deceits being practised in other ways.' *Faux* marble, then, was wrong not simply because it sought to deceive onlookers, but because, as the background against which a family went about its daily business, it created an unwholesome and ever-present influence. Like dangerous miasmas in the air, it leached into the very fabric of existence.[70] Those who tolerated deceits or ugliness in their everyday life became accustomed to it. The threshold to wrongdoing was lowered.

Before the mid-nineteenth century, bad taste was rarely viewed as evidence of moral turpitude.[71] Evangelicals such as John Barclay condemned the beautifully appointed room as well as the garish one: both testified to worldliness, an ungodly laying up of treasure on earth. For earlier generations in the eighteenth century, taste, by definition, went hand in hand with refinement.[72] It was an attribute of the literate, those who subscribed to polite journals such as the *Spectator*, attended Italian operas and picture galleries, and displayed their knowledge in genteel conversation. While there was a vague sense that taste (like art) would promote virtue, refinement, tinged as it was with the air of feminine luxury, served to threaten as much as to strengthen the nation's moral fibre.[73] Most often, taste was viewed as innate, not as a matter of conscious choice. It was a quality theoretically open to everyone, but in practice possessed only by a select, usually well-born few. Although taste could be cultivated, the chance for mass conversion was slim. The dictum of the painter Sir Joshua Reynolds reflected the accepted view: 'Could we teach taste or genius by rules, they would no longer be taste or genius.'[74]

Victorian design reformers took the opposite position: taste could be learned by the mass of people – indeed, instruction in taste was a moral necessity precisely because things had the power to influence people for good or for ill.[75] If building a house in bad taste could do as much damage to society as taking a mistress or defrauding one's investors, the aesthetic atrocities committed by otherwise well-meaning people could not be tolerated.[76] Good taste did not represent self-indulgence or Georgian frippery; it was rather, as one decorating manual put it, the 'embodiment of qualities which the world cannot do without – qualities whose first practical action is rather to cultivate mercy than to foster sentiment'.[77] Following the 'requirements of Taste', promised the author of *The Science of Taste* (1879), would 'exercise a salutary effect in elevating the character'.[78]

The moralization of possessions reflected a broader, post-evangelical mindset, which granted to household objects sway over those who came into contact with them. An evangelical would never have considered the design of one coal scuttle or another immoral. Sin was an attribute of humans, not their possessions. But design reformers endowed goods with new meanings: what one owned, bought, and treasured helped to shape – and hence also to communicate – something of the moral make-up of a person. It was a habit of mind that, despite their many differences, linked emphatically practical men such as Cole to theorists like John Ruskin; it spread well beyond the narrow circles of design reform.[79] Even before Karl Marx, exiled to London after the failed revolution of 1848, developed his famous notion of 'commodity fetishism', many Victorians would certainly have agreed that the household good was a 'very strange' thing, though unlike Marx, they would have rooted the source of that strangeness in the commodity's moral properties rather than in its ability to obscure the social relations of its production.[80]

Cole was well aware of the strategic force of a moral appeal to British consumers. He had himself blazed the trail that Syrie Maugham would later follow. Raised in a devout household coloured by his mother's Quaker upbringing, Cole had abandoned church-going in the late 1820s after his mother's death.[81] To brand a table top decorated with cabbage roses as immoral, Cole understood, implicated the purchaser of that item in an act that, if not a path to hell in itself, was at the very least not respectable. Amidst the exuberant excesses of early industrial production, the language of morality offered a powerful means of drawing distinctions: between good and bad, false and true.[82] But design reform's moral idiom was not just a rhetorical club to bludgeon the public into furnishing properly. Cole and his fellow reformers sincerely believed that meretricious designs corrupted the body politic, and that bad taste promoted immorality. Confronted by the riot of patterns, objects, and materials made possible by the machine, design reformers sought to discipline abundance. They preached a gospel of fixed principles and absolute rules in the place of wobbly Georgian notions of 'fluctuating' taste.[83] They looked with nostalgia upon the era of the medieval Church, which in its role as the patron of architecture, embroideries, and stained glass, had enforced artistic standards.[84] If the Church had once served as the guardian of art as well as morals, the torch had now passed to the agents of design reform. Design reform's rules were intended to provide a guide to consumption as the absolute strictures imposed by severe religion increasingly lost their hold.

16 The 'Silenus' jug, designed by Minton & Co. in 1831. One of Minton's most popular designs, the 'Silenus' jug depicted Bacchus' triumphal procession. It was displayed in the Chamber of Horrors at Marlborough House as an example of an object whose form was both 'ungraceful and broken by ornament'.

In Marlborough House, Henry Cole and his allies opened a Museum of Ornamental Art, comprised of exhibits left over from the previous year's Great Exhibition and items from the royal collections.[85] They displayed goods they found sound and worthy, demonstrating right-minded principles of design. The public was admitted free on Monday and Tuesday; otherwise, there was a 6d. charge; more than 125,000 visitors attended in 1853, more than 100,000 the following year.[86] Artisans were welcome to handle the objects on display for a small fee, providing that they washed their hands in advance. But by far the most popular attraction among museum visitors – displayed in the corridor approaching the exhibition rooms so that no one could miss it – was the so-called Chamber of Horrors, a collection of specially chosen objects intended to humiliate inept consumers and duplicitous manufacturers, presented under the rubric, 'Instances of Bad Taste'.[87] Accompanying each item in the catalogue were critical remarks offered, according to one reporter, 'with the view of . . . improving the judgment of the people in general'.[88] A pair of scissors in the shape of a stork was based upon 'false principles', the museum's visitors learned, because the bird's beak opened the wrong way.[89] So far as carpets went, 'flatness should be one of the principles for decorating a surface continually under the feet'.[90] Design reformers believed fervently in the virtues of 'conventionalized' ornamentation, which represented nature by means of stylized images, rather than 'naturalistic' or imitative renderings drawn from life, which were doomed always to disappoint.[91] Ornament – in other words – should be simple, chaste, in line with the object's function and, for the English, Protestant.[92]

17 Papier-mâché tray, manufactured by Jennens & Bettridge of Birmingham, c. 1850. This is likely the tray criticized in the Marlborough House catalogue for its absurd pairing of a pirated painting with a mother-of-pearl and gilt border – the net result being that 'the picture, on which most labour has been bestowed, is thrown away, as it must be hidden when the tray is used'.

18 'Conventionalized' ornamentation. 'Daisy' wallpaper designed by William Morris, 1864.

19 'Naturalistic' design. A furnishing fabric from 1850 of roller-printed and glazed cotton. This chintz, displayed in the Chamber of Horrors, was condemned for its 'direct imitation of nature'. The guest who lowered himself onto a sofa upholstered in this fabric had to fear that he might be impaled on a protruding twig.

Many visitors entered the Chamber of Horrors only to find one of their own previously prized possessions displayed there. 'It was amusing,' reported one journalist, 'to hear the people admire the "false principles" when they first entered the room, from an impression that the articles were hung there in commendation.'[93] Most members of the public, he continued, found the label of 'false principles' at first difficult to understand. They could not comprehend why a rose so beautifully copied could be wrong, but through the museum's instruction, came to see the errors of their ways: '. . . for the first time in their lives they began to think about art and its meanings'. His was an optimistic appraisal. Others found the museum displays bewildering, or even off-putting. In Charles Dickens' weekly *Household Words*, Henry Morley satirized the reaction of a man, a Mr Crumpet, driven half mad by his visit to the museum. Not only had Crumpet decorated his own house in horrors, but he could no longer abide his friends' dwellings. When Crumpet calls upon his friend Frippy, the proud possessor of a house done up in the ridiculed style, the trauma inflicted upon poor Crumpet by his museum visit is evident: 'if your carpet were what it represents itself to be, I couldn't walk to the door without treading upon half-a-dozen thorns, and perhaps, dislocating my ankle among the architectural scrolls that I see projecting out of it'.[94]

Cole and other design reformers had for a decade carped at manufacturers, but never before had they taken their case directly to the public. And never before had the case against bad design been so heavily loaded with the charge of immorality. Cole's own manner was peremptory and designed to provoke, characteristic of his habit of 'thrusting aside and trampling down those who did not agree with him'.[95] In Dickens' indignant description, he was a 'professed pugilist', a government officer 'ready to fight all England', who appears in the novel *Hard Times* to indoctrinate schoolchildren in the 'new discovery' that horses did not belong on wallpapers, nor flowers on carpets: 'What is called Taste, is only another name for Fact'.[96] The reaction from Birmingham was predictable. Manufacturers raged at a government that sponsored efforts to defame industry; it was an attack of the Court upon the productive classes.[97] Retailers claimed that they had lost orders – that clients had visited the Chamber of Horrors and cancelled their purchases. One manufacturer described the effect of the design reformers' educational efforts on his business. His customer's wife had gone 'to see what is taste at Marlborough House, and there discovered that everything that had been ordered to be done was in the worst possible taste. The gentleman proceeded immediately to countermand his order, mentioning at the same time the discovery he had so fortunately made just in time to save his credit as a man of taste'.[98]

The Museum of Ornamental Art had scarcely been open six months when 'Argus' – an anonymous but widely distributed critic – took up the cudgels for the manufacturers. In a series of pamphlets published throughout 1853, entitled 'A Mild Remonstrance against the Taste-Censorship at Marlborough House', Argus lambasted the principles of design reform generally, and Cole, Richard Redgrave, and Owen Jones, whom he branded the 'Triumvirate of Taste', more specifically.[99] In eighty pages of closely argued and never mild prose, he mocked their cherished ideas about conventionalized or stylized decoration, took issue with their conception of taste, and repudiated their methods. 'If you may dogmatize on matters of Taste in art and ornamentation, why not in matters of Opinion, political, civil, religious and domestic? If you may, unquestioned and unchecked, expose to public ridicule the productions of a Manufacturer on the unproved plea of bad taste, why may you not post up for public reprobation the name of the Author of an unpalatable book?'[100] Argus insisted that there were no absolute standards of taste that could be applied to manufacture. 'Taste in the abstract, i.e. pure and perfect Taste . . . [was] antagonistic to Commerce . . . .'[101] Tastes were individual, and manufacturers had the right to produce whatever would sell.

But for all of Argus' protests, he agreed with the Taste Triumvirate on one crucial point: the morality of the nation was indeed at stake in the design of manufactured goods. The 'ultimate end of Taste', Argus wrote, was 'the Progress of Humanity towards general enlightenment, morality, and Religion'.[102] However, the design reformers, with their odes to conventionalized ornamentation, were barking up the wrong tree. There was no higher call, Argus urged, than to imitate the Lord's own creation. He cited the eighteenth-century moral philosopher Archdeacon William Paley – scourge of the evangelicals – in his defence. Naturalized ornamentation was the superior choice. 'The Natural in Ornamentation [is] better fitted to disseminate enlightenment, refinement, morality, and Religion.'[103]

The force of Argus' appeal was not lost upon the besieged manufacturers. By distributing Argus' pamphlet to his clientele, one manufacturer sought to offer reassurance 'that we carpet manufacturers, calico printers, and paper-hanging manufacturers, are "not so bad as we seem"; but that the character for bad taste, absurdity, and ignorance, applies more to our critics than to us'.[104] Argus' outrage gained a hearing, too, in the pages of the press. While the *Morning Advertiser* agreed with Cole and company that British taste required improving, they advised caution (following Argus), lest the government concentrate in its own hands the power that rightfully belonged to the people.[105] The design reformers struck back in Prince Albert's *Court Journal*, claiming that Argus must be a manufacturer of one of the objects in the Chamber of Horrors. If he could 'detect a poetic idea in a piece of opaque glass, tortured into the form of a lily', they could do little for him. Argus – they sniped – was the kind of man who approved of shirts emblazoned with ballet girls and hearthrugs patterned upon lions: 'you do not want to be taught, you would rather stumble about than tread firmly'.[106]

Livid manufacturers succeeded in getting the Chamber of Horrors shut down, but the issue of the public's taste was put – permanently – on the nation's agenda. The problem was, of course, that middle-class Britons appeared to delight in the new possibilities that mechanization offered them. They wanted possessions they could not afford, and do not seem to have been much bothered if imitation was all they could achieve. Better, they thought, to have *faux* marble than no marble at all. Moreover, they liked the whimsical character of soup tureens in the form of boars' heads and andirons fashioned as snakes, and sought novelties with which to fill their houses. If man was no longer condemned to a life of penance, why should he not take a modicum of pleasure in the material world?

THE MORAL INFLUENCE OF FURNITURE

Whether most middle-class people absorbed the tenets of design reform in detail is, as we shall see in the next chapter, very doubtful. But by the 1860s and 1870s, the larger idea – that domestic goods helped to shape character – was well established. Good taste, John Ruskin told his Bradford audience in 1864, was 'essentially a moral quality'. Because 'what we *like* determines what we *are* . . . to teach taste is inevitably to form character'.[107] Treatises on the 'moral influence of furniture' even appeared in the pages of furniture trade journals, incongruously nestled next to the newest techniques for veneering, which design reformers abhorred. 'Tawdry' objects were, the *Furniture Gazette* instructed its readers, 'missionaries in the cause of ugliness and meanness – doing an amount of real mischief, the extent, nature and ramifications of which could scarcely be described in a volume'.[108] Linked as it was with morality, house decoration even became a pressing concern for the sober reformers who gathered at the Social Science Association's annual meeting. Alongside sessions on police supervision and the spread of infectious fevers was one on house decoration; it was as 'morally injurious to keep company with bad things, as it is to associate with bad people'.[109] The decorator George Audsley's paper made clear the debt that design reform owed to evangelical ideas about self-discipline and restraint. The British, he argued, should elect 'to be guided by the canon of simplicity rather than by the dictates of passionate luxury, by self-denial rather than indulgence'.[110]

As a host of self-appointed taste-makers churned out tract upon tract to guide shoppers, what was right and what was wrong in decoration became a lively subject for debate. If treasure stored up on earth no longer put its owners in the way of eternal damnation, Victorians nonetheless remained preoccupied by the question of *how* one was to consume. The collision between older religious ideas and new consuming desires, together with the furore aroused by design reform, left middle-class Britons in search of answers to these novel dilemmas of the marketplace. Was religiously inspired Gothic furnishing really the best style of decoration? Did three-dimensional patterns sicken visitors or could they be tolerated in heirloom chintzes? If the individual had once been enjoined to inspect his or her own conscience for evidence of wrongdoing, scrutiny now increasingly centred upon inanimate objects. Possessions were evaluated not only for their value or durability, but also for the effects they might have on the house's inhabitants – an idea that may appear ludicrous to us today, until we reflect upon the fad for the Chinese practice of feng shui, which takes as its starting point the idea that the physical environment moulds the person.[111]

For most Victorian believers, it was the doctrine of incarnationalism, probably more than design reform, which forged the link between morality and household possessions. From the 1860s, the harsh evangelical doctrine of the Atonement had fallen from favour.[112] For the increasingly prosperous middle classes, the hell-fire to which their newfound fortunes exposed them burned too hot. The question of whether or not one would be saved became odious when, as Boyd Hilton puts it, 'the rich and powerful were unable to bear this suspense any longer'.[113] Rejected was the idea that humanity was born irredeemably wicked; out went the spectre of Christ, tortured on the cross to pay for mankind's sins. Instead, men were enjoined to live in the power of Christ's life. As a generation of clerics and their congregants turned against the old evangelical ideas about self-denial, which they variously dismissed as 'Calvinistic' or 'puritanical', the image of God changed, too, from the cruel and capricious deity of the Atonement who would punish the innocent for the sins of the guilty to a merciful deity who forgave man's failings. In this new schema, sackcloth and ashes were neither necessary nor inherently virtuous. As one Baptist minister, preaching in the 1860s, put it: 'We have left the old Puritan error. We no longer despise the beautiful and artistic, but claim them as divine things, and enlist them in divine service ... all man's life and work can be dedicated to heaven'.[114] Beauty and godliness went hand in hand.

The idea that beauty could be divine (or its corollary, that ugliness was evil) served to direct new attention to the quotidian matters of the household. Among the earliest home decoration gurus were clergymen cast in the incarnationalist mould: optimistic about the possibilities of human progress, unlikely to dwell upon the fires of hell, focused upon the pleasures (and virtues) of self-cultivation. The backlash against the doctrine of the Atonement came first in Scotland.[115] Where once the most rigorous evangelicalism had been fervently embraced, the northern pulpits had yielded to the kinder, gentler prophets of the Incarnation. Among them was the Ayrshire native Andrew Boyd, who had trained as a barrister before deciding upon a career in the ministry. For twenty-five years, Boyd preached at St Andrews, where his sermons were notable for their 'literary and practical rather than dogmatic' nature.[116] Why, he wondered, in a thinly veiled dig at the militant Church, were so many people who profess to be Christians 'like grim Gorgon's heads warning people off from having anything to do with Christianity'?[117] In a series of popular books, he derided the premium that evangelicals had placed upon asceticism while insisting upon the significance (as he put it) of 'external things'.[118]

Boyd's essay, 'Concerning the Moral Influences of the Dwelling', printed in his best-selling *Recreations of a Country Parson* (1861), dealt not with the staples of evangelical tracts – with original sin and the regenerated will – but with the interior and possessions. Although Boyd's decorating advice did not extend beyond a vaguely expressed preference for Gothic styles, and a detestation of 'the vile old willow-pattern', he cast the activity of furnishing as a morally elevating, even morally necessary, pursuit.[119] 'I do not hesitate to say that the scenery amid which a man lives, and the house in which he lives, have a vast deal to do with making him what he is.'[120] Entering your property by means of a 'battlemented gateway under a lofty arch' gave a man a different feeling from the 'common five-bar gate'.[121] He described with relish his own study, decorated in green to complement the rich finish of his oak furniture. The man who lived among beauty was more likely to take pleasure in life and do good – pursuits that in Boyd's writings were posited as complementary rather than antagonistic activities. Goodness, for Boyd, was as much a result of what was without as what was within: 'We are all moral chameleons; and we take the colour of the objects among which we are placed.'[122]

If man was indeed a moral chameleon, the improvement of taste was not only a practical or an aesthetic, but an urgently religious matter. The idea for the first series of mass-marketed decoration manuals came (unlikely as it may at first seem) from an Anglican curate. In 1876, the Reverend W.J. Loftie proposed to the publisher Macmillan a series of books on home furnishing to be entitled 'Art at Home'.[123]

Loftie, a man of wide-ranging literary and antiquarian interests, had taken holy orders at the age of twenty-six, and held curacies throughout England before being appointed assistant chaplain at the Chapel Royal, Savoy – a position he occupied for twenty-four years.[124] His duties left him plenty of time to indulge his interests in British art and architecture, the history of London, as well as the 'recreation' he reported to *Who's Who*: searching out unrestored churches.[125] But even before Loftie turned his attention to despoliation of ecclesiastical monuments, he made his name as an expert in home decoration. He penned the first of the 'Art at Home' books himself; the edited series would eventually run to twelve volumes, including one tract on the dining-room by Loftie's wife, Martha.

Loftie's book, entitled *A Plea for Art in the House*, sought – like Boyd's – to provide a religious basis for home decoration. The cultivation of taste, Loftie lectured his readers, was not only a 'moral but even a religious duty'.[126] Acknowledging that this idea might at first seem 'paradoxical', he invoked the authority of none other than Bishop Joseph Butler, one of the most influential figures for early nineteenth-century evangelicals. If life was, as Butler had said, a 'state of probation', and home life the highest ideal type of heaven, it was, Loftie concluded, everyone's duty to 'do something towards raising ourselves and others, and bringing heaven nearer to earth'.[127] In Loftie's version of religion, which strayed far from Butler's own conception of perpetual trial and punishment, moral beauty and material beauty went hand in hand. Heaven was domesticated and hell left far behind. But beauty imposed strictures of its own. The best taste, at least to Loftie's mind, was biblical. Loftie lauded a scheme for a dining-room done up in the most sombre shades of grey, complete with a motto from the Book of Job, stencilled in Old English script slanting up from the fireplace: 'Man is born unto travail as the sparks fly upward.'[128]

Even as severe religion lost its hold in mid-nineteenth-century Britain, the habit of thinking in moral terms strengthened. The business of furnishing attracted the efforts of the godly – men like the Congregationalist Elias Henry Davies, of the Rhondda, whose furnishing firm allowed him 'to serve his generation according to the will of God'.[129] For the trade paper magnate John Benn, the improvement of the nation's taste was a moral issue, in which he was 'gifted with indomitable persever-ance'.[130] Raised by evangelical missionaries in the East End of London, himself a devout man, Benn chose to make the domestic interior, rather than the parish, his field of crusade. The paper he founded, the *Cabinet-Maker*, became a byword for good taste. Even as he compulsively redecorated his own house and those of the nation, Benn remained a 'cheerful Puritan', as his biographer put it; his unpublished autobiography was entitled 'The Joys of Adversity'.[131] Late nineteenth-century Bradford's most fashionable furnishing firm, Christopher Pratt & Son, was estab-lished by a family of Methodist missionaries and ministers. From their Bradford store, the Pratts sent out a line of sons and nephews as missionaries to Africa, while themselves chairing the local branches of the Vigilance Committee, Purity League, and Religious Tract Society.[132] In the furnishing business itself, the elevation of morals was never far from the surface. Pratt & Son advertised their fitted bathroom with the words of John Wesley: ' "Cleanliness is next to Godliness", said Wesley, and it might almost be inferred from this that a useful bathroom paves the way to heaven.'[133] The firm's own history described the relationship that the Pratts cultivated with their clients in pastoral terms: 'An intimacy was . . . engendered between the firm and its clients which became almost sacred'.[134] Amid rising standards of living and evidence of declining belief, families such as the Davies, the Benns, and the Pratts, alongside design reformers, sought in the realm of consumption a means (to paraphrase Noel Annan's famous formulation) of making people good in the absence of organized religion.[135]

The conviction that better rooms made better people – or that well-fitted bathrooms propelled their users to heaven – undoubtedly provided new justifications for consumer expenditure. The diary of the young Mary Eliza Joy, whose career as one of the first woman decorators will be followed in Chapter 3, demonstrates how readily incarnationalist convictions could underwrite consumer pleasures. Reared in the tradition of the evangelical Sunday, the eighteen-year-old Joy began, in the 1860s, to question its strictures. 'Once upon a time I thought it a heinous sin to buy anything on a Sunday,' confided Joy to her diary in 1866; 'now I see it is not. Beauty makes all things and all places and all seasons holy.'[136] Turning the old condemnation of wealth on its head, *Queen*, that bible of refined female taste, in 1875 judged that 'the owners of a pretty house are likely to be more estimable characters than others less happily situated'.[137] In the *Contemporary Review*, the Reverend Foster Barham Zincke assured his readers that 'every improvement in the house is an improvement in morality'.[138] As household goods became (in popular parlance) household gods, the choice of particular materials, patterns, and furniture styles opened householders to moral acclaim or censure from family members, acquaintances, and friends. Gwen Raverat, Charles Darwin's granddaughter, recounted a conversation between two of her uncles. At the turn of the century, Uncle Lenny, a military man, built a house in the Ashdown Forest, complete with (his architect had insisted) heavily leaded, small-paned pseudo-Gothic windows. He awaited the visit of his brother, Horace, with trepidation. Horace lived in an exquisitely furnished but not grand house. Lenny greeted his brother with a disclaimer. 'Well, Horace, I suppose you think these windows are not only ugly but immoral.'[139]

The idea of furnishing as a moral proving ground found wide reception, as despairing critics of the notion acknowledged. With their moral natterings, wrote an angry correspondent to the *Globe*, writers on home decoration had turned furnishing into 'a long series of anxious experiments'. People of limited means had to make compromises which left them open to the 'lofty-souled critic . . . ready at any moment that may give him the opportunity to explain the "moral" grounds of his objection to this, that, or the other'.[140] At the Society of Arts, the painter Thomas

Purdie criticized the overheated rhetoric of design reform: 'language has been perverted from its original meaning; ethics and aesthetics have been jumbled together; bad taste has been confounded with moral turpitude'.[141]

But those who objected to the practice of endowing furniture with moral meaning found themselves in the minority. For years to come, the issue of morality would remain central to the business of home decoration. Whether furnished with belongings that reflected right-minded principles of design or simply judged according to a standard of goodness, rooms took on a semi-religious aspect. So widespread were churchly objects, acknowledged one advice manual, that a purchaser had to 'be constantly on his guard . . . or he will have a church corona over his dining-table and an ecclesiastical scuttle for the reception of his secular coal'.[142] Rooms decorated in the 1870s recalled one antique dealer, had a 'dim religious effect'.[143] The writer Richard Church, boarding with an Anglo-Catholic couple in the years before the First World War, recollected their 'semi-ecclesiastical'

20 An ecclesiastical corner cupboard. Manufactured by Cox & Sons in the 1870s, this Gothic cupboard evoked a baptismal font.

21 A Gothic hall seat, advertised for sale by the firm of C. & R. Light, London, 1880s.

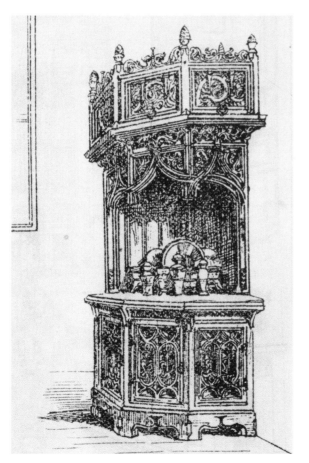

drawing-room, sparsely furnished with white walls, a severe scheme relieved only by pictures of the Madonna and saints.[144] By the Edwardian period, when conceptions of decoration had changed, religiously inflected furnishing had come to be seen as *démodé*, a musty relic of an earlier era. For up-to-date modern novelists such as H.G. Wells, such rooms summoned up the world of country clerics and their families – the sorts of people who littered their bedrooms with needlepointed texts announcing 'Thy Grace is Sufficient for Me'. In rented accommodation, Wells' heroine Marjorie, fresh from London, marvels at the 'faint and faded flavour of religion that pervaded the bedrooms'. The 'moral element' was the room's strongest impression.[145]

* * *

The well-upholstered, overstuffed Victorian domestic interior invites psychological speculation. It may, at first, appear a subconscious compensation for the privations that militant Christianity inflicted upon the individual. But that interpretation is too simplistic. Rather, what needs to be explained is the long coexistence of consumerist longings and moral concerns: 'the conciliation', as George Eliot put it in describing the evangelical banker's wife Mrs Bulstrode, of 'piety and worldliness, the nothingness of this life and the desirability of cut glass'.[146] How to be good *and* well-to-do: this was the question that confronted the British middle classes from the mid-nineteenth century onwards. At the dawn of the age of mass consumerism, worldly pleasures had first to be cleared of the charge of self-indulgence. The idea that possessions could be evaluated along a moral yardstick – a notion endorsed by design reform and underwritten by incarnationalist theology – found wide reception among Victorians, both agnostic and religious. By redefining consumption as a moral act, and the home as a foretaste of the heaven to come, the British middle classes sought to square material abundance with spiritual good.

If the history of the Victorian interior has taken us – unexpectedly – back to the pulpit, let us revisit the young Syrie Barnardo in her father's house on the edge of Epping Forest. At the age of sixteen, Syrie indulged in her first conscious act of decoration, embellishing the stolid mahogany mirror that hung above her dressing-table with a length of pink silk ribbon. By the 1920s, her individual style would make her a household name, the avatar of a distinctly British form of modern design characterized by sleek, monochromatic lines in place of Victorian clutter and colour. But if Syrie's trademark white-upon-white seems a world away from the black-upon-black in which she was raised, the distance between self-denial and self-expression was not as great as we might imagine. Most significantly, evangelicalism forced a concentration upon the self which was, in the generations that followed, modified but not abandoned.[147] 'This conformation of the English mind, this habit of turning in upon the self, this primacy of the moral being, this need to perceive that moral self first of all', counted for the Frenchman Hippolyte Taine among the most noteworthy of English qualities.[148] Above all else, Augustus Hare noted critically, evangelicalism caused 'an individual to dwell upon himself and his own doings . . . thus causing him to invest that self and those doings with a most undue importance'.[149] In the seemingly inhospitable terrain of early nineteenth-century soul-searching, the modern individual took root.

CHAPTER 2

CATHEDRALS TO COMMERCE

SHOPPERS AND ENTREPRENEURS

The origins of the modern home decoration magazine can be traced back to the mind of an evangelical businessman. Launched with a great fanfare in 1897, *The House* was Britain's first interiors magazine, the ancestor of all of the glossy titles, from *House and Garden* to *Wallpaper**, that today beckon from the news-stand. Its founder, John Benn, was a legend in a nation of shopkeepers – a man with a proven genius for spotting a market. By the 1890s, Benn had already scored a number of triumphs in the world of trade papers. His first paper, the *Cabinet-Maker*, started in 1880, had within a few years outclassed its rivals, becoming the standard-bearer for all that was good and worthy in the realm of Chippendale. To the *Cabinet-Maker* Benn had, in 1890, added a complementary organ, the *Furnisher and Decorator*; later would come the *Hardware Trade Journal* and the *Export World*, cornerstones of a veritable trade paper empire that would eventually catapult John Benn from his humble origins as a furniture draughtsman on to the stage of Edwardian progressive politics.[1] But by 1903, *The House* itself was nearly defunct, a drain upon the Benn family finances and, as John Benn's son Ernest would remember it, a 'disastrous failure' in an otherwise unblemished late Victorian success story.[2] The country was simply not ready for such a publication, Ernest Benn explained; his father was two decades ahead of his time.

Or was he? From the first issue, *The House* presented its role as that of a 'friendly critic to the family'.[3] The magazine sought to save the prospective furnisher from embarrassing mistakes. The best course for most would-be home decorators – or so *The House*'s editors advised – was to turn their interiors over to men who had made the house their profession; in that way 'many a decorative disaster would be avoided'.[4] While *The House* offered its readers instruction in amateur arts, it firmly counselled that the significant decisions be left to the expert because this was 'work requiring as much careful thought and as much knowledge as the solution of a problem requires of a mathematician'.[5] Divergence from the path of design reform was not tolerated in its pages. To 'Bel', who wrote in to ask how to imitate stained glass, the columnist Penelope delivered a stern rebuke: 'Imitation, as such, as you will have gathered from the articles in THE HOUSE, cannot be considered artistic, and I should, therefore, not recommend you to imitate stained glass in the way I gather you wish to do.'[6] *The House* sought to defend the country's residences from their inhabitants.

Visitors to Henry Cole's Chamber of Horrors in 1853 would have found Benn's vision of the tasteless British public familiar and even instructive. But fifty years later, the rigid principles of design reform, bolstered by Benn's evangelical beliefs, seemed very old-fashioned. Rather than arriving too early at the banquet of consumer desire, Benn had come with a dish that was at least three decades out of date. By the 1870s, the sharp decline in the price of food and other necessities had put money in many Britons' pockets, and furnishing was all the rage. Even as shoppers deployed the language of moral good, they flocked to a new generation of retail stores to exercise their newfound buying power with little regard for the strictures of design reform.[7] To the despair of those who wished to control it, Britain's first mass consumer revolution could not be contained by the commandments of taste.

At the outset of the Victorian period, affluent couples decorated once, generally at marriage. By the later nineteenth century, a middle-class family might renew their décor every seven years or so, while constantly embellishing rooms with newly purchased bric-à-brac.[8] In 1862, it seemed to the barrister William Hardman, himself mired in a renovation project, that 'everybody is putting his house in order in this great Metropolis'.[9] Entire industries sprung up to foster and serve this demand: advice manuals to instruct in the art of doing up the house, slick catalogues that reproduced photographs of real or fantasy interiors, and, most importantly, the stores. The windows of the magnificent new furnishing emporia invited shoppers to imagine themselves surrounded by objects of finery. As mechanization and other innovations had increased the supply and types of goods available, so, too, had it reduced their cost. The prosperous middle-class couple might buy a lacquered Japanese cabinet for their new drawing-room; the servant girl, an enamelled teaspoon of her own. Their purchases fuelled the construction of the largest stores ever known.

Whether demand creates supply or supply generates demand is one of the great chicken-and-egg questions of capitalism. But in the mid-nineteenth century, there was no doubt that the public's wants were the engine driving consumption. Manufacturers complained bitterly about consumers' insatiable desire for novelties and new patterns. The old-style furniture suppliers – with their cramped, often insalubrious premises and limited range of items – had to expand their stock or face extinction. In the increasingly cut-throat business of late Victorian furnishing, victory would belong to the great urban palaces of home decoration. Cathedrals to consumption, shops such as Maple's or Glasgow's Wylie & Lochhead became places of pilgrimage for the middle-class men and women who filed through their sumptuous galleries. They were the brainchild of a new generation of entrepreneurs: men who viewed furnishing chiefly as an art rather than as a moral discipline. In a relatively short time, the proprietors of Britain's furnishing stores would not only satisfy shoppers' longings, but devise new ways to prise open their wallets with lavish advertising campaigns and innovations to tickle their fancy. They knew what the Benns never recognized. The customer had come to expect flattery and a wide selection, rather than criticism and restraints.

THE NOVELTY OF ABUNDANCE

The clutter we associate with Victorian interiors came at the end of the nineteenth century, not before. The rooms of the 1830s and 1840s were relatively spare, as befitted their religiously minded (and financially straitened) inhabitants. But as the century wore on, rooms became ever more crowded with possessions in a bewildering variety of styles. Patterns battled for attention; no surface was left unadorned. A foreigner unfamiliar with the British custom of lining up plates on picture rails, quipped a critic, might believe that the English ate their dinners vertically – off the wall.[10] The satirist 'Corney Grain' lampooned drawing-rooms so full of bric-à-brac that 'You had to go in and out pick-a-back'.[11] For the new people of

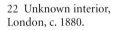

22 Unknown interior, London, c. 1880.

23 The Bower family home, Springfield Cottage, near Bedford, c. 1900. Dr David Bower, a Scotsman, purchased Springfield House Private Asylum in 1879. Springfield Cottage was built for him when he married in 1888.

24 Charles Kettlewell's dining room at St Margaret's Mansions, Victoria St. A case study in abundant furnishing and native exotica: spears and bows, a wide variety of stuffed birds and (apparently) a wind-up minstrel show doll. Photographed by Bedford Lemere in 1888.

plenty, what counted as sufficient was constantly under revision. One advice columnist, while cautioning against too much furniture in the dining-room, described as
appropriate a pirate's trove of belongings that would bewilder modern tastes: 'a
good dining-table, two armchairs, deep and roomy, with arms, ten or twelve ordinary chairs, a sofa, sideboard, dinner-waggon, occasional table, and writing-table, is
quite as much as is really necessary, unless the room, even with this amount of
furniture, looks bare, and then a bookcase or two in convenient recesses, a screen,
or an old-fashioned bureau for china, may have a place'. [12]

What had formerly been luxuries were now necessities, placed within the range
of every middle-class budget courtesy of rising standards of living and the fruits of
the machine. These were the first dizzying decades of mass production, and British
manufacturers let loose upon the world a riot of textiles, carpets, and pottery.[13]
Mechanization, along with the invention of cheap aniline dyes, meant that designs
which previously required hand block-printing with expensive colours could be
produced by the thousands on steam-operated cylinder machines.[14] So rapidly had
textile manufacture developed, commented the reporter George Dodd in 1844, that
the quantity of work turned out was now measured in miles, rather than, as previously, in yards.[15] One well-known potter brought more than a thousand original
designs to town in 1848; designers were, in the words of one critic, 'worked like
mill-horses'.[16] Patterns proliferated, designs multiplied; the removal of excise taxes
on glass and paper opened new vistas for decoration. In 1834, British wallpaper
manufacturers recorded an output of 1.2 million pieces; by 1851 they were
producing 5.5 million; in 1860, 19 million, and in 1874, 32 million.[17] The young

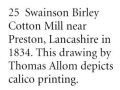

25 Swainson Birley
Cotton Mill near
Preston, Lancashire in
1834. This drawing by
Thomas Allom depicts
calico printing.

Hippolyte Taine observed in the 1860s that the British competed fiercely to develop new products: 'Everyone tries to devise some refinement to flatter a desire, a whim, or a mania . . . Genius is expended in making and selling some special set of horse-brushes'.[18]

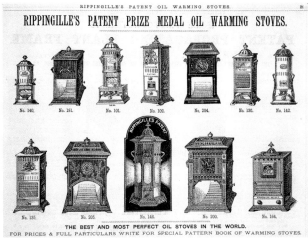

26 A profusion of oil-warming stoves, c. 1882.

27 Papier-mâché bedstead designed by Mr Fitzcook and manufactured by John Bettridge & Co., Birmingham. Displayed at the 1862 International Exhibition.

British consumers, manufacturers often complained, set a high premium on novelty.[19] Adjustable furniture enjoyed great acclaim, as, too, did a bewildering variety of objects made of papier mâché, including (improbably enough) an elaborate half-tester bedstead.[20] Decoration could be symbolic: a Lilliputian cow might perch upon the handle of a pot for butter, a sitting hen pointed out a container of boiled eggs.[21] Despite the censure of design reform, the British public relished fanciful items, especially those whose form was radically divorced from their dreary function. The Industrial Revolution had turned the world upside down – the charred landscapes and smokestacks of the Midlands were proof of that. But it also made possible a fantasy world that had previously existed only in the most feverish dreams. Wallpapers, brought within the range of middle-class purchasers by the reduction of paper duties, were 'calculated to cause intense amazement to the beholder on a first view'.[22] A trip to the shops, *circa* 1880, yielded pencil cases shaped like pigs, as well as in the form of the notoriously sober Mr Gladstone and his

28 Symbolic decor-
ation – a 'Jackfield' cow
creamer, c. 1860.

29 Three-dimensional
wallpaper designed by
James Huntington,
c. 1860.

30 A fire-screen set
with stuffed birds,
c. 1850.

foppish sparring partner, Lord Beaconsfield. There were pepper boxes in the shape
of owls, a boar's head intended for a soup tureen, scissors modelled after birds,
japanned baths decorated with ocean-scapes of seashells and stones, and a stuffed
monkey skin for a lamp stand.[23] Whether ghoulish, impractical, or fanciful, there
was a use for it at home. A visitor to the modern middle-class household, one disapproving observer commented in 1879, 'may knock for admittance with the head of
a goat, wipe one's "feet" upon a Newfoundland dog, approach the hostess over a

carpet strewn with bouquets, converse with one foot upon a bengal tiger, and . . . be called upon to interpose the Bay of Naples between an elderly lady and the fireplace'.[24]

The breadth of selection offered in turn-of-the-century shops far outstripped what is available on the floor of our modern retail establishments. To capture a fickle public, manufacturers produced an incredible variety of goods. By the turn of the century, Messrs Hoskins and Sewell, among the largest bedstead-makers in the world, had placed 7,000 *different* examples on the market.[25] One Glasgow shop advertised that it offered furniture in all styles: if a customer wanted a bedstead just like grandfather had, it was available on the spot as, too, was the very latest rendition of Queen Anne.[26] H.J. Benjamin & Sons, a furniture warehouse in the East End of London, stocked nearly 300 varieties of sideboards from pieces inspired by the exoticism of the Moors to those faithful to the rigours of the medieval style.[27]

Furniture today is both standardized and, to a large extent, mass-produced. Neither was the case in the nineteenth century.[28] Until the First World War, furniture production relied largely upon hand-work. Between 1841 and 1881, the number of workers employed in the wood, furniture, and carriage trades soared, from 171,600 to 269,300, a reflection both of the greater demand for furniture and the still limited use of the machine.[29] Between 1819 and 1913, Britain's furniture output increased nearly fourfold.[30] Although saws might be used to cut out pieces

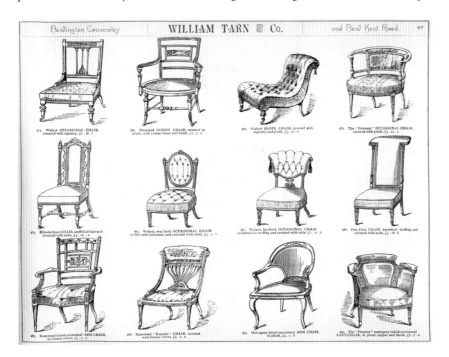

31 A small selection of the chairs available from William Tarn & Co., London, late nineteenth century.

and veneers, the process of assembly and finishing remained the work of skilled or semi-skilled craftsmen. Unlike in the United States, where large factories dominated the industry, the furniture trade in Britain belonged to small workshops. Its centre was London, supplemented by scattered pockets throughout the country, including the High Wycombe district, which was renowned for its chair-making (after the First World War this became the country's major furniture-making centre), and Birmingham, home to the iron and brass bed industry. In 1860, High Wycombe reportedly produced one chair a minute the entire year round.[31]

32 The machine shop of Heal's cabinet factory, 1899.

Through the 1860s, most of the prominent West End furniture emporia were largely supplied by their own in-house workshops and designers. However, by the 1870s the practice of subcontracting and piece-work had taken over. Called upon to give evidence to the government's 1888 Select Committee on the Sweating System, Blundell Maple, proprietor of one of the country's largest furnishing establishments, acknowledged that his firm bought goods from as many as a thousand different shops, located either in the furniture quarter around the Tottenham Court Road or in the East End.[32] By the 1880s, the East End, heavily reliant on sweated immigrant labour, housed the lion's share of the capital's workshops; the divorce of manufacturing and retailing was nearly complete. The social investigator Ernest Aves has left us a vivid picture of the state of the East End industry, *circa* 1889.[33] Every type of furniture was produced there, from exclusive, inlaid products destined for the drawing-rooms of the élite to the cheapest and roughest dining-room sets sold by hawkers on the street. According to Aves, the trade was becoming more competitive every year. The typical producer was a man of very limited means, with three to six employees, scant capital, and no machinery to speak of. He bought the already sawn timber with the earnings of the previous week, and planed, shaped, dowelled, and glued it in his own workshops. Turning and carving were out of his line; if the design required, he sent the piece out to specialized workers. The warehouse dealer received the producer's output 'in the white' – that is, unpolished and not yet upholstered – jobs that would be executed by other contractors. Before it reached the showroom floor, every piece of furniture had thus passed through a number of different workers' hands.

Machines cost money, and such a large investment only made sense where a firm could be guaranteed an ample market for one particular design or another. But given the public's well-known taste for novelty, furniture dealers reduced the selection of stock at their peril. Consumer demand played a crucial role in shaping the furniture trade, reinforcing its small workshop structure even as other industries such as engineering and cotton conglomerated and mechanized.[34] Because a host of independent producers competed to turn out new designs, what counted as fashionable changed rapidly, too. Describing a visit to the furnishing section of the department store Whiteley's in 1881, one reporter observed that the 'goods were almost entirely fresh in style since our last visit; the leading character of the energetic management being to secure the very "last thing out"'.[35] So long as labour remained abundant and cheap, and easy to exploit, as was the case in the East End because of immigration, machinery was unnecessary. The earliest firms to employ the machine extensively were the wealthier outfits, which could afford the initial outlay and made a fashionable virtue of their limited inventory.[36] The first type of furniture to be mass-produced was – ironically – probably of the Arts and Crafts variety around the turn of the century. The Arts and Crafts' simple and austere lines, ostensibly a rebuff to the machine-carved ornamentation popular among vulgar middle-class buyers, in fact proved remarkably adaptable to mechanization. 'This class of work,' wrote one trade paper of an Arts and Crafts oak buffet, 'lends itself admirably to machinery.'[37] By 1909, the Gomme Company of High Wycombe was manufacturing 'imitation rush seats' for a line derived from William Morris' signature product, the Windsor chair.[38]

Innovation 'to create an effect' was at a premium in the furnishing and allied trades.[39] In the 1840s, the Patent Decorative Carving and Sculpture Works in London burned designs into wood with a red-hot iron brand to create the appearance of carved Jacobean oak. The number of patents granted for furniture rose exponentially after the 1850s, as inventors (motivated in part by new trademark legislation) sought novel ways of designing better reclining chairs or collapsible bedsteads.[40] Workshops proved sites of experimentation. In 1861, the cabinetmaker John Dyer patented a technique he had discovered for creating inlay work

33 An easy-chair fitted with spring seat and back, Ashworth & Penfold, Manchester, 1875.

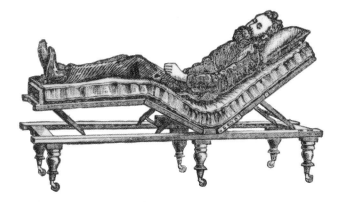

34 Blackman's wood-carving machine, 1875.

without the use of the saw. He coated cheap deal (or pine) furniture with wax, on to which he applied stencils, polishing the final product to a high sheen. Xylography, invented by Thomas Whitburn in the early 1870s, was a process for printing engravings or electrotypes on to a wood surface.

From the empire came new materials for the decorating trade, ranging from exotic timbers such as bamboo and rattan, harvested from a climbing palm native to the East Indies, to the first blooming of laboratory-created materials such as gutta-percha, a species of resin derived from latex.[41] Gutta-percha was the wonder substance of its day. It was 'discovered' in Singapore by Dr Montgomery, an assistant surgeon to the Residency, who one day queried a native woodcutter about the hatchet he employed.[42] The axe's handle was of a curious material, one which – the man told him – could be moulded into any form when it was dipped into boiling water, but dried hard as ivory. Like india rubber, gutta-percha came from the sap of a tree, the Isonandra Gutta, native to the steamy jungles of Singapore and Penang. So marvellous was the new substance that the Society of Arts in London, to which Dr Montgomery submitted his find in 1843, awarded him a gold medal. Within three years, a Mr Charles Hancock had already patented gutta-percha for use in an extraordinary variety of ventures, from telegraph wire insulation to cricket balls. In the domestic arena, gutta-percha took the place of any kind of ornamentation that would otherwise have been made of wood, from decorative elements and mouldings on furniture to inkstands, from imitation fringe to picture frames, bowls, and door handles.[43] Mixed with rubber and another substance called jintawan, gutta-percha proved suitable for stuffing or forming the seats of chairs, cushions, and mattresses. The gutta tree – chopped down for its sap rather than, like rubber, tapped – was nearly extinct by the 1890s.[44]

Gutta-percha mouldings, *faux* inlay, burnished Jacobean oak: innovation flourished precisely here, in attempts to imitate costly processes or materials in novel ways. For design reformers, modern construction seemed to grow more false with each passing day. Whitburn's imitation marquetry earned him the scorn of the critic Robert Rawlinson, who quoted Dr Johnson's rejoinder to the comment that a piece of highly embellished music he had just heard was very difficult: ' "Difficult", said the doctor, "I wish it were impossible" '.[45] Manufacturers, rather than defending, as had Argus fifty years before, the prerogatives of individual taste, tended instead to blame the public. Even if they themselves were converted to the cause of design reform, the average British consumer still demanded wide variety at a small price. Because of sweated labour, competition among the firms, and ersatz materials, prices for decoration and furnishings had declined in the 1870s and 1880s. What was prohibitive today might tomorrow be cheap. Consignments of Japanese tooled leather paper put aesthetic friezes within the reach even of poor families.[46] Nevertheless, the public, or so manufacturers had it, required 'a lot of show for a little money'.[47] Objects that were richly ornamented sold better than those which were plain.

By 1897, when *The House* made its début, there could be little doubt, at least for true believers in design reform, that the obstacle to more beautiful homes was the British public and specifically, its unquenchable taste for novelty and effect. With articles on how to furnish tastefully for 'five hundred', Benn's magazine was directed to middle- and upper middle-class consumers. Beauty was its guiding principle.[48] '[T]his magazine' – announced an advertising circular – 'is designed and produced to appeal to cultivated people who desire to make their homes beautiful, comfortable, healthful and entertaining.' Evident in the velvet glove of beauty, however, was an iron fist of aesthetic discipline. Avoiding home decoration errors, *The House* told its readers, required wholesale reform on the part of the British consumer. First and foremost, consumers had to abandon the notion that they were capable of furnishing their own houses tastefully. 'Individual preferences' were inherently suspect; home decoration should proceed according to established rules.[49] Contrary to consumers' undisciplined desires, *The House* stood for fixed ideas, principles to be incarnated, in line with Benn's own moral ways of thinking about design.

But in the marketplace of late Victorian Britain, the dogmas of design reform could hardly compete with the intoxicating promise of 7,000 different bedsteads. Those beauty-seeking subscribers who were not alienated by *The House*'s criticism of consumers may simply have lost interest in Benn's inflexible message. Given the staggering plenitude of the nation's furnishing emporia, the commandments of taste were precisely the wrong prescription for success in the periodicals trade. Fixated on the rightness of their doctrines, unwilling ultimately to license consumer desire, the Benns had missed the boat. The cause of design reform foundered on the shoals of the consumer.

A RETAIL REVOLUTION

Early on a September morning in 1881, a large crowd began to gather around Whiteley's department store in Westbourne Grove. William Whiteley's antics were already the stuff of legend: he was, he liked to claim, the Universal Provider, capable of producing, on short order, everything from a pint of fleas to a white elephant. But the shoppers who congregated in front of Whiteley's magnificent plate-glass windows had never seen anything like what the Universal Provider had on offer that day. It was as if the inhabitants of an opulent South Kensington home had momentarily left their well-appointed chambers, pushed their chairs back from the dining-room table, or retired from the elegant drawing-room. In one window was a Chippendale dining-room, complete with place settings of blue-and-white china, and carved and gilded chairs. In another, an exquisite drawing-room in ebonized woods upholstered in rich velvet and tapestry. Furniture stores had long displayed their wares in settings, but never before had the rooms been rendered so lifelike and complete. Whiteley's windows afforded a tantalizing peep into the houses of strangers.[50]

Extravagant window displays would become, by the turn of the century, part of the retailers' repertoire. But in the 1880s, Whiteley's techniques were revolutionary: an effort to create demand rather than struggling to keep pace with it. The extremely wealthy had long enjoyed recherché furnishing shops such as J.D. Crace & Sons, whose Wigmore Street showrooms, richly appointed in the style of the early French Renaissance, catered to the whims of dukes and marquesses.[51] But these were exclusive establishments, far beyond the means of middle-class shoppers. To understand the shock of Whiteley's windows, we have to pay a visit to the average provincial furnishing house of the era. The largest shop in all of north Wales was S. Aston

& Son, which opened its new premises in the town of Wrexham in 1882. The customer entered the store through a narrow pair of doors flanked by a display window on each side. A step down led into a dimly lit shop of approximately 400 square feet, piled high with furniture, with a counter for drapery and ironware. Rolls of linoleum and cheap rugs were arrayed at the back of the store in a passage leading to a staircase to the first floor. Upstairs could be found more furniture, along with such practical items of housekeeping as washtubs, clothes-horses and buckets.[52]

Shops such as Aston's were not establishments to dazzle, nor even to create longings. They were not, for starters, particularly hygienic. The cabinet-maker James Hopkinson, who opened a shop in the booming city of Liverpool in 1851, took a dim view of his competition. Liverpool should have offered superb horizons for the general dealer in furniture. However, there were 'many dirty looking shops in the town which do not *succeed, simply*, because they are not kept sweet & clean'.[53] Given the structure of the cabinet-making business, it was probably the smell rather than sawdust that was the problem. Because business was organized along lines of production, upholstery and undertaking – trades that deployed the same raw materials – often occupied the same premises. A firm might sell furniture, provide upholstery, and outfit funerals. Hence, shops such as William Brock & Co., Ltd in Exeter – house furnishers, cabinet and bedding manufacturers, carpet warehousemen, undertakers and removal contractors – or H.G. Dunn & Sons, Ltd in Bromley, Kent – house furnishers, undertakers, and removers – sold not only the upholstered parlour sets that were a staple of middle-class interiors, but caskets as well. The sound of nails being pounded into coffins offered a grim reminder of the fact that the rewards of the righteous were not to be enjoyed on this earth.

35 Breckel's Cabinet Manufacturer, Upholsterers, Undertakers, &c. High Street. From *Tallis's London Street Views*, 1838–40.

36 R. & J. Newton,
Upholsterers,
Appraisers &
Undertakers, Wardour
Street. From *Tallis's
London Street Views*,
1838–40.

With retail choices such as these, doing up a house in the mid-nineteenth century was a very different enterprise from what it would become even a few decades later. There was, for instance, no advice literature to inspire the budding furnisher. Such books as did exist handled the subject of making do on £100 or £250 a year: they largely treated economy, rather than style. *The House*, a periodical founded in 1875, dealt not (as would Benn's magazine of the same name) with matters of decoration and taste, but with the practicalities involved in running a home: 'It is not everyone who knows how to clean his carpet. How few are there in the world who have learnt how to boil potatoes.'[54] The local upholsterer, a stock figure of fun in Victorian fiction, was not a man to inspire aesthetic confidence. Willing to say anything to make a sale, his province was the matching nine-piece suite, purveyed alongside its associated draperies and furbelows. He sold furniture as if by weight, and gave little thought to the resulting effect. Anthony Trollope's heroine, Alice Vavasor, was cursed with the verdant vision created by a tasteless tradesman: 'Her father had had the care of furnishing the house, and he had entrusted the duty to a tradesman who had chosen green paper, a green carpet, green curtains, and green damask chairs. There was a green damask sofa, and two green arm-chairs opposite to each other in the two sides of the fireplace. The room was altogether green, and was not enticing.'[55]

Where might Alice Vavasor have gone, around 1860, to remedy the upholsterer's monochromatic scheme? For 'the maximum of selection with the minimum of locomotion', Alice would have visited an arcade or bazaar.[56] While Paris, Vienna, and Berlin had long had glass-covered arcades to entice passers-by, this form of commerce – distinguished by small shops, many with living quarters, arrayed on either side of a covered passageway – only came to England after the Napoleonic Wars. The selection in such arcades far exceeded what individual shops could provide. However, the standards of display often left much to be desired. At the Lowther Arcade, which ran from St Martin's churchyard into the Strand, were goods, or so reported the journalist George Augustus Sala in the 1850s, 'heaped in wild confusion', among them French coffee-pots, toothbrushes, paperweights, china mantelshelf ornaments, and plaster statuettes. It was the 'Bagdad of housekeeping odds and ends'.[57]

If arcades were in essence covered streets, bazaars were modelled on the exchanges where merchants and traders had, since the late sixteenth century, gathered to transact business.[58] The bazaar was an authentically English invention.[59] Housed in cavernous buildings, often constructed of cast iron and glass, bazaars featured counters let to individual traders. The first bazaar, founded in Soho in 1816, provided stalls to the relatives of those who had fallen in the French wars; its purpose was charitable.[60] The concept soon spread through London and provincial towns. The Pantheon on Oxford Street, opened in 1834, was the most magnificent of the bazaars. Decorated throughout with paintings, the domed building cost more than £40,000. A visit to the Pantheon was more than a shopping excursion; as one lady shopper remembered, so beloved was the Pantheon that 'one was sure of meeting friends there'.[61]

37 Soho Bazaar, 1816.

A BAZAAR.

38 New Pantheon,
Oxford Street, 1834.

The great bazaars were victims of their own success, as the principles of commerce which they embodied took shape in a retail revolution. By the 1870s the Pantheon had closed, as had the Lowther arcade, while the Soho limped on.[62] Meanwhile, the idea of bringing together a variety of goods in an elegant setting, of encouraging browsing, novelty items, and cash sales, and of providing, for the customer, a place to meet one's friends, flourished in the department stores and emporia of the late nineteenth century. The 'spirit of bazaars', noted one critic in 1862, 'spreads far beyond their covered limits, which indeed influences the shop and the drawing-room, commerce and society . . .'.[63] This new spirit, as applied to the furnishing trade, entailed nothing less than a reorganization of commerce. In particular, those long-time companions, upholstery and undertaking, were at last separated.[64] The Glasgow firm of Wylie & Lochhead, founded in the 1820s, operated for more than three decades as an undertaking and cabinet-making business. In 1852, Wylie and Lochhead advertised themselves as 'Warehousemen, Funeral

39 Wylie & Lochhead, c. 1860s.

40 Wylie & Lochhead. The interior of 45 Buchanan St, 1875.

Undertakers and Coach Proprietors'. In 1855, the firm opened a new warehouse on Buchanan Street, featuring both an arcade and a gallery. Not only the look of the building, but the complexion of the business had changed; according to their 1857 stationery, Wylie and Lochhead were 'Cabinet Makers, Upholsterers, Carpet Warehousemen, Paper Stainers, General House Furnishers', with (in the smallest possible letters), 'Funerals Undertaken'.[65] In 1863, the funeral business was formally severed from the furnishing emporium and relocated to new quarters.

Separating death from home decoration had more to do with the wishes of customers than with any internal development of the furniture industry or question of profitability. The undertaking business was undeniably lucrative, for the advantages of steam power applied to woodworking accrued to coffins as well as to cabinet-making. However, when the emphasis shifted from production efficiency to enticing customers, coffins could not coexist with cosy corners. The furnishers that thrived in the later nineteenth century were those that could capitalize on the middle-class shopper's demand for a full-service establishment – firms that offered curtains and carpets, paper hangings and bibelots, dining-room furniture and bedsteads, all under the same roof. Old-fashioned enterprises such as Heal's of London, founded in the 1830s as a bedding and bedroom furniture business, discovered that the new era required that they expand their range of merchandise, or be left behind. In the 1880s they added sitting-room furniture to their repertoire; by the turn of the century, they stocked fabrics and bric-à-brac.[66] They advertised, produced catalogues, ran accounts on credit, and eventually built a brand-new, luxuriously outfitted building. The modern furnishing establishment, as we know it today, had been born.

41 Maple's in 1852.

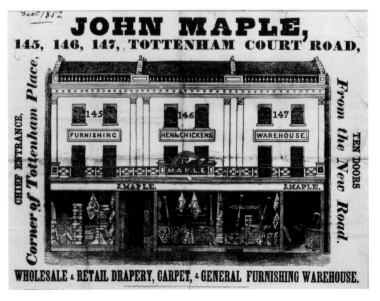

By the 1860s and 1870s, Tottenham Court Road had become the centre of retail furnishing for the middle classes. There, the renowned English names – Maple & Co., Jas. Shoolbred & Co., Heal – had their flagship stores. In the 1870s, the most famous of the London furnishers was undoubtedly Maple. John Maple had opened a small draper's shop on Tottenham Court Road in 1841; by the 1850s, he sold chiefly household furnishings. Maple's enterprise was an old-style venture that did little to attract consumers: 'A shop enveloped in shadows with windows packed full of stocks'.[67] The proprietor himself paraded outside the shop, thwacking the goods displayed on the pavement with a walking stick; his salesmanship consisted of importuning passers-by – 'almost laying hold of the arms of people in his eagerness to make them buy something'.[68] But John's jovial and high-living son, Blundell, would turn Maple into one of the largest furnishing houses in the world; the Maple name became an institution, a symbol of quality and respectability.[69]

By the time the journalist Percy Russell visited Maple's in 1874, the shop had grown to five floors and its store-front stretched the length of twenty-five houses.[70] It employed about 2,000 people, in addition to those cabinet-makers who filled orders according to the firm's specifications. Maple's was, Russell wrote, a 'kind of vast exhibition extending in all directions, closely but artistically packed with every description of furniture'.[71] The atmosphere was one of hushed calm – in Russell's words, the store cultivated a 'bank-like appearance'. Along one of the store's great avenues could be found a set of recessed rooms, complete with windows draped in rose-tinted fabric, and furniture of all sorts arranged in room settings. Maple's warehouse was the size of a modern townlet, encompassing the space of fifty-two ordinary dwellings. Everything that one required to furnish a house, with the excep-

42 Entrance to Maple's, c. 1900.

43 Exterior of Maple's,
photographed in 1902

tion of fine arts, pianos, and books, could be found there. The firm could boast of
nearly 34,000 customers in 1891, and of profits of £284,000 in 1896.[72] It was, as its
own advertisement proclaimed, 'One of the SIGHTS of LONDON to American
visitors and others'.[73]

    If Maple & Co. was the largest of the new-style furniture emporia, with branches
in Brighton, Bournemouth, Paris, and eventually Buenos Aires and Montevideo, it
faced stiff competition from other enterprises. Shoolbred & Co., Britain's largest
draper in 1850, later moved into the lucrative furniture market. Then there were the
older houses, such as Holland & Sons, cabinet-makers and upholsterers, dating
from 1815, or fine craftsmen such as Gillow's of Lancaster and Oxford Street, which
had – since the early eighteenth century – executed furniture to order, according to
the customer's specifications.[74] Because the records of most firms have been only
sporadically, if at all, preserved, we know very little about them. A vast concern as
early as the 1860s, Shoolbred has, for instance, disappeared almost without a trace,
its sole legacy a small set of catalogues and dispersed furniture where once there
existed four floors, thousands of pieces for sale, and probably hundreds of
employees. On Hampstead Road near Tottenham Court Road was Oetzmann & Co.
– its slogan, 'Furnish Throughout' – founded in 1848. Oetzmann, like Hewetson's,
catered to smaller budgets. Messrs Story & Co. laid claim to Kensington High Street,
whereas Liberty & Co. aimed for the exotic-minded and artistic trade. And those
were only the major West End ventures, *circa* 1880. Among the cheaper East End
trade, the firms of William Wallace & Co. and B. Cohen & Sons, manufacturers,
wholesalers, and dealers, reigned supreme.

44 The interior of Oetzmann in the late nineteenth century.

So great was the market for furnishings – and so significant the profit to be made – that co-operative and department stores, too, entered the fray.[75] For those about to be posted to the colonies, the Army and Navy Stores supplied lines of lightweight, collapsible camp furniture, alongside the staple ensembles and knick-knacks for the stay-at-home customer.[76] The department stores, too, competed with the exclusively

45 Portable furniture for officers, as advertised by Heal & Son in 1863. The furniture depicted was everything required for an officer's tent; the entire ensemble packed into the box shown in the foreground of the drawing, with a total weight of 200 lb.

46 A watercolour of a sitting room in the Malvern Hills Station by A.W.H., 1858, Canterbury, New Zealand. Red curtains, wallpaper, and imported furniture brought the comforts of home to a colonial outpost.

furnishing retailers. As Whiteley's windows promised, the Universal Provider offered four floors of furniture from which a customer might choose. On the ground level were dining- and drawing-room suites arranged in stylish groups of Chippendale, early English, and French Regency. The first floor featured bedroom furniture, the second, simply iron and brass bedsteads. At Whiteley's, or so its catalogue boasted, one might furnish a house of eight rooms for a little more than £250, 'all items excellent quality'.[77] Furnishing was dear to the founder's heart. Rather than accompanying his family to church on Sunday, William Whiteley stayed at home, according to the society gossip, Mrs Adams-Acton, to 'indulge in a thoroughly congenial occupation – one in which his soul delighted – that of making a systematic tour of the house, and subjecting its contents to the closest scrutiny while making an exhaustive list of all deficiencies'.[78] His motto was 'Work to Live'.[79]

Shops like Maple's, Whiteley's, or Glasgow's Wylie & Lochhead transformed shopping from a necessity to a pleasure, offering luxurious amenities for their customers, including reading rooms where they might peruse the latest periodicals at leisure and tea salons where they could rest tired feet or even host a lunch party.[80] The stores became a destination in themselves, a place to while away an afternoon. Their windows, remembered the Londoner Mary Hughes, were an education; she and her mother spent hours admiring the exotic fruit and china jugs displayed behind plate glass.[81] The writer Osbert Lancaster's aunts were fierce partisans of particular stores: 'It is difficult to realise how very personal was then the relation-ship, even in London, between shopkeeper and customer and the enormous impor-tance, comparable almost to that attained by rival churches, which late Victorian and Edwardian ladies attached to certain stores'.[82] To attract a clientele, the stores built new premises, each more lavish than the one before. Wylie & Lochhead's new warehouse on Buchanan Street in central Glasgow, opened in 1885, was inspired by the style of the Italian Renaissance, and graced with ornamental terra cotta. In the centre of the new store was an atrium, surrounded by three floors of galleries, where curtains, upholstery, carpets, paper hangings, and furniture for the dining-room,

47 A showroom at Waring & Sons, Deansgate, Manchester, 1897.

drawing-room, hall, and smoking-room were on display. The main staircase that
swept visitors from the ground floor was made of stone, its railings carved from
walnut.[83] For those who knew the old Wylie & Lochhead, furnishers and undertakers, the contrast could hardly have been more striking.

London's stores were of course the grandest in the country, testimony to the
imperial ambitions of their proprietors at the height of Britain's world domina-
tion.[84] Courtesy of the fast trains, they drew customers from hundreds of miles
away, promising them not only the widest selection of goods, but also – as in
twenty-first-century Las Vegas – the landmarks of world civilization in easily
digestible forms. Arthur Lasenby Liberty's oriental warehouse on Regent Street
provided shoppers with the exoticism of foreign travel without leaving the comforts
of the West End: customers could spend days rummaging around the electrically lit
Eastern Bazaar in the basement, visiting the Curio Department with its Chinese
armour, and taking tea in the Arab tea room on the first floor.[85] By the turn of the
century, Harrods, which had started as a wholesale grocery, was one of the world's
most majestic department stores. Its telegraphic address read 'Everything, London',

evidence of the store's ambitions as well as its stock.[86] Harrods' interior was a wonder: the richly plastered ceilings, parquet floors, marble walls, walnut fittings, and stained-glass windows had taken five years to complete, and its escalator – the first moving staircase in Britain, unveiled in 1898 – drew visitors eager to experience the new sensation.[87] For the young Eric Newby, brought to the store by his mother, Harrods was not a shop, but 'a whole fascinating world . . .'.[88] Whiteley's new building, a 1910 retort to the American Gordon Selfridge's imposing department store on Oxford Street, was crowned with three gilt domes.[89] Over the main entrance was a reproduction of Venice's Santa Maria della Salute, heavy artillery in the retailing arms race. Whiteley's lighting was adapted from the lamps that adorned Napoleon's tomb at the Hôtel des Invalides; it made 'a charming and restful appeal to the eye'. Shoppers had the use of hundreds of telephones, then an innovation; there were rest-rooms, promised the store's management, 'where ladies may rest as free from interruption as if they were in their own homes'.[90] Whiteley's sent out a quarter of a million invitation cards to announce the store's opening.[91]

In order to keep up with retail giants such as Whiteley's and Harrods, furniture firms expanded with dizzying speed, adding department upon department, floor upon floor, until they, too, came to resemble small hamlets, complete with model flats and even, in some cases, model houses fully decorated on the premises.[92] When their new building was finished, Messrs Story & Co. occupied a full acre in Kensington. Oetzmann extended its premises with a seven-floor annexe along one side of Drummond Street.[93] But the gigantomania of the Edwardian Gilded Age knew no bounds. The new premises of Waring & Gillow – opened in 1906 – dwarfed even Maple's operations. Waring, a Liverpool store, had opened a London branch in 1893; its acquisition of the famed Gillow business in 1897, along with the firms of T.J. Bontor, oriental carpet importers and Collinson & Lock, renowned cabinet-makers, put it at the head of the pack. The firm had showrooms in Liverpool, Manchester, Lancaster, and Paris, but its new London store, ornamented in the style of the Belle Epoque with wrought-iron balconies, carved stone pilasters, and graceful round windows, would become the standard-bearer. Waring & Gillow's building occupied an island of 40,000 square feet on Oxford Street, encompassing forty departments devoted to every phase of furnishing and decoration, providing for nearly every middle-class pocketbook.[94]

Waring & Gillow's new store was sumptuous, one of the sights of Edwardian London. Its opulence would stun us today. While modern furniture stores are larger (the average Ikea outlet in the UK runs to nearly 70,000 square feet), their displays are rudimentary and their fittings crude by comparison.[95] Waring's crowning glory was a rotunda half the size of St Paul's, adorned with palm trees and exotic flowers, fitted out with cases to display rare silver and china, its walls hung with romantically faded Persian rugs.[96] From the magnificent Rotunda, shoppers could wander through the most elaborate set of specimen rooms ever built. Reconstructed down

49 Waring & Gillow
after the opening of
the new store on
Oxford Street, 1906.

to the last detail on Waring's premises was the state room at Blenheim Palace, complete with panelling, balustrading, and an elaborate painted ceiling.[97] The *Daily Express* called Waring's New Galleries 'the ninth wonder of the world', and visitors who delighted in the possibilities of time travel, all the rage after the publication of H.G. Wells' *Time Machine* (1895), must have agreed.[98] The Knole gallery, with its Jacobean embroideries and carved chimneypieces gave on to a neoclassical Louis-Seize salon, decorated with gilded furniture and intricately moulded plaster friezes. A rose arcade connected a classic English study of the eighteenth century to a cosy Dutch panelled drawing-room of the Golden Age, graced with a characteristic delft-tiled fireplace. The £100 cottage could be contrasted with the £200 house, and both compared unfavourably with a French regency salon – and these were but a handful of the thirty-plus model rooms on display.[99] Best of all, everything was for sale.

The man who engineered Waring & Gillow's rise had been (like Ambrose Heal and Blundell Maple) born into the furniture business. Samuel J. Waring's father owned a cabinet-making shop in Liverpool. It was a modest, but well-respected enterprise, notable for the quality of the furniture it produced. But the young Waring, imbued with the ideas of a new English aesthetic renaissance, had bigger ambitions. He urged his father to allow him to open two branches in London. The old man assented, but grudgingly – and when the stores on Sloane and Oxford Streets lost money in the first two years, Waring Senior docked his son's savings to pay for the losses.[100] But Samuel Waring was not deterred. An inveterate risk-taker, he responded to his father's provocation with a still greater venture: to gain attention for the new stores, he provided interior decoration for the Hotel Cecil at a serious loss. The gambit paid off. Not only did more hotel contracts come his way, including for the Carlton and the Ritz, but the home business boomed, especially around the turn of the century. Waring laboured around the clock. He employed two shifts of secretaries to work alongside him; his second crew arrived at eleven o'clock at night. 'He can be described, on the facts, as a slave-driver,' wrote a friend, 'even though it were impossible to drive other people as hard as he drove himself.'[101] 'Mr Sam', as Waring was known to his employees, worked himself well beyond the point of exhaustion.[102]

Waring & Gillow was a monument to all that was beautiful and artistic in furnishing. If Waring, on his regular rounds through the showrooms, saw an article that failed to meet his exacting standards, he returned it to the workshops to be improved or, if that proved impossible, destroyed. Although he lived like a plutocrat with a yacht and an exquisite town house at Portland Place, he treated his dwellings as store windows; everything in them was for sale, and the furnishings changed all the time. Nor was he often at home. For many years, he travelled 50,000 miles annually to 'plant the flag of British decorative art throughout the world'. Before the First World War, Waring & Gillow had opened branches in Brussels, Madrid, Buenos Aires, and Montreal.[103] His detractors called him a 'hustler', but he was, in the words of one of his employees, 'ever aglow with the inner fires of aspiring optimism'.[104]

Less than fifty years separated the unsavoury cabinet-making shops from palaces like Waring's, but if retailers had once seemed flat-footed in the face of consumer demand, by the end of the nineteenth century they were giving the public a run for their money. It was, the novelist and advice columnist Mrs Jane Panton confessed, 'a relief to turn my back on London', as 'I always spent far more money than I could afford in the gay and brilliant shops . . .'.[105] As the race for customers intensified, advertising vied with luxurious amenities for pride of place in the retailer's budget. Beginning in the 1860s, large furnishers such as Shoolbred's and Maple's took out advertisements in the papers and periodicals to alert the public to their new inventory.

These were omnibus notices aimed at the general reading public, and probably of moderate effectiveness so far as the rapidly developing practice of advertising went.[106] Later in the century, the stores refined their techniques. In 1875, one furnishing firm dispatched 5,000 telegrams to well-to-do families, all timed to arrive at the dinner hour, announcing 20,000 new bedsteads.[107] Newly married couples whose weddings were reported in *The Times* could expect, by the 1890s, to receive circulars from furnishing firms: '"He loves her" – that's his business! "She loves him" – that's her business!! "They'll soon want furniture" – that's our business!!!'[108] Playbills were filled with advertisements for furnishing houses such as Oetzmann, as well as notices taken out by smaller concerns like that of the decorator Mrs Frank Oliver, whose galleries on New Bond Street and East Street, Brighton, offered 'Artistic Home Decoration' and classes in decorative painting.[109]

From the 1890s, women's periodicals contained advertisements for the London furnishing houses, as of course, too, did the home decoration magazines founded after the First World War. The periodicals and the stores enjoyed a cosy relationship, founded upon their mutual interest in creating 'interest' and in a quick turnover: a magazine's own decorating columnist gave favourable notice to the new products of a particular emporium, which in turn took out a quarter-page, or larger, advertisement in the back of the journal.[110] The same was true of decorating advice manuals. Mrs Panton's *Homes of Taste: Economical Hints* (1890) specially recommended black-and-white photographs for the hall from the Autotype Fine Art Gallery – advertisers in the volume's endpapers – and promoted Land's Art Wall-Papers and furniture from Smee & Cobay and Oetzmann, whose notices appear in the book's last pages.[111] Whether endorsement or advertisement came first, the effect was the same: decorating problem and solution followed in quick succession.

Enterprises such as Heal's on Tottenham Court Road were advertising pioneers, expert in the business of linking their wares to intangible but desirable qualities. To sell blue-and-white toiletware, Heal's offered a brochure decorated with pagodas in a Chinese motif. The 'Legend of the Willow Pattern' recounted the tragic fable of Koong-Shee, who died after running away with her lover, thereby conferring an aura of romance upon the oriental-inspired jars and make-up pots decorated with the doomed couple.[112] No less inventive was the free pamphlet 'The Evolution of "Fouracres"', the tale of a young couple, the Challoners, and their old house. Part short story, part advertisement, part advice manual, 'The Evolution of "Fouracres"' described the travails of the Challoners to find suitable furnishings for their half-timbered home – that is, until they visited Heal's. Contained therein was an advertisement within an advertisement, a self-referential piece of congratulatory marketing. Mrs Challoner knew that Heal's was the place for her when she saw the willow-patterned toiletware and read about 'the immortal Koong-Shee'. 'It seemed to me that the attitude of mind which will go to the trouble of reproducing exactly the dear old blue and white "Willow Pattern," . . . and in addition extract the last bit of romantic interest out of the idea by giving the story of Koong-Shee as an introduction to a catalogue, is bound to be in sympathy with "Fouracres" and its furniture.'[113]

In preaching a gospel of beauty, men such as Sam Waring or Ambrose Heal sought in their own fashion to elevate public taste. But unlike the design reformers, their appeal was romantic rather than didactic. Instead of browbeating their customers, successful retailers aimed to cultivate them. In the 1930s, amid the hardships of the Slump, the proprietors of a successful chain of furnishing shops explained their healthy trading profits as a consequence of the company's 'liberal policy . . . in treating its customers as partners and participators in its success'.[114] But if the customer was always right (a slogan that Gordon Selfridge made famous), he or she could nonetheless be educated. From their historic specimen rooms to the exhibitions they staged, the shops offered the public an instruction in taste – defined not as a set of immutable rules but as the *sine qua non* of individual distinction; not discipline, in other words, but liberation. Many an 'aesthetic conversion' had been experienced at Heal's, wrote the noted adman Joseph Thorpe, whose booklet for the firm detailed his own coming to tasteful consciousness, courtesy, of course, of the store on the Tottenham Court Road. This shop, advertisements promised, was a setting to ennoble you; the immense variety contained within its portals offered purchasers an opportunity to assemble the ingredients of an exceptional life.

* * *

In 1901, the year of Queen Victoria's death, Samuel Waring was hatching plans for the most extravagant furnishing store ever seen. But even as the great shops flourished, *The House*, which should have caught the wave of the future, remained stranded in the evangelical past. By 1902, even the admen had deserted John Benn's journal. Whereas early issues carried notices from London's finest emporia, advertisements in later years indicated that Benn had to cast further afield for patrons. Alongside the old standard-bearers like Williamsons' antique dealers of Guildford, 'frequently visited by members of the royal family', there appeared 'Walpole's Sale for Bargains in Household Linens' and 'Wood! Wood! Wood!!! These are only a few of our Cheap Lines'.[115]

Unable to stanch *The House*'s losses, the Benns sold the paper in 1903 to the philanthropist Mrs Alice Hart. Under her guidance, the journal, now retitled *The House Beautiful and the Home* and reformatted as a smaller and less showy journal, made explicit the message that had always lurked beneath the surface. Featured in the first issue was Canon Samuel Barnett, missionary to the East End of London and a founder of the settlement house Toynbee Hall. Canon Barnett denounced the crass, home-obsessed materialism of his age.[116] Where, he lamented, had the moral spirit of the House Beautiful gone? The sentiment was Mrs Hart's own. As the magazine strayed ever farther from the subjects of home decoration, with only the occasional article on the 'dainty' or 'old English' styles, the editor of the Chicago-based *House Beautiful* wondered critically whether Mrs Hart's publication deserved its name. Mrs Hart retorted: 'There is a wide difference between a beautiful house and the House Beautiful. A beautiful house may be created by architectural design, by artistic furniture and pictures, by harmoniously coloured carpets, curtains, and wall-papers; but to possess "The House Beautiful" it is necessary to have as its inmates the "grave and beautiful damsels", Piety, Charity, Discretion and Prudence.'[117]

That was the last issue. By the early twentieth century, as Canon Barnett rightly recognized, the alliance of morality and acquisitiveness that had propelled many Victorian shoppers had come under serious strain. The pleasures of self-expression – of communicating one's own creativity – had become much more compelling than any notion of mere correctness. The new prophets were 'lady art advisors' of the women's press who harnessed the dynamic force of the shops to their own mantra of self-fulfilment. In 1881, the same year as Whiteley's stopped traffic with its windows, the decorating columnist Mary Eliza Haweis proclaimed a new age in decoration, in violation of everything design reform represented: 'There is no ought in beauty, save your own feeling of delight.'[118] Possessions could demonstrate their owner's fancy, his sense of humour – even, eventually, her individuality in the face of mass society. The selection and arrangement of furniture was, most people agreed by the late nineteenth century, an art no less significant than painting or sculpture. And as art entered the house, so, too, did the house enter art.

CHAPTER 3

ART AT HOME

HOW THE HOUSE BECAME ARTISTIC

The Reverend Hugh Reginald Haweis chose a wife with an artistic temperament. For his grandfather, the evangelical founder of the London Missionary Society, artistic flair would not have been an asset in a wife. But Hugh Reginald Haweis was a different sort of minister.[1] As a young man, he had taken the incarnationalist turn, bringing many of his parishioners along with him into a kindler, gentler Christianity. His church, St James in Marylebone, was at the forefront of the new spirit. The author of *Music and Morals*, Haweis believed in the power of music to inculcate virtue. He played his violin in church and invited theatrical ladies endowed with winning voices and suspect reputations to join the choir. He was the first minister in Britain to introduce magic-lantern pictures during his services, all of which added up to an 'unheard-of secularity', as a congregant remembered.[2] The church was packed.

Haweis' bride, Mary Eliza Joy, was the eldest daughter of Thomas Musgrove Joy, a portrait painter of moderate renown in his own lifetime, completely forgotten today. Thomas Joy's career had peaked in the 1840s, when he was commissioned to paint Victoria's children, and declined precipitously thereafter. Mary Eliza had herself early demonstrated artistic abilities; at the age of eighteen, she had exhibited a painting in the summer show of the Royal Academy. But the life of a painter held little attraction for Mary Eliza, who remembered her father's struggles. She elected to make her name instead as a domestic advice-giver, one of the many who lined up to help the newly prosperous spend their money 'artistically'. The Reverend Haweis encouraged his wife in her journalistic endeavours, and put his own connections in the publishing world at her service. Her books, interspersed with children, followed in quick succession: *The Art of Beauty* (1878), *The Art of Decoration* (1881) and *Beautiful Houses* (1882). By the year 1884, when the Haweises took up residence in Dante Gabriel Rossetti's former house in Chelsea, they seemed the very embodiment of the harmonious Victorian alliance of art and morality.

Mrs Haweis' choice of a career was inspired, for if painting remained a very difficult craft for Victorian ladies to ply, she caught the crest of the tidal wave of art in

50 The Reverend
Hugh Reginald Haweis
in 1892.

51 Mrs Mary Eliza
Haweis in 1895.

the home. The last quarter of the nineteenth century appeared, at least to some who lived through it, a supremely artistic age. The boundaries between art, home, and commerce, breached first by Henry Cole's South Kensington Museum and later, more flamboyantly by aesthetes such as Oscar Wilde, threatened to dissolve completely. 'Art,' wrote the architect E.W. Godwin in 1878, 'is every day widening in its influence, appealing to a larger audience, becoming more popular. From Cabinet ministers weighed down with serious affairs of State to young ladies who have just learnt how to arrange a little blue china on a mantelpiece, we receive lectures on art'.[3] So profound had the association between art and furnishing become in Britain that the architect and critic H.H. Statham, speaking at the Social Science Congress in 1877, felt compelled to assert the distinction between the high and the decorative arts: 'I protest against the assumption that this worship of furniture and china is an indication of an advanced perception in regard to art'.[4] Despite the protests, home decoration remained within an artistic idiom through at least the 1920s.

How can we explain this proliferation of art? The leading intellectuals of the day have often been given credit for the awakening of middle-class artistic sensibilities. And yet men such as John Ruskin and William Morris are only the best known, not necessarily the most influential, of art's advocates. The cast of characters is far broader than has been recognized. A powerful web of connections linked the spheres of high art, home decoration, and the shops. Crucial to the propagation of the art gospel were figures such as Mrs Haweis and her rivals among the 'lady art advisors'. Now forgotten, they were the foot soldiers of the new movement, responsible for the torrents of artistic advice that flooded the British market. But more important still was their work in defining what art meant. In the face of aesthetes such as Wilde, whose sacrilegious utterances and heterodox lifestyles threatened to tarnish the name of art and drag interior decoration down with it, they reclaimed the cause. Art was not only virtuous, it also – they told their readers – betokened individuality. The lady art advisors would endow artistic furnishing with an irresistible purpose; they made it something that no self-respecting middle-class household could do without.

THE ART OF DECORATION

Today, we know where art resides. When we wish to see it we go to museums and galleries. But in late nineteenth-century Britain, 'art' entered the lives of the middle classes through their things. People became artistic in their own minds not simply because they visited the National Gallery or the South Kensington Museum, but in the selection and arrangement of their possessions.[5] Museums still sparked desires, of course, but they by no means fulfilled the public's artistic needs. The new English Renaissance came to fruition in the shops. At furniture emporia such as Glasgow's Wylie & Lochhead, or Bradford's Christopher Pratt & Sons, clients could select from a range of artistic fabrics, fittings, and furniture drawn from all corners of the world. In the new art journals and ladies' periodicals, decorators on paper (as they were known) promised to cultivate in their readers 'a taste for true art'.[6] 'Artistic' became a term of praise for a well-furnished dwelling, and 'inartistic' a much-dreaded censure.[7] From the ubiquitous 'art furniture' displayed in store windows to the 'artistic' effects achieved by those who decorated according to the popular 'Art at Home' series of household manuals, the home had become *the* haven for art.[8]

What exactly art furnishing entailed was a matter of individual discernment. A wide variety of furniture was sold under the rubric – including Sheraton and Chippendale reproductions, Louis-Quatorze, Jacobean, Liberty's fabrics, and spindly sideboards in black lacquer – as well, of course, as such self-consciously

52 'Artistic Joinery' as advertised in *The Cabinet Maker*, 1881.

53 Maple & Co.'s 'very
artistic writing table'.

'artistic' productions as Wallace & Co.'s 'Alma Tadema' boudoir suite, stained
golden-green with tawny yellow velvet seats.[9] The only imperative was that the
furniture should not match, an important departure from the mid-Victorian
period, when the monotonous nine-piece parlour suite had reigned. In his ode to
'Modern Decoration', 'Corney Grain' identified the guiding principle:

> To furnish in the modern way,
> This recipe remember pray!
> You fill up each corner with something odd
> a Japanese monkey or a Hindoo god![10]

Certain kinds of object, the odder the better, communicated an artistic flair. It was
the 'delightful irregularity' of Japanese bric-à-brac which appealed to all those who
rebelled against the oppressive order of the matching room.[11] This was the era of the
'rubbish plate', those assemblages of acorns, broken watch pieces and old button-
hooks pasted to a tin plate, then gilded and hung on the wall.[12] Blue-and-white
oriental china, preferably displayed on plate rails, and painted drainpipes (known as
'art pots') became staples of the artistic interior, as too did screens and 'art squares',
otherwise known as small carpets.[13]

Artistic furnishing was less a collection of particular furniture than a state of
mind. On this point the 'art at home' writers agreed. It was not about spending lots

54 A Japanese exhibit by Messrs Holme & Co. of London and Yokohama. Displayed in the Oriental Court as part of the 1883 furniture exhibition.

55 James Macbeth (1847–1891), *An Elegant Lady*, 1873. This watercolour depicts an aesthetic interior, complete with blue-and-white china and Japanese screens.

of money, nor about purchasing specific objects. There was 'no need to pretend to be Japanese' in order to be artistic.[14] Moreover, too many screens in the parlour and your home resembled a restaurant.[15] Those who would furnish artistically had to strive for a distinctive effect. Such a decorative scheme required discernment and, as Mary Eliza Haweis liked to remind her readers, the skills of a painter. If some evangelicals had viewed the arts as a source of spiritual danger, their descendants thought very differently. Those who had once fled from Art had turned on their heel – and were now in hot pursuit. As the *Architect* observed in 1881: 'A most remarkable change has of late come over the English mind in respect of art. It is not in the Grosvenor Gallery that it has been manifesting itself – certainly not in the Royal Academy. It is in our thousand and one shops, and workshops, and manufactories . . .. The sense of being, as English people, at least alive to this thing called art is immensely exhilarating.'[16]

The *Architect* was mocking middle-class pretensions, but as the critics were laughing, art became enshrined in the retail sector. Art appeared not only at the top end of the market in the designer Christopher Dresser's Art Furnishers' Alliance, but in the cheap East End trade as well. In Britain's rapidly expanding suburbs, pioneering tradesmen opened up stores with pictorial art on one side and 'art products' on the other.[17] Art provided more than a few struggling businessmen with a recipe for success. After a failure in the second-hand clothes business, the writer V.S.

56 Story & Triggs' line of inexpensive artistic furniture.

Pritchett's father ventured into the art needlework and art pot trade, where his particular style of 'fussing, addicted draftsman and perfectionist' – he viewed himself as an 'artist-priest' – served him well.[18] Shops bombarded the public with rival artistic claims.[19] In just one issue of the ladies' magazine *Hearth and Home* for 1895, more than 70 per cent of the advertisements for furnishing claimed to supply artistic products.[20] 'An artistic achievement in Furnishing is not only possible,' promised the firm of Norman & Stacey in 1902, 'but absolutely assured.'[21]

As shops set out to cultivate their customers' tastes, the distinction between art and commerce eroded. Reporters who visited the richly decorated West End emporia frequently described them as 'museums' or as 'art collections', and the stores encouraged the comparison – perhaps because they had the better of it.[22] After visiting Waring & Gillow's sumptuous galleries, the editors of Britain's leading antiques magazine commented: 'There are many museums and public galleries far less rich in historic examples and far less important from an artistic and educational point of view.'[23] The store's 'curators', as the heads of department were termed in some establishments, had budgets placed at their disposal of which Britain's perpetually cash-strapped museums could only dream.[24] Furnishing emporia pioneered the display of period rooms decades before museums did.[25] The mission of a modern furnishing firm, wrote one ladies' paper in 1904, is less the 'mere supply of ameublements than the privilege of bringing the art of "all the ages" within reach'.[26]

57 Maple & Co.'s 'artistic easel' – a peculiarly Victorian redundancy.

58 The 'Rossetti Library', designed by Wylie & Lochhead for the Glasgow International Exhibition in 1901. With woodwork of mahogany, a carpet hand-tufted by the peasants of Donegal, and richly leaded windows, this room 'recalls the style associated with the Pre-Raphaelite School, and especially with Rossetti, after whom it is named'.

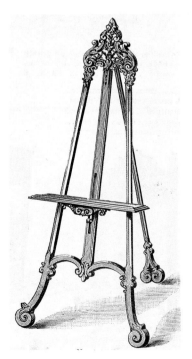

59 The London house-
furnishing firm of
Oetzmann & Co.
colonizes the fine arts
business, 1875.

By the end of the century, furnishing shops had entered into direct competition with London's picture galleries: nearly half of house furnishers in the metropolis had opened departments for the sale of pictures.[27] For those whose budgets did not permit the purchase of original images, Whiteley's issued *The Hundred Best Pictures for Home Decoration*, a collection of the greatest hits of Western art selected to complement British décor.[28]

Furnishing impresarios were fêted as artistic innovators for a democratic age. Arthur Lasenby Liberty, wrote one reporter in 1900, 'is as much the founder of an artistic school as ever were Velásquez, or Rubens, or Turner. What is far more important, Liberty has founded a cult that is more wide-reaching than that of any of the men mentioned, for his work . . . is not devoted, like that of most other founders of artistic schools and systems, solely to the service of the opulent.'[29] Samuel Waring's motto, as

60 *The Hundred Best Pictures*, as purveyed by Whiteley's.

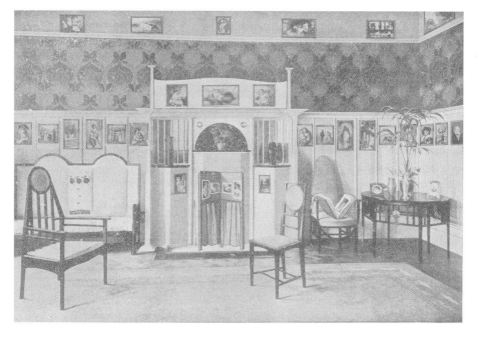

he liked to say, was not merely 'Art in the Home', but 'Art in Everybody's Home'. His aim was to appeal 'to the artistic instinct that is in everyone, small and great'.[30] Interviewed in 1907, Waring claimed that in his lavish new store on Oxford Street 'The artistic consideration was frankly made the dominant one.'[31] Like Liberty, he spoke in terms of a 'movement': 'Today I believe the world is a more artistic world for our influence.'

But the domestication of art was not solely the achievement of entrepreneurs such as Waring and Liberty. British artists, especially those in the avant-garde, played a crucial role in redefining the boundaries of art. Even as French modernists claimed the life of the street as their purview, their British counterparts focused attention upon the interior and home decoration.[32] From aestheticism to the Arts and Crafts to Roger Fry's Omega workshops, Britain's art movements famously blurred the distinctions between the applied and fine arts.[33] Thus the fad for all things Japanese – a significant influence upon Impressionism in France – found its chief British expression in the decorative arts.[34] Artists' own houses and studios became showpieces as never before, written up in the papers as important and self-conscious emblems of an individual style.[35] Whistler intended his 'White House' to demonstrate that the entirety of the décor – not just the paintings – should be regarded as art; he hoped to capture a slice of the interior decorating business that

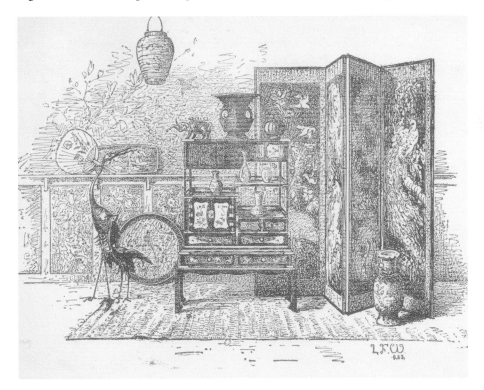

61 Japanese furniture and decoration, as sold by Liberty & Co., c. 1890.

had proven so profitable for William Morris and Edward Burne-Jones.[36] So famous
was Sir Frederic Leighton's Moorish-inspired house in Kensington that it spawned
the adjective 'leightonesque' as a means of describing rooms.[37]

From the circles of fine art came the personnel for the English home decoration
renaissance. Charles Eastlake, author of the influential *Hints on Household Taste*
(1868), was the nephew of the first director of the National Gallery, and himself
became Keeper of the Gallery in 1878.[38] A number of ladies born or married into
fine art families opted, like Mrs Haweis, to pursue their talents outside the
unfriendly confines of the Royal Academy. The wife of the portraitist Harrington
Mann numbered among the first female interior decorators. Two daughters of
William Frith, the renowned painter of the age and himself the son of an auctioneer,
ran a bric-à-brac shop in South Kensington.[39] Frith's eldest, Mrs Jane Panton,
married a brewer. From her remote location in the Cornish countryside, where she
languished in 'rural isolation', she nonetheless managed to set an artistic standard.
Retailers scrambled to gain a mention in her best-selling books. Her manuals,
including *Homes of Taste: Economical Hints*, *The Gentlewoman's Home*, and *From
Kitchen to Garret: Hints for Young Householders*, demonstrated how even those with
modest incomes could decorate artistically.[40]

Art periodicals, founded to encourage the public's appreciation of the fine arts,
devoted an ever increasing number of pages to the subject of home decoration. The
Magazine of Art's 1880 series on the 'Treasure-Houses of Art' makes the point
clearly: it dealt not with museums, but with private homes; not with pictures, but
with décor. Mr Alfred Morrison's collection of paintings, on which he had spent a

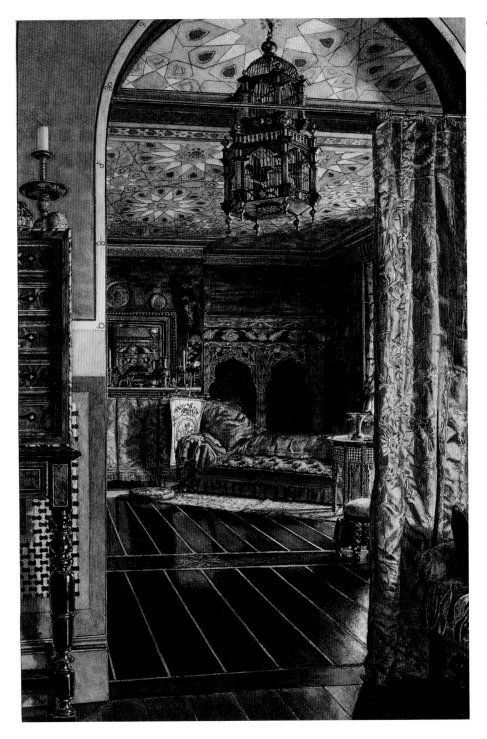

63 An artistic show-place – Sir Lawrence Alma-Tadema's drawing room, with his famed collection of textiles accorded pride of place. Anna Alma-Tadema, *The Drawing Room, Townshend House*, 1885.

small fortune, scarcely merited a mention from the reporter who paid a visit: 'Oil paintings, chiefly modern, adorn the walls of the staircase. We must not omit to speak of the superb softness of the carpets . . .'[41] From its inaugural issue, *The Artist* reviewed furnishing manuals and dispensed domestic advice.[42] In a question-and-answer column entitled 'Domestic Art Notes', 'Tartine' offered solutions to readers' queries about the proper application of paint and decorating with oriental rugs. In 1881, *The Artist* changed its name to *The Artist and Journal of Home Culture* to reflect art's widened purpose: 'Art in England is every day, to its own great benefit, becoming more and more a matter of "home culture" while not at the same time less a subject of technical and professional study.'[43]

This British penchant for the art of the home – widely recognized at the time – gave some critics comfort. If Britain had neglected the fine arts, as understood on the Continent, she had excelled in household art.[44] The days of Reynolds and Gainsborough might be long gone, but a host of anonymous craftsmen and designers with a quintessentially English genius for the arts of the home had sprung up in their place.[45] The British contribution to world art would be the home; a well-chosen wallpaper, in other words, was a more noble contribution to the aesthetic progress of mankind than the too-often mediocre paintings that filled the Royal Academy. Writing in the *Magazine of Art*, the designer Lewis Day excoriated a pictorial art that consisted of 'immortalizing dead herrings or living nobodies'.[46] If people wished to be artistic, better that they should decorate with taste. Trade papers heralded the home arts as a right-minded step towards democratization. As the *Furniture Gazette* put it: 'Decorative art is really the only art that is within the means of the largest proportion of the people . . . The home is the fit altar at which to offer up our artistic efforts . . .'[47] Mrs Haweis, like so many others, saw hope for a true artistic regeneration from below. It would come not from the realm of high art, with its snobbery and exclusions (here she avenged her father's name), but from the shops. 'We shall do without our artists – as they pretend they can do without us! – and we shall have better art!'[48]

But while those who stood to profit from the tidal wave of art cheered it on, others viewed the prospect of a nation of 'domestic museums' with horror. The cosy relationship between art and the shops had, they argued, redounded to the shopkeepers' advantage, but to art's peril. Rather than improving the public taste and preparing the way for a finer fine art, household art had, or so charged its detractors, sapped fine art of its vitality. People who viewed themselves as standard-bearers for the fine arts against the incursions of the trivial lambasted the pretensions of so-called 'art advisors' such as Mrs Haweis: 'Decoration is not the whole of art, nor the highest field of art. To hear some people's conversation one would suppose that brass finger-plates for doors and brass fenders were of more value than all the works of Phidias.'[49] Even Whistler, who had plunged wholeheartedly into the home decoration business, decried the way in which art had become 'a common topic for the

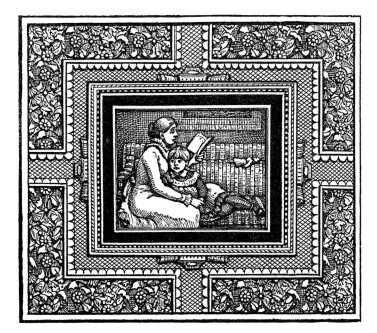

64 *Proper Picture Hanging*, published in G. L.'s *The Science of Taste* (1879). The picture is lost in the elaborate decorative border treatment.

tea-table'. In his 'Ten O'Clock Lecture', delivered in 1885 at the Prince's Hall in Piccadilly, he denounced the 'false prophets, who have brought the very name of the beautiful into disrepute'.[50] The hyper-inflation of art talk, he charged, had made a mockery of true art. Art in the house was nothing more than a fad.

And yet, the juggernaut rolled on. The phenomenon of art at home long outlasted its Victorian critics. By the turn of the century, the siren song of art had echoed through the ranks of the lower middle classes, sweeping up Britain's rapidly growing numbers of clerks, shopkeepers, and schoolteachers in its wake. The pages of the *Happy Home*, a penny weekly aimed at the lower middle class, are typical: the China craze, the antiques fad, the 'art pot', the screen – all are bandied about in the year 1895 for an audience conversant with the phenomena.[51] High art's 'homely' quality encouraged imitation down the social scale. Nearly twenty years after Whistler's execution of the Peacock Room, one decorating columnist advised that an artistic effect in the dining-room might be achieved with china blue paper, woodwork painted white, and cupboards full of blue china: 'It is a kind of cottage realization of the magnificent dining-room which was decorated by Mr. Whistler for Mr. Leyland.'[52]

Although a new generation of twentieth-century design reformers would eventually seek to banish the word 'artistic' from the English vocabulary, arguing that four decades of art manufacture had done little to raise design standards, art proved difficult to purge from the business of home decoration.[53] Well into the twentieth century, readers were writing in to columnists of the ladies' papers in search of an

65 Artistic furnishing down the social scale. The drawing room, 188 Rugby Road, Leamington, 1911–21.

artistic scheme.[54] For the editors of *Ideal Home*, Britain's leading inter-war home decoration magazine, art remained a term of praise: 'The homes of the people,' the magazine's editors noted in 1920, 'are more artistic than they have ever been before.'[55] Through the 1920s, furnishers continued to deploy the term 'art' in their advertisements and wares, and to attract customers in search of the artistic. More than fifty years after Arthur Lasenby Liberty opened his oriental warehouse on Regent Street, Liberty & Co. was still – according to one lady visiting from Bristol – 'The most artistic and fascinating bit of London'.[56] Only in the 1930s did the prefix 'art', worn fusty in the face of the adjective 'modern', drop decisively away.

HOW THE ARTISTIC HOUSE SURVIVED THE AESTHETES

In the mid-nineteenth century, the combined forces of incarnationalism and design reform had served to redeem consumption from the realm of sin. And yet, if the pleasures of shopping had gained a powerful moral rationale, the strict rules of design reform failed to win Henry Cole's cause many adherents. That was the hard lesson that John Benn learned as Britain's first home decoration magazine declined and then disappeared. Morality, as Mrs Haweis could have told *The House*'s proprietor, was no longer the compass that guided shoppers through the luxurious new emporia. Furnishing had acquired a new set of associations at the end of the nineteenth century. Decoration was, above all, an art to be pursued. Rooms were like pictures, counselled Mrs Haweis; their composition required 'equal skill and forethought'.[57] But what had happened to the old moral concerns? How did they fit into the artistic world of home decoration? At the end of the Victorian era, a battle raged to shape the fundamental relationship between people and their possessions. This is where art enters the story, as a well-located waystation on the long road from sin to self-expression.

Mary Eliza Haweis liked to claim that she had invented the rage for artistic home decoration.[58] As a young bride in the 1860s, she struck the first blow against the drab terraced London street when she scaled a ladder to paint the balcony railings of her Welbeck Street house scarlet.[59] In her *Art of Decoration* and *Beautiful Houses*, she instructed ordinary middle-class householders in painterly tricks, showing them how to create the illusion of space and how to harmonize the colours of a room with the complexion of its hostess. Above all else, readers learned – thanks to her guidance – to seek 'the cachet of individuality' in the place of rules and strictures.[60] Her own taste was renowned. After the publication of her fashion manual, *The Art of Dress*, society ladies shrank from meeting Mrs Haweis, lest she cast a critical eye over their raiment. So exquisitely sensitive was Mrs Haweis to the inharmonious arrangement of a room that badly decorated dwellings, or so her husband claimed, made her physically ill.[61]

Mrs Haweis was not a modest woman, but in her claim to have pioneered the artistic home more was at stake than her own reputation. In the early 1880s, the cause of art in the home had become entangled in many people's minds with the self-proclaimed aesthetes, who seemed to have sprung up, like their favourite blossom, the sunflower, with extraordinary speed.[62] Under the mantle of 'Art for Art's Sake', aesthetes turned the quest for beauty into an ideal unto itself; art, in other words, did not need to promote morals in order to achieve legitimacy. The most eminent of the aesthetes were painters such as Albert Moore and architects such as E.W. Godwin, whose contributions to the historical pastiche redbrick style known as 'Queen Anne' furnished picturesque dwellings for the cause. But many others in the enlightened middle classes had hastened to embrace the new aesthetic style. Prominent among them were the free-thinkers who, dressed in faded shades of grey and green, attended the open days at the Grosvenor Gallery, founded in 1877, and eagerly discussed Whistler's infamously abstract *Nocturnes*.

Like the hippies of the 1960s, the signature characteristic of the aesthetes was their lifestyle, a term not yet invented. The aesthetes took up residence in the new 'Queen Anne' suburb of Bedford Park, with its Norman Shaw houses, or, if they had

66 Bath Road, Bedford Park. Lithograph by B.F. Berry, published in 1882.

more money, colonized Chelsea and Hampstead. Their preferences in house decoration, rather than their politics or their principles, brought them to the public's attention.[63] In thrall to William Morris, that 'ruthless tyrant in the drawing-room', they spurned vulgar manufactures, plumping instead for Indian textiles and Japanese fans.[64] They haunted the antique shops of Wardour Street in search of silver salt-cellars and Chippendale chairs, and rhapsodized on the joys of blue-and-white china. A favourite museum was Sir John Soane's house in Lincoln's Inn Fields, whose eccentricities gratified the aesthetic disposition.[65] The flashiest of the leading aesthetic lights was Oscar Wilde, in the late 1870s fresh from a showily successful career at Oxford. In his first British lecture tour, Wilde took the House Beautiful as his subject. The average parlour furniture of the day, Wilde told an audience in the town of Derby, looked as if it had been manufactured 'for purposes of offence and defence', while the habit of scattering antimacassars over upholstery suggested 'an eternal washing day'.[66]

In extolling the virtues of beauty, the aesthetically minded may not, at first, have seemed out of step with the prevailing spirit of moral materialism.[67] The argument that art elevated character was, after all, an ancient one. A tenet of Romanticism, it had been given extensive play during the 1835 hearings of the Select Committee on

Arts and Manufactures, by the London Art Union, and in the writings of Pugin, Ruskin, and Morris.[68] The idea that furnishing could improve the moral tone of the household had been common currency for decades; calling furniture an art, as the Reverend Loftie did in his *Plea for Art in the House*, fitted neatly within this framework. Typical were the lectures that Lucy Crane, sister of the illustrator Walter Crane, gave at the Methodist Sunday School Institute in Halifax in 1882. In an age of bad taste, when ugly objects competed with virtuous designs for the public's attention, art – Crane argued – stood for authenticity. 'Does it not become a sort of moral obligation to exercise a *wise* choice, to express a *just* opinion?'[69] Art and morality were self-reinforcing propositions; art provided a powerful rubric under which material abundance could be justified. 'The higher order of art,' explained the china collector Herbert Byng Hall, is 'the constant handmaid of religion.'[70]

And yet, if 'Art for Art's Sake' had been for a time accommodated within a moral framework, the slogan itself had always contained the seeds of conflict. As prominent aesthetes increasingly divorced the search for beauty from the incarnationalist religious quest that the Reverend Haweis espoused, art – rather than promoting morality – threatened to undermine it. In the mid-1860s, when Mrs Haweis took a paint-pot to her railings, 'artistic' connoted eccentricity or originality, depending upon your perspective.[71] But the rapidity with which the young don Walter Pater attracted converts signalled a worrying new development. In 1866, Pater, a fellow of Brasenose College, Oxford, had proclaimed his conversion to 'the religion of art'. Art did not exist to bolster religion, as the Pre-Raphaelite painter Ford Madox Brown or the Reverend Loftie might have believed. It was for pleasure rather than virtue. Pater, whose Morris-papered and china-filled home would become a meeting-place for young aesthetes, had by the 1870s become a 'cult figure' in Oxford.[72]

Pater avoided controversy, but his disciples – especially Oscar Wilde – embraced it.[73] As an undergraduate at Oxford, Wilde had crowned three years of dandyism at Magdalen College with the infamous pronouncement: 'I find it harder and harder every day to live up to my blue china.'[74] This was both a more subtle and a more lethal joke than is often recognized. It at once mocked the virtue that Victorians had invested in their possessions – as we have seen, a key means by which prosperity and morality were reconciled – and also suggested that humans could fall short of the perfection of the material world in ways never imagined by incarnationalists such as the Reverend Loftie. To the clerical authorities at Oxford, where the spirit of Pater seemed in the ascendancy, this was a gauntlet thrown down. At the church of St Mary's, Dean John William Burgon denounced Wilde from the pulpit: 'When a young man says not in polished banter, but in sober earnestness, that he finds it difficult to live up to the level of his blue china, there has crept into these cloistered shades a form of heathenism which it is our bounden duty to fight against and to crush out, if possible.'[75]

Courtesy of Wilde, the relationship between aestheticism and morality played

67 George du Maurier
in *Punch*, 30 October,
1880.

THE SIX-MARK TEA-POT.

Æsthetic Bridegroom. "IT IS QUITE CONSUMMATE, IS IT NOT?"
Intense Bride. "IT IS, INDEED! OH, ALGERNON, LET US LIVE UP TO IT!"

out on a very public stage. More than three years after the original Oxford
contretemps, George du Maurier revisited the incident in a cartoon for *Punch*.[76]
He made some changes. A teapot has replaced blue china; Wilde's line has been
given to the Aesthetic Bride. As her husband (a caricature of Wilde) looks fondly
on, she proclaims: 'Oh, Algernon, let us live up to it!' In altering Wilde's remark,
Du Maurier had softened the most cutting of his barbs – the sentiment, heftily
criticized by Dean Burgon, that mankind was already failing to measure up to its
possessions. Wilde's challenge was turned into pure satire. But lest there be any
misunderstanding about where he stood, Wilde took up the issue again in the
following year. In a Dublin lecture on 'The House Beautiful', he begged to disagree
with Ruskin and the design reformers about the immorality of sham materials:
'The morality of art was merely beauty – its immorality, ugliness.'[77] In his essay, 'The
Critic as Artist', he carried the point further. Aesthetic discernment was not merely
different from morality; it was superior. 'Even a colour-sense is more important, in
the development of the individual, than a sense of right and wrong.'[78]

To lose your faith was hardly exceptional in late Victorian Britain, but to deni-
grate the moral conscience was, for most people, unforgivable. Because of Du
Maurier's cartoons and parodies such as F.C. Burnand's play *The Colonel* and
Gilbert & Sullivan's *Patience*, we remember the aesthetes today more for their fool-
ishness than for their apostasy. But their critics were doing more than simply poking
fun; ridicule, in this case, disguised a ferocious indictment. The onslaught began in
the mid-1870s with a series of attacks in the press. No fan of the South Kensington
enterprise, the *Saturday Review* depicted the aesthetes as the second coming of
Henry Cole. They were failed artists who had parlayed their lack of talent into
aesthetic expertise.[79] But these 'disciples of Cole' had outdone their master: the
'aesthetic friend' had managed to gain admittance into the middle-class house. Like
a clergyman, he had made himself at home in the family's most private sanctuary
and had become the arbiter of its manners. With his strong views on colour, the
'aesthetic friend' had rearranged the furniture and reoriented dinner-table discussion. Assuming the posture of 'religious gravity', he had arrogated to himself the
right to pronounce upon their household gods.

As paraded through the press, the aesthete appeared the sordid inversion of the
evangelical. His 'intensity' recalled the 'enthusiasm' of the fervently religious. His
raptures over blue-and-white china were a backhand allusion to the godly ecstasies
of the newly converted. Cliquish and inbred, aesthetes believed themselves among
the elect. In her memoirs, the novelist Lucy Walford recalled an encounter with one
young aesthetic woman: 'every time she said "Oscar Wilde" I had an inward convul-
sion; it was the breath of a worshipper at a shrine'.[80] But while the evangelicals were
pure, the aesthetes were manifestly corrupt. The *Saturday Review* accused the
'aesthetic friend' of revelling in decay, anticipating the charges levelled against the

68 James Hadley's
Aesthetic Teapot, 1882.

Decadents of the 1890s.[81] Aesthetes were unwholesome and unmanly; their ranks, according to the *Architect*, included 'young ladies of both sexes and all ages'.[82] Where all of this was leading was not difficult to see. In 1882, the Hadley Porcelain Company offered for sale its Aesthetic Teapot, a satire in china on the dual godless challenges of Darwinism and aestheticism. On one side, a foppish aesthetic man emblazoned with a sunflower; on the other, a masculine young lady armed with a lily. Inscribed on the bottom of the teapot was 'Fearful consequences through the laws of Natural Selection and Evolution of living up to one's teapot'.[83] If there was anything worse than turning into a teapot, it was the collapse of sexual difference.

What began as a campaign against aesthetic immorality threatened to engulf all of those who had lauded the saving graces of the House Beautiful. Writing in the *New Quarterly Magazine*, Frances Power Cobbe savaged the conviction that 'sage-green walls' will 'purify the conscience and exalt the soul'. Raised in an evangelical household, Cobbe had forsaken the Church of England but not her morals. At work in the 1870s with the women's trade union movement, Cobbe claimed that the worship of beauty had caused Britons to neglect the misery outside their artistically decorated dwellings.[84] Cobbe's criticisms implicated people far removed from advanced aesthetic circles; even the Reverend Boyd could feel himself in the dock. Materialism, rather than promoting goodness, had become a substitute for it. The pursuit of beauty was mere hedonism. Hedonism in turn bred heathenism, a crime worse than agnosticism. In case any doubt remained as to her meaning, Cobbe drove her point home. Just like the Brahmins with their holy ladle of the sacramental Soma, the British who 'fall into ecstasies over their salt-cellars' were worshipping false idols.

So unsavoury was the image of the aesthetes by the early 1880s that even the movement's friends began to distance themselves from the cause. At the Bedford Park Club, an oasis of lower-income aestheticism, the suburb's developer, Jonathan Carr, denounced the 'harm aestheticism has done to art'.[85] Arthur Liberty, who, more than any other retailer, had profited from his associations with the likes of Godwin and Walter Crane, publicly acknowledged the excesses of the aesthetic movement.[86] Richard D'Oyly Carte, famous as the producer of Gilbert and Sullivan's operettas, had himself moved in aesthetic circles in London.[87] Now he sought to portray the movement's apparent irreligion as a perversion of its original character. Before dispatching *Patience* on a national tour, D'Oyly Carte wrote an explanatory pamphlet to be distributed before each performance. The 'pure and healthy' teachings of the real prophets of beauty, he instructed his provincial audiences, had given way to the excrescences of the 'high priests' of so-called aestheticism – 'unmanly oddities' with an 'unhealthy admiration for exhaustion, corruption and decay'.[88] Even Mrs Panton, presumably safe in her 'rural isolation', was on the defensive. She admitted that some might object that 'Souls are not saved by dadoes' and that 'friezes do not take one an inch nearer heaven'.[89] However, she 'boldly' gainsaid the critics, maintaining the moral posture that the Reverends Boyd and Loftie had staked out: people who cared for their houses were much better 'mentally and morally' than those who did not. Of course, Mrs Panton acknowledged in her autobiography, she never played cards on Sunday.[90]

For the promoters of the art of the house, aestheticism became a dirty word. Rarely – if ever – were the hoards of art products on sale in the stores described as 'aesthetic'.[91] Styles pioneered by the aesthetes, such as the lacquered overmantel or the dado, were advertised under the label of 'art'. Even those designs most closely associated with aesthetic designers such as E.W. Godwin went uncredited.[92] The assiduous avoidance of the obvious indicates the disrepute into which the aesthetic cause had fallen – a development that Wilde's conviction in 1895 on charges of 'gross indecency' simply cemented. The *Daily Telegraph* was not alone in viewing Wilde's downfall as a repudiation of 'some of the artistic tendencies of the time'.[93] It was a good thing, wrote H.J. Jennings, the author of *Our Homes and How to Beautify Them* (1902), that the aesthetic school – 'effeminate, invertebrate, sensuous and mawkish' – had been laughed out of existence before it succeeded 'in making the very name of art contemptible!'[94]

As the perversities of the aesthetes were trotted out for public notice, 'artistic' advisors such as Mrs Haweis sought to establish their efforts on a new footing. She offered the obligatory disavowal: the aesthetes were 'selfish and soporific'; their style was 'weakly and feminine'. But the real problem, she advised her readers in *The Art of Decoration*, was their lack of originality. Aesthetic houses were 'a bore': 'The chairs are few, hard, square and heavy, and covered with dingy velvets laboriously made to look poor and imperfect in web and recalling in colour mud – mildew – ironmould – nothing clean or healthy.'[95] Still, Mrs Haweis could understand why people had flown to the fashions of Queen Anne. For those who had no taste, the standard of 'severity' prevented decorative disasters; for those who had little money, it required only a small outlay; for the self-made, its simplicity demonstrated self-restraint and a becoming modesty. It seemed, in other words, safe. But in following the aesthetic credo, the English had, 'sheeplike', succumbed to the pressures of conformity. Their houses did not do what houses should: they failed to 'represent our individual tastes and habits'.

For Mrs Haweis, art connoted morality, but more importantly, it stood for self-expression. People who wished to make art had to 'cultivate and use their own faculties'. Houses should reflect moods; they should express their inhabitants' likes and dislikes: 'A man's house, whilst he is in it, is a part of himself.'[96] More than a pleasure, this was also a duty. Each person could 'aid the nation by self-culture'. In insulating home decoration from the charges of self-indulgence and decadence that clung to the aesthetes, Mrs Haweis turned the art of the home into a civic virtue. She summoned up the spirit of mid-century Victorian liberalism. Those who cared how their walls were covered struck a blow for the 'right of individual

69 A riotous late
Victorian arrangement.

thought and action'.[97] They withstood the tyranny of the dreaded upholsterer and
the rules of design reform. An artistic home, no less than a successful business,
provided a way for a man both to distinguish himself from the crowd and to
improve the nation.

Mrs Haweis did not invent a new pedigree for art on her own, but her solution to
the problem that aestheticism posed was one that gained favour among the virtuous
home-decorating public. 'Artistic' increasingly meant not abiding by rules or
conventions, but relying upon personal inspiration.[98] It signified originality rather
than dogmatism, eclecticism rather than adherence to a single decorative creed. In
her first year as the decorating columnist for *Queen*, Mrs Talbot Coke, an avid
proponent of the artistic interior, declared that she knew 'nothing of art rules or
what is "correct"'; she was guided, rather, by her own preferences.[99] Asked by the
illustrated paper, *The World*, to offer its readers guidelines upon 'The Principles of
Modern Decoration', the architect Halsey Ricardo gave an answer that despite its
title owed more to the spirit of the shops than to the ghost of design reform. The
home, if it was to be a shrine to art, had to be 'individualistic'. It should be restful,
not garish. It should give an 'amiable sidelight into the character' of its owner.[100]

Making a good impression had always been important, especially in the middling
ranks of society. But the emphasis upon self-expression was new. Art at home had
proliferated in a period that saw not only political democratization but increased

70 A corner of the drawing room at Newlands, the home of Joseph Collier Phythian, who ran his father's manufactory, c. 1880's. Watercolours by the lady of the house are displayed alongside an artistic arrangement of ceramics, textiles and photographs.

social mobility. In the early nineteenth century Britain was still largely a society of orders; the vast majority of people lived and died in the class into which they had been born. This was the Britain that the evangelicals knew, and the model of society they endorsed: God had assigned each person to a station in life: his will was immutable. However, with the development of the industrial economy, this system of rigid social hierarchy came under strain, as the centre of gravity shifted from inherited land to industry and, even more significantly, to commerce and finance.[101] Writing in 1848, John Stuart Mill observed that 'the habits or disabilities which chained people to their hereditary condition are fast wearing away'.[102] Although rags-to-riches transformations remained exceptionally rare, more modest upward movements – from the skilled trades to lower middle-class white-collar jobs– came within the realm of expectations for the socially ambitious.[103] Victorian etiquette manuals took for granted a measure of social mobility that would have astonished Georgian readers.[104]

For those in the urban middle classes, the relative openness of late Victorian society presented opportunities, but also problems. The enterprising and very fortunate could exploit commercial capitalism's flexibility to join a new metropolitan élite, where the *nouveau riche* entered into partnerships with the landed gentry, and Jewish financiers rubbed elbows with Oxbridge gentlemen.[105] But with a more fluid society came more insecurity. 'All the way up and all the way down the scale there's the same discontent,' wrote H.G. Wells in 1905. 'No one is quite sure where they stand, and everyone's fretting.'[106] There was the danger of sinking into a subordinate social position; at the turn of the twentieth century, one in three sons of the upper middle class spent some part of his career in manual labour, the ultimate degradation for those who prided themselves upon their separation from physical toil.[107] Moreover, as the definition of a 'gentleman' widened, it became increasingly difficult to tell people apart.[108] In the anonymous big cities, and especially in London, a bustling metropolis of some seven million souls, cases of impostors and mistaken identity abounded. In a single month in 1904, one newspaper reported five instances of mistaken identity: 'It seems not enough nowadays that a man should pursue an honest calling, and be an ordinary peaceful, law-abiding subject of the King. To be really lucky, a man must be born without a double.'[109]

When a family name no longer sufficed to communicate identity, how could one person be distinguished from another? For the élite of previous centuries, distinctiveness was a prerogative conferred, like land and title, by lineage. But in this new era, individuality – as Mrs Haweis recognized – had to be earned. As the other signs of belonging diminished, material belongings gained in significance. An artistically furnished room did not simply express one's status; it conferred status. The question of the day, claimed Mrs Talbot Coke in 1892, was not 'Who are they?' but 'What *have* they?'[110] Who one *was* still mattered enormously, as it does today. But what one *had* came, by the late nineteenth century, to define the self in new ways, and on a hitherto unimaginable scale. Aristocrats, though oftentimes conspicuous consumers, did not secure their status by their household possessions. Similarly, bibles and sober dress did not make evangelicals. But for the middle classes, the acquisition of blue-and-white china and Moorish fretwork arches provided the essential tickets of admission to an 'artistic' way of life. Things preceded identity; what you owned told others (and yourself) who you were.

＊　＊　＊

For the Reverend Hugh Reginald Haweis and his wife Mary Eliza, the year 1884 marked a moment of triumph. The couple had taken up the lease on 'Queen's House', Rossetti's eighteenth-century dwelling in Cheyne Walk. Mary Eliza's *Beautiful Houses*, an escorted tour through a dozen 'well-known artistic houses', had received favourable notices in the papers. Mrs Haweis had become, she wrote to her mother, what the newspapers called 'the queen of a very clever set'.[111] The Reverend Haweis' book on American humorists was already into a second edition; his *Story of the Four Evangelists*, a more conventional effort for a man in his position, was nearly complete. Their four children were thriving. And Mary Eliza was poised to make Rossetti's home a showplace for her ideas about decoration – a laboratory for conjuring up the *Zeitgeist* of art. Snubbing the pale-wall conventions of Queen Anne, she returned to the vivid colours that Rossetti himself had favoured;

71 The Reverend
H.R. Haweis in front
of Queen's House,
c. 1880s.

she shopped for furniture and sought out old lace. For six months, Mary Eliza commandeered a small battalion of plasterers, painters, and carpenters under the flag of originality.

But the individuality and independence that Mary Eliza Haweis had urged upon her readers would, within a few years, prove too much for her own husband. The trouble began in 1890, when Mrs Haweis threw herself 'heart and soul' into the cause of women's suffrage – a logical extension, we will see in the next chapter, of her theories of decoration, but still a risky endeavour for a minister's wife. Despite his humanitarian notions, the Reverend Haweis resented his wife's political causes, her success, and the salons she hosted for her friends.[112] The 1890s saw the Haweises undoing all that they had made in the previous decade. The couple's children were drawn into their feud. Hugh Haweis complained to his sons that their mother was making herself ridiculous: 'Her abilities, if guided, as I guided them in the past and so got her a name, could still make her shine in this new world.'[113] In 1894, off on a lecturing tour in California, the Reverend Haweis wrote in a letter to his wife that she was 'not what I married'.[114] My 'household gods', he charged, have been 'broken'.

Rossetti's house had become a battleground in the war of the sexes. The Reverend Haweis complained that Queen's House was a drain on the couple's finances. His wife, for her part, was determined to remain in the house that she had created. As fast as Mrs Haweis could earn money with her articles and books, the Reverend Haweis spent it. He squandered large quantities to keep his mistress, who had borne him a child, silent. Even as Mrs Haweis cheerily advised her readers on turning a deep packing-case into a very good settee, the couple teetered on the verge of financial ruin.[115] In 1897, Mrs Haweis was forced to leave Rossetti's house for lodgings in Brighton. Before she departed, she drew up a minutely detailed plan so that she might, when finances permitted, reproduce her beloved home in miniature. She also cut her husband out of her will. Mrs Haweis died the following year at the age of fifty. Her obituary acknowledged her mettle in terms more suitable to a captain of industry than a lady decorator: 'She was never anxious to please everyone, troubled herself little enough with people's prejudices and was quite immovable in her opinions . . .'.[116]

If this book has so far touched on the different roles that men and women played in the enterprise of furnishing and decoration, these differences have remained unthematized. But if we are to understand the crisis of the Haweis marriage, and the dynamics of consumerism in middle-class families more generally, we must peer still more closely into the houses and shops of the late Victorian period. Today, women comprise the target audience for all things to do with the domestic interior. Whether choosing wallpapers or selecting bathroom fixtures, women are solicited by advertisers and courted by retailers. The married man's interest in his home is widely understood to be grudging, at best. 'Why do I have to make all the decisions,' complains a woman to a defeated-looking man in the parking lot of a DIY store. This exchange, captured in a 2003 television commercial for cricket, ends with a male voice-over: 'It's just not cricket.'[117] The guiding hand in home decoration is – we tend to assume – female. But was home decoration always a female pursuit? Did women in previous centuries exercise control over the domestic environment? Who took charge of the task of furnishing the home?

CHAPTER 4

IN POSSESSION

MEN, WOMEN AND DECORATION

In September 1867, the long-suffering upholsterer Mr Edmonds, proprietor of a well-regarded furnishing shop in the town of Newbury, received the latest letter from one of his most demanding clients. The upholstered door that Edmonds had supplied for the customer's dining-room was all wrong: 'I wish the baize door to be *red* instead of green, and of showy quality; not fine, nor with brass nails or any other ornamentals.'[1] No sooner had the door been replaced than Edmonds received word that his client had purchased Russian pine bookcases for the room. Though the bookcases were nicely carved and designed, their purchase threw the room's original decorative scheme into disarray.[2] This turn of events provided an opportunity for Edmonds' client to pester the beleaguered upholsterer with tedious new assignments – where to put the bookcases, how to paint the woodwork. The correspondence continued until the following year, when Edmonds' client died unexpectedly, perhaps to the upholsterer's relief.

Such preoccupation with decoration, the taste for 'showy quality', suggests patterns of behaviour and longing that we tend to associate with women. But Edmonds' client was a man, a Mr J.F. Winterbottom – and a married man at that. If this fact surprises, it is because the history of the domestic interior has most often been written as a history of women.[3] There are, of course, good reasons to associate women with consumption for the house. Women, and Victorian women in particular, have been defined by their domesticity.[4] And yet, middle-class Victorian men were, in an unprecedented fashion, also domestically minded.[5] The gradual separation of workplace from residence had made the home a welcome sanctuary from the money-grubbing world outside. Preoccupied by moral concerns, devoted to their children, men – or so claimed John Stuart Mill – no longer gave their 'spare hours to violent outdoor exercises and boisterous conviviality with male associates; the two sexes now pass their lives together'.[6]

Contrary to what most books on the subject have assumed, the Victorian interior was neither chiefly the responsibility, nor even the prerogative of women. Through the late nineteenth century, amid the rage for furnishing that overtook the middle

72 Defined by domes-
ticity. William Henry
Hunt, *Woman Sewing
in a Bedchamber*, 1837.

classes, men played a crucial role in the fitting-out of the home. Most often, husbands and wives made decorating decisions collaboratively. But men did not merely follow; more often than not, they seem to have led. The archives yield up in abundance stories of husbands like Mr Winterbottom, whose preferences determined the arrangement of interiors. This interest in decoration was not restricted to married men; bachelors, no less than spinsters, evinced concern for their rooms, and stores offered lines of furniture designed with the single man in mind. Until at least the 1880s, the business of furnishing was almost entirely a man's world. The earliest home decoration manuals were written by married men for married men. Decorators were men; the cause of design reform was led by men; upholsterers were men, as were the clerks on the shop floor.[7]

But by the 1920s and 1930s, home decoration had become nearly exclusively a woman's domain. Men played a limited role in choosing possessions for their houses; smart lady decorators such as Syrie Maugham set the fashions. This represented a dramatic change from the Victorian era, but one which has been obscured by the assumption that women's claim on the house remained much the same throughout this period. We begin, therefore, with men such as Mr Winterbottom, in order to investigate why Victorian masters of the house took such pains over their decorative schemes. Why many men seem to have abandoned home decoration after the turn of the century, how women claimed it, and to what degree, if any, a struggle ensued are the questions we take up next. What changed, we will see, was more than the hand that furnished the house. Along with the emancipated 'New

Woman' of the late nineteenth century came a new ethos of domesticity characterized specifically by the novel belief that a woman's décor served to reflect her
personality.

AN ENGLISHMAN'S HOME

Sir Edward Coke's famous dictum – the Englishman's home is his castle – reflected
the realities of a husband's authority within his own four walls. At marriage, a
woman ceased, according to the dictates of common law, to exist as a separate legal
entity. Until the sweeping reforms of marriage law enacted in 1882, a married
woman's property became her husband's, she could neither sue nor be sued, make
neither contracts nor a separate will without his consent.[8] A small minority of
women, usually from wealthy families, had separate property bestowed upon them
in the form of trusts; on these funds a woman could, subject to the trust's limitations, draw.[9] Otherwise, any property a woman inherited during the marriage came
under her husband's control, as did her earnings (if any). Moreover, after the
ancient and nearly obsolete right to dower (usually a one-third interest in her
husband's freehold lands) was repealed in 1833, wives had no absolute right to
inherit from their husband's estate.

Constrained by restrictions on property-holding, married women were debarred
from contracting debts in their own name. Common law dating from the age of
Henry VI had allowed wives to pledge their husbands' credit for goods deemed
'necessary'. However, women could not be held liable for the debt.[10] So long as shopping remained a local, face-to-face, personal transaction with tradesmen who knew
their customers' finances, this arrangement sufficed, though it was not without its
hitches. Husbands who could not control their wives' spending were forced to place
embarrassing advertisements in local newspapers disclaiming their purchases. But
with the advent of high-speed trains to London and other major cities and the blos-
soming of the retail sector, the problems raised by the law of 'necessaries' became
more serious.[11] Husbands could disavow their wives' purchases, claiming never to
have authorized them, and unlucky tradesmen were left with little recourse other
than to sue for the payment of debts. The county courts became a staging-ground
for family dramas featuring putatively extravagant wives and stingy husbands, each
blaming the other for stacks of unpaid bills. Called upon to assess responsibility,
judges often faulted the innocent tradesman, charging that shopkeepers had
unwisely extended credit without sufficient security. Tradesmen thus tended to
regard women, especially those who were shopping far from home, with suspicion.
Not until the 1930s did married women gain the right to contract debts in their own
name.

Furnishing was an expensive proposition, and women – as Virginia Woolf
reminded her readers – were poor.[12] Outfitting a house in the 1860s might require

that a middle-class man spend as much as his entire annual salary.[13] Some men decorated their residences before marriage. Men of means were the most likely to do so. Titus Salt, Jr, son of the famed mill owner and himself a wealthy man, bought his Gothic-inspired furniture the year before he married.[14] A furnished house signified prosperity and stability; it helped a man to attract a desirable wife. Men who advertised for a wife noted their business or income, their appearance, and – if they had one – their 'nice' or 'comfortable' home.[15] In his 1864–5 novel, *Can You Forgive Her?*, Anthony Trollope satirized the efforts of a Mr Cheesacre, a wealthy but uncouth farmer, to find a wife. In courting the moneyed widow Mrs Greenow, Cheesacre threw open the portals of his prized residence, 'Oileymead', to ensnare his catch, displaying 'every bit of china, delft, glass, and plate in the establishment', and beseeching his intended to 'feel the texture of the blankets'. After proposing marriage, Cheesacre pressed the beleaguered Mrs Greenow for an answer: 'Come then, say the word. There ain't a bedroom in my house, – not one of the front ones, – that isn't mahogany furnished!'[16]

Before the 1880s, those who wrote about home decoration largely directed their advice to the man of the house. Robert Kerr's 1864 treatise on dwellings of 'the

73 Shopping together: *Mr Silverlock's Shop in New Oxford-Street*, 1847.

better sort' was baldly titled *The Gentleman's House*, and the 'views of the ladies' were accorded a paltry one out of 470-odd pages.[17] While women might pride themselves upon their taste, too often (or so design reformers warned) they fell under the upholsterer's spell.[18] According to the prodigiously self-promoting designer Christopher Dresser, it was 'almost impossible that women who have not had special advantages of education can be good judges of what is necessary to good taste in house furnishing'.[19] Women who wished to inform themselves looked to the ladies' periodicals in vain; neither the *Lady's Newspaper and Pictorial Times* nor the *Englishwoman's Domestic Magazine* devoted columns to the topic, nor did they attract furnishing advertisers.[20] In *A Plea for Art in the House* (1876), the Reverend W.J. Loftie assumed that men were his audience.[21] The earliest women writers on the subject followed suit. Rhoda and Agnes Garrett were pioneering suffragists. And yet they wrote their *Suggestions for House Decoration* (1877) for the benefit of men. The 'amateur' to whom they refer throughout is male; their book would, they promised, 'enable him to speak with more authority to the upholsterer or the paper-hanger'.[22] Women's sovereignty in the furnishing of the house, even as the Garrett cousins imagined it, was limited. Only when it came to the drawing-room were 'the ladies of the family . . . told that it is now their turn to have their taste consulted'.[23]

In practice, furnishing probably most often began as a collaborative endeavour between man and wife, but one in which husbands ultimately made the decisions. There were of course those husbands who turned over to their wives complete authority in furnishing. Thomas Carlyle entered into his marriage with Jane Welsh full of fierce language about the man's 'rule in the house', but in practice he left her in charge of all household matters; decoration fell within her purview, as did the battle with the bugs that infested their Cheyne Row home.[24] There were also harmonious couples who made decisions about purchases together. According to the wife of the painter E.M. Ward, she and her husband 'were entirely of one mind . . . and as we both had a passion for antiques and old masters, after our work was over we would take long walks through the streets, examining old furniture'.[25] In many families, houses were, in all likelihood, divided into spheres of influence: because the drawing-room was, as the Garretts noted, widely seen as the ladies' chamber, a wife's preferences might rule; similarly, the study or library (if the house had one) reflected her husband's desires. To women, in addition, belonged the minor tasks of bric-à-brac, of furbelows and valences – in the words of the Garretts, the job of getting right the 'small and comparatively insignificant details'.[26]

But in the case of a dispute, men had the last word. An 1878 article in the *Cabinet and Upholstery Advertiser*, a leading trade journal, related what happened when husbands and wives disagreed. A newly married couple visit a furniture store in search of a bedroom suite. The wife adores an ornate Eastlake set; her husband 'who dislikes show or gaudiness of every kind, is particularly pleased with a rich but plain black walnut one . . .'. And in an incident which, according to the journal, 'happens

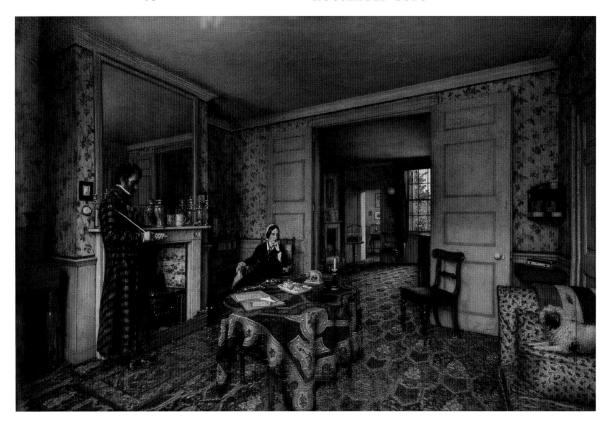

74 Robert S. Tait, *Thomas and Jane Carlyle in the Drawing Room of their House in Cheyne Row*, 1857–8.

almost every day', 'The husband . . . is a very decided man when he is inclined to be; and although he does not care to offend his wife by appearing mean or contemptible in her loving and confiding eyes, still, on this occasion, he is obliged to tell her frankly what suite of furniture he shall take.'[27] The home may have been woman's sphere, but she did not there reign. Coventry Patmore, author of that notorious tribute to nineteenth-century femininity, *The Angel in the House*, did not – according to his biographer – permit his second wife the liberty of arranging her heavenly domain, bought with her fortune: 'Patmore . . . ruled the home as his own, managed the property, inaugurated changes, and was in all respects the complete master.'[28]

Control over decoration was not simply common practice, but, in some quarters, the ideal. 'I can scarcely imagine a task more agreeable for a gentleman of means, taste, and leisure than to set himself to the consistent decoration and furnishing of a Gothic villa,' wrote the critic J. Beavington Atkinson in the *Art Journal* in 1867.[29] After the Irish poet Katharine Tynan's first literary success in 1885, her father decided that she needed a room of her own in which to write and receive visitors. Andrew Tynan was a gentleman farmer, with a large dairy concern outside Dublin to manage. But the job of decorating Katharine's room was a task he entrusted to no

one else.[30] Father and daughter spent days poring over wallpapers, weeks more in the auction houses in search of suitable furniture. Contrary to his daughter's aesthetic taste, he insisted upon a large looking-glass for her room. He chose for her a davenport in walnut wood.

Stories of acquisitive men and husbands who were intimately involved in the details of furnishing abound throughout nineteenth-century records. In the archives of the Scottish interior decoration firm of William Scott Morton & Co. for 1881–2, we meet Mr David Anderson, a very 'particular' man who haunts the shops in search of dining-room chairs, and wishes his decorator to accompany him; Mr Robert Stewart, who commissions some 'velvety cushions' from the firm; C.E. Willet, who proposes a 'red crape material' for curtains; Mr W.H. Henderson, who wishes his mantelpieces 'nicely arranged'; Mr James Templeton, who firmly believes that the 'yellow green' colour should be used all over his room.[31] Women who wrote to decorating columnists for advice often made explicit reference to their husbands' preferences and demands. 'Marta's' husband refused a Brussels carpet as '"dreadfully inartistic"' while 'Myrene's' would '"never permit a pile carpet."'[32] 'Idri's' husband 'only likes plain walls'.[33] Some men exercised their will in a fashion

75 The college living room of an unidentified undergraduate man, c. 1890, as photographed by Henry Taunt. Taunt's photographs of Oxford record the attention that male students lavished upon their rooms.

76 The discerning
man of the house,
ensconced in his
library. From Lewis
Day's 'How to Decorate
a Room', *Magazine of
Art*, 1880–1.

that was, to say the least, idiosyncratic. 'Pauline's' husband was literal-minded. 'I find it very difficult to put myself in your position,' *Hearth and Home*'s decorating columnist wrote to her, 'because I can't grasp the idea that the name of the house including the word "oak" compels you to a dining-room painted oak brown. Indeed, I can fancy nothing more gloomy. But if your husband really *is* firm about it, the yellowy shade of light oak will be one degree less hopeless than your present dark brown . . . .'[34]

Even in those unusual marriages where wives enjoyed the financial upper hand, decoration could still be a man's due. Dinah Mulock was the author of the wildly popular romance, *John Halifax, Gentleman.*[35] Still unmarried at the age of forty, Mulock appeared destined for spinsterhood. And then one day – true to the spirit of her own romantic novels – she opened the door of her Hampstead cottage to find a surprise visitor who changed her solitary life. The visitor was George Craik, the young nephew of a friend of hers. Craik had been injured in a railway accident. Mulock devoted the next months to nursing him; the pair married the next year. The Scottish novelist Lucy Walford recounted with amusement her visit in the 1870s to the Craiks. The romance novelist and her husband were in the midst of decorating their new house; a grey-felt carpet had just been laid down in the drawing-room. When Mrs Craik deplored the carpet, Walford expressed surprise. Her hostess' earnings, notoriously, had paid for the house. Mrs Craik explained: '"It is my husband's taste I have to conform to, — " and she put on a demure look.'[36] Mrs Craik, the elder, richer, and more famous of the two, conspicuously deferred to her husband to right the obvious imbalance. And for George Craik, the conferral of decorating supremacy proved a means of establishing his authority within the marriage.

Why, apart from the expense, did men care so much about grey-felt carpets and nicely arranged mantelpieces? Motivations, we can assume, varied dramatically. There were, for instance, those men who sought through their décor to safeguard the righteousness of their households. The home, as envisioned by evangelicals, had redemptive power; there, the man could throw off the temptations to which his work had exposed him. In very religious households, men were the arbiters of display, though the prevailing asceticism did not provide much scope for manœuvre. By contrast, the coming of incarnationalism after the mid-nineteenth century, combined with rising prosperity, made decoration a pressing issue for the paterfamilias. If beauty was a moral virtue, as the Reverends Boyd and Loftie had claimed, men were obliged to attend to even the most minute details of room decoration. This was not simply a matter of protecting his family from possessions that might exercise a pernicious influence. It also implicated a man's moral cultivation. In the process of beautifying his surroundings, the house – or so the advice manuals promised – worked a change upon him. Painting one's walls and studying the form of furniture became acts of grace, which 'humanized' the amateur home decorator.[37]

Houses also served to convey a man's wealth and standing. Where and how a man lived might do more to advertise his position than could his occupation or profession, especially if he were involved in a grimy business such as factory management or a lucrative but not quite respectable line of work like stockbroking.[38] In 1875, the designer Christopher Dresser complained that his clients often exaggerated the amount that he had charged to impress their friends: 'The work perhaps proves satisfactory, when the host, with the view of extolling himself, says that "Dr. Dresser did this for me, but he is a very expensive man. The thing has cost me so and so."'[39] For the men of the Forsyte family, the novelist John Galsworthy's emblematic, upper middle-class clan, old gold lacquer and Worcesterware functioned as the visible emblems, even the guarantors of status. Retired from the (in his mind) 'deplorable' profession of land agency, Swithin Forsyte counted on his ormolu-encrusted

77 Colonel Harold Esdaile Malet (1841–1918), *Interior at Cox Hoe*, 1867–8. Over the course of an itinerant military career, Malet, an enthusiastic amateur watercolourist, made a habit of drawing the places where he lived. Using photographic montage, he inserted himself twice into this picture.

furnishings to attest to his gentlemanly qualifications: 'out of the knowledge that no one could possibly enter his rooms without perceiving him to be a man of wealth, he had derived a solid and prolonged happiness such as perhaps no other circumstance in life had afforded him'.[40]

For men who wished to demonstrate their refinement, the home became a show-place. It was not uncommon for a visitor, upon calling for the first time on an acquaintance, to be conducted through the premises by the man of the house, who directed his guest's attention to the improvements he had made.[41] Writing to a friend in 1862, one Bloomsbury man boasted about the renovation of his drawing-room, to be papered in pink, white, and gold. 'In doing this we are taking a very bold step, as people are always nervous about colour in Drawing-rooms. I am having a paper prepared to my own taste.'[42] William Morris drew his best clients from the ranks of successful entrepreneurs. For a class charged with 'philistinism', an artistic interior offered a defence: its inhabitants proclaimed their love of beauty.[43] But even those men whose taste fell far short of the high-minded ideals of the day prided themselves upon achieving a genteel effect. In his autobiography, Frederick Locker-Lampson recollected a visit to friends in Pentonville, who had just (in the 1880s) purchased a garish mid-Victorian-style carpet in deep pile crimson and orange. The husband of the couple was, as his wife readily acknowledged, very 'particular': 'You can't conceive how awfully fidgety Edgar is about his carpets – it's perfectly ghastly.'[44]

A taste for collecting old Worcester-ware or Regency clocks might accompany a man's interest in decoration, but the middle-class men we have thus far encountered had not assembled collections in any systematic sense. They simply took charge of the job of furnishing their house. The distinction between collectors and furnishers is important, because though some men continued to collect, by the 1920s and 1930s the consumer landscape for home furnishing had shifted. Men played a limited role in choosing posses-sions for their houses; home decoration had become predominantly a woman's domain. According to *Furnishings*, the leading trade journal of the 1920s: '... woman is the purchaser of at least 90 per cent of the furnishings for the home.'[45] Marketing campaigns featured female shoppers, while stores courted their clientele by emphasizing women's pref-erences in walnut or French china.[46] The fashionable furnishing business was, as the

78 Relegated to package carrier – from 'My Wife's Shopping', a tale of a drawing-room refurbishment published in *The House*, 1898.

Cabinet Maker put it on the eve of the Second World War, a 'woman's world'.[47] Apart from their neatly arrayed collections of pipes and pottery, men's part in domestic decoration – if indeed they had one at all – had been reduced to do-it-yourself home repair.[48]

What explains the transformation? The decade of the 1890s witnessed a change in the relationship between a man and his possessions that though gradual was nonetheless significant. Suspicious commentators had long mocked the fad for artistic furnishing as insufficiently masculine.[49] In the *Saturday Review*'s scathing depiction, the 'aesthetic friend' who insinuated himself into the household 'screams with a pretty feminine horror at the mention of mauve or magenta'.[50] Even before Wilde's trials discredited the public face of the 'House Beautiful', Mrs Talbot Coke, decorating columnist for *Hearth and Home*, distinguished between two kinds of men. Her preference was for (in her words) a 'real man', who loved sport and outdoor life. 'As to another class of man, the handy man who "does his own draperies" (I know one who also makes his own lampshades, poor thing) . . . I could never feel the same unwilling respect I do for one who will have none of my artistic notions in his own den, but only wants to "know where to find his things", and be able to smoke undisturbed and unreproved.'[51]

Oscar Wilde's 1895 conviction on charges of 'gross indecency' transformed Mrs Talbot Coke's innuendo into overt public disapproval. If a whiff of femininity lingered around aesthetes and, by extension, home decoration before Wilde's public humiliation, afterwards the link between effeminacy and homosexuality was forged solid. During most of the nineteenth century, there was of course no homosexual identity or consciousness as we today know it.[52] Men might have sex with or love other men without thinking of themselves either as embodying or rejecting a set of traits. But in the aftermath of Wilde's trials, it is possible to catch a glimpse of a homosexual identity in the making – one which would, in the twentieth century, turn the home into a place for uncloseted self-expression and allow men to transcend provincial prejudices by allying themselves with good taste.[53] But the cause of gay liberation, even as it would eventually open the closet door, also led heterosexual men to narrow their aesthetic worlds. Too conspicuous a pursuit of the House Beautiful left a man open to ridicule, possibly even misperception. The men who wrote in to decorating columnists in the 1890s and after sought, above all, to avoid creating the wrong impression: they wanted manly furniture. 'Little Paddy' aimed at the 'good and plain style of the male apartment', but it eluded him. Mrs Talbot Coke blamed his cream ground floral paper: 'It is that which gives the "sentimental spinster" look you so amusingly deplore.'[54]

While Wilde's disgrace did much to alter the public perception of masculinity within the home, men's relationships to their houses were already changing. By the end of the nineteenth century, the enthusiastic domesticity that had characterized mid-Victorian men was under increasing strain. For a small but vocal minority of men, domestic life had come to seem a suffocating burden, full of financial encumbrances and daily tedium. They rejected the cosy virtues of hearth and home in what the historian John Tosh has termed a 'flight from domesticity', seeking refuge in clubs and sporting associations.[55] Even among avid family men, however, the growth of the suburbs meant that many husbands were increasingly absent from their homes. Between 1880 and 1939, entire new districts shot up around Britain's major cities, built on speculation by developers who recognized the needs of the growing middle classes for more spacious accommodation at lower rents, with the benefits of greenery and fresh air.[56] The first building boom, which lasted until the First World War, was responsible for the creation of single-class suburbs like Twickenham and Chislehurst on the outskirts of London. After the war, building resumed at a feverish pace to house the middle class's latest additions to its ranks: the legions of white-collar workers and new professionals who, thanks to newly affordable mortgages, could for the first time buy their own homes.

'Suburbia', a term coined in the 1890s, described a social phenomenon – in the Liberal politician C.F.G. Masterman's phrase, a 'civilization'.[57] Its manners and mores were very different from those of the early suburbs, the puritanical enclaves created by high-minded evangelicals in Clapham and Streatham. This new suburbia meant getting and spending. Unlike the older suburbs, close enough that a man might walk to work, the new suburbia took the nineteenth-century process of the separation of home and work to its logical conclusion. The bowler-hatted suburban man caught the 8.05 train to town, and did not return until six or even seven, perhaps after dinner at his club. His wife was left in charge of their detached or semi-detached Tudorbethan house, furnished with goods bought on credit from the stores and tantalizingly shielded from passers-by with gardens, walls, and lace curtains. For contemporary observers, the husband's absence from his own home jarred. In 1909, Thomas Crosland, a firebrand social critic of the day, scornfully described suburbia as a 'country whose population consists almost wholly of women, children, and tax-gatherers'. Crosland continued: 'This absence of responsible male population throughout the day may be reckoned a much more serious matter than appears at first sight . . . . Practically it gives over the household and all that dwell therein to the unquestioned rule of woman, which is not good.'[58] A few years later, Philip Gibbs, a harsh judge of the 'New Man', agreed: 'Gradually he effaces himself in a home governed by the feminine influence.'[59]

Men did not abandon the pursuit of home decoration altogether. Those men who worked at home – especially the clergy and some professionals such as doctors – continued to take charge of the furnishing and decoration of their homes. Ursula Bloom describes her father, Harvey, a country clergyman in the Church of England, as an avid connoisseur of antique furniture, with a 'genius for interior decoration'.[60] Like his nineteenth-century predecessors, Harvey placed a high value on a well-designed room. His diaries indicate a network of similarly inclined country clerics: 'I then went to see Tredington Rectory, to visit the Rector Edwards and see their pretty furniture.'[61] Some of the keenest furniture-hounds were doctors, whose profession brought them into the homes of the sick and elderly, and, as disgusted dealers noted, they took antiques as payment in kind: 'We could . . . give the names of some doctors who can classify chairs as readily as diseases and medicines.'[62]

Perhaps because they lived for so long with no fixed home (and did not fear the taint of effeminacy), military men, too, continued to cultivate a reputation for discernment in domestic matters. Beryl Booker's father, retired from the 11th Hussars in India, was known by friends and neighbours for his good taste. At their house in Cambridge Square, he 'made a clean sweep' of Victoriana, stripping the fireplace of its polished oak and bevelled glass overmantel, evicting the Brussels carpets, and adding fresh chintz covers to the chairs.[63] In his autobiography, Colonel Montague Cooke extolled the virtues of tasteful home decoration, observing that 'even as a youth, I have ever appreciated loveliness in all its forms'.[64] Some military men even made a second profession out of their furnishing habits. In her trawl around London's shops, published in 1924, the journalist Elizabeth Montizambert discovered a number of shops for antiques run by ex-officers, singling out the Old

79 Dr Frederick Treves, Welbeck House sitting room, 1899. Treves, the son of an upholsterer, was a well-known surgeon. The Hunterian professor of anatomy at the Royal College of Surgeons, he is remembered today as the doctor to the 'Elephant Man'.

80 Major Joicey,
59 Cadogan Square,
drawing room. In
1890, Major Joicey
commissioned Bedford
Lemere to photograph
his flat.

81 Lieutenant
L. Walker Munro's
drawing room at
Lady Cross Lodge,
Brockenhurst, Hants,
1890.

Farmhouse Salon and the General Trading Company managed by a Major Christie Millar for praise.[65]

Herbert Kitchener, the ruthless hero of Omdurman, was known for his voracious appetite for china and curios and his talent for flower-arranging. From 1906, he was accompanied by a constant companion and ADC, Captain O.A.G. Fitzgerald. Kitchener's tastes were luxurious, and his methods unorthodox. When re-doing his Indian bungalow (as Commander-in-Chief), he ordered his military aides to craft a decorative ceiling of papier mâché from discarded official files. From India he wrote to Lady Roberts: 'I shall set up as a House Decorator when I leave here.'[66] Kitchener's acquisitiveness literally knew no bounds; he looted without regret and, on occasion, even pilfered choice specimens from other people's houses.[67] After Kitchener's death at sea in 1916, *Country Life* noted (without, presumably, arousing any untoward suspicions) that his few leisure hours were spent on the 'beautifying of his home, Broome Park, Kent'.[68] Field Marshal Lord Grenfell, Kitchener's old rival in the Egyptian campaign, was possessed by a similar fixation: 'I have,' he acknowledged in his will, 'been a slave to my furniture for years.'[69]

THE STRUGGLE FOR THE HOUSE

If a number of men retreated on their own accord from the house, still others were pushed out by their wives. The struggle for the house began with the campaign for reform of the marriage laws. In the 1850s the artist Barbara Leigh Smith, daughter of the radical MP for Norwich, petitioned Parliament to improve married women's lot. Raised in an unconventional household, Leigh Smith was 'never happy in an English genteel family life', and she diagnosed married women's inability to hold property as a critical part of their problem.[70] Her petition, signed by more than 26,000 people, marked the beginning of a concerted campaign for reform, though the issue of married women's property eventually stalled in Parliament. Opposition to married women's property and education, wrote the feminist Josephine Butler, was above all rooted in a 'secret dread' that women's claims would 'revolutionize society [and] our *Homes*'.[71]

The first Married Women's Property Act of 1870 – co-sponsored by John Stuart Mill but defanged in the House of Lords – granted English wives some limited authority over registered investments, inherited property, and their own earnings, but fell far short of the reforms that women's rights campaigners had urged. Instead of granting women the right to hold property on the same terms as men, the 1870 Act provided limited protection from the abuse of feckless husbands. Not until twelve years later, in 1882, were all married women vested with property rights. Even then, Parliament did not grant wives comparable rights to their husbands', but simply extended to all women the prerogatives that wealthy wives with separate property settlements had long since enjoyed. They could hold property and make a will without their husbands' agreement.[72]

Against the backdrop of the parliamentary crusades, the right to make a home became a feminist rallying cry. This was a new domesticity, a more militant domesticity – which points up the degree to which Victorian women's rights within the home were neither as secure nor as extensive as has been assumed. As women entered the public sphere in unprecedented numbers in the service of social purity campaigns or to demand entry into higher education and the professions, they also demanded new domestic privileges. In *The Duties of Women*, Frances Power Cobbe asserted that the home, famously women's sphere, was also her prerogative. Cobbe, exiled from her girlhood Irish home by common law governing property, staked a woman's claim to home-making: 'The making of a true home is really our peculiar and inalienable right, – a right which no man can take from us; for a man can no more make a home than a drone can make a hive . . . . It is a woman, and only a woman, – and a woman all by herself, if she likes, and without any man to help her, – who can turn a house into a home.'[73] For Cobbe, the objective was not the woman's own 'aesthetic gratification' – a proposition she had roundly criticized in her attacks on the worshippers of salt-cellars – but the comfort and moral soundness of those who came to her drawing-room.[74] Hers was a feminism rooted in women's moral supremacy.

Although men still commanded the heights of retailing and design reform, and would do so until the 1980s, women in the late nineteenth century increasingly took the lead in the 'business' of decorating. The first woman decorators opened shops in the 1870s; by the 1920s and 1930s, they had been joined by many others.[75] In these early years, feminism and home decoration were complementary pursuits. To identify the early female decorators as pioneers of emancipation may appear a contradiction in terms. To our eyes, Laura Ashley and Martha Stewart scarcely seem forces for women's liberation. But women's entrance into the field of professional decoration was relatively slow and hard-fought. The Incorporated Institute of British Decorators excluded women as members until the end of the First World War; as late as 1930, only a handful of the professional society's 1,070 members were women.[76] The designer Lewis Day characterized house decoration as a profession for men: 'His is a manly art, and remains for the most part in the hands of men.'[77] The first female decorators came either (like Mary Eliza Haweis and Jane Panton) from artistic circles or – like the first female physicians – from wealthy families that could afford to finance the costs of training and setting up shop.[78]

In Britain's most famous suffrage families, the women's cause and the business of home decoration became mutually sustaining enterprises – intertwined aims best understood within the context of a new domesticity. Of the talented Garrett sisters, Elizabeth (1836–1917) would become the first female doctor in Britain, Millicent (1847–1929) the leader of the liberal suffrage cause, and Agnes (1845–1935), an

82 Rhoda Garrett, as depicted in 1883 in the *Cabinet-Maker*.

83 Rhoda and Agnes Garrett.

early woman decorator.[79] Unmarried at the age of twenty-six, Agnes decided that it was time to embark upon a career. Her father, a prosperous malter, wanted to make a place for his clever daughter in the family business.[80] But Agnes' brothers protested: they wanted the business for themselves and believed that any public role for Agnes in the brewing enterprise would shame the family. That possibility foreclosed, Agnes and her cousin, Rhoda, decided to go into business on their own. Like Agnes, Rhoda was an ardent suffragist and had already become known as a fiery public speaker.[81] House decoration, they decided, would permit them both to earn money and to advance the feminist cause.

But many obstacles lay in wait. Despite her father's objections, Agnes moved to London to study under the furnisher Daniel Cottier who had agreed to teach her the decorating trade.[82] Rhoda came to London, too, though for her it was still riskier, since she was older than Agnes, and virtually penniless. Cottier, though he took the cousins' money, taught them little, perhaps because, like so many of his colleagues, he believed that decoration was no profession for women.[83] After some struggle, they eventually found a sympathetic patron in J.M. Brydon, an architect of the 'Queen Anne' persuasion who had a few years earlier opened his own decorating and furnishing business. Their apprenticeship lasted three rigorous years. The Garretts travelled the countryside sketching the interiors of old houses, and they worked in Brydon's office. But despite their skill as designers, the decorating firm they approached in the early 1870s declined to give them work. The manager mocked their proposal, claiming that they would be fatally handicapped by their

inability to swear at workmen or climb
ladders. At that point, one of the cousins
responded: 'As for swearing at the
workmen, they would not need that if it
were ladies who made requests; and as for
the ladders, bring one here and see whether
we can climb it or not!'[84] In 1875, the
Garrett cousins opened their own shop
dealing in old oak and other furniture at 2
Gower Street, Bedford Square and in 1876,
published a book on house decoration for
the middle classes. They exhibited some of
the furniture they designed at the first Arts
and Crafts Exhibition Society.

   The Garretts built their furnishing business against the backdrop of their campaign
for the vote. Agnes served as an honorary
secretary to the National Society for
Women's Suffrage, while Rhoda spoke from
the platform about the obstacles and 'almost
overwhelming prejudice' she had faced in
attempting to learn her trade. Rhoda was
much in demand as a speaker, but her
health, even then, was fragile.[85] Despite
Agnes' best efforts to shield her cousin from
the 'slings and arrows which are the reward
of pioneers', Rhoda died of tuberculosis in
1882 at the age of 41.[86] Agnes carried on the
business on her own, establishing a reputation for unyieldingly high standards, and a
speciality in panelled rooms. 'I like all my
work,' she told a reporter in 1890, 'to bear
the individual impress of my mind.'[87] She
undertook the decoration of private homes,
her clients including the composer Sir
Hubert Parry and the scientist Lord Kelvin,
and executed the interiors of the Ladies'
Residential Chambers in Chenies Street,
which provided accommodation at a
moderate rate for working women in
London. Agnes Garrett never married, and

84 A drawing room chimney piece designed by the Garretts,
probably in their house at 2 Gower St, London.

continued her business for almost fifty years, training two generations of pupils to follow in her wake. She was, as one reporter observed, 'bound heart and soul' to her profession.[88]

The connection between suffrage and home decoration was not limited to 'moderates' like the Garretts. In 1885, the year of the match girls' strike, Emmeline Pankhurst – later founder of the militant Women's Social and Political Union, ruthless organizer, passionate orator, inveterate window-smasher and imprisoned hunger striker – opened a furnishing shop in London.[89] As a young woman, she had lived in Paris and moved in artistic circles. After her husband lost his campaign for a seat in Parliament, the struggling family moved to London, where Mrs Pankhurst decided to go into business. She wanted to make money, and thought a business permitted its owners greater freedom of opinion than did a professional career.[90] Her store, Emerson & Co., was located in Hampstead Road, home to cheap food stores: a worse choice for the artistic enamelled milking-stools and picture frames she proffered would be difficult to imagine. Still, she had high hopes, as her daughter Christabel later remembered: 'With a shop she would lay the financial foundation of a great movement of social and industrial reform and, of course, the enfranchisement of women.'[91]

Although Mrs Pankhurst's Hampstead Road enterprise was not a success, she persisted in the business, opening a shop on Berners Street, a more refined location off the Oxford Street thoroughfare. There, she added stock: Persian plates, oriental brass, embroidered hangings. She designed white-painted furniture with fretwork, and engaged a carpenter to make it according to her designs. When her lease on Berners Street ended, she took a still more expensive shop on Regent Street. Even after she closed her failing London enterprise in 1893, home decoration remained for Emmeline Pankhurst a calling to which she would return again and again, despite the fact that her shops rarely, if ever, earned money.[92] After her husband's death, in need of a source of income, she opened another store in Manchester selling 'artistic' wares. 'I think you could do something better than that!' was her daughter Christabel's reproof.[93] Only when the family moved from Manchester in 1906 to devote themselves full time to the suffrage cause did Mrs Pankhurst finally abandon her store.

The Garretts and the Pankhursts are the best-known suffrage pioneers. But there were many other purveyors of this new and more militant brand of domesticity, whose lives bear out the link between a struggle for the house and agitation for women's rights. So prominent were decorating ladies like Mrs Haweis and the Misses Garrett that house decoration garnered considerable attention at the turn of the century as a suitable occupation for women. It was the second type of employment (after teaching) discussed in *Woman*'s regular 'World of Breadwinners' column of 1890; other periodicals, including *The Young Woman* and *Our Home* carried similar notices.[94] In the pages of the trade periodicals, we catch a glimpse of lady decorators who have left little trace: Miss Coleman, Mrs Mary Masters, Miss Millicent Cohen, a pupil of the Garretts.[95] 'Flitting' between two shops in Manchester and London around the 1890s was the formidable Miss Charlotte Robinson, who, once employed, demanded the right to carry out her schemes 'without further interference or suggestions from her customers'.[96] Some of these decorators were society ladies, like Mrs Eugenia Merry, who opened a shop called Madame Aileen.[97] Others appear to have been sisters who joined their capital to found a business together: the Misses Helen and Isabel Woollan, 'decorative artists' at 28 Brook Street, or Miss Caroline Crommelin and Mrs Florence Goring-Thomas.[98] Miss Stapylton-Smith dealt in antiques, decorated and had, by the late 1890s, qualified as an appraiser and valuer for probate.[99] Mrs Charles Muller set up a model flat on Sloane Street to show callers what a 'cozy and tasteful home should be . . . '.[100]

While decorators catered principally to the well-to-do, 'decorators on paper' – always women – served the middle classes. Beginning in the 1880s, domestic art advisors such as Mrs Jane Panton in the *Lady's Pictorial* or Mrs Talbot Coke in *Hearth and Home* offered their readers suggestions on how to finish curtain rods with pine cones or rescue an outdated decorative scheme. They provided individually tailored advice to subscribers who wrote in to them, printing their replies at the back of the magazine.[101] The redoubtable Mrs Talbot Coke was married to a general, always on the move (she lived in twenty-five homes in as many years), and the mother of seven children. And yet, by her own proud reckoning, she devoted six

85 A corner of the Misses Woollan's shop on Brook St, London.

86 Charlotte Talbot Coke in 1888.

hours every day to answering the letters that poured in by the thousand. Possessed of an 'abnormally sound constitution, both mental and physical' and 'inexhaustible energy', Mrs Talbot Coke was at her writing desk by six o'clock every morning.[102] In the pages of *Queen*, where she got her start, and then at the magazine she founded, *Hearth and Home*, Mrs Coke appealed to the socially ambitious woman reader navigating the perilous shoals of originality and good taste. Mrs Coke was fortunate enough to possess family heirlooms, thereby establishing her pedigree, while at the same time remaining a woman of 'energy and inborn love of work', values prized by her middle-class readers.[103] Her own taste was, it went without saying, impeccable.

During her more than two-decade-long rule at *Hearth and Home*, Coke liked to claim that her name was a 'talisman' to conjure with in the shops.[104] That was no exaggeration. Not only did she advise her readers to buy certain fabrics or styles from particular retailers, but furniture stores advertised their products as 'recommended' or 'designed' by Mrs Talbot Coke, thereby contributing (as the designer Gustav Haite acknowledged) to an improved selection in the shops.[105] She claimed credit for the invention of the cosy corner, a late nineteenth-century cushioned recess by the fireplace shielded with Moorish fretwork arches and heaped with oriental pillows, and soon ubiquitous in middle-class homes.[106] Of all the columns in *Hearth and Home*, including those on dress and health, hers attracted the most voluminous correspondence. She created a sense of intimacy with her readers, welcoming back her 'old friends' with inquiries about their former rooms and demanding that new correspondents send her photographs of completed arrangements. She urged her readers to act 'boldly', liberally sprinkling her answers with exclamation marks and French phrases, but did not hesitate to chastise those she thought had gone astray.[107] Bad news she dispensed with élan: 'How I wish I could be truthful and at the same time pleasant after all the nice things you say about my columns! But it is useless my pretending that autotypes will ever satisfy the eye in such a panelled room as yours, and with all your fine old china and old furniture.'[108]

87 Mrs Talbot Coke's own house – Trusley Hall.

By the turn of the century, the decorators on paper had captured the middle-class market. Decorating advice, once scarce in the ladies' press, now became a standard feature. Every woman's paper employed a decorating columnist, whose advice – and persona – was carefully calibrated to the sensibilities of her audience. In the down-market *Lady's Companion*, 'Torfrida' advised ladies whose decorative reach exceeded their financial grasp. Behind her Nordic pen-name, she wrote, was a woman just like her readers: she lived in a cottage, did her own housework, and had decided to go in for poultry-keeping to make extra money.[109] A sofa was beyond her means, though she had a piano on hire purchase. With £52, she had managed to furnish her cottage throughout, a feat made possible by a brave disregard of all the rules. In days gone past, a drawing-room hung with deepest red wallpaper or a dining-room done in green would have scandalized observers, but such strictures no longer applied. 'Freedom of opinion,' Torfrida exulted, 'is now allowed to each individual.'[110]

Lady art advisors such as Torfrida and Mrs Talbot Coke understood that the house had become, in late nineteenth-century Britain, increasingly feminine territory and – above all else – personal, a reflection of a woman's individuality. 'All decoration is,' as Coke put it, 'an opening for individual opinion.'[111] Blithely disregarding the shibboleths of design reform, Coke endorsed the sham if that was the most expressive option. She was not interested in what was right, but what her correspondents wished to have. 'Because I do not like a glass shade over a clock or ornament, I should be sorry to say it is "wrong".'[112] She preached self-expression

88 A cosy corner, as
advertised by Graham
& Biddle, 1887.

88 A cosy corner, as
advertised by Graham
& Biddle, 1887.

rather than fidelity to the rules: 'It is such a help when anyone tells me she "likes
bold designs and conventional as possible", for I would always rather fall in with
views (any not absolutely vulgar) than force a certain decorative dogma on
unwilling recipients.'[113] Mrs Coke could be censorious or disapproving, but she
always indicated a way that a lady might show herself to best advantage. According
to the journalist Mrs C.S. Peel, English women the world over followed Mrs Coke's
counsel. 'Wherever English women were,' Peel wrote, 'there were decorative schemes
chosen for them by Mrs Talbot Coke.'[114]

   To those who had wearied of the rules of design reform, Mrs Talbot Coke's appeal
was obvious. Her 'heterodox and "free-lance" notion as to decoration' unshackled
the timid and self-conscious, licensing a broad range of furnishing caprices in the
name of individuality.[115] As a chorus of admiring press notices attested, her evident
sympathy for the 'mere average woman' and her eclectic sensibilities helped to
distinguish her from 'the exponents of so many doctrines and theories'.[116] In 1892,
Winter's Magazine drew an illuminating contrast between Mrs Talbot Coke and
Oscar Wilde. Where Oscar Wilde and his kind 'manifested a certain insincerity', Mrs
Coke demonstrated a wholesome and unselfish womanly desire to help those 'struggling to work out their own artistic salvation'. As a consequence, her counsel had
'penetrated into places' that Wilde could never have reached.[117] According to the
Globe, she had won for herself the confidence of 'half the matrons in the
kingdom'.[118] 'Perhaps no living woman,' observed *Winter's Weekly*, 'has so

89 Mrs Talbot Coke's
determinedly asym-
metrical arrangement
of a mantelpiece in
Queen, 1887.

completely set her seal upon the taste of to-day as Mrs Talbot Coke.'[119] Her influence, measured in terms of contemporary sales, probably far exceeded that of
William Morris, whose 'severe' style she firmly rejected.[120]

For their efforts, 'lady art advisors' like Coke were roundly mocked by male taste-
makers such as the designer Lewis Day.[121] They displayed, charged Day, 'mingled
pretentiousness and triviality'.[122] Their practical advice amounted to nothing more
than jargon, and was so indistinct as to be useless: 'Every room must be strewn
about with pots, "Benares", "repoussé", or whatever may be the newest thing . . . .'
Their columns bore the tarnish of the shops. 'The advice is always buy, buy, buy!'[123]
Day's criticism marked one more episode in the long battle between female
amateurs and male professionals fought over the course of the nineteenth century.
But unlike the case of midwives displaced by doctors, this time the men were on the
losing side. Decorators on paper had joined the power of the exploding periodical
press to that of the retail revolution and new rights for women.[124] The monopoly
that men like Day had hoped to exercise over design principles was slipping away,
and the middle-class consumer would not be his to control. To those who meant to
'take art seriously', Day warned, the lady art advisor represented a menace. Mrs
Talbot Coke did not let the charge pass unrebutted. Given Day's unyielding adherence to the dogmas of design reform, retorted Coke, it was no wonder that the
rigidly righteous – or as she called them, the 'unco guid' – found her individualistic
message a threat.[125]

THE NEW WOMAN AT HOME

In 1892, Mrs Talbot Coke pasted into her scrapbook a letter of which she was espe-cially proud. A month earlier, she had sent a copy of her new book, *The Gentlewoman at Home*, to the sixty-seven-year-old Reverend Andrew Boyd, whose treatises she had long admired. Charlotte Coke did not know Boyd personally, but his incarnationalist sermons seem to have struck a chord with her.[126] To the unex-pected gift of a decorating manual for gentlewomen, Boyd responded with courtly grace. He had not yet had a chance to finish Mrs Coke's book, but a quick browse through its pages enticed him. *The Gentlewoman at Home*, he wrote, 'is the kind of book I delight in . . . . I remember what my countryman Archbishop Tait used to say, that "it is debasing, & even demoralizing, to live among ugly 'things'". You and I agree with him.'

In presuming that Mrs Coke wished to demonstrate the moral virtues of decora-tion, Boyd demonstrated his attachment to a mid-Victorian idea that the lady art advisors had long since passed by. The religious and ethical concerns that Boyd fore-grounded in his published sermons were entirely absent from *The Gentlewoman at Home*.[127] What 'moral support' Mrs Coke offered her readers came in the form of enthusiasm for 'bold' colours and patterns; she aimed to buck up those ladies whose individualistic convictions might flag in the face of opposition.[128] She viewed herself as a preacher in the cause of individuality, who defied 'the most determined sleeper to even desire to close an eye when she mounts the pulpit steps'.[129] Decorators such as Lewis Day, Mrs Coke believed, were like clergyman who made 'reforming oneself appear an utterly hopeless task'. She, by contrast, thought that everyone could be saved, decoratively speaking, simply by expressing their own tastes.[130]

From Frances Power Cobbe to Mrs Talbot Coke, women had evolved from the guardians of morality to the innovative and industrious creators of the House Beautiful. Domesticity had gained a new meaning. As the old-style nineteenth-century angel in the house, woman had neither the right nor the means to deter-mine its contents. For the 'New Woman', by contrast, domesticity meant creativity rather than self-sacrifice, and reflected the strengthened position that came from new opportunities in higher education, the professions, and, eventually, the vote.[131] Where women were once content with 'puerile pursuits' such as cross-stitch, reported Mrs Talbot Coke, 'the active minds, clever fingers, and bolder grasp of to-day seek a wider scope wherein to find full expression'.[132] Women's artistic training in the home had, according to one paper, emboldened them: 'Women . . . know that they have gained independence by an almost unconscious education in art, and in their way are no more cowardly regarding criticism than Raphael was when he designed the hangings of the Vatican.'[133] In 1911, amid the militant campaign of picture-slashing and window-breaking led by Emmeline Pankhurst, the suffragette

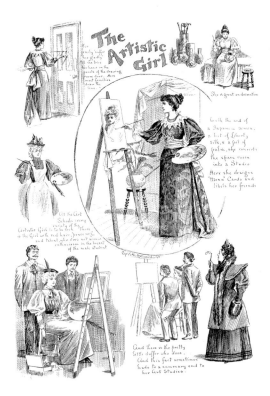

90 As depicted in a *Hearth and Home* cartoon of 1895, the 'artistic girl' trod the path from painting the drawing-room door panels to decorating pots and furniture to art school.

journal, *Votes for Women*, reported on a trade exhibition of modern furnishing: 'No one is more keen about the home than the Suffragette.'[134]

With their prospects in the wider world of professions and property finally improved, middle-class women took charge of the home. The vast majority of those who wrote to the decorators on paper were women, though there were a few men, like 'Little Paddy' or 'Medicus' who wanted rooms fit for their sex (Day, for his part, believed these male correspondents to be fabrications). Men's preferences, when they were aired, came chiefly in their wives' letters.[135] In the late 1890s, the poet Rosamund Marriott Watson, no fan of the amateur decorator and her paintbrush and stencils, observed with disapproval that 'there is no escaping the evidences of increased feminine activity'.[136] John Benn's magazine, *The House*, launched in 1897, was aimed at women, though it sought, too, a readership in the 'cultured "master", who, be he married or single, believes with Sir Edward Coke that a "man's house is his castle", and is constantly studying to make it a palace of delight'.[137] By contrast, the raft of home decoration periodicals that made their début after the First World War, among them *Ideal Home* and *House and Garden*, largely dispensed with the appeal to men.

The middle-class interior has often been depicted as an upholstered cage, in which women frittered away their creativity and ambition on Berlin-work or furbe-lows.[138] But neither restraint nor its opposite pole, liberation, is a sufficiently subtle concept to capture accurately women's stake in interior decoration. The women who wrote to the decorators on paper talked most often about the *pleasure* their rooms gave them.[139] Thanking Mrs Talbot Coke for her advice, 'Giroux' exulted that her renovated drawing-room 'has been "a daily joy ever since"!'[140] Forced by unspecified 'circumstances' to move from a grand house into smaller quarters, another woman wrote: 'I am happy in this little nest, made beautiful by your advice, happier than two years ago I ever believed possible for me to be again.'[141] The delight these women took in the material world marks their distance from the evangelical ideal of the home as a moral training-ground. Mrs Coke, though stringently observant of propriety, encouraged in her correspondents the sentiment that 'money spent on one's home is a daily, hourly pleasure'; her own 'hereditary instincts' verged, she confessed, 'towards extravagance'.[142] A trip to Maple's, advised Mrs Conyers Morrell of the *Lady's Pictorial*, might turn up 'some specially covetable article, the annexation of which, if possible, would be a life-long joy'.[143] What melancholy her readers felt, Mrs Talbot Coke proposed might be remedied, by a new colour or a new wallpaper: 'I don't think it is the red paint in the hall, but the dismal red-and-green paper which depresses you.'[144]

Like men, middle-class women wished their interiors to attest to their social position. Women's magazines were full of letters from readers who (because of their husbands' business failures or death) had suffered one of the reversals of fortunes common enough in the boom-and-bust late Victorian economy, yet wanted – at all costs – to keep up appearances.[145] The home, always a sensitive barometer of status, offered a last retreat for those who had fallen on hard times. Familiar was the story of a widow in straitened circumstances, forced to sell all of her furniture aside from a table in the window, upon which an aspidistra plant, visible through a small parting in the lace curtains, proved to passers-by that she had not lost her dignity.[146] Buoyed by the notion, common in the advice literature, that good taste costs no more than bad, decorators on paper gave comfort to their downwardly mobile readers. To 'Perdita', compelled to sell her silver, Mrs Talbot Coke offered encouragement: 'I know houses full of silver where nothing is a bit nice. Once you get over the idea that you must have things "just like everybody else", you will see what pretty things can be bought for very little.'[147]

As was true of men, women also wanted to demonstrate cultivation and distinction through their homes. Many a provincial lady aimed to be the first in her town to have an 'artistic' overmantel festooned with blue-and-white pottery. Married later in life, Jeanette Marshall set about making her Clapham home, The Limes, a showpiece of modern taste. She even contributed her own savings to pay for the furnishing of her new home. Her husband, Dr Edward Seaton, did not need his

91 The home as a setting for pleasure – A.I. Rossi's *The Love Letter*, c. 1900.

bride's money, but the determined Jeanette insisted, at least in part because some of her husband's furniture did not accord with her own advanced sensibility. Although Seaton had before their wedding in 1891 declared his conversion to the aesthetic interior, his duties as a medical officer in Surrey took him away from the home for much of the day. In pace with fashion, Jeanette's tastes had moved well beyond the aesthetic style. With her sister, she bought second-hand inlaid, Sheraton-style furniture for her apricot-and-ivory rooms, and carved walnut for her blue rooms. If Edward protested at all (which he probably did not), photographs of The Limes indicate who carried the day. It was, after all, in substantial measure her money.[148]

Women's sense of themselves seems from the 1890s onward to have been tied up increasingly in their décor. The Sisyphean task of furnishing and refurnishing might be understood within this context. Your parlour told you and others who you were: this was the prescription of the advice literature, but it also reflected lived experience. Where the male collector viewed his 'things' with objective disinterest, women's investment in their domestic possessions was personal. Despite advances in public life and improvements in their legal status, women's life possibilities were still constrained: in the absence of an office or an occupation, women's things constituted the tools of their trade, the ingredients of their personality. A woman's furnishings were, to quote the middle-class spinster Miss Florence Gardiner, 'dear . . . from association, or on account of the memories they recall'.[149] While a middle-class man might identify with his profession, women – in the words of the society dressmaker Lady Duff Gordon – became 'a part of their surroundings'.[150] A beautiful woman reclining on a sofa, wrote Mary Eliza Haweis, 'becomes for a time a part of the sofa, and the sofa part of her'.[151] Together, a woman's things made up a composite portrait of their owner. As an advertising brochure from the furniture store Shoolbred's read: ' "L'état c'est moi" exclaims a Mussolini or Lenin. "L'ameublement c'est moi", declares your up-to-date hostess.'[152]

Middle-class women in the early twentieth century were still a work in progress, forged (among other ingredients) from the raw materials of the home. The contrast with lower middle-class men is instructive. In Edwardian-era autobiographies and diaries, men of the lower middle classes depicted themselves in soul-searching transition – as immigrants to a new land of gentility, their selves under construction. They were acutely aware of, and indeed often embarrassed by, the homes in which they had grown up. Their accounts provide detailed descriptions of the dwellings and furnishings of their youth. But their own adult homes are left almost entirely undescribed. The central drama of lower middle-class men's lives consisted of their professional aspirations: their work told the world who they were.[153] For middle-class women, the home was the prize they had won and, for a time, they would define themselves by what they put in it.

92 Mrs Thomson in her flat at 2 Macclesfield Chambers, 1898. The fact that Bedford Lemere's interiors almost never included individuals suggests that Mrs Thomson may have insisted that she be photographed in her sitting room.

* * *

As befitted a man whose love life brought him many times over to the brink of ruin, H.G. Wells believed that men and women were incurable antagonists. Wells' novel, *Marriage*, published in 1912 as his second marriage faltered, is an exposition of that elementary premise. Trafford is a brilliant young chemist destined for a research career of great significance. Marjorie is a spirited young lady who, like so many of Wells' heroines, chafes at the restrictions in her parental home. The couple elopes. By the world's reckoning, Trafford has married up; his own family is not quite respectable, and Marjorie is an industrious and ambitious variant of the species

New Woman. But the flaws in the marriage become evident immediately. Obsessed with furnishing and decoration, Marjorie gives way 'to spending exactly as a struggling drunkard decides to tipple'.[154] Not content with the Bokhara hangings and brass-footed work-boxes purchased for her newly-wed dwelling, she fixates upon larger and more picturesque houses in more central locations. She decorates with abandon, acquiring *cloisonné* jars, lacquer cabinets, and post-Impressionist paintings – none of which her husband can afford. Unable to rein in his extravagant wife, Trafford is forced to abandon his research career and enter the synthetic rubber business.

Marriage, as Wells described the novel in his autobiography, is an archetypal tale: the story of how 'masculine intellectual interest met feminine spending and what ensued'.[155] Marjorie is not a sympathetic character, but neither is she a villain.[156] Her four children are not sufficient to keep her occupied or satisfied. The narrow confines of her life thwart her. 'You cannot consume your energies merely in not spending money.'[157] But neither is Marjorie corrigible. Trafford's misery in his business career prompts the couple to flee to Labrador to try to save the marriage. In that icy wilderness, Marjorie redeems herself after Trafford is attacked by a lynx, and they decide, full of resolve for a new future, to return to England. But even at the novel's climax, when her husband asks her to cease her 'Jackdaw buying' and become a 'non-shopping woman', Marjorie cannot stop imagining her life in terms of furnishing.[158] She translates all experiences into acquisitions. The life they would live upon their return was, for Marjorie, 'framed in a tall, fine room, a study, a study in sombre tones' with 'rich deep green curtains' and 'furnishings of old brass' and, to commemorate their year in the arctic Canadian north, 'a touch of the wilderness about it; a skin perhaps'.[159]

Consumption was, in Wells' depiction, a physical need for women, an ingrained biological imperative much like child-bearing: 'Men were released from that close, continuous touch with physical necessities long before women were.'[160] But, as we have seen, men's independence from the world of possessions was of rather more recent vintage than the author of *Marriage* allowed. His Edwardian presumptions – the product of a very specific set of historical developments – have shaped our own views, and coloured what we take for granted.[161] Too often have we read present-day arrangements back into the past world of consumption. Because we assume home decoration to be a preoccupation of women and gay men, so, too, must it always have been. For the Victorians, by contrast, acquisitiveness in the matter of furnishing was both a male and a female trait. Taste-makers like the Reverend Loftie took to task men such as his neighbour 'Brown', who had lovingly and expensively furnished his sitting-rooms with mid-Victorian Gothic monstrosities.

In the nineteenth century, women's sphere may have been the house, but the angel who resided there – without property rights and earning power – had little control over its disposition. Middle-class women could only fight, and win, the battle for the house when their standing in society at large had improved. The house proved an easier castle to besiege than would education and the professions. New conceptions of domesticity, married women's separate property, suburbanization, and the downfall of Oscar Wilde all combined to cause men gradually to abandon decoration as women claimed it as their right. For the pioneering first generation of lady art advisors, for women such as Mrs Haweis and Mrs Talbot Coke, the domestic interior offered a potent means of self-expression, even the key to individuality. But their gospel of the home had its limits. As the insatiable Marjorie would discover, the pleasures of furnishing all too often proved short-lived, even as the habit of thinking in terms of things endured.

CHAPTER 5

HOME AS A STAGE
PERSONALITY AND POSSESSIONS

Of all the journalistic innovations for which Edmund Yates could take credit over the course of a long and infamous career, the series of celebrity profiles he commissioned for *The World* were among the most successful. The scion of a renowned theatrical family, Yates was well acquainted with the perils of notoriety. As a young man, he had been responsible for introducing the gossip column into the pages of the respectable papers.[1] His scathing profile of Thackeray, published in *Town Talk*, propelled the upstart to the centre of a literary contretemps. Thackeray demanded Yates' expulsion from the Garrick Club, charging that the young journalist had violated the club's regulations by airing private conversations in public. After reviewing the evidence, the club agreed, and demanded an apology. When Yates refused, he was expelled.

In the years to come, Yates turned Thackeray's accusation into a livelihood – first in a series of gossip columns, then at the helm of the paper he founded in 1874, *The World: A Journal for Men and Women*. One of *The World*'s 'most attractive features', in Yates' description, was the series that began in the summer of 1876 entitled 'Celebrities at Home'.[2] For the price of 6d., the portals of Britain's great and good swung open for inspection by *The World*'s readers. Never before had the homes – and possessions – of public figures been exposed in print. So novel was the idea (and so notorious *The World*'s editor) that Yates had to establish a firm set of ground rules. To counteract fears that unscrupulous reporters might scour the house for skeletons in the cupboards, Yates assured his celebrities that only those who wished would be profiled at home; in addition, they had the right to inspect the article in proof before it went to press.

What had begun as a ploy to ensnare an audience for the new periodical exceeded all expectations. Gladstone, Disraeli, the Earl of Shaftesbury, Lord Randolph Churchill, and John Bright all consented to an interview, as, too, did the Post Office reformer Sir Rowland Hill, the fiery evangelist Charles Spurgeon, and Thomas Carlyle.[3] At his home in Portman Square, Wilkie Collins showed off a massive writing-table 'furnished with a small desk of the same design as that used by Charles

Dickens'.[4] Even the notoriously reclusive poet laureate Alfred Tennyson agreed to a profile at his Haslemere retreat, where *The World* discovered high-backed chairs 'typifying the poet's sterner moods', along with comfortable sofas 'that indicate a tendency to yield sometimes to the soft seductions of more effeminate inspirations'.[5] The at-home profile became *The World*'s trademark. It was eagerly copied by Yates' competitors. Such were the auspices under which the ladies' magazine, *Hearth and Home*, visited Mrs Haweis in 1892, as she meditated upon the 'effeminate and unnatural affections of so-called aesthetes' and the 'importance of freedom of opinion in art'.[6] By the end of the nineteenth century, 'at home' articles were a staple of the periodical press.[7]

93 Marie Corelli's writing desk – from an at-home profile published in the *Lady's Realm*, 1897/8.

The popularity of the 'at home' feature lay in the late Victorian public's increasingly avid appetite for celebrity gossip. But what made the 'at home' genre work was the conviction, much discussed from the 1890s onward, that the domestic interior expressed its inhabitant's inner self, especially in the case of women.[8] While Mrs Haweis' dress and conversation exposed something of her nature, entry into her home yielded a new kind of intimacy, bordering on voyeurism. The 'at home' profile offered a glimpse into her most private place, both deliberately constructed and unintentionally revealing. The perceptive visitor could play the detective, reading meanings into Disraeli's fondness for ormolu and gilt, or Wilkie Collins' Dickensian

94 Alfred Parsons,
*Darwin's Study at
Down House near
Beckenham, Kent,* 1881.

writing-desk.[9] Reared in the theatre, Yates intuitively understood the power of
setting to communicate a person's essence.[10] Facing imprisonment in 1885 on a
libel charge, he invited a party of reporters to escort him to Maple's to choose
furniture for his Holloway jail cell.

The idea that interiors reveal personalities is such a truism of contemporary
culture that it is difficult to imagine that it was not always so. But while the well-to-
do in previous eras lavished attention on their mansions and country houses, such
refurbishments more often attested to the dynastic ambitions of a family than the
inner self of a particular lord or lady.[11] And if a few individuals such as the architect
Sir John Soane had, in the Georgian period, aimed to transform their dwellings
into monuments to their unique sensibilities, their efforts lay far beyond the imagi-
nings or budgets of the vast majority, whose concern was comfort and propriety
rather than romantic creativity.[12] When Soane's neoclassical town house in
Lincoln's Inn Fields was opened to the public in 1837, the year Victoria acceded to
the throne, its benefactor's ostentation, rather than his originality, was all the talk.[13]
Not until the 1890s did Soane's mansion attract scores of admirers, who saw in his
innovative colour schemes and mirror-encrusted rooms not just the eccentricity
and profligacy condemned by earlier critics, but inspiration for their own decorative
arrangements.[14]

What had changed during the Victorian period was not just the purchasing power of middle-class Britons but understandings of the self. In the mid-nineteenth century, Victorians had most often conceived of the self in terms of character – a religiously inflected term that chiefly connoted a moral condition. A man's character might be built through painstaking instruction and introspection; however, the path to improvement was tortuous.[15] By the 1890s, there was a new, seemingly secular way of thinking about the self, expressed in the concept of personality.[16] If character was demonstrated by self-control and self-denial, a display of 'personality' required individuality. Personality was malleable, creative, and complex; it accompanied a new, psychological conception of the mind. A man's personality might be captivating, magnetic, domineering, delightful, or vigorous; the range of adjectives indicates the term's wide reach, and its capacity for making fine distinctions.[17] Unlike character, which was silent, personality was constantly on display. 'It would be difficult,' wrote the poet Rosamund Marriott Watson, 'to over-estimate the intimacy of the relations between ourselves and what, for want of a better word, may be called our setting. Like hermit crabs we gather round us a medley of objects, present and recollected, that become a part of our personality.'[18]

Artistic advisors such as Mrs Haweis, in emphasizing the joys of self-expression in the place of design reform's strictures, had anticipated the concept of personality. However, they could not have predicted the feverish quest for individuality, defined as the leitmotif of personality, which would ensue. The two decades from the 1890s to the First World War witnessed the apogee of the 'individual' decorative scheme. In increasingly heterogeneous middling strata, a personality – expressed in a distinctive interior – became a necessary asset. And yet the task of communicating one's individuality would prove a far more perilous undertaking than middle-class furnishers had envisioned. What if one inadvertently broadcast the wrong message? When furnishings made the person, every decision could become a cause for regret.

THE AGE OF INDIVIDUALITY

Mrs Thomas Keeling – the protagonist of E.F. Benson's novel, *An Autumn Sowing* (1917) – understood what it meant to make a decorative statement. Her husband, a successful department store entrepreneur, had turned over the decoration of their home to his wife, in concert with the head of the Keeling Store's furnishing department, the 'artistic' Mr Bowman.[19] Mr Bowman favoured Jacobean chairs and grandfather clocks, while Mrs Keeling's preferences ran to draped pictures on easels and plush-framed mirrors.[20] For Mr Bowman, his collaboration with Mrs Keeling yielded little but frustration. Into his Gothically inspired entrance hall, Mrs Keeling added a painted wheelbarrow complete with a gilt spade, stuffed full of shell-encrusted Polynesian leather aprons. To make the hall even more 'quaint', she introduced a small stuffed crocodile on its hind legs, proferring a copper tray for visitors' calling cards.[21]

95 An interior, graced
with a cosy corner, in
the old village of
Bournville, late nine-
teenth century.

96 A 'quaint' bamboo
plant stand with four
small hanging pots
with ferns.

E.F. Benson was famous for his social
satire, but in the matter of Mrs Keeling's
decorative scheme, no exaggeration was
necessary. Since the 1890s the excesses of
individuality to be found in British middle-
class dwellings had been a subject for admiration or despair, depending upon one's
perspective. Several decades before, the
artistic home, distinguished by 'its utter
disregard of uniformity', had initiated the age
of individuality.[22] But however outrageous
Mrs Haweis' vibrant hues and packing-case
furniture had appeared to contemporaries,
art at home marked merely a beginning. In
the new epoch, 'quaintness', defined as 'the
quality of being unusual', was the desired
effect. As one trade journal put it, quaintness
was 'a side-light from the lamp of beauty',
permitting 'us to express in a thousand

pleasant ways a constant playful violation of the monotony of classical taste'.[23] Whether expressed in a stuffed crocodile card-holder or a wall stacked high with antler horns, quaintness signified the ability of the individual to mould the material world according to her own fancy.

This new confidence that possessions could communicate their owner's individuality made for a giddy period of acquisitive experimentation. No scheme was off limits. The spinster in Sussex who wallpapered her bedroom with blackbordered In Memoriam cards or the hostess who placed her guests in 'spring', 'summer', 'autumn', and 'winter' rooms according to their age, belong to the human comedy of fashionably eccentric furnishing at the *fin de siècle*.[24] So, too, do the young couples who decorated their drawing-rooms according to the prevailing fashions of pan-Asianism, with occasional pillows of Indian embroidery to cushion the backs of visitors crouching in unfamiliar postures at inlaid Persian coffee-tables.[25] Or their parents, proud Conservatives, who communicated their political ardour with furniture from the Bath Cabinet Works' 'Primrose League' line, inlaid with the registered Tory primrose, made in satinwood, rosewood, and mahogany.[26] Why not a Tess of the d'Urbervilles room, wondered one Thomas Hardy enthusiast, envisioning a décor imbued with the 'spirit of the West Country and the gloom of the book'.[27]

97 A smoking room fitted out in the oriental style by Hampton & Sons, 1890s.

98 Mrs Wallace
Carpenter's Moorish
fantasy at 28 Ashley
Place, London, 1893 –
complete with women's
quarters above, where
ladies could look down
without being seen. The
firm H. & J. Cooper
designed the room.

Rooms took on fantastical qualities. The misanthropic poet John Payne, translator of the *Arabian Nights*, decorated his Kilburn drawing-room in the manner of a sultan's chamber, with lacquer furniture and dusky-coloured walls. A perfectly ordinary semi-detached suburban house, Payne's dwelling looked no different from those of his neighbours – until the lucky visitor ventured inside. 'I might have been in Persia or Arabia,' marvelled the biographer Thomas Wright. What had begun as a trip to the north London suburbs ended in exotic climes. Vases of beaten Egyptian copper framed the fireplace. Moorish lamps of pierced brass cast a gentle light. Above all else, however, eclecticism reigned; nestled cheek by jowl with genuine oriental splendours were the cheap Japanese paper fans that Payne favoured. In the middle of the drawing-room table stood a porcelain statue of a Chinese man, whose jointed head, tongue, and hands responded to the slightest vibration with alarming gestures. According to Wright, 'The room was indeed a picture of Payne's mind – Greatness, here and there invaded by littleness.'[28]

Mrs Keeling's fictional stuffed crocodile had many real-life analogues. Furniture made out of animals was, as one magazine reported in 1910, a 'veritable craze'. Pincushions, candlesticks, matchboxes, inkstands, and lamps had all been fabricated of hooves, to 'quaint, interesting, and decidedly attractive' effect.[29] Called upon to

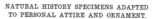

HOOF TROPHIES AND PRESERVATION OF HOOFS.

The hoofs of animals are particularly suitable for preservation as trophies, and for adaptation. An Illustrated Pamphlet, *Observations on the Preservation of Hoofs and the Designing of Hoof Trophies*, by ROWLAND WARD, F.Z.S., will be forwarded on receipt of two stamps.

HOOFS OF ANIMALS

Can be utilised in an endless variety of ways, and more than fifty different original designs for Hoof Trophies can be seen at 167 Piccadilly. Horseshoes kept in memory of favourite animals can be used with much effect in the same manner.

As a Letter-weighing Machine.
(Registered No. 24473.)

To hold a Match-Box.
(Registered No. 24421.)

Door Stop.

As a Table-Bell.
(Registered No. 24422.)

DECORATION OF SPECIAL ROOMS IN COUNTRY HOUSES.

Trophies of the Hunting Field, of Favourite Horses, of the Gun, the Fishing Rod, etc., can be characteristically grouped and arranged to decorate Libraries and Smoking Rooms, or Special Rooms devoted to Trophies of Sport, with much unconventional and naturalistic effect that is very attractive.

ROWLAND WARD, LIMITED, 167 PICCADILLY.

NATURAL HISTORY SPECIMENS ADAPTED TO PERSONAL ATTIRE AND ORNAMENT.

Bird and Insect Jewellery, Hats of Unique character, rare Furs, Muffs, Jackets, Rugs, Repairs, Redressing, Relining, Skin Dressing, Furriers' Work and Trade, Feather Work and Dressing.

BIRD STUFFING AND THE STUFFING OF SMALL ANIMALS

In the simplest and most inexpensive way are undertaken with the same rigid attention to the best artistic result as is bestowed on the most elaborated and costly designs and combinations of rare specimens.

HERONS BIRDS AS FIRE AND OTHER MOUNTED SCREENS.

PORTIONS AND NATURAL FEATURES OF BIRDS & ANIMALS

That are capable of being converted into most interesting and useful Trophies, Articles of Personal Adornment, Articles of Furniture, and objects of minor uses or Decorations, are often wasted in country houses, but should be preserved. For instance—Hoofs of Favourite Horses, Slots of Stags, exceptionally fine-plumaged Game, and other Birds, Small Animals, and Pet Animals of remarkable beauty or interest can be made, as the case may be, into unique specimens, and in common trade, of Ladies' Hats, Muffs, Collarettes, Trimming, etc.

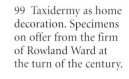

99 Taxidermy as home decoration. Specimens on offer from the firm of Rowland Ward at the turn of the century.

100 W.D. James' hall at West Dean Park, Singleton, Chichester, Sussex. Bedford Lemere photographed James' house in 1895, nine years before the architect Edwin Lutyens removed the white bear.

rearrange the hall of one *arriviste* client, the architect Edwin Lutyens removed an enormous palm tree, two screens, a large white stuffed bear, and an old sedan chair. Even then, he acknowledged in a letter to his wife, there 'was enormously too much in the room'.[30] For her part, Mrs Talbot Coke recommended armaments for the hallway. Among those 'quaint savage weapons of warfare' from which her readers might choose were 'curved Afghan guns, Eastern scimitars, graceful spears, and quaintly moulded rhinoceros hide shields from the Soudan'; best of all were munitions 'sent from stirring scenes of strife', which could be 'carelessly grouped' with carved oak panels, one or two dark old oil paintings, and hanging brass lamps.[31] For the possessor of the moderately sized vestibule who wanted to avoid animal carcasses, spears, and shields, 'the very thing', *circa* 1900, was a 'life-size negro, dressed in the latest fashion, and sprawling in a cane chair'.[32]

Among the most potent means of injecting individuality into a room was colour. Where design reformers had focused on right-minded form as the key to good taste, the prophets of individuality embraced colour as the building-block of distinctiveness. The development of aniline dyes in the 1850s had inaugurated entire new palettes, while the exploitation of colonial labour put even formerly expensive

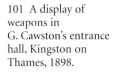

101 A display of weapons in G. Cawston's entrance hall, Kingston on Thames, 1898.

102 A colour palette, pre-1914.

natural dyes within reach.[33] Colour permitted infinite variability, since each person could deploy it in different ways. Pale lettuce greens could be juxtaposed with saffron yellows, or harmonized with darker, forest-tinted tones. Her own inspiration, Mrs Talbot Coke frankly confessed, came from the years she spent in Cairo, where none of the rules that restricted the English imagination obtained.[34]

The ideal was not simply the original, but the unique. Interviewed by the *Daily News* in 1914, Miss Winfield, a lady decorator with premises on Wells Street, noted that her clients were 'more anxious than ever to have schemes that no one else has.'[35] This desire for the unique was not confined to those who could afford the services of decorators. Ladies' periodicals made reference to their readers' demands for designs they would not see elsewhere – an ambition with which Mrs Coke heartily sympathized: 'Yes, I can well imagine in a "local centre" the joy of having something in the way of decoration, which no one else has.'[36] Only furniture 'designed in a manner "out of the ordinary"', retailers noted, could expect a favourable reception among middle-class buyers.[37] For those who could not afford to buy new items, there was always the panacea of recycling or a fresh coat of paint. 'Marion', decorating columnist for the down-market *Lady's Companion*, reported that a friend of hers rearranged her drawing-room every other week before receiving visitors.[38] In the disapproving appraisal of the eminent Victorian Frederick Locker-Lampson, 'Now people ruin themselves to be fantastical.'[39]

Commentators such as Locker-Lampson, who remembered fondly the old ways, objected to the blurring of social distinctions that the end of the century seemed to

103 The sitting room at 5 Crofts Bank Road, Urmston in 1914. This was the home of Henry Cuthbert, a butcher and amateur photographer. He and his family lived above the shop premises.

104 Replete with individual touches – the drawing room of the large flat, Warner Estate, Markhouse Road, Walthamstow, c. 1902.

have brought. Money 'talked', as the contemporary saying had it, with an ever louder voice.[40] The exploits of the Edwardian *nouveau riche* made headlines, but just as significant was the apparent narrowing of the divide between the upper reaches of the middle class and its lower echelons.[41] Crucial to this 'levelling' were material possessions. Suburbia was, in the journalist Philip Gibbs' disparaging phrase, 'a great straggling territory' inhabited by people who – whether stockbrokers or city clerks – were 'all struggling for social advancement'.[42] Gibbs, the son of a civil servant and a self-described member of the 'shabby genteel' Victorian middle class, took a dim view of the changing social order.[43] Buoyed by 'a wave of material prosperity', lower middle-class Britons had 'adopted the manners and customs of that class which used to be called "the Upper Ten"'. Even the inhabitants of £35 houses could equip themselves with the 'little luxuries and little refinements of modern civilisation'.

Much of what Philip Gibbs derided in the spending habits of suburbia echoed the charges that the American economist Thorstein Veblen had aimed at his countrymen fifteen years earlier. In his *Theory of the Leisure Class* (1899), Veblen argued that consumption lay at the heart of social stratification. Insecure in their newfound wealth, America's Gilded Age élite spent money in order to consolidate their status. Their 'conspicuous consumption', as Veblen termed it, set the standards for the entire society, as wasteful goods (such as sterling silver table services in the place of utilitarian pot metals) came to represent reputability. People who wanted to rise in the estimation of their fellow citizens had to follow the lead of the leisure class. 'The motive that lies at the root of ownership is emulation.'[44] The middle classes accumulated possessions as a means of aping their social betters.

However well Veblen's theory of consumption described the United States (a proposition hotly disputed by scholars ever since), it cannot be shipped across the Atlantic without substantial modification.[45] Social climbing undoubtedly played some part in the late Victorian and Edwardian furnishing frenzy; the fact that Lady So-and-So had ordered a particular carpet was certain, retailers reported, to ensnare some middle-class buyers.[46] But emulation was only one piece of the puzzle. The British middle classes had formed their identity as much in opposition to the aristocracy as in imitation of it.[47] In selecting their furnishings, Britons in the 1860s and 1870s were concerned above all to promote the moral integrity of the household and to make the right impression; copying the élite sent the wrong signals.[48] Later in the century, as furnishing became equated with art, middle-class buyers sought to express their creativity through their things, prizing possessions for their beauty or quaintness – qualities that have no place in Veblen's schema. Consumption was not always simply a matter for show; as the attention paid to bedrooms indicates, furnishing could be private and 'inconspicuous'.[49] Moreover, emulation was not a one-way street.[50] Britain's reigning family had notoriously bourgeois tastes. After her marriage, the future Queen Mary was horrified to find that her husband had decorated their palaces from Maple's, the epitome of the middle-class marketplace.[51]

What was entirely missing from Gibbs' and Veblen's social diagnosis was any mention of individuality – an omission especially striking given the term's omnipresence in other arenas. Where they detected conformism, their contemporaries claimed individuality as the hallmark of the age. Neither Gibbs nor Veblen would likely have set much store by the idea of 'uniqueness' or 'creativity', especially when applied to stuffed crocodile card-holders; in their accounts, terms such as 'beauty' concealed myriad instances of emulation. Their perspective lay firmly in the aggregate, not in the mind of the individual shopper. And yet, to accept their analysis would be to ignore the framework within which the owners of the Primrose League suite or the inhabitants of the pan-Asian room conceived of their activities. The rage for individuality needs explaining.

When Mrs Haweis urged her readers in the early 1880s to cultivate individuality, she saw the distinctive interior as a solution to the problem of mass society. She, like the other late nineteenth-century promoters of self-expression, understood that amid a rapidly growing middle class, cultural attributes such as taste, no less than occupation, religious sect or political affiliation, would serve as a means of claiming status. The explosion of the service sector from the 1890s, together with the coming of a second 'industrial revolution', heralded by new technologies and careers, turned Mrs Haweis' prediction into reality.[52] By the First World War, more than 25 per cent of Britain's population counted as middle class. This was, however, a heterogeneous group, defying easy categorization, ranging from industrialists and bankers as rich as the aristocracy to professional people such as physicians and solicitors, to the burgeoning numbers of shopkeepers, clerks, stenographers, and commercial travellers. Appearances, everyone agreed, counted for more than ever before; one needed, above all, to make an impression. Those who wished to be noticed, as the historian Guy Chapman observed, had to take a page from the adman: 'One must, in short, advertise oneself by a better house, by more generous entertainment, by new and richer clothes . . . .'[53] How a person spent his money was as important (if not more so) than how he had earned it.

If Mrs Haweis had posited individuality as an ideal, by the Edwardian period it had become a necessity. Individuality, rather than the exception, was the norm among middle-class Britons; stores and advice manuals raised the distinctive and unique over the merely correct.[54] However paradoxical the idea may at first appear, individuality had become an essential feature of bourgeois life, something that anyone who wanted to count themselves as middle class – from the lowliest shopkeeper to the grandest manufacturer – had to have. Where the poor were still conceived of in the aggregate, the middle class took pains to underscore their own singularity. The interest in a unique, rather than just an artistic, decorative scheme needs to be understood in this context. This was especially, but not exclusively, the case for the upper middle class, who felt their social inferiors nipping at their heels. However, even lower middle-class Britons strove for originality.[55] A room in the oriental style, capable of communicating an exotic side-light, could be created for less than £50, advised the *Lady's Companion* in 1897.[56] The residents of suburban terraces endowed their front windows with the emblems of individuality; the writer W. Pett Ridge catalogued the sights to be seen on one modest crescent: 'Bamboo stands with ferns in giant egg-shells. Webster's dictionary. A stuffed cockatoo. St. Paul's Cathedral in white wax. Bust of the late Mr Spurgeon. Portrait of Her Majesty. The Three Graces under glass shade.'[57]

105 A down-market take on the oriental style – *Lady's Companion*, 1897.

Long the cradle of the family, the home became something more in the Edwardian period: the domestic interior literally helped to create the individual. C.S. Lewis was one of many who credited his boyhood home, considered apart from his family, as 'almost a major character in my story', viewing himself as 'a product' of its corridors and rooms, attics and noises.[58] For E.M. Forster, by contrast, it was the lack of a home that had proven the crucial source of his personality. When Forster was fourteen, he and his mother had been forced to leave Rooksnest, their beloved Hertfordshire home.[59] Later in life, Forster saw this moment as a turning point. Had he remained in the house, the novelist later recalled, 'I should have become a different person, married, and fought in the war'.[60] To explain why the home became the crucible for the self, we must turn to the relationship between the domestic interior and the concept of human interiority. The home was the staging-ground for the new idea of personality.

INTERIORS AND INTERIORITY

In January 1882 a man who would become synonymous with the very definition of 'a personality', first stepped on to a New York stage. The 'Apostle of Aestheticism', as the American press dubbed Oscar Wilde, had sailed across the Atlantic to lecture the New World on 'The English Renaissance in Art'.[61] Although warmly received by his New York listeners, very little of what Wilde had to say was genuinely original. He trumpeted the genius of the Pre-Raphaelite Brotherhood, extolled the contributions of happy artisans, and exhorted Americans to love art for its own sake – all ideas with which an educated British audience would, by the early 1880s, have been very familiar. Only on one point, which the young Irishman chose to cite in the original French, did Wilde venture beyond the truisms of the Grosvenor Gallery. '"La personnalité . . . voilà ce qui nous sauvera."'[62]

In 1882, the term 'personality', as a description of the self, was still exotic territory in Britain. Personality had an archaic meaning, referring to the characteristics that distinguished a person from a thing.[63] Some people used it interchangeably with personage, especially when referring to great men. However, personality in its modern sense, meaning 'the quality or assemblage of qualities which makes a person what he is, as distinct from other persons', remained a rarity. The term had first been used in this fashion in 1795. But for much of the nineteenth century, personality scarcely made any inroads into British conversations – especially when compared with the omnipresence of the word 'character'. Wilde himself did not use the word 'personality' in his lecture on house decoration, the successor to his English Renaissance speech.

By the turn of the twentieth century, however, what was once a Frenchified curiosity had become mainstream. Not only was personality a founding concept for the new discipline of psychology, but theologians, resuscitating older conceptions of divine personality embodied in the Trinity, deployed the term in sermons and religious tracts as well.[64] Even as medical doctors searched for the biological roots of personality in the workings of the endocrine gland, expensive dressmakers became noted for their success in 'making personalities' through individualistic confections.[65] While metaphysical philosophers pondered the meaning of the self in turgid prose, the gains to be derived from a 'sparkling' or 'powerful' personality were proclaimed in advice manuals. Many Edwardian mothers would probably have agreed with the goal that the novelist Marie Connor Leighton set for her children: 'I want you to grow up to have personality.'[66] One of the most significant changes that had taken place in her lifetime, reflected the journalist Mrs C.S. Peel in 1933, was the 'decline of the aristocracy of birth and of wealth, and the rise of the aristocracy of brains and personality'.[67]

But if the term 'personality' abounded in ladies' magazines and self-help guides, in psychology textbooks and at the pulpit, there was much less agreement about what precisely it entailed. 'Personality is one of those terms,' acknowledged the *Times Literary Supplement*'s reviewer, 'which are both indispensable and indefinable.'[68] Even the basic lineaments of the concept provoked debate. Was personality the outer manifestation of a person's inner self, a souped-up variant of character that took account of physiology as well as fortune? Or did the very mutability of personality attest to the absence of a durable, essential self at the core of each individual?[69] Put differently, could a man change his personality as easily as his topcoat?

The notion of an ever-changing self dependent upon dressmakers and advice manuals troubled church luminaries. It implied both a selfishness and an atomism incompatible with Christianity. In response, religious authorities asserted the 'synthetic unity' of the self in God, extolling Christ as the model of an ideal personality.[70] But despite a flood of treatises with titles such as *Atonement and Personality* and *Personality Human and Divine*, the definition of personality, as it circulated through the popular press, remained – at base – secular, even amoral. When Mrs Talbot Coke offered to help her correspondents learn how to 'shed one's own personality on any and every home', she could not have been confused with a philanthropic Lady Bountiful.[71] Goodness took a back seat to individuality. While God and morality might form a part of the self, they by no means held a monopoly on the constitution of personalities.

If God had been demoted, material belongings had been elevated. One's things did not merely express one's status, or inner longings, or fancies. Nor was it simply, as design reformers had suggested, that specific objects could affect a house's inhabitants for good or for ill. Rather, self and material belongings had become even more closely intertwined. As the American psychologist William James observed in 1890, 'between what a man calls *me* and what he simply calls *mine* the line is difficult to draw'.[72] Possessions were the very stuff out of which the self was made. Perfect congruence was, or so advertisers suggested, a possibility. Most admirable of all were those inhabitants of a graceful dwelling who could say: 'If you know our house, you know us, our house *is* us.'[73]

In defining personality, the home enjoyed pride of place among other possessions.[74] Where clothing was ephemeral, the home's influence was indelible and pervasive. The house, wrote Mrs Talbot Coke, 'is one's mind, the home of one's soul: one's ego'.[75] For the first generations of women endowed with a modicum of control over marital property, the home proved a potent symbol of independence, a place where creativity could flourish. In her 1911 treatise, *The Ideal Home and Its Problems*, the journalist Mrs Eustace Miles took issue both with the dictionary definition of 'home' and with Ruskin's famous paean to the 'place of Peace': 'Home is neither simply a locality nor simply a place of restfulness. Home is the expression of individuality also.'[76] Bolstered by advice-givers and retailers, women conceived of the domestic interior as a training-ground for personality – their own of course, but even more importantly, that of their children. As childhood was reimagined in psychological (though not yet, in Britain, in Freudian) terms, the furnishing of nurseries drew new attention.[77] Where Victorian parents had once thought cast-offs from the rest of the dwelling good enough for children's rooms, Edwardians purchased special lines of purpose-built furniture.[78] The ideal nursery was designed to foster originality and independence of mind through its material objects; for little girls, the ubiquitous dolls' house provided an apprenticeship to the psychic realm of womanhood.[79] The sensory impressions gleaned even in early childhood served to shape individual consciousness.

Those who were children in the late Victorian and Edwardian periods bore witness to the new significance accorded the home. Their houses were of consummate importance, more significant in some cases even than the people who inhabited them. They penned autobiographies rich in material details of interiors, beside which the recollections of the previous generations appear arid.[80] Some, like Dorothy Pym, the author of *Houses as Friends*, structured their memoirs around the homes they occupied, lavishing pages of description upon the tints, furnishings, and atmosphere of rooms, even as they neglected the most basic biographical details of their lives.[81] Others deployed the language of the unconscious, marvelling at the hold that the dwellings of their youth exercised over their adult imaginations.[82] Though he never again visited the house where he had lived for three years as a small child, the writer Herbert Palmer returned to it over and over in his thoughts: 'it is strange how that house is fixed in my mind and how often I think about it and wish I were back in it'.[83] 'The influence of houses on their inhabitants,' wrote Lytton Strachey, 'might well be the subject of a scientific investigation.'[84]

When the writer Violet Trefusis claimed that 'places have played at least as important a part in my life as people', she was expressing an Edwardian commonplace.[85] And yet, as Trefusis – a lifelong creator of fantastical interiors – was only too well aware, the separation between people and places implied in her observation was hazy at best.[86] Places were very much the embodiment of their inhabitants. 'Everything in a human dwelling is bathed in personality,' observed Mrs Eustace Miles, 'everything has a voice that speaks of the character and individuality of the person to whom the room belongs.'[87] The relation between the individual and her possessions was, as William James and the lady art advisors knew, fundamentally reciprocal. Writing in 1898, the columnist 'Penelope' commented upon the change from early in the century: 'Rooms, and their furniture, now express convictions and opinions, and well might one alter the old aphorism into: "Show me your room and

106 The ideal nursery, decorated
to spark a child's imagination. From
Matilda Lees Dods,
The Ideal Home, 1914.

I will tell you what you are." '[88] Whether you liked it or not, your possessions offered a peek into your soul.[89]

Since rooms could be read like faces, it was all the more important that their owners communicate the message intended.[90] On this score, retailers and the lady art advisors broadcast a cheerful message. Taste was not innate, as eighteenth-century sages had believed, nor rule-bound, as design reformers had preached. Every woman could achieve a distinctive effect if only she put her mind to it. The drab needed not resign themselves to a life of dreariness; they had only to convince themselves that they deserved better. Rather than bemoaning their lot, those down on their luck could view hardship as a test of their ingenuity. A tasteful room, 'full of the strange indefinable charm of being just like the woman who owns it', did not require lots of money.[91] Properly understood, taste could even trump class. Though money might 'make the man', it did not make the room: 'priceless consolation to those with taste and but little of this world's goods!'[92]

The rewards ascribed to redecoration were considerable. Not only the approbation of one's fellow citizens, but self-fulfilment lay in store. Rooms promised to boost a flagging personality. Mrs Eustace Miles advised the lady of the house to provide herself with different-coloured rooms to suit her varying moods; in this way, she could prepare herself 'against every mental emergency'.[93] The bedroom, like the nursery, acquired new prominence. If life was a performance, the bedroom was the backstage, where the self could be coaxed into putting on a good show.[94] 'It is here we are alone with ourselves and our undisguised tempers, and we are far more likely to be upset in this frame of mind by shortcomings on the part of our surroundings, or soothed into amiability by their general harmony.'[95] Happiness was a matter of living amid harmonious surroundings. Originality was recast as a matter of will.

But for all of their breezy optimism about the infinite corrigibility of rooms and personalities, the lady art advisors could not deny the frustration, even despair, which accompanied most of their correspondents' decorative endeavours. Mrs Talbot Coke acknowledged that nearly two-thirds of the letters she received contained 'expressions of dislike for the writers' possessions', a report that her competitors at *The Lady* and the *Lady's Pictorial* confirmed.[96] No sooner had a woman furnished than doubts began to creep in. 'Lorena' found her dining-room 'unendurable'; another correspondent 'detested everything in the drawing-room' – complaints whose vehemence indicates the painful disenchantment that succeeded shopping trips.[97]

Rooms, bound up as they were with the self, created desires that could not, by their very definition, be completely satisfied. Women's oft-expressed regret about their possessions stemmed, at least in part, from the impossibility of permanently incarnating oneself in one's things.[98] This discontent affected women most because they were, after the turn of the century, the prime household consumers but also

107 The ideal bedroom. Displayed at Heal & Son's Tottenham Court Road premises, this specimen room showcased an especially theatrical flourish: a curtained-off bed alcove.

because they had, on the whole, fewer means of self-expression than did men. In this context, 'dull', 'cold', 'uninteresting', and 'vulgar' – all adjectives that women despairingly applied to their homes when they wrote to decorators on paper – became personal indictments. The worst thing that a husband could tell his young wife about her furnishing, or so the novelist Horace Annesley Vachell warned, was: 'You know, angel face, your drawing-room is not the least like *you*.'[99]

The overcrowded room may, in part, have reflected these disappointments.[100] Only the truly wealthy could afford to harmonize their interiors with a restless personality. For everyone else, purchases proved rather more durable than the frame of mind that had spawned them. New objects were wedged in to improve an effect found unsatisfactory. An unfortunate wallpaper pattern could be covered with lithographs and paintings; tapestries and antimacassars helped to camouflage out-of-date furniture. Too many such improvements, however, and the hapless furnisher, rather than stamping her imprimatur on the room, lost control of its constituent elements. The women who wrote in to the lady art advisors complained of 'warring' pieces of furniture. They had not mastered their interiors after all; instead, their belongings had gained the upper hand. 'The pursuit of the elaborate and the rococo,' the architect John Elder-Duncan warned his readers, 'ends in our goods possessing us, not in our owning our possessions.'[101]

Individuality proved elusive for many. No matter how many mirrored overman-
tels or stuffed birds they imported into their rooms, their houses still looked
'common'. Some of those who set out to be distinctive found, to their dismay, that
others were expressing their individuality in much the same way. Mrs C.S. Peel
noted the obvious similarities between the house of her godmother – 'a fashionable
ladyship' – and that of a town councillor's wife in Dewbury: both had indulged a
taste for hand-painted pots and clutter.[102] In seeking to demonstrate personality,
they had achieved a surprising degree of uniformity. This could happen to the
genuinely eccentric as well as to the mildly adventurous. Imagine the chagrin that
the orientalist scholar John Payne must have felt when he discovered that the more
daring of his Kilburn neighbours had adopted the *Lady's Companion*'s oriental
scheme. There had always been an irony at the heart of the lady art advisors' fervent
endorsements of originality.[103] To what degree was a scheme truly individual when
it had been prescribed in the back columns of a magazine? A few of their correspondents, at least, were well aware of the problem. To preserve the fiction that they
had dreamt up original designs on their own, they asked the decorators on paper
not to divulge their town or personal details, lest their friends learn the source of
their 'inspiration'.[104]

Individuality was more easily preached than practised. In explaining where their
disappointed readers had gone wrong, the lady art advisors diagnosed over-hasty
purchases and failures of 'intuition'.[105] They did not broach the larger frustrations
that propelled their audience; they did not note that enshrining selves in objects had
proved a tricky proposition. More critical observers, such as the journalist Philip
Gibbs or the Christian Socialist historian R.H. Tawney, suggested that the problem
lay at the empty heart of consumer society itself.[106] 'The overthrow of the old
Puritanism of England and the adoption of a pagan creed of pleasure,' wrote Gibbs,
'has been the change from one tyranny to another.'[107] While the English might
attempt to enjoy themselves, they were haunted by scruples that the 'Latin races' did
not possess: 'The New Nation is always having twinges of conscience, and is always
searching its soul, like a woman who has lost her religion but cannot escape from
spiritual questionings.'[108] Gibbs denounced the futile 'feverish quest of pleasure' –
unanchored by discipline or duty – prophesying 'some great national disaster which
will shock us to the very foundations of our social system'.[109]

Gibbs' book was published in 1913. To anyone who picked up Gibbs' diatribe in
the following decade, his invective against the 'tyranny' of pleasure must have
seemed as remote as the last Edwardian summer. There was so much more to worry
about than the shortcomings of one's furniture. The war would mark a change in
the ways in which Britons thought about their interiors, though the conflict itself
was only one among a number of factors. Even in the heyday of the unique decorative scheme, there had been a tension between individual whimsy and the idea of

good taste. However, in the inter-war period, middle-class Britons increasingly opted for safety in the place of originality. Many of us still believe, of course, that our rooms represent our personalities, but we endow our possessions with fewer expectations than did the Edwardians. In the end, good taste (which the poet John Betjeman in 1933 labelled 'ghastly good taste') won out over individual taste.

* * *

Even before the First World War forced a change in the ways in which Britons thought about their domestic interiors, there were those who protested against the ascendancy of individuality. Born into a family of warriors, Mrs Talbot Coke's youngest son, Desmond, was more inclined to the pen than to the sword.[110] Aside from an obligatory stint on the Western Front, which ruined his health, Desmond Coke did not choose – unlike his father, his eldest brother, and his four sisters' husbands – to fight Afghan tribesmen at the Khyber Pass or to defend Britain's interests in South Africa. Before the war, Coke lived in a Bayswater attic, where he wrote novels about young men estranged from their fathers, and collected eighteenth-century silhouettes; afterwards, he served as a house-master at

108 The antique collector Desmond Coke.

Clayesmore School.[111] At the end of his *Confessions of an Incurable Collector*, Coke penned his own obituary: 'If it could be remembered of me, at my death, that I loved beauty and tried modestly to save it from oblivion . . . I shall not feel, remote and leisure-demanding idiot, as I am, that I have failed totally in the career I set myself, not narrowly, of Art.'[112]

Though Coke and his mother had both devoted themselves to Art, they meant very different things by the term. For Mrs Talbot Coke, art was the visual embodiment of individuality; it could be expressed in the draping of a mantelpiece or the arrangement of a difficult room. She was a woman perfectly in tune with her time, an entrepreneur who turned her flair for decoration into a household name. For her son, by contrast, art required beauty; it was endangered, not omnipresent, a scarce commodity that necessitated expertise and an 'eye' for genuine articles. Desmond Coke was out of step with the age that his mother had helped to create.[113] There were, as he saw it, 'two modern maladies': 'We look inside ourselves too much: we give out far too many words for what we say.'[114] Only by means of 'solitary collecting' could one break free from the self-conscious nature of modern life.

In the years before the First World War, it was Mrs Coke's vision of art and personality that predominated. Individuality was intimately bound up with possessions, foremost among them, the home and its furnishings. In 1902, *Tatler* summed up the obvious: 'We all want to be original and have something distinctive and characteristic about our belongings.'[115] However, Desmond Coke was not alone in his criticism: not everyone accepted the idea that the purpose of possessions was to communicate their owner's personalities. Some of those who objected most vociferously were – like Desmond Coke – antique collectors. They rejected the reign of individuality, and paid little heed to conventional notions of good taste. Antique collectors were the most passionate about their belongings, for they believed that things spoke for themselves.

CHAPTER 6

DESIGNS ON THE PAST
ANTIQUES AS A FAITH

At the close of the year 1898, the Cardiff pharmacist Robert Drane took himself severely to task. Drane was the proprietor of the Queen Street apothecary, a mahogany-panelled shop on one of the busy thoroughfares that conveyed Cardiff's booming population into the centre of the city. It was a profitable enterprise. But if the treatment of skin ailments and syphilis was his bread and butter, Drane's overriding passion was for the finer things of life. In the auction rooms of Cardiff and Bristol, Drane, who never married, was most at home. An authority on old Worcesterware, he amassed a collection of porcelain, silver, glassware, books, and religious objects. When it came time to add up his purchases for 1898, Drane documented nearly £600 in expenditure, a substantial sum even for a bachelor without a family to feed. With remorse, he noted in his diary that his New Year's resolution – 'not to spend so much money on such things' – had crumbled in the face of temptation. Such 'is the measure of my selfishness and *folly*'.[1]

In an era in which consumption had largely shed the moral taint that once dogged shopping expeditions, Drane's recriminations seem oddly old-fashioned. At the turn of the twentieth century, things were widely viewed as the essential ingredients of personality. What regret middle-class consumers felt about their possessions stemmed from the inability of material belongings to live up to the extravagant expectations their owners had of them. Drane's penitence was something different. It was neither the despondency of the dissatisfied shopper who wrote in to the lady art advisor, nor was it a simple echo of early Victorian piety. Although he had been raised in a strict evangelical household – his father was a Congregationalist minister – Drane did not attend church; his pursuit of religious icons and occasional nightmares about hell were the only tangible reminders of his severe upbringing. Moreover, Drane's self-flagellation about his 'things' did not impede the pace of his acquisitions. The day after he vowed to restrain his expenditure, he bought antique wine cups and a Worcester cider jug, noting ruefully that this was a 'GOOD BEGINNING in Extravagance to the New Year!?'[2] In 1899, he spent still more than he had in 1898.

109 Robert Drane in 1913.

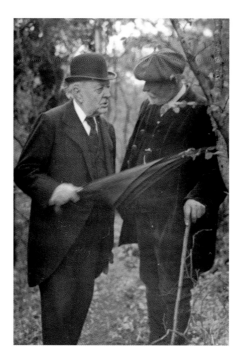

However unlikely Drane was as the harbinger of a trend, the retail apothecary stood at the centre of a new phenomenon. In the years between the whimsical stolidity of Victoriana and the advent of tubular steel furniture, the newest thing was the antique.[3] Shoppers who rejected the goods of their own time embraced the antique, combing salerooms, auction houses, bazaars, and curiosity shops for objects that predated the machine. Particularly prized was the furniture of the eighteenth century, treasured for its elegant symmetry and restraint. The works of Sheraton, Chippendale, and their less famous contemporaries, which unappreciative Victorians had once relegated to servants' quarters and attics as too old for notice, were unearthed and proudly displayed.[4] Of course, very few could afford an original Sheraton sideboard, which ran to hundreds of pounds. But by the turn of the century, all of the major furniture stores had opened antiques departments that stocked goods within the reach of middle-class shoppers. To satisfy the demand for antique furniture, manufacturers created the first mass-market reproduction industry.

The allure of the old in an age so self-consciously modern was an irony that did not escape the sharp-eyed wits of the time. Some commentators attributed the fashion for antiques to a protest movement against the grotesqueries of Victorian manufacture. Others remarked upon the charms of nostalgic fantasy in a period dominated by rationality and science. Both sentiments undoubtedly contributed to the craze for furnishings of an earlier day. But what is most striking, given the trajectory this book has traced from evangelical self-restraint to the reign of personality, was the antidote antiques offered to those who had wearied of novelty and endless reinvention. To collect antiques was to exercise restraint, even to practise self-denial. Lesser objects had to be left on sales tables in the quest for better specimens. Desires went unquenched for months, even years. Except by millionaires, antiques collections could not be built overnight; they required discernment, dogged determination, and, above all, the tireless pursuit of the rare and excellent. As personality became the dominant means of conceiving of the self, antique collectors sought refuge in possessions – and values – that no longer seemed to have a place in the wider world.

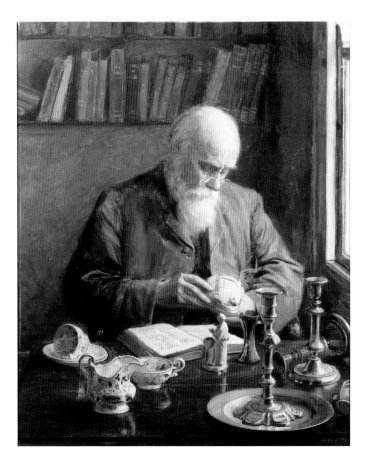

110 Walter Bonner Gash (1869–1928), *The Connoisseur*. As in Gash's painting, the connoisseur was invariably imagined as an elderly gentleman.

For Drane, as for other antiques enthusiasts, collecting old objects served as a critique of a fast-living age. In a nation in which the established social hierarchy seemed increasingly imperilled, an eye for antiques became a mark of distinction not easily replicable. It signified the triumph of substance over mere style. People who 'went in' for antiques liked to describe their predilection as an innate characteristic, a refutation of the idea that good taste could be learned by all. They tended, more than other twentieth-century Britons, to exist in a shadowland between the sacred and the secular. In some cases, such as Drane's, the long shade of militant religion was visible, as guilt about self-indulgence vied with material desires for the soul of the collector. For others, however, the material and immaterial worlds coexisted peacefully, indeed reinforced one another; they lived in a world of spirits who spoke from the afterlife, summoned by raps upon historic tables. Either way, antique-fanciers agreed that old objects had a life of their own. They were survivors from another era with their own stories to tell; they could not be moulded to the whims of mere mortals.

ANTIQUES AS A PROTEST

Before the 1880s, the suggestion that one should buy old furniture would have been greeted by most middle-class citizens with derision.[5] Even in the grandest early nineteenth-century interiors, little value was attached to the authenticity of the furniture; lavish new productions were often treasured above the finest objects of the past.[6] The first systematic study of antique furniture was Henry Shaw's 1836 *Specimens of Ancient Furniture Drawn from Existing Authorities*.[7] However, Shaw's book was intended as a guide for artists, an instruction manual for wayward history painters who might be tempted to insert a Regency sofa in their depiction of a Tudor hall. There were, of course, a minority of buyers, mostly antiquarians or bohemians, who appreciated the furniture of yesteryear.[8] In the 1860s, the infamously eccentric Pre-Raphaelite painter Dante Gabriel Rossetti decorated his Cheyne Walk house in eighteenth-century furniture; it was also home to a motley collection of armadillos, kangaroos, and exotic snakes.[9]

Before there was the antique, then, there was simply second-hand furniture. Those who wished to buy used furniture could find plenty of specimens in their local auction house. It was not a high-toned business. The better auctioneers, such as Messrs Christie, Manson and Woods, largely made their money from the sale of pictures.[10] The haphazard array of goods on offer at most auctions – parrot cages

111 William Luker, Jr,
*A view of the city
auction rooms in
Gracechurch Street,*
1900.

In the City Auction Rooms.

and boxes of cigars, a pocket compass and eight pairs of stays – presented a sorry contrast with the orderly atmosphere of the new furnishing emporia. After visiting the auction firm of Debenham & Storr's on one July afternoon in the 1850s, the *Daily Telegraph* reporter and man about town George Augustus Sala observed that the 'mere perusal of the catalogue is sufficient to give one vertigo'.[11] Even more off-putting, in Sala's opinion, was the crowd the auction houses attracted; most of the serious buyers were Jews, whose stranglehold on the second-hand business was a matter of legend if not fact. Colonized by the 'hook-nosed, ripe-lipped, bright-eyed, cork-screw ringleted, and generally oleaginous-looking children of Israel', auctioneering was, Sala concluded, 'the Bohemianism of commerce'.[12]

The first sign of a more general taste for the old came in the realm of smaller household wares, especially china. In the mid-1860s, Lady Charlotte Schreiber, a widow who had scandalized her family and society by marrying her son's young tutor, began 'ransacking' (the word was Lady Charlotte's) the Continent's private villas and shops in search of fine porcelain and china.[13] The 'china mania', as it was known, caught the imagination not just of moneyed collectors such as Lady Charlotte or Frederick Leyland, but of ordinary folk as well. Specimens of Bow, Bristol, Worcester, and Chelsea were abundant and still relatively inexpensive. Even William Ewart Gladstone succumbed to the fad, stockpiling a distinguished collection of Wedgwood porcelain; his brother-in-law, Sir Stephen Glynne, died of a heart attack while searching for antiquities in the ragamuffin surroundings of Shoreditch High Street.[14]

112 Messrs Fenton's Old Curiosity Shop, Bury St Edmunds, c. 1865. Among the shop's wares were pottery, china, armour, as well as Greek, Roman and Egyptian antiquities and prehistoric artefacts.

Curiosity shops, a feature of city life since the eighteenth century, offered happy hunting grounds for seekers after the unusual.[15] By the 1870s, Wardour Street in Soho was a byword for curios, though forgery was rife. Woe betide the naïf who stumbled into a dimly lit Wardour Street store in search of a Jacobean bowl – and emerged in the daylight clutching modern Sheffield silver plate. The mania that had begun with china soon spread to silver, pewter, other items of bric-à-brac, and eventually to furniture. Antiques, claimed the American expatriate Henry James, were the 'most modern of our current passions'.[16] In 1897, James published a novel, *The Spoils of Poynton*, which took as its subject an antique collector's 'strange, almost maniacal' obsession with her treasures, a predilection with which his readership would have been increasingly familiar.[17] With the founding of the richly illustrated periodical the *Connoisseur* in 1900, the antiques trade gained its first exclusive organ, to be joined by the *Antique Collector*, *Old Furniture*, and a host of smaller publications in the inter-war years.

By the turn of the twentieth century, antiques were no longer an eccentric taste, and suppliers abounded. In 1870, the London trade directories had registered just twenty-one 'Antique Furniture Dealers'.[18] In the early twentieth century, however, the trade expanded exponentially: by 1910, London alone could boast more than 150 antique dealers, while towns such as Portsmouth became known for their richly stocked shops.[19] Some of the newly minted antique dealers had started in the curiosities business; Frederick Litchfield, who ran the Sinclair Galleries in Soho,

113 Mr Bowerman's antique shop in Burford, Oxfordshire, early twentieth century.

grew up in the bric-à-brac shop his father managed.[20] Other shops were the product of opportunistic expansion into a field that seemed to promise wide profit margins. The Welsh firm of Solomon Andrews & Son, which began as a baking and confectionery concern in the 1850s, soon ventured into the business of furniture removal and undertaking, department stores, coach and omnibus building, the provision of omnibus and tramcar services, and – by 1912 – antiques, with premises in Cardiff's Morgan Arcade.[21] Alongside the much-maligned Jews, the antiques business boasted its fair share of gentlemen entrepreneurs, such as George Marshall, the scion of a prosperous banking family, who opened the Hereford Antique Furniture Company when his venture in fruit-farming failed.[22]

The shopper in search of antiques during the Edwardian years was spoiled for choice. There were the venerable haunts of yesteryear, though for the connoisseur who remembered the old days, the increased competition for prized objects was hardly welcome. As the authors of *The Bargain Book* noted with some dismay in 1911, the Friday outdoor sales at the Caledonian Market had become 'weekly fashionable gatherings of the town'.[23] The truly adventurous could avoid the crowds by scouting for hidden treasures in distant villages, where good bargains might still be made with provincial folk.[24] Those who had no interest in tramping through villages could visit one of the established furnishing stores instead; every Edwardian furniture emporium had an antiques department, the largest and grandest of which belonged to Waring & Gillow. Competition from the furnishing retailers had a salutary

114 A bird's eye view of the Caledonian Market, 1911.

115 The Soho Antique
Gallery, London,
photographed by
Bedford Lemere in
1886.

effect on the rest of the trade, though disreputable pockets still remained. At the
Sinclair Galleries, once a Wardour Street fixture, Frederick Litchfield – whose land-
mark *Illustrated History of Furniture* (1892) had established his name with the
broader public – presided over a treasure-house; the store occupied five large floors
on Shaftesbury Avenue illuminated by electric light, where carefully authenticated
objets d'art could be examined at leisure.[25]

   But if the business had begun to shed its raffish image, shopping for antiques
remained a very different experience from what customers in department stores had
come to expect. In many antique shops, items were not marked with prices, an
unsettling experience for customers who knew that the dealer's mark-up might be
200 per cent, or more.[26] To ensnare buyers, some proprietors spun fanciful tales
around their objects, embellishing elderly specimens with noble pedigrees and
endowing quotidian things with fables of 'romantic discovery'.[27] One lucky antique
dealer, Mr Mathuen, could claim a shop in the eighteenth-century inn frequented
by Dick Turpin.[28] The visitor who inquired would be conducted to Turpin's hiding-
place. Though not every shop offered such an atmospheric setting, most retained an
individual character, derived from the proprietor's own tastes and specialities.[29]
Enterprising shop owners cultivated personal relationships with their customers.
Their best clients received items sent upon approval. The pharmacist Drane, never

116 Charles Spencelayh, *The Old Dealer*, exhibited at the Royal Academy in 1925.

one to worry about giving offence, found his own, uniquely appropriate way to respond to these solicitations. He returned poor specimens with a poison label attached.[30]

What – bemused observers asked themselves, surveying the bustling trade – could explain Britons' newfound penchant for the antique? One likely culprit was that Victorian whipping-boy: manufacture. As the antiques trade boomed, its success seemed, at least in part, to stem from dissatisfaction with modern products. Manufacturers, their critics charged, had little to offer discriminating palettes.[31] Perhaps, as some retailers speculated, the sinewy forms influenced by French art nouveau had alienated more conservative British householders. Or was it that buyers were simply fed up with the unending cycle of historicist pastiche that characterized Victorian furniture? Compared with the spare elegance of an eighteenth-century cabinet, a pseudo-Jacobean item on gilded feet was hard to love. Modern decoration, observed Rosamund Marriott Watson, was like Mary Shelley's monster, 'compacted mainly from fragmentary relics of the dead'. It 'has no real life of its own, no harmonious entity, no perceptible potentialities in the future'.[32]

But whatever the failings of modern manufacture, the turn towards the antique reflected a deeper discontent with the status quo. In every era there are lamentations about an earlier, simpler age.[33] However, the late Victorian period witnessed the most profound transformation of time and space the world has ever known.[34] A person born in the 1840s saw the coming of the railway, which whisked passengers to their destinations at superhuman speeds; the telegraph, telephone, and the radio, which offered instantaneous communication; and eventually, if they lived into their seventies and eighties, the automobile and the aeroplane as well. A journey that had formerly taken days could be made in one morning; a message that once took weeks to arrive now took no time at all. Writing in 1890, one woman observed: 'These are days of hurry . . . everything must be had and done at once; folks have "no time".'[35] Even those who relished the new possibilities for travel and communication nonetheless found the change disconcerting. In a world in which the present moved too quickly, the past offered sanctuary. As a boy, Desmond Coke had accompanied his mother on her shopping trips through London's finest emporia. But his own preferences were anchored firmly in history.[36] 'Old things,' he wrote, 'seem to me the only refuge that any human soul can find from this new tyranny. They give leisure, they bring peace.'[37]

Like many other lovers of the antique, Desmond Coke felt nostalgia for a time that he had not known. W. Carew Hazlitt, grandson of the famous critic, understood the phenomenon, perhaps because he devoted much of his own life to the memorialization of his grandfather's legacy. Casting 'love-sick glances' at the past, 'bourgeois collectors' sought to 'live more or less with the generations which have gone before them'.[38] They accumulated information about daily life in other eras,

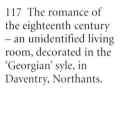

117 The romance of the eighteenth century – an unidentified living room, decorated in the 'Georgian' syle, in Daventry, Northants.

charting the marriage customs that governed dowry chests and the meals that had been eaten off pewter plates, anticipating the interest in social history that blossomed during the 1920s and 1930s.[39] For most, the century of choice was the eighteenth, hailed as the golden age of British craftsmanship. The eighteenth century was close enough in time to spark the imagination, yet distant from the concerns of the modern world. It was the 'first really domestic century', familiar to those whose formative years were passed amid the Victorian ethos of hearth and home.[40] However, the eighteenth-century room bore 'no traces of the nerve-tearing "strenuous life"'.[41] So beloved had the eighteenth century become that the *Antique Collector* felt it necessary to remind readers of what their own, sober-living grandparents had been only too aware: 'there were many gross evils in the age'.[42]

But if nostalgia for the past contributed to the antiques phenomenon, most antique-lovers also had their feet firmly planted on the shifting sands of late Victorian society. Antiques offered an important counterpoint to the ideas explored in the previous chapter: that good taste 'cost no more'; that a scintillating personality lay within the reach of all. Antiques stood instead for absolute hierarchies of value. Whether one preferred an 'Eastern' parlour to its Morrisian variant was a matter of individual taste. The same could not be said of a mid-Victorian bowl and a piece of old Wedgwood. The relative rarity of old things created rigid systems of worth, bolstered by the systems of exchange in which the antique was always embedded. While a person might have treasured the mid-Victorian bowl for sentimental reasons, few antique collectors would have disputed that a Wedgwood piece would in fact have been preferable.

To cherish antiques was to proclaim a taste that required cultivation beyond the means of the vast majority. For those who embraced them, antiques offered a form of distinction, cultural capital all the more precious for the fact that it retained exclusivity in an increasingly homogeneous world. As the *Connoisseur* made clear, the possessors of fine specimens were frankly to be admired, a markedly undemocratic sentiment in an era that witnessed Lloyd George's attack on inherited privilege and unearned income. A man who had inherited his furniture could luxuriate in a pedigree, surrounded by 'reminders of his ancient lineage'.[43] He who had to 'buy all his furniture', as the infamous remark about Michael Heseltine went, began (and arguably still begins) with a disadvantage.[44]

Were antiques then just another prop for self-fashioning, albeit in a more rarefied context? Some of those who flocked to antique shops sought simply to furnish their house with genteel items, cherishing the aura of pedigree that antiques conferred.[45] With expert assistance, a wealthy man could acquire 'household gods which tell of a longer past and a closer relationship with the well-to-do than he can legitimately claim'.[46] But the antique inherently resisted the role assigned to other household possessions. Its rarity, on the one hand, and the expertise required of its collectors, on the other, offered a rebuke not just to the social climber, but to the entire notion of personality. Within the large numbers of Britons who embraced the antique as a protest against their own era was a smaller coterie of dedicated fanciers. Both collectors and furnishers, they were distinguished by the rigour of their dedication. For them, antiques were more than a nostalgic pursuit, more even than a protest against the homogenizing force of consumer culture; they were also a faith.

ANTIQUES AS A FAITH

When the Cardiff businessman F.C. Andrews sent Robert Drane a silver castor for inspection in May 1906, he must have braced himself for a frank evaluation. Andrews was still a novice in the world of antiques; he would not open his own shop, the Welbeck Galleries, for another six years. Drane, by contrast, was already a well-known personage among the city's antique-fanciers, as famous for his expertise in old things as for his cutting remarks about their owners. Those who dared risk the pharmacist's tart observations carried their treasures into his shop for

118 Drane's pharmacy, early twentieth century.

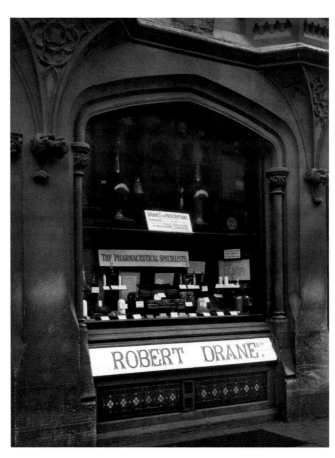

inspection and valuation – an early, stationary, and not so polite version of *Antiques Roadshow*. To the ignorant and unwary, he manifested contempt rather than pity. The possessors of objects he deemed fine would be congratulated on their knowledge and discerning eye; if they impressed the pharmacist sufficiently, they might even be honoured with an invitation to visit Drane at home among his collections.

In the matter of Andrews' silver castor, Drane did not mince words. The castor was as 'bad as badness can be. It is ignorant, illshapen, cheap, mechanical and false in every respect except the fact that it is of standard silver.' The castor, Drane judged, belonged to the 'order of things made by the hundred weight for the fool at home' and the 'transatlantic buyer'. 'No man of any knowledge or taste would have it at any price.' Drane's morally charged language, once common currency among Victorians, ran contrary to the more tolerant aesthetic of the originality-seeking Edwardians. The pharmacist ended his letter, as was often his habit, with a biblical citation refashioned enigmatically for the occasion. While Andrews would certainly have understood that Drane's closing remark was another insult, whether he could have deciphered its precise meaning is doubtful. Drane wrote: 'It was said of Ephraim that he was "joined to his idols" with the comment "Let Him alone" – and so say *I* – altho' not perhaps "all of *us*."'[47]

Whatever Andrews made of Drane's reference, it reveals much about the pharmacist himself. Drane's quotation came from the prophet Hosea, who foretold disaster for the idol-worshipping tribe of Israel ('Ephraim') shortly before the Israelites disappeared into the desert never to be heard from again. For those who were 'joined' to false idols, Hosea warned, there was no hope and no help: 'Let Him alone.' Like Hosea, Drane saw clearly the difference between right and wrong – in china as in life – and was quick to pass judgment upon those, like Andrews, who could not. But as the pharmacist slyly acknowledged in the last line of his letter, the same harsh judgment did not apply to 'all of us'. For the true cognoscenti, worshipping at the altar of fine antiques was no sin. There were false idols and then there were real ones. The pharmacist, too, was a worshipper of idols, but his, at least, were not untrue.

Antiques, Drane warned his callers, were not an appropriate pursuit for the ostentatious or the unserious. Distinguishing false idols from the real thing required expertise and a certain flair for objects. So robust was the demand for old items that the market was glutted with fakes to lure the unsuspecting. In books with titles such as *Antiques Genuine and Spurious* (1924) or *The Gentle Art of Faking Old Furniture* (1931) antique experts unmasked the tricks of the trade. Unscrupulous dealers 'aged' furniture with faked wormholes, burns, or more creatively still, by encouraging rabbits to scamper across their surfaces.[48] There were fraudulent silver bowls fashioned out of genuine spoons, sham gate-leg tables briskly brushed with wire bristles, 'Cromwellian' sideboards constructed from church pews. And the list went

119 A fake antique
chair, composed
entirely of old frag-
ments. 'To an expert,'
wrote Herbert
Cescinsky in *The
Gentle Art of Faking
Furniture* (1931), 'the
whole chair *looks*
wrong, both from the
point of detail and
proportion.'

on. Capitalizing on the fad for direct sales, some dealers went so far as to plant
phoney objects in out-of-the-way cottages and country houses, paying a commission to the householder who reluctantly agreed, upon a knock on the door, to part
over and again with their treasured 'family heirlooms'.[49]

To the delight of connoisseurs such as Drane, the antique thwarted those who
intended to use it for mere show. In an age full of 'ignorant pretenders', as the pharmacist put it in his diary, where 'everywhere and in everything the rage is "to save
and to get" with trumpery display', this at least was the province of a discriminating
few.[50] Even the lady art advisors, normally buoyant in their sense of the possible,
urged caution. Those who filled their houses with 'shaky sham oak, and venerable-
looking rubbish' in the hope of conveying a distinguished name, warned Mrs
Panton, should not expect success.[51] Books that purported to offer guidance to the
amateur antique collector could not have been very reassuring; in *How to Collect
Old Furniture* (1904), Frederick Litchfield acknowledged that no amount of advice
could substitute for genuine expertise, especially when it came to expensive fakes.[52]
While an 'original' or 'eccentric' interior could be achieved by the man or (more
likely) woman on the street, the same was not true of a home filled with genuine
antiques. Rather than attending auctions or straying into country villages, Litchfield
advised the would-be furnisher to place himself in the hands of a 'reputable'
dealer.

While self-cultivation was a hallmark of the early twentieth century, the antique
pointed up its limits. There was thought to be something innate about true connoisseurs,

which distinguished them from their fellow citizens. 'A collector, like a poet,' observed one periodical, 'is born, not made.'[53] Those in the know spoke of a 'natural eye' or a 'collecting instinct', much as we today might refer to a 'collecting gene'.[54] How he came by his 'infallible instinct in the matter of glass' the antique dealer Thomas Rohan could not explain; he certainly had not been schooled in matters of taste.[55] W. Carew Hazlitt believed that the penchant for old things ran in families, passed down like eye colour or an aptitude for mathematics. 'There must be a sort of inborn instinct to make one a true collector. It is a faculty and a quality belonging to the constitution and the blood, and is seldom acquired, although it may be developed by experience and education.'[56] It was, in other words, characterological rather than a matter of personality, a throwback to older models of the self that had prevailed in the mid-nineteenth century.

Serious antique collectors fancied themselves a people apart. In a sense, they were right. Antiques, by and large, were not a pastime for the young or the newly married. A trade that rejected the 'pep, push and din' of the modern age offered little appeal to the vast majority who revelled in the motor car and cinema.[57] As women increasingly colonized the furnishing business, antique collecting – an expensive pursuit – remained a predominantly male preserve. Though Drane on occasion entertained women collectors, his world was largely made up of men who shared his passion, ranging from the Cardiff fishmonger Joshua John Neal to Judge Owen, a local dignitary. Women constituted only 15 per cent of the clientele of one Bradford

120 J. Walter Butters and his walking stick collection, 1905. Walter Butters (1838–1907) was a builder by trade.

antique shop between 1912 and 1915, a figure that was probably typical of the country as a whole.[58] Bachelors seem to have been disproportionately represented among antique collectors. Desmond Coke, the only one of Mrs Talbot's seven children not to marry, saw antique collecting as an alternative to matrimony: 'If I had not spent always a good third of my yearly income on antiques . . . I might have had . . . a limousine, a week-end cottage, a wife and a pot-belly'.[59] A 'tendency to collect, manifested in early manhood,' observed the Liberal aristocrat George W.E. Russell in 1906, 'is a heavy blow and deep discouragement to the operations of the matrimonial market.'[60] Collectors, notoriously, were 'married' above all to their collections; whether in addition their tastes extended to the opposite sex was a matter Russell left in doubt. In certain circles in Cardiff, the pharmacist Drane was known as the 'old hermaphrodite' – in the parlance of the day, a synonym for homosexual.

Whatever irregularities may have characterized the private lives of collectors, the pursuit of antiques required – or so connoisseurs liked to say – the exercise of old-fashioned virtues. Chief among these was self-denial. The person who wished to decorate with antiques had to be patient, forsaking the nearly-right object in search of the perfect specimen.[61] They had to be content, too, with sparsely furnished rooms. In contrast to furniture emporia, which promised instant gratification to those in possession of a sufficient bank balance, the quest for good antiques could last years. Discipline was the collector's mantra: 'Any impatience on his part will result in his own undoing; for old furniture is not come by easily, or, in other words, if he wants certain articles he must be prepared to acquire them one by one if necessary.'[62] According to Litchfield, the *nouveaux riches* were too often in a hurry – eager to 'entertain distinguished guests during the coming autumn or winter' – to accumulate a worthy collection.[63]

And yet, as Drane was only too painfully aware, the antique collector's brand of self-denial was a far cry from the selflessness that Drane's evangelical father had urged upon his charges – the 'humble and hearty surrender of yourself to Him'.[64] Viewed in the clear light of his own year-end reckoning, the pharmacist's collections appeared, even to himself, excessive, indeed selfish. Drane was not alone. So familiar a theme was the antique-lover's obsession with his possessions that it became the subject of a popular play, and later a series of novels, by Horace Annesley Vachell.[65] In *Quinneys'* (1915), Vachell dramatized the inner workings of an antique dealer's household. Enchanted with his lacquer cabinet – 'I can say my prayers to it' – the dealer, Joe Quinney was not an easy man to live with.[66] His days were dedicated to the pursuit of beautiful objects; his wife and daughter lived in the shadow of his quests. To Joe's wife, frustrated by her husband's love-affair with 'graven images', Vachell awarded the play's most memorable line: 'It is things – things – THINGS you care for . . . .There's only one person in all the wide world you care for, and that's yourself!'[67]

What Vachell played as comedy was for Drane a deadly serious matter. While the pharmacist had long since abandoned the evangelicalism of his youth, his diaries bear witness to a struggle over what precisely his possessions ought to mean to him. Unlike the Reverends Loftie and Boyd, who viewed beautiful surroundings as another way of worshipping God on earth, Drane had rejected the Established Church in favour of rationalism and scientific observation. The cardinal tenet of Protestant Christianity – '"Only believe and you shall be saved"' – he judged 'the hysteric cry of the fool, the quack, or the fanatic'.[68] But neither had the pharmacist entirely left behind the framework of his upbringing. He twisted biblical phrases to suit his dealings with objects. When a piece of pottery he was offered for sale cracked upon his usual test – a dip in the fire – Drane reworked Jesus' words into a maxim for the collector. 'Blessed are they who believe for they shall surely be deluded,' he wrote in his diary, 'therefore search and see if these things be so or not and hold fast only those which are good.'[69]

As in the case of Mr Andrews' silver castor, the distinction between false and true gods lay at the heart of the pharmacist's world-view. Drane's possessions were not just metaphorically, but in actual fact, his household gods. He had no others. Unlike those eminent agnostic Victorians such as Leslie Stephen, who lost their faith but placed their trust in the moral powers of man, Drane despaired about society. He had a host of complaints: vulgarity was in the ascendant, men of means lived among rubbish, people gave themselves false airs and graces, housemaids were photographed in lace-trimmed evening attire, display had gained over 'genuineness'.[70] 'Public life' was 'mainly a fraudulent pretence. Anybody will do who has sufficient "push" and unconscious ignorance.'[71] It was not just that the social hierarchies that had formerly governed life were collapsing. Even worse, authenticity itself was gravely imperilled, perhaps even on the verge of extinction.

Where people were often false, the right objects were always true. Drane sought comfort and pleasure in his things and in his animals; he was a keen naturalist, and raised hares, 'natural-born gentlemen', in captivity. While Drane might have agreed with Oscar Wilde about the difficulty of living up to one's china, he, like the lady art advisors, would have taken very strong exception to the sybaritic values Wilde espoused. He condemned 'selfish gratification' in himself as in others. Of a Mr Williams whom he had met in the resort town of Torquay, Drane observed: 'a "gentleman" in the World's sense, a selfish unprincipled scoundrel in mine. . . . At 45, Batchelor, unattached, living between a club and an hotel, with ample means and no obligations.'[72] Given Drane's awareness of his own indulgences, perhaps the pharmacist's harsh view of Mr Williams was another form of self-reproach. If so, Drane took solace in the fact that strangers commented upon his likeness to Gladstone, especially in the eyes. The pharmacist shared the window to the soul of the nineteenth century's irreproachable moral force.[73]

Antiques were, for Drane, a faith: he believed in them as he trusted neither established religion nor his fellow man. In his possessions, he found the virtues that seemed in woefully short supply in the world: purity and authenticity, sincerity and timelessness. His diaries – all thirty-three volumes of them – served as a record of his household gods; he scrupulously noted all acquisitions. Where evangelicals had turned to diary-keeping as a means of repentance and self-discipline, Drane reflected not just upon the state of his soul, but the nature of his purchases. Indebted to the spiritual testaments of the past, Drane's diaries were also strikingly self-conscious documents, clearly intended to justify his collections to posterity. He never entirely freed himself from guilt about his expenditure. However, he had, with his distinction between false and true idols, developed a credo that sustained him: the very transcendence of his objects redeemed them from the charge of mere indulgence.

If Drane was eccentric, he was typical of an eccentric breed. Devotees of the antique invested their possessions with a mystical aura. They styled themselves as an Elect, united in their pursuits against the forces of the infidel. 'The "worship of the Antique",' claimed the *Connoisseur and Collector's Journal*, 'is a cult which is only possible to men and women of high cultivation and refined intellect.'[74] Religious language was put to use in markedly secular ways: the enamelling on a set of chairs 'was simply sacrilege'; the man with little to spend could find 'his earthly paradise' in Hepplewhite furniture; collectors entitled their memoirs 'confessions'.[75] A case full of finely preserved books, exclaimed one man, would make him 'believe Heaven to be possible but hardly necessary'. For true believers, their antiques were literally other-worldly. The poet Rosamund Marriott Watson put her faith in a fine old Chinese tea set from the seventeenth century, which (like a flying carpet) whisked its possessor away from her earthly cares: 'In the world of blue china there are no right angles of incidence, no stubborn facts, but only a sweet unreasonableness – a happy and blessed inconsequence; it is fairy-land, in fine, driven back to its last intrenchments.'[76]

In seeking fairy-land amid the monotonous terraced landscapes of early twentieth-century Britain, devotees of the antique had plenty of company. In an age celebrated for the ascendance of science, the occult flourished.[77] Fairies and sprites cavorted through the drawing-rooms of respectable middle-class people. Spiritualists plied their craft before hushed audiences, while inter-galactic magicians journeyed to distant planets in search of extraterrestrial life. This was not simply a repudiation of science, as the presence of a number of scientists among the occultists indicates. Rather, interest in the supernatural represented an acknowledgement, widespread in some progressive-minded circles, that neither scientific rationality nor orthodox religion fully explained the mysteries of humanity; something more was needed. Antique-lovers such as Drane or Marriott Watson offered their own answer to the conundrum of man's place in the universe. By endowing their possessions with sacred significance, they drew together the secular and the spiritual, uniting the material and immaterial worlds. Antiques, observed the Bournemouth dealer Thomas Rohan, offered 'a light that can never die'.[78]

Spiritual quests would figure prominently in the lives of antique-enthusiasts well into the twentieth century. Ethel Deane, who created *Queen*'s popular collecting column, experimented with Christian Science; alongside her best-selling *Byways of Collecting* (1908), she also wrote a Christian Science romance novel.[79] The *Antique Collector*'s contributors wrestled with the legacy of orthodox Christianity. Alfred Docker, who wrote articles on colour prints, sought to develop 'a new and workable religion' in the place of Christianity as it was practised.[80] He called for a Christianity 'subject to verification by reason' and 'uplifted by moral or ethical impulse' in place of the 'untrue, misleading, and incorrect' dogmas of the Established Church.[81] 'Heaven cannot be made for us; we must make it for ourselves.'[82] Docker's colleague, Dr Margaret Vivian, was the *Antique Collector*'s authority on antique porcelain boxes. Like Drane, Vivian was the child of a clergyman; she, too, had repudiated Christianity in her youth.[83] She remained a defiant agnostic until one day, when she was a medical student, there appeared before her a spirit from the Other Side.[84] From that moment of spiritualist revelation, objects became mediators between the netherworld and planet earth, redolent with spirits and psychic adventure.

As Margaret Vivian and Robert Drane saw it, antiques were not inanimate objects. The lives that old objects had touched in previous times remained vested within them. Antiques had outlasted their creators and would survive their possessors. The Bournemouth dealer Thomas Rohan urged his clients to think of themselves as 'trustees' of their objects; he cited the words of the apostle Paul: 'We brought nothing into this world and it is certain we can carry nothing out.'[85] This quality of transcendence distinguished old objects, sparing them the taint of indiscriminate materialism. Vivian, like Drane, felt keenly all that was wrong with British society. She had hopes, though, for a better world: an afterlife that was not merely heaven, but a utopia where the faults of the world were remedied. On the Other Side, virtue was rewarded with plenty. The unselfish were granted fine houses.[86] After death, that bedevilling force, 'the desire for material things' disappeared, and money along with it. Nonetheless, the residents of the Other Side – Vivian reassured her readers – enjoyed material goods 'far more wonderful' than anything that could be purchased on earth.[87]

THE SECRET LIFE OF THINGS

Mrs Talbot Coke had been dead four years when her son, Desmond, was 'seized' with a 'sudden, very poignant memory' of her. Leafing through a bookseller's catalogue in 1926, he saw listed for sale a volume of the sumptuously illustrated Regency journal *Ackermann's Repository*. Remembering the pleasure that his mother found in *Ackermann's*, Coke sent for the book, only to find upon its arrival that the copy he had ordered was inscribed in his mother's hand. She had given it to a friend many years earlier. It was as if the book had spoken to him, reached out through the catalogue's thin pages, and claimed its proper place in Coke's home. Such experiences – and he acknowledged that he had many of them – had convinced Coke that old objects had a will of their own: 'I say further, in full possession (I hope) of my mental faculties, that they do, in some way beyond our understanding, find their way to those who have a special love for them, and settle comfortably beside their fellows.'[88]

Well might Coke have reassured his readers as to his sanity, for this vision of a world of purposeful objects doggedly seeking out their rightful owners ran quite contrary to the way in which one's possessions were supposed to function in the twentieth century. Whether the aim was to communicate creativity or to express individuality, household objects – as a generation of lady art advisors had instructed their readers – existed to do their owners' bidding. The furniture in Maple's was as subordinate to the human will as a rod of steel in the firm grasp of a smelter or a skein of cotton in the hands of a mill girl. Even the finest objects could be smothered by an unfavourable arrangement; the woman of ingenuity and flair could, by contrast, transform the most unpromising article into a thing of beauty. Rooms were canvases or stages – blank slates, by whatever metaphor – while furnishings were raw materials. The lady who was dissatisfied with her drawing-room had no one to blame but herself.

And yet, Coke was not alone in his conviction that the apparently inanimate world was anything but. For his fellow collectors, the notion that objects had a life of their own was an article of faith. Their belongings possessed human qualities: a cabinet was 'suspicious' and a piece of china was 'reproachful'.[89] The feeling of Wedgwood put Gladstone in mind of a 'baby's flesh'.[90] Aficionados described their objects in familial terms.[91] New acquisitions were equated with new children, likely to displace existing treasures in the affections of their proud parents.[92] Specimens in prime condition attracted wonderment and admiration, while the drive to social work took shape in rescuing neglected or marred examples. Connoisseurs revelled in objects that they had discovered 'in the rough' and – like the evangelizing minister of old – 'raised from a debased condition'.[93] Horace Vachell reported that one middle-aged spinster of his acquaintance kept her 'cripples', or damaged treasures, locked in cabinets, which she referred to as 'infirmaries'.[94]

How objects came to be imbued with life force was an issue on which collectors disagreed. Some followed Marx and Ruskin in identifying hand-work as the source of the commodity's 'strange' properties. Only objects made by hand had 'a perennial life'; those that had been fabricated by machine, by contrast, were dead.[95] Others, probably the majority, took a broader view. For them, what animated the antique was its longevity.[96] Old objects had, against the odds, survived the centuries. Like a benign version of Dracula, they drew life force from their long-dead consorts. Ghosts clung to their surfaces. An old screen, wrote Rosamund Marriott Watson, 'exhales a phantom fragrance of pot-pourri and rustling, lavender-scented silks'.[97] Some antiques almost literally spoke for themselves. 'Do not the guns of Wellington's artillery sound in the distance as I contemplate that glorious group of Buen Retiro?' marvelled the china collector Herbert Byng Hall.[98] The dealer Thomas Rohan wrote a novel from the perspective of a Chippendale chair.[99]

But even beyond the narrow circles of collectors, the suspicion that domestic objects were not entirely under human control lingered well into the twentieth century, offering a defiant counterpoint to the cheery assumptions of decorating magazines. Second-hand furniture figured as the catalyst for many a ghost story and fairy-tale, contributing a crucial point of connection between the supernatural and a world in which inanimate objects obeyed the rules. C.S. Lewis' wardrobe is just the best known of a host of magical articles of furniture. Some, like Lewis' portal to Narnia, provided gateways to realms of fantasy; others summoned up long-dead spirits. He who carted home an antique bureau, warned the anonymous author of the short story 'An Old Bureau', had to prepare for a sleepless night.[100] The narrator, a man who believed he had made a bargain, soon found that the bureau concealed a mid-Victorian tragedy. No sooner had he drifted off to sleep than a ghost appeared before him. It was the bureau's former owner, a little girl whose illness had forced her father to seek work in another town. She died before he returned home, as, too, did her grief-stricken mother. Her father had committed suicide.

At the epicentre of the enchanted world of domestic objects was the haunted house. Judging from early twentieth-century memoirs, there must have been few Britons who did not have some experience of a haunted house. There was the classic, Victorian variety: the ghosts of former residents who stubbornly refused to relinquish their former habitations, clanking in chains along a dim hallway.[101] These were the kind most likely to be seen by housemaids and children.[102] But more often there were indefinable auras attached to a dwelling, both good and bad. Her strong feeling upon entering a house, one woman acknowledged, was the 'one superstition, which no common sense can eradicate'.[103] Some houses, wrote the journalist Mrs E.T. Cook, gave 'something of the feeling of standing by a new-made grave'.[104] Other houses, by contrast, welcomed visitors 'like gentle fingers on an aching head'.[105] Such houses were more than dwellings; as Dorothy Pym, the author of *Houses as Friends* (1936) put it, they became dear companions.[106]

In the increasingly crowded twentieth-century literary marketplace, the house with a life of its own offered a popular commercial vehicle. Most of the century's notable authors penned such a story: a very partial list (to the 1950s) includes Arnold Bennett, E.F. Benson, Elizabeth Bowen, John Buchan, E.M. Forster, Ellen Glasgow, Elizabeth Jane Howard, D.H. Lawrence, Elizabeth Taylor, Muriel Spark, H.G. Wells, and Hugh Walpole. Even Virginia Woolf tried her hand at the genre.[107]

Not just established authors, but dabblers from other fields joined the fray. For the provost of Eton, M.R. James, the ghost story offered an escape from the tedium of academic disputes and a light-hearted diversion from his scholarly work on illuminated manuscripts; it was the only fiction he wrote.[108]

The haunted house tale was not, of course, new. Victorian audiences had thrilled to stories about haunted houses; in many households, the arrival of the Christmas editions of *Household Words* or *Review of Reviews*, special issues devoted to spooky apparitions, was an eagerly anticipated event.[109] So redolent of Victoriana was the ghost story that critics such as Edmund Wilson marvelled at its survival in an era of electricity. Elizabeth Bowen, herself a practitioner, disputed Wilson's presumption: ghosts 'do well in flats, and are villa-dwellers. They know how to curdle electric light, chill off heating, or de-condition air.'[110] And yet, there could be no doubt that the nature of haunting had changed since Victorian times. Fully materialized ghosts were less central to the genre than had been the case in the previous century. For clanking chains twentieth-century authors substituted vague and indefinable feelings of dread. In the place of blood-curdling sights came insinuations and psychological torture. The best stories, noted M.R. James, elicited feelings of familiarity and recognition; the reader should say to himself: 'If I'm not very careful, something of this kind may happen to me!'[111]

If the Victorian ghost story had spooked readers by stripping away the cosy, self-congratulatory domesticity of hearth and home, its twentieth-century descendant had another purpose.[112] Edwardian and inter-war tales took aim at a more modern set of pieties: they mocked the idea that the domestic interior lay within mankind's control. Redecorating, in James' 'Diary of Mr Poynter' (1919), opens the door not to self-expression, but to the malign spirits of the past. The Dentons, a bachelor and his maiden aunt, are furnishing their house. They draw the inspiration for their curtains from a fabric scrap pinned within the pages of a seventeenth-century diary. So far, so good: decorating columnists had long urged their readers, in the name of originality, to seek out the 'fine, old chintzes of the past'. The Dentons' scheme meets with success; the pattern, reminiscent of curly tresses of hair, is 'so restful and yet so far from being dull'.[113] It is also, needless to say, one of a kind. It is not until nightfall that the curtains turn upon their new owners. The pattern is literally monstrous, the relict of a horrible two-hundred-year-old murder. The Dentons have curtained their windows with a pattern drawn from a dead man's hair. It could have happened to anyone with an interest in old chintz.

The haunted house laid bare the dark side of the home decoration manual. The premonitions that people reported upon entering a house for the first time echoed unhappily the advice that one should seek to 'create an impression'. Ghostly apparitions defied even the most valiant attempts to express one's individuality. Houses were not cooperative, but obdurate, wilful, even possessed.[114] Most importantly, the appearance of a room provided no indication of the horrors that lay within. Old-fashioned interiors were most perilous, suffused as they were with the spirits of the dead. But even a 'cheerful' interior was not free from mischief; evil forces infiltrated 'exquisitely furnished' bedroom suites as boldly as musty and decrepit country houses. Sooner or later, even the inhabitants of a room containing 'a handsome fire-screen with golden peacocks, and a deep Turkish carpet, soft and luxurious to the feet' – a chirpy description that could have been borrowed from a lady's magazine – would succumb to the terrors of the night.[115]

Given the discontent that so many Britons felt with their interiors, the haunted-house tale offered literary consolation. Houses conspired against their inhabitants; they thwarted even the best intentions. 'We all know the type of house which has so aggressive a personality that it completely submerges the owner,' admitted the *Times Literary Supplement*.[116] Unless one could make a clean sweep of it – and even then the ghost story promised no happy ending – the past filled the material world.[117] Most people, even those who wanted nothing to do with antiques, inevitably lived in houses surrounded by objects given and inherited.[118] Those who had to make do in furnished lodgings had more serious problems. This was the dilemma that Jennifer Wayne, an English teacher in Bristol, faced during the Second World War. Forced in 1940 to move to new accommodation, Wayne took rooms in a Victorian terrace. The rooms were awful, claustrophobic and damp, but she nonetheless hoped that 'with "a few deft touches"' – that staple counsel of the decorating manuals – she could manage to 'lift them out of their oppressive gloom'. But the furniture got the better of her: 'Most sinister of all, in a curious way, was a round polished Victorian mahogany table. It sat in the middle of the room, darkly shining and unfriendly.'[119] If things had a life of their own, what was the mere mortal to do?

* * *

In the first days of July 1916, as the Battle of the Somme raged murderously across the Channel, Sotheby's consigned to the gavel a marvellous collection. Displayed in the firm's London auction rooms were silver and works of art belonging to the late Mr Robert Drane, of Cardiff. The sale occupied the better part of three days. It was not a propitious year for the antiques trade. The war had thinned the ranks of the nation's dealers and collectors, even as taxes reduced the scope for luxuries among the country's well-to-do. But such was the quality of the pharmacist's collections that Drane's objects realized a considerable sum for his executors. Especially noteworthy was the price fetched by his sixteenth-century Evangelist spoon, topped by the figure of St Mark. It sold for £66, more than ten times what the pharmacist had paid for it.[120]

After prophesying his own demise for many years, the old pharmacist had finally died at the age of eighty, just before the outbreak of the war. His body was transported from Cardiff to the family vault in Norfolk; the renegade son was laid to rest alongside his God-fearing parents. The notice in the newspapers was unsparing in its detail: 'There were no flowers, but an old member of the church threw a spray of roses into the grave.'[121] Before dispersing Drane's collection to auction and to the Cardiff Museum, his executors took care to photograph his rooms as the pharmacist had arranged them. They mounted the pictures on grey matting, a handsome display which they presented, along with Drane's thirty-three volumes of diaries, to the city's archives. The official who received the bequest must have felt alarmed by their contents. 'Diaries of an old hermaphrodite,' he wrote on the accession tag. 'Do not distribute freely.'

At first glance, there is little to distinguish Drane's posthumously photographed sitting-room from the overstuffed interiors of the 1890s. Every surface is decorated, from the panels of the doors to the tops of tables. Cabinets bear up stolidly under the weight of multiple jars and vases. The room is jam-packed. A superficial glance at the photographs would not have identified the pharmacist as a man at odds with his time. Quite to the contrary: everything about Drane's rooms bespoke just that attention to display which he abhorred. A connoisseur could have readily identified Drane's treasures – could even have known just what they had meant to their possessor – but to the man on the street, the distinction would not have been apparent. Antiques enthusiasts construed their acquisitions as a sacred activity, separate from the vulgarity of their own age. But in an era defined by self-expression, even the most cantankerous of antique-worshipping pharmacists inevitably made a statement.

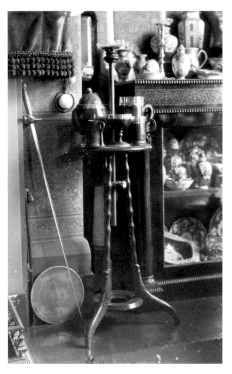

121–3 Robert Drane's house, 1914.

CHAPTER 7

MODERN LIVING

THE TRIUMPH OF SAFETY FIRST

In 1924, Sir Edwin Lutyens, the architect of New Delhi, unveiled the most eagerly anticipated house of the day. The dolls' house Lutyens presented to Queen Mary was a gift from the grateful British public in honour of the royal couple's patriotic wartime service. But Lutyens and the thousand-odd craftsmen who contributed pieces also intended the house to celebrate the best of British design and manufacture. Queen Mary's dolls' house showcased all the latest in interior design, amenities, and newfangled household inventions. The house's furnishings and decorations, commissioned from the country's top tradesmen and artists, were sumptuous. The style was pure eighteenth-century pastiche, some Chippendale, some Sheraton, some Louis-Quinze, some Louis-Seize. There were striped-silk upholstered *fauteuils* and rococo console tables, garlanded beds hung with needle-work tapestries and Palladian chimneypieces. Electric lifts connected the house's four floors; each of the five bathrooms featured hot and cold running water and flushing toilets. Electric lights illuminated its forty rooms, the gramophone played, the grandfather clocks chimed on the hour, and a tiny Hoover vacuum cleaner stood at the ready in the scullery.[1]

Queen Mary's dolls' house exemplified the paradoxes of modern life in inter-war Britain.[2] The country was, in some senses, a byword for modernity: it was the most unabashedly industrialized and urbanized nation in all of Europe. The mechanization of Queen Mary's dolls' house was fitting, for the British could take credit for the popularization, if not the invention, of many of the signal innovations of the nineteenth and twentieth centuries, including the railway, the Tube, and the radio. But measured against the late-comers to the industrial revolution, and especially the Germans, the British seemed after the First World War to be living in the past. England's contribution to the modern movement was trifling. Nowhere was this more true than in the field of domestic design.[3] By the early 1920s, the design revolution had swept through Scandinavia, France, Austria, and Germany. The best of Swedish design in 1924 meant blond wood and streamlined rectangularity, the best of German and Austrian design, tubular steel. According to the French guru of

124 Queen Mary's dolls' house being packed for dispatch to Windsor Castle, 1923.

125 The saloon of Queen Mary's dolls' house. Inspired by the architecture of Inigo Jones, this room features gilt 'Georgian' sofas, copied from the Chippendale furnishings at Harewood House, silk-hung walls, and a Palladian panelled ceiling.

modernism, Le Corbusier, the house was 'a machine for living in'. Ornament, or so the Austrian architect Adolf Loos had claimed in 1908, was a 'crime'. But whatever the upheavals on the Continent, the British seemed impervious to modernism at home.[4] Through the 1920s, in Queen Mary's dolls' house as in more pedestrian residences, British manufacturers and their customers remained faithful to the styles of their ancestors.

Endowed with sentiment and personality, the British house was not easily transformed into Le Corbusier's machine for living. Modern furniture required a particular lifestyle of its owners: fast-living, transitory, homogenized. One critic complained that it gave ordinary domestic life 'the atmosphere of a perpetual cocktail party'.[5] Few among the British middle classes were willing to forsake ornament. They had enthusiastically imported Indian and Japanese bric-à-brac into the home alongside Louis-Seize reproductions, but they balked at the intrusion associated with their former enemy's extreme modernism. Unlike on the Continent or in the United States, where metal furniture was adopted for home use, it proved a dismal failure in Britain. By and large, the British middle classes did not wish to live in the modern way, in 'a flat without a past', accompanied only by a cactus for comfort. Their homes remained important ways of making statements about who they were – clues not easily conveyed in cold steel.

126 Modern living in Sussex – Serge Chermayeff's house in Bentley Wood, Uckfield, 1938.

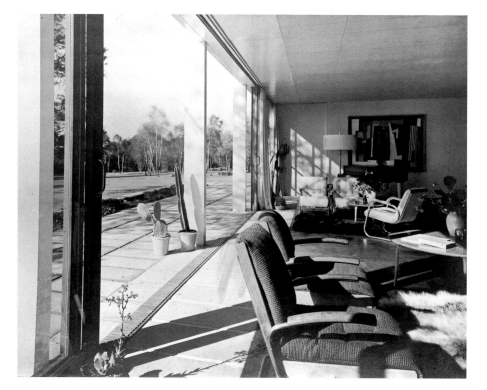

Frustrated modernists complained that the British clung mindlessly to the tried-and-tested styles of previous eras. According to the Russian-born architect Serge Chermayeff, the countrymen of his adopted land were mired in a 'retrospective stupor'.[6] And yet, lamentations such as Chermayeff's should not obscure the very real changes that had transformed British interiors. Inter-war homes looked different from their Edwardian counterparts. Most importantly, those who furnished in the 1920s and 1930s aimed to avoid the appearance of eccentricity – a marked departure from the Edwardian period, when originality had reigned. As the lady art advisors recognized, there had always been a conflict between the desire for uniqueness and the demands of good taste. By the inter-war years, the conventions strengthened as the promise of individual recognition through home decoration correspondingly diminished. Unlike in the mid-nineteenth century, when design reformers failed to win an audience for their principles, uniform standards of taste would eventually prevail in twentieth-century Britain. When the rules of good taste were joined to the powerful forces of social differentiation, self-expression became above all a matter of class belonging.

COMFORT IN STEEL?

More than sixty years after the Great Exhibition, Henry Cole's spiritual descendants gathered in London. For the designers and progressive-minded businessmen who founded the Design and Industries Association (DIA) during the First World War, the situation was not encouraging.[7] The taste of the public in the early twentieth century was as bad as ever. Since the original design reform campaigns of the mid-

127 The continuing allure of three-dimensional wallpaper. 'Delphinium & trellis', designed by A.J. Baker and machine printed by C. & J.G. Potter in 1914.

nineteenth century, fakery had decisively prevailed. Despite a half-century of hectoring advice, British consumers still decorated their walls with paper printed to resemble tiles and illuminated their windows with transparent sheets of 'stained glass'. A new initiative for design reform was needed. For inspiration, the DIA's members looked abroad to the German Werkbund, which, with its radically stream-lined furnishings and fittings, was revolutionizing continental design.

Outside a small group of design-oriented cognoscenti, the Werkbund was hardly known in Britain. Edwardians had used the term 'modern' to refer to the latest thing; a modern room, *circa* 1912, was one furnished harmoniously throughout with eighteenth-century reproductions. In 1915, the DIA sought to persuade the Board of Trade to host an exhibition of Werkbund objects with the aim of stimulating British industrial design. When the Board of Trade refused, the DIA's founders followed a two-pronged strategy: a campaign to stamp out imitation alongside a crusade to bring the best of the continental modern movement to the British public's attention.[8] However, their fight on behalf of 'fitness for purpose' met with little success. Confronted with DIA diatribes against biscuit boxes fabricated in the shape of bags of golf clubs, the chairman of Maple's objected to the 'crank touch' of the organization. The 'middle-aged middle class' who might have been expected to support the DIA demurred that 'they heard all that twenty years ago and it had no result then and will have less now'.[9]

Nor did the Design and Industries Association seem, at first, to make much headway with their efforts on behalf of modern furnishing. The '1924 Dining Room' displayed at that year's British Empire Exhibition at Wembley bore little

128 The 1924 Dining Room, designed by Lord Gerald Wellesley and Mr Trenwith Wills. British Empire Exhibition, Wembley – Palace of Arts.

resemblance to the functional ensembles on offer in Parisian department stores. Adorned with painted wall-panels of ostriches and Grecian urns, the room featured balloon-back armchairs grouped around a polished oblong table. In *The Times'* acerbic assessment, the model room aspired to innovative elegance but achieved only vulgarity – a 'Brixton lady assuming what she conceives to be cabaret dress and manners'.[10] It was not until 1928 that the average Londoner had an opportunity to see 'modern' furnishing on display. On the verge of bankruptcy, the Tottenham Court Road emporium Shoolbred's & Co. agreed to host a 'modernist furnishing' competition with the hope of attracting crowds to its premises. Eighty-three designers, from locales as far-flung as Shanghai and New Zealand, participated in the contest. The winning suites, boasting the trademark rectangularity of modern furniture, drew 10,000 visitors – enough to initiate Britain's modern experiment, but not to stave off Shoolbred's demise.[11]

Advocates of the modern insisted that the new era required a new style. They deplored the vogue for reproductions, which, in the psychological language of the day, they analysed as evidence of an 'inferiority complex'.[12] The British were too enchanted with their glorious history, and, as a consequence, fearful of the future. 'Can't we be ourselves in 1932?' asked the interior decorator J. Ronald Fleming.[13] Modern work, by contrast, was 'an expression of sanity'.[14] Dispensing with the pretence of the past, modern furnishing addressed the ways in which people now lived. Because of the widespread housing shortage after the war, city-dwellers had been forced into more cramped accommodation; even when house construction boomed in the later 1920s and 1930s, many middle-class families found themselves with smaller rooms. For women forced to do without domestic servants, the clean lines of the modern interior would create less work. Devoid of the nooks and crannies that were 'the breeding grounds of germs in the past', modern furnishings were healthier.[15]

For those who embraced the new style, the epicentre of modern furnishing was Heal's, the colonnaded emporium on Tottenham Court Road. Heal's began as a bedding store in the 1830s, but by the turn of the century had joined the ranks of the country's best-known furnishing emporia. At its helm was Ambrose Heal, the fourth generation of his family to run the business. Intelligent and opinionated, Ambrose Heal had little interest in simply maintaining the status quo. As a young man, he had been imbued with the reforming zeal of the Arts and Crafts movement. Apprenticed to a cabinet-maker at Warwick, he joined the family business as a designer in 1893. Before the First World War, his designs had made Heal's a centre for fine workmanship in the severe style, though the firm's salesmen grumbled about the 'prison' and 'workhouse' furniture that filled the store's galleries.[16]

In 1928, the year of the Shoolbred's exhibition, Heal was fifty-five, feared by his designers for his 'eagle' eye; 'a Victorian by temperament', in the words of one, 'an utterly ruthless man'.[17] Based upon appearances, a more unlikely character to

129 Ambrose Heal in 1933, painted by Edward Halliday.

market the modern would have been hard to find. He dressed in fine tweeds, exquisite handmade shirts, and wore folding steel spectacles from the eighteenth century.[18] However, Heal was also a founding member of the DIA. Like his fellow reformers, he had grown frustrated with the handicraft bias of the Arts and Crafts. Only with the machine could the British hope to produce furniture that kept step with the requirements of a post-war generation. After the world-wide crash, Heal launched a modern line, complete with steel-framed plywood-seated chairs and laminate dressers, accompanied by annual in-store exhibitions on 'Modern Tendencies'.

130 A view of the Modern Tendencies exhibition at Heal's, probably from 1934.

Heal's Modern Tendencies exhibitions served to introduce the discriminating customer as well as the merely curious passer-by to the latest ideas in interior design. Unlike Shoolbred's venture, Modern Tendencies featured British products, most of which had been designed or commissioned by Heal's. Tubular, chromium-plated steel abounded, put to work in dressing-tables, chairs, and even dining-room tables, but so, too, did goods wrought of the more familiar weathered oak. Objects were arranged in fully furnished room settings in order that the prospective purchaser could absorb the implications of the modern style. For collectors, Heal's offered specially signed editions. To entice those short of cash, the shop unveiled a Modern Tendencies flat in 1932 entirely outfitted for £195, alongside its deluxe £350 model.

The best publicity of all, however, was the example provided by one of Heal's own employees. Long before she racked up successes with *One Hundred and One Dalmatians* and *I Capture the Castle*, Dodie Smith was the manager of Heal's toy department, and, as her diary reveals, Ambrose Heal's mistress.[19] The success of her first play, *Autumn Crocus*, brought Smith a flat to suit her 'very decided ideas' about home decoration.[20] Decorated entirely in black, white, and silver, the flat represented the very latest in stage-set modernism. Its walls were bare of pictures; the few ornaments allowed, black glass flower vases and silver candlesticks, fitted the bichromatic colour scheme.[21] The reporters who visited her in the top-floor flat marvelled at the happy synchronicity between the woman – 'a modern phenomenon' – and her dwelling.[22] Hers was a 'flat without a past', a spare assemblage of modernist items purchased to suit the rooms, with no family heirlooms to spoil the effect. Each room (including the bathroom) had a telephone. In place of the ubiquitous Victorian aspidistra, Smith cultivated cacti, plants that 'in their obliging habits are suited to the long absences of their owners which are part of modern life'.[23] Dodie Smith's surroundings were a backdrop that framed their owner, but did not demand anything of her.

But what Dodie Smith proclaimed an advantage hardly seemed desirable to many middle-class consumers. Heal's attempts to promote metal and glass furniture fared especially badly.[24] Metal was, if at all, appropriate for hospitals, laboratories, ships, maybe for offices, but certainly not for the sitting-room. Worst of all, modern furniture lacked comfort. A woman who had been willing to experiment with the modern style returned two settees to the manufacturer with an angry note: 'Both your settees are extremely uncomfortable. The springing is as hard as armour plating and the backs too upright to allow room for a cushion.' Thanks to the settees, her country sitting-room had been transformed into that most industrial of locales – a train: 'My friends say sitting on the smaller one is like sitting in a third-class railway carriage.'[25]

131–2 A satirical take on tubular steel from W. Heath Robinson and Kenneth Browne, *How to Live in a Flat*, 1936.

The new furniture, or so its critics claimed, represented nothing less than an attack upon the British national character. 'Modern tendencies' summoned up the cocktail party and the aspirin, jazz and the motor car: a menacing combination of American hedonism and Teutonic conformity.[26] Such purely functional interiors were alien to British sensibilities. The man on the Clapham omnibus might be willing to tolerate discordant modern music on the wireless, or futuristic art on the Tube.[27] However, he drew the line at tubular steel, which ran contrary to everything that home meant. A chrome dining-table suggested 'a Nudist colony in November rather than a gathering of rational human beings': 'cold, stark, and repulsive, a negation of comfort and all the gentle things of life'.[28]

The high-point of the modern movement came in the years 1929–35, when Gordon Russell founded his showrooms on Wigmore Street, Heal staged Modern Tendencies, and architects such as Serge Chermayeff, Wells Coates, and Oliver Hill turned their talents to interior design.[29] However, outside a few prominent shops, steel and angularity hardly gained a foothold in Britain. Most retailers refused to stock the newfangled items: the market for modernism was small, and they could not afford the slow turnover.[30] Magazines, catering for reader interest, preferred to showcase newly built Jacobean or Georgian residences.[31] In the late 1930s, the Lines

133 Heal's dining room, displayed at the Exhibition of British Industrial Art in Relation to the Home, Dorland Hall, 1933.

Bros. Co. put an international-style dolls' house into production alongside their popular cottage and Georgian models. Faced with slow sales, however, they withdrew it from the market. Even intellectuals – whom retailers viewed as the natural constituency for modern furniture – proved resistant to the new styles. The

134 Untrammelled Victorianism – the dining room at 1 Kensington Palace Gardens before Wells Coates began his refurbishment.

135 Modernist splendour – 1 Kensington Palace Gardens after Wells Coates' renovation, 1932.

136 Minimalism for dolls: the Lines Bros.' ultra-modern dolls' house, c. 1937.

maverick philosopher A.J. Ayer was typical. In 1933, Ayer was a lecturer at Christ Church, Oxford, and an avid Labour Party supporter. When he and his wife furnished their first flat, they chose the style of the Second Empire, with an elegant, if uncomfortable, sofa and two armchairs purchased second-hand in London.[32]

To the extent that modern furniture was adopted in Britain, it took on a different shape from furniture on the Continent or in the United States. Manufacturers offered 'modernity robbed of angularity', as one advertisement from the late 1930s read.[33] In the hands of British designers, metal furniture acquired scalloped arms and ornamented legs in place of the severe, functional simplicity upon which European modernists had insisted.[34] Steel remained, at any rate, a rarity: designs were much more often executed in wood, following Scandinavian and art deco models. Retailers were painfully conscious of the 'alien' stigma that had attached to tubular steel, all the more damning as the Continent fell prey to political extremism. They laboured to convince their customers that modern (or, as they increasingly called it, 'contemporary') furniture was, in its essence, British.[35] Ambrose Heal traced the origins of his own modern lines to that exemplary Englishman, William Morris.[36] Whiteley's reassured shoppers that the 'introduction of WROUGHT IRON into modern furniture is the adaptation of an Old English handicraft'.[37]

137 Heal & Son's Roman Chair, c. 1933. This chair aroused the ire of the *Architectural Review*'s critic, who complained that Heal had replaced the 'simplicity and functional efficiency' of Breuer's steel with 'senselessly scalloped arms and bowed legs, sharp points, dust traps and more than a suggestion of antiquarianism'.

138 A specimen flat at
Heal & Son from the
1930s.

This watered-down version of modernism could hardly compete with the thriving trade in reproduction styles. The most prosperous clientele opted for the styles of the Empire and Regency, refashioned in exotic woods ('Sheraton in sycamore') and updated for modern living.[38] In 1936, Fortnum & Mason introduced a line of Queen Anne furnishings, which though 'unmistakably modern have about them a very pleasant flavour of the eighteenth century'.[39] In the middle-class trade, by contrast, Jacobean and Elizabethan styles predominated.[40] Customers who visited the gigantic new Clapham Junction premises of Hastings' Furniture Store in the mid-1930s were greeted with furniture that harked back to another era.[41] Especially popular were 'frank reproductions', in the description of one trade journal, 'complete with scratches, dents and other blemishes covered with an imitation patina of age'.[42] In their catalogues, Brookes Home Furnishers in Coventry heralded the 'Elizabethan' draw table and the 'Cromwellian' type of chair, constructed of oak and leather.[43]

Even the much-lampooned early Victorian style came in for a modest revival. The summer of 1931 saw two duelling Victorian exhibitions. On Bruton Street, Cecil Harcourt-Smith, the retired director of the Victoria & Albert Museum, oversaw the erection of a model Victorian home in aid of St Bartholomew's Hospital. So well attended was the Bruton Street exhibition that it was extended for a month,

139 The vogue for the Regency – the 1834 room, designed by Ronald Fleming, at the 1934 Ideal Home Exhibition.

140 Interior of a showhouse built by Messrs Edmonson Ltd, Meadway Estate, Southgate, 1930.

141 Furniture for the home by Brookes Sem-Par Ltd, 1930s. A Jacobean draw table confronts an art deco sideboard.

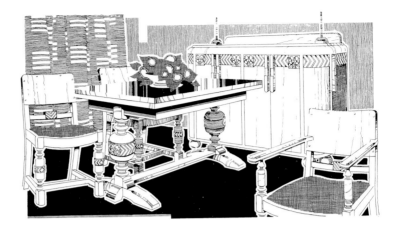

prompting calls in the press for a permanent Victorian installation.[44] Across town, Heal's, too, assembled a collection of mid-Victorian oddities, including Gothic clocks, papier mâché bedsteads, and horsehair and rosewood sofas, in the Mansard Gallery.[45] While Ambrose Heal's Victorian display could hardly have pleased his fellow DIA members, he was, above all, a shrewd retailer. Sales in the shop's antiques department had been flagging, and Heal hoped for a spark. Among a coterie of fashionable young shoppers, what was anathema to the previous two generations had found new favour. In the parlance of the day, Victorian furniture was 'amusing', something to tickle the fancy without being taken seriously.[46] Anything in papier mâché was at a premium, the more ridiculous the better.[47]

142 The Victorian Exhibition at Heal's, May 1931.

The complimentary reviews for Victoriana offered a striking contrast with the hostility that had greeted tubular steel. The enemies of the modern style drew the obvious conclusion: the fad for Gothic clocks and wax fruit under glass domes signalled a repudiation of functionalism.[48] For the British, they proclaimed, the house could never be merely a machine for living in; homes were repositories of feeling and personality. But in interpreting the British rejection of modernism as a matter of immutable national character, commentators misconstrued the situation. During the inter-war period, what home – and especially decoration and furnishing – meant to middle-class Britons was changing. The experimentation that had characterized the Edwardian period no longer appealed to most householders; after the Victorian exhibition closed, Heal's sold off its remaining stocks of antique furniture at a loss. The quest for novelty and originality had come to an end. If the home was not a machine, neither was it any longer a place to run risks. Where the spirit of 'safety first' held sway, modernism was doomed to fail.

SAFETY FIRST

It was not just tubular steel that the British rejected. That was the hard lesson of the Art in Industry exhibition staged in the winter of 1935 at Burlington House. The show got off to a promising start. For the first time in its 167-year-long history, the Royal Academy had agreed to sponsor an exhibition of craft-work. For the champions of the decorative arts, the Academy's participation was an auspicious sign: the nation's foremost bastion of fine arts had, however tardily, come to recognize the importance of design.[49] By the time the exhibition closed, however, the Royal Academy's authorities had probably come to regret their new alliance. Not only had the exhibition cost £20,000 to stage – a hair-raising sum at the time – but the displays in Burlington House had been lambasted in the popular as well as the trade press. Rather than signalling the auspicious marriage of art and industry, the exhibition had fallen prey to 'freakishness'. According to the *Cabinet-Maker*: 'Perhaps it is our education that is at fault, but quite a number of the things on exhibition seem to us to belong to what Barnum would have called a raree show.'[50]

Worst of all, critics concurred, were the specimen rooms decorated by the country's leading designers. No one who visited Burlington House could have forgotten the model library furnished by Robert Lutyens, son of the famous architect and himself an interior designer. The room's focal point was a table suspended from the ceiling by rods fitted with electric lights. While the table avoided the inconvenience of knees jostling table legs, most visitors thought the innovation merely bizarre. To connoisseurs of the new modern style, the specimen rooms were 'cowardly', 'vulgar', and full of unaffordable furniture, another missed opportunity in Britain's misbegotten romance with the past.[51] Traditionalists were no more

pleased. The 'cult of the extraordinary', one trade journal opined, 'is allowed too much scope'.[52] What might have been suitable in 1912, wrote the critic Joseph Thorp, was now 'an affront to the intelligence of serious people'.[53] Behind the exhibition's failure, the *Architect and Building News* detected the 'evidence of some restricting dead hand – or shall we say an Edwardian hand'.[54]

The critics' references to Edwardian influences were not accidental. In the Edwardian period, a library table that dangled from the ceiling might have been greeted with acclaim and purchase orders – the very definition of 'quaint' as applied to furniture. However, by the mid-1930s, the notion of eccentric furnishing was hopelessly outmoded, as redolent of the pre-war years as an abundance of servants and low rates of taxation.[55] Bizarre decoration, wrote one inter-war authority, 'is generally to be avoided'. She singled out silver ceilings, 'violent' pairings of purples and magentas and strange lighting as especially 'nauseating and tiresome' effects. 'A home must not be given the self-conscious air of a mannequin or of a West-end teashop.'[56]

Inter-war consumers sought, above all, to decorate in good taste, a standard that now ruled out designers' flamboyant experiments, as well as individual fancies. In furnishing, as in choosing a mate, caution and the observance of proprieties were required. 'Daring' furniture might 'infatuate', one women's magazine warned its readers, but its appeal would soon wane.[57] Better to stick with tried-and-tested items. One quick-witted company introduced a 'Majority' line of furnishings to capitalize on this sentiment.[58] Although nostalgics lamented the passing of the age of individuality, their complaints did not register more broadly. In middle-class homes, as in middle-class politics, the slogan of the day was 'Safety First', the theme that Prime Minister Stanley Baldwin had appropriated for his Conservative Party from a road safety campaign.

When Buying Furniture insist on seeing the
"MAJORITY" Lines

Obtainable from   your Retailer

One of the
75
"Majority"
Lines

Insist
on seeing the
" Majority "
labels
when buying
furniture

3 ft. 6 in. "Majority" Suite in Figured Oak.

144 Furnishing with the majority: the 'Majority Suite' in oak, from the *Home Furnisher*, 1924.

That the most notorious Edwardian idiosyncrasies did not survive the carnage of the First World War was probably to be expected. More than 875,000 men had been killed. Another 1.6 million were wounded, of whom 755,000 were permanently disabled. Widows and orphans numbered in the millions. The public censure meted out to wartime profiteers put an end to lavish display; excess expenditure was stigmatized as unpatriotic. The furnishings of the Edwardian period were – or so wrote a 'Schoolmaster in Khaki' to the *Evening News* in 1916 – part and parcel of the corruption of the pre-war period. 'Our fathers were content to exist and stagnate in an atmosphere of antimacassars and leather-lined armchairs stuffed with horsehair. They lived ugly lives, and their furniture was typical of them. . . . Only lately have we learnt the much-needed lesson – that neither vice nor ugliness (which is much the same thing) is a necessary part of our lives.'[59]

The war had imposed a new simplicity. Well into the 1920s, furniture was expensive – a consequence of the shift to wartime production and the inflation that followed. Even basic items such as bedsteads, carpets, and chests of drawers had tripled in cost. For the professionals of the Edwardian era who called themselves the 'new poor', the commodious houses of the past were an impossible luxury.[60] 'Mary Wylde', the pen-name of a literary Kensington housewife, insisted upon remaining in her late Georgian house, but lamented that she was the last of her friends to do so. Rising rents and the shortage of domestic servants had already conspired to drive the rest out. Most had been forced to 'squeeze themselves' into flats, and to get rid of their bulky furniture. The jam-packed interior, loaded with china and curiosities that required dusting, was a thing of the past.[61]

While the war had a sobering effect, it was not the sole agent of change. The catastrophe of 1914–18 hastened a codification of taste that was more broadly rooted. Critical to the story was the widespread diffusion of home decoration periodicals and advice manuals. No fewer than twelve new home magazines were founded in the inter-war period – some by multinational publishing empires such as Condé Nast, others by a new breed of home professional.[62] *Ideal Home* was the brainchild of an estate agent; *New House* was affiliated to a mortgage company; *House and Home* was an auxiliary of *Dalton's Weekly*, the nation's leading property advertiser. The new home magazines had a very different mission from their literary predecessors. They aimed to encourage home ownership, and sought especially to create a clientele for the Tudorbethan semi-detached houses that were springing up all over the countryside.[63] Houses, in their pages, were places for repose and a means of fitting in with one's neighbours, not beacons of originality. Where late Victorian and Edwardian consumers had taken an 'unwholesome delight in the grotesque or merely startling', the home-makers of the present day – or so the magazines proclaimed – had embraced the decorative wisdom of the ages.[64] The post-war middle class aimed to create homes that carried on the 'best English manner': 'neither brilliant nor mediocre, but solid, seemly, and distinguished'.

By contrast with the lady art advisors, the raft of home magazines founded after the First World War elevated good taste above individuality. But good taste did not require, as it had in Benn's ill-fated *House*, adherence to abstruse principles imposed by the arbiters of design reform. Rather, it was an expression of common sense – a faculty that the new periodicals confidently assumed their audience already possessed. The magazines systematized middle-class conventions under the rubric of style. They addressed their readers as informed participants, referring to standards of which 'many of us' were aware: carpets in very small rooms should be devoid of patterns; curtains should either just cover a window's woodwork or extend to the ground; patterned walls called for plain curtains, and vice versa.[65] A 'peaceful, neutral background' was the solution to most of the problems that plagued the post-war home-maker, from small rooms to the expense of refurnishing.[66]

Of course, publications such as *Ideal Home* helped to disseminate the very standards they claimed to take for granted. Inter-war magazines reserved their highest praise for simple, restful rooms in which colour was used sparingly.[67] Though 'style' was a matter of 'individual choice', acknowledged the *Ideal Home*'s Marquis d'Oisy, 'the more conventional idea . . . will, if in excellent taste, be restful and continue to give satisfaction for a lifetime'.[68] *Ideal Home*'s first serialized column was entitled 'Furnishing on Established Lines'. Readers were counselled to reckon with the realities of their situation. She who possessed only a small bedroom should not attempt anything 'out of the commonplace'. 'Striking' schemes were reserved for Mayfair's 'dignified boudoirs'; for the denizens of cottages, a grey hair carpet was appropriate.[69] Readers who asked Jack Dare, *Modern Home*'s interior decorator, to formulate colour schemes for their rooms received a palette of beiges (cream, buff, oatmeal, and linen) in response.[70]

In promulgating a decorative orthodoxy, home magazines drew upon the guidance of a novel type of expert: the interior decorator.[71] Before the First World War, the professional house decorator was a relative rarity. Most who furnished did so on their own, drawing upon advice manuals, as well as the counsel of friends, relatives, shopkeepers, and the decorators on paper. However, in the 1920s and especially

145 Understated cottage charm. A house in Hampstead Garden Suburb, 1925.

1930s, interior decoration (as the business was now known), gained new legitimacy. Unlike the lady art advisors such as Mrs Talbot Coke, who vehemently insisted upon their amateur status, interior decorators were professionals, equipped with their own language, hierarchy, and rules. The successful interior decorator possessed not just an individual, artistic flair, but a sound command of the essential principles.

Interior decoration became a fashionable trade full of headline-grabbing characters. Among the new interior decorators were society lionesses forced to turn a flair for furnishing into a livelihood. Like the famously brainy Sybil Colefax, a friend of Virginia Woolf's, they had money troubles, or, like Colefax's competitor, Syrie Maugham, they had to earn their own way because of marriages gone bad.[72] Others, such as Basil Ionides, were architects who turned to interior decoration as a full-time proposition. Many of the young men who became interior decorators were barely closeted gays. Ronald Fleming returned from the Battle of the Somme via the Paris branch of the New York School for Architecture and Decoration. Handsome and intelligent, he dressed in ready-made suits, never ate soup at dinner, and shocked the crowd at the Venice Lido when he appeared in a bathing costume without a top. Dismayed by the prospect of a varnished oak coffin, he ordered his own casket to be covered in orange-red velvet adorned with rows of small gilt nails.[73]

Despite their flashy personae, the country's leading interior decorators largely promoted conventional designs.[74] At Fortnum & Mason, and later at his own firm, Kelso, Ronald Fleming helped to define British traditionalism: chintz paired with dark woods. Though some of the best-known names experimented with tubular steel, they largely abandoned it after a few years. Colefax enshrined the country house idiom, while Syrie Maugham imported the glamour of the movies into urbane drawing-rooms.[75] Since few could afford their services, their influence was felt indirectly. Interior designers gave talks on the BBC and interviews to the home magazines.[76] All of the major furnishing emporia added an interior design department to their operations. Margaret Covell, who managed the interior design division at Peter Jones, was infamous within the trade for her lightning-quick adaptations of 'smart' fashions.[77] Prudence Maufe, her formidable counterpart at Heal's, translated Syrie Maugham's signature style into a Mansard Gallery exhibition, Whites and Off-Whites.

Books by interior designers helped to create the conventional wisdom upon which the home magazines relied. Ionides' two books – *Colour and Interior Decoration* (1926) and *Colour in Everyday Rooms* (1934) – sought to guide the amateur to a more scientific understanding of colour, complete with italicized maxims ('It is better to have good things than pretty ones') and detailed prescriptions for the perfectly colour-coordinated room.[78] According to Ionides, each colour imposed its own requirements; there was little room for individual fancy. He offered systematized colour tables to direct the novice. What suited the simple whitewashed sitting-room was not at all appropriate for a south-facing room painted lime yellow. For the humble white room, Ionides prescribed cut-glass ornaments, brown holland upholstery piped with bright yellow, cream-coloured alpaca cushions edged with gold cord, white curtains trimmed with yellow braid of artificial silk, and red charcoal drawings in pink frames.[79] The yellow sitting-room, by contrast, required old coloured Empire fashion prints, yellow glass or gilt ornaments, ivory and straw-coloured striped damask cushions, smoke-coloured curtains lined with green Japanese silk, and sage green and straw-coloured upholstery. Ionides' objective – he frankly confessed – was perfection, rather than novelty because in 'this course safety lies'.[80]

Inter-war advice manuals not only passed on conventional design wisdom, they showed their readers exactly what it looked like. When she started at *Queen*, Mrs Talbot Coke had to persuade its editors to include sketches of her arrangements. Fifty years later, the photo had become the bedrock of the home decoration industry, a practice made possible by the refinement of half-tone printing at the turn of the century.[81] Magazines courted their audiences with lavish portfolios of illustrations, and stores built their advertisements around photos. *House and Garden* ran a 'Little Portfolio of Good Interiors'; *Modern Home* countered with its coloured, drawn plates. Photos provided readers with a template that could be copied; they showed very concretely how things were to be done. The camera was, as the architect Oswald Milne saw it, a 'magic carpet' that whisked readers to the 'sanctuaries of others', where they could 'gather new ideas and see examples of the best and most modern taste'.[82] Speaking in 1934 to his fellow architects at the Royal Institute of British Architects, Edward Maufe (Prudence's husband) credited the press and secondary education with 'a levelling up – perhaps you may prefer "levelling down" of the standard of taste'.[83]

As taste was 'levelled' and homogenized, the abundance of furnishing choices once available to Victorian consumers diminished. In part, this was a function of the mechanization of the furniture industry, a process begun in the 1890s but only fully realized in the 1920s. It also reflected changes in the retailing sector. Before the First World War, the centre of gravity in the furnishing trade had belonged to the large emporia such as Maple's or Waring & Gillow in London, Christopher Pratt & Son in Bradford, and Wylie & Lockhead in Glasgow; middle-class residents of smaller towns often travelled to furnish.[84] In the 1920s and 1930s, however, these grand meccas of interior decoration were struggling.[85] At Waring & Gillow, which had staked its reputation on the artistic and the individual, the situation was dire. The last time the publisher Ernest Benn saw Samuel Waring was in 1937, when the entrepreneur, in desperate need of money, called upon his old friend to try to raise funds. Waring died deeply in debt, having lost control of the business.[86] The Slump was to blame, but so, too, was the growth of chain stores. In 1920, there were 200 branch shops, with 4 per cent of the furnishing market; by 1939, multiple stores had captured nearly 20 per cent of total sales, with 800 branches in total.[87] Establishments such as Aston & Co. offered their customers convenience and generous hire-purchase terms. The selection in their moderately sized premises, of course, could not rival that of the mammoth London stores, but they nonetheless succeeded in winning customers. From its undistinguished beginnings in Wrexham, Aston had by the 1930s grown to an empire of fourteen shops; the firm recorded its highest ever profits in the economically strapped years of 1933 and 1937.[88]

If the stores were more modest and the goods less diverse, that was a fair reflection of the customers who patronized them. The British middle class of the 1930s was markedly different from its Edwardian counterpart. It was larger, increasingly engaged in technical and scientific occupations, and more likely to work for others.[89] Laboratories and engineering plants snapped up grammar school graduates, creating professions that had not even existed three decades earlier, such as technician and draughtsman. On the eve of the First World War, the stereotypical upper middle-class man was a lawyer, a doctor, or a clergyman; by the early 1950s, the ranks of clergymen had thinned, while the numbers of engineers and science-based professionals had boomed. Whether upper or lower, the middle classes were increasingly, in the 1930s, employees. The proportion of self-employed among the middle classes declined, while the numbers of managers soared.

Measured in terms of incomes, politics, and attitudes, the British middle class of the 1920s and especially 1930s was a far more cohesive entity than had been the case in the Edwardian period. The war had accelerated the process of social levelling. Most middle-class people earned between £250 and £500 a year; however, even those who made less tended to spend their money in the same way, devoting larger sums to rent, and increasingly to mortgages, in order to live in a middle-class fashion. As salaried employees with secure jobs, middle-class Britons were spared the cyclical and structural unemployment that ravaged working-class communities. Unemployment rates for the middle class never rose above 6 per cent even in the worst years of the Slump; working-class people, by contrast, faced a one in four chance that they would lose their livelihoods. Frightened by the spectre of socialism and strikes, hunger marchers and unrest, the middle class became politically unified as well, throwing its support behind Baldwin's Conservative Party.

Above all else, though, what defined the inter-war middle class, as contemporaries saw it, was home ownership.[90] By 1939, nearly 60 per cent of middle-class families owned their own houses.[91] Very few of these new home owners had themselves been raised in home-owning families. At the turn of the twentieth century, only 10 per cent of the country's houses were owner-occupied, and most middle-class families rented their accommodation. However, by the 1920s, and especially the 1930s, the economic and social calculus had changed. A sharp fall in construction costs during the early 1930s fuelled a speculative building boom which,

146 New suburbs springing up in the countryside – Telscombe Tyle Estate, near Peacehaven, on the Sussex coast, 1931.

combined with readily accessible mortgages, made home ownership a possibility for a sizeable majority of middle-class families. Magazines such as *Modern Home, Ideal Home*, and *House and Home* catered to this market. By the outbreak of the Second World War, more than four million new houses had been built in Britain, an increase of 50 per cent on the country's entire housing stock in 1919.[92]

Both in the speculatively built 'new towns' and in towns whose suburban periphery had expanded dramatically, middle-class Britons developed new social strategies. In towns such as Hertford where large numbers of newcomers settled on the suburban edges, tensions between transplants and the older, established middle-class families could be acute. Organizations such as Masonic lodges, Rotary clubs, women's institutes, and chambers of commerce grew rapidly during this period because they provided a 'neutral' meeting-place where a town's middle-class residents could mingle. In the 'new towns', the situation was different, though the solution was similar. There, everyone was a transplant, either from the North or from more proximate town centres, whose decaying housing stock could not rival the amenities on offer in the suburbs. The social life they cultivated tended to downplay religion, which had fractured the pre-war middle classes, in favour of depoliticized associations such as sporting clubs or Masonic lodges. In both cases, observes the historian Ross McKibbin, a new brand of sociability took hold, aimed at 'the elimination of tension and anxiety from personal relations by the elimination of anything which seemed aggressive or caused "embarrassment".[93] Smoothing over potential conflict required a good sense of humour and a willingness to adhere to standards of decorum.

Avoiding embarrassment necessitated, above all, caution. Hence the emphasis on good taste and 'quiet' or 'neutral' décor.[94] The Tudor-style dining-room fitted with oak furniture, oatmeal-coloured walls, and linen curtains was the decorative analogue to a safe repertoire of conversational topics.[95] The possessor of an *outré* room filled with eccentric objects, by contrast, was someone who might initiate conversations about sex or religion. *Modern Home* advised its readers to examine their furniture with a 'cold and critical eye', as if they were 'a stranger seeing it for the first time'.[96] This was a point of view that both the stores and the advice literature urged. Advertisements took the form of overheard conversations – 'Joan has such good taste' – in order to remind potential customers that they were the subject of constant scrutiny.[97] Oatmeal-coloured walls indicated that a person knew the conventions. Tubular steel signalled a dangerous disregard for the feelings of one's visitors.

147 'Appropriate' furnishing, as prescribed by the decorating manual, *Furnishing and Refurnishing* in 1938.

It just isn't appropriate to have a bed like this in cottages. And that means it's in bad taste.

Caution encouraged uniformity. By the 1930s, middle-class style meant plain furnishings constructed of natural timbers, 'quiet' walls, pastel-coloured carpets, and soft furnishings, which were either unpatterned, or decorated with small, formal motifs. Colour was to be added in 'touches' – through a brilliant purple candlestick or a discreet statue placed upon a table.[98] Sidney Campion – child of the proletariat and a self-made journalist and barrister – learned about these middle-class mores when he moved his family to the prosperous suburbs. For years Campion had dreamt about living in a 'Temple of Colour'. As a first step, he wall-papered his kitchen in pale peach with an apple-green dado. Undeterred by the horrified response of friends and neighbours, he chose three colours for the lounge: sunshine yellow, pale pink and pale blue, which he supplemented with a satin wall-paper trim.[99]

Under the broad rubric of middle-class style, there were of course important differences of type.[100] Urban sophisticates were more likely to enliven their neutral décor with 'amusing' touches, such as Victorian papier-mâché trays or metal-legged dressing-stools, while the residents of the new suburbs opted for more standard Jacobean-flavoured rooms. The 'intellectual customer', advised one trade journal, was the most difficult to cater for. Intellectuals liked to think that they were different from other people: 'Never tell an intellectual what other people are buying, or what other people like.'[101] In a sea of conformity, the unique decorative scheme became a badge of honour for people who repudiated bourgeois mores. The actress Colette O'Niel lived out the 1930s in a rustic cottage located in Blagdon on Mendip, complete with a bedroom in a converted hayloft, scented by incense dispensed from a filigree silver censer.[102] The painter W.B.E. Rankin decorated his dining-room with black varnished walls and white paintwork.[103]

But these differences within the bourgeoisie paled in comparison to the broad consensus of style that bound them together. The advice offered by upscale maga-zines such as *Ideal Home* or *House and Garden* did not differ significantly from the decorating tips retailed by more modest periodicals such as *Home Furnisher* or *Modern Home*. Both extolled the virtues in 'well-made simplicity', echoing the language in which retailers catering to middle-class customers advertised their products. Solids were preferable to patterns (except sedate chintzes), woods to metal, restraint over ostentation; the sufficient took precedence over superfluity. So similar had suburban tastes become, judged Osbert Lancaster, that the distinctions between the stockbroker and the clerk were, by the 1930s, 'all quantitative not qual-itative. One lived in a gabled mansion standing in its own ground at Sunningdale, the other in a semi-detached villa at Mitcham, but both residences were bogus Elizabethan and both householders caught the 8.28 every morning.'[104]

Margaret Bulley's *Have You Good Taste?* (1933) exemplified the new consensus of the 1930s.[105] Inspired by the psychology of aesthetics, Bulley, a pioneer in the field

148 Mrs Holman's
living room in the new
suburb of Rottingdean,
1932.

149 Which chair is in
good taste? The one on
the right, according to
Margaret Bulley's *Have
You Good Taste?* (1933).

of art education, assembled nineteen matched pairs of household objects, including chairs, teapots, jars, and bookcases, in styles that ran the gamut from Persian medievalism to tubular steel. With the assistance of Cyril Burt, professor of psychology at the University of London, Bulley's paired photographs became the subject of an experiment carried out by the BBC and its magazine, *The Listener*. Readers were called upon to make their own selections of the 'better' and 'worse' objects solely on the basis of the pictures, without reference either to provenance or price. Six thousand members of the British public, drawn from all walks of life, responded to Bulley's test.

Of course, the test depended on an 'expert' determination as to which choice was actually better. Bulley had her own ideas. Good taste, as she saw it, was not simply a matter of the 'set standards' that Cole and his ilk had urged, but required the 'discernment, even if faint, of a living principle'. It could be learned. She rejected both function and expense as absolute tests. A machine-moulded wine glass could achieve grace where the hand-blown object failed. At the same time, however, Bulley's principles did not admit of relativism. The scion of a prominent Congregationalist family, she brought a 'moral purpose' to her writings.[106] The hierarchies between objects were fixed; to have good taste meant to prefer the severe early eighteenth-century armchair to a gilded, heavily ornamented French production. The six art critics to whom Bulley submitted her choices agreed with her unanimously – and so, it turned out, did the vast majority of the British middle class.

If good taste was in theory open to all, the BBC's survey demonstrated to whom it was most likely, *circa* 1933, to belong. Beneficiaries of a university education 'were distinctly superior in taste', noted Cyril Burt, to those who had only attended elementary school. The chauffeurs, gardeners, fishmongers, and waitresses who wrote in to express their preferences were more likely to favour the 'worse' objects over the 'better' ones. Women had better taste than men, artists had worse taste than art critics, and psychologists (with the exception of Burt himself) had the best taste of all of the professionals. But most remarkable of all was the homogeneity that Bulley's survey had elicited. Nearly 75 per cent of the answers submitted were correct. Given that the 'educated sections' of the populace were over-represented and the working-class respondents fared poorly, more than 80 per cent of the BBC's middle-class audience may have manifested 'good taste'. The experiment proved, wrote the art historian Alan Francis Clutton-Brock, that there was 'at the present time . . . an educated standard of taste which is not entirely capricious or confined to individual judgments'.[107]

Design reformers such as Henry Cole would have reckoned such results a triumph. Long mired in a morass of bad taste, the British middle classes – satisfied readers of Bulley might have concluded – had emerged from the spell cast by the quaint and eccentric to embrace a more coherent and pleasing aesthetic. Whether

good taste could be disseminated more broadly, however, was a different question.[108] Despite her oft-professed belief that taste could be learned, Bulley herself
was not an easy guide. She spoke in abstractions, favouring 'organic unity',
'rhythmic relationship', and 'emotional directness' while damning pomposity and
the 'dissipation of energy'. Burt, meanwhile, was a convinced eugenicist, who
believed in the heritability of IQ.[109] The evanescent quality of inter-war good taste
excluded the uninitiated more effectively than had the design reformers' arcane
rules.

As individuality lost ground to good taste, the inter-war aesthetic landscape
narrowed. Rooms still expressed personalities, but the range of expression had
become more limited. Writing in the women's magazine *Eve*, the journalist Julia
Cairns sought to reconcile the seemingly contradictory dictates of self-expression
and style: 'At times you feel it very strongly this ability to permeate your own
personality through the furnishing effects of various rooms. And this is the reason
why Fashion demands simplicity, therefore you need in no way forsake her.'[110]
Personality, in other words, did not require originality, as the lady art advisors had
once insisted. Rather, personality could be accommodated within the principles of
fashion, the dictates of good taste – and the standards of one's class. In inter-war
Britain, fitting in was more important than standing out.

* * *

The most popular picture at the 1940 Royal Academy was the work of an unrecon-
structed Victorian. Entitled *There'll Always Be an England*, Charles Spencelayh's
painting depicts a pipe-smoking older man comfortably ensconced in a modest
sitting-room. The man's furniture is old-fashioned; a grandfather clock presides
over the disarray. His walls are hung thickly with pictures, the surfaces of his tables
are crowded with a jumbled assortment of objects, including a tea caddy, a globe,
and a stuffed bird under a glass dome. In an artistic era defined by abstraction, the
seventy-five-year-old Spencelayh, a former miniaturist, was resolutely old-fashioned.
Other than a calendar with a picture of George VI on the wall and an air warden kit,
there is little to identify the setting as a mid-twentieth-century scene.

Although the inter-war middle classes had, by and large, rejected the 'Age of
Bric à Brac', after a year of war the reign of Victoria no doubt struck a nostalgic
chord. Perhaps the quintessence of England was, after all, an overcrowded Victorian
sitting-room.[111] Aerial bombardment destroyed or rendered unusable nearly half a
million (or two in every seven) houses in Britain; many more were significantly
damaged. Sixty thousand Britons died in air-raids on the Home Front; another
million and a half were left homeless. Suffering and material privation became the
common lot. Shortly after he won the Royal Academy prize, Spencelayh's own house
in Lee was destroyed by bombers. Three storeys high, the dwelling was packed full
of nineteenth-century furniture and curios. There were grandfather clocks on each

landing (six in total), walking-sticks and umbrellas, oil lamps, stuffed animals in glass cases, tattered silk top hats, and a room devoted exclusively to metal and china jugs. Seven removal vans had been required to transport Spencelayh's belongings to the house in 1937. After the bomb, the Spencelayhs fitted all of their treasures into three.[112]

Amid the turmoil and sacrifices of the war, possessions became both less and more important to their owners. The rationing of even basic foodstuffs made the furnishing frivolities of the past seem almost unimaginable. 'Your black-out curtains need not be ugly,' advised *Ideal Home* optimistically in November 1939.[113] The long-trumpeted glories of redecoration disappeared from the pages of home magazines, which emphasized instead, on cheap regulation paper, the patriotic virtues of making do. 'Self-expression in small ways stopped,' wrote Elizabeth Bowen of wartime life. 'You used to know what you were like from the things you liked, and chose. Now there was not what you liked, and you did not choose.' And

150 Charles Spencelayh, *There'll Always Be An England*, 1940.

yet, Bowen observed, belongings – because they represented a time lost – simultaneously gained in significance. 'People whose homes had been blown up went to infinite lengths to assemble bits of themselves – broken ornaments, odd shoes, torn scraps of the curtains that had hung in a room – from the wreckage.'[114] Lives were turned into tangible bits and pieces that could be salvaged from bomb craters or smuggled across the border. Refugees from Nazi-occupied Europe arrived in Britain with battered suitcases that contained the last material remnants of a civilized existence.

151 A bedroom in the Midlands after a night raid, 21 November 1940.

Syrie Maugham had fled Paris in advance of the German army. Years later, her friend Beverley Nichols wondered what had become of the striking furnishings she had assembled at her villa in Le Touquet. One item in particular – an enormous screen composed of thin, slatted strips of mirrors, the centrepiece of Syrie's all-white decorative scheme – haunted his memory. Syrie was long since dead, but that mirrored screen was so much like her. It recalled a childhood of evangelical stringency that had yielded a career dedicated to the pursuit of beauty and fortune; it reflected the long, and sometimes tormented, road from sin to self-expression that Syrie had travelled alongside many of her fellow Britons. The mirrored screen put Nichols in mind of an altar, in whose recesses 'there must linger, however faintly, the essence of the prayers that have drifted round it through the ages'. But there was, he hastened to add, a crucial difference: 'No prayers were offered to the mirrored screen; of all decorations it was the most blatantly secular.'[115]

The mid-Victorian collision of piety and material prosperity that underlay Syrie Maugham's career had paradoxical consequences. To reconcile good with abundance, taste was recast as a moral necessity, and, later, as an artistic accomplishment. Under the guidance of Mrs Talbot Coke and the lady art advisors, the home – once a site for instilling the virtues of self-restraint and humility – became a stage for self-fulfilment. After the First World War, Mrs Coke's son Desmond recollected the best advice his mother had given him: 'It'll only be the things you resist that you'll ever regret.'[116] That supremely materialistic, even licentious sentiment was, he recognized, likely to shock old-fashioned moralists (especially coming from a mother to a son), but it summarized his mother's experience. By the 1930s, the moral restraints that had plagued Britons a century earlier no longer pricked most people's consciences. But that did not mean that unfettered self-expression had won out. What to Mrs Coke had seemed an infinitely capacious arena for individualistic display had become instead a place to demonstrate how little we differ from the people next door.

EPILOGUE
YOUR NEIGHBOUR'S HOUSE

A visitor to Britain at the start of the twenty-first century might well have concluded that the age of unrestrained materialism and self-expression had at last arrived. The Reverend Mark Rylands certainly thought so when he railed against his fellow citizens' godless obsession with home improvement.[1] Britain was in the midst of a boom in prosperity every bit as remarkable as the one that had propelled the Victorians down the road to modern consumer society in the mid-nineteenth century. The property market was roaring; a new generation of home decoration mavens – in glossy magazines, furnishing manuals, newspaper supplements, DIY superstores, but most insistently, on the television – had sprung up to advise buyers and renovators. Peak-time television schedules were clogged with programmes about houses and homes. On any given week in 2003, ten separate shows vied for audiences in the coveted 8–10 p.m. slot. Home renovation, DIY disasters, construction projects, and property transactions became the subject of half-hour, and then one-hour-long shows. Newly launched property programmes attracted two million viewers, while established shows could count on audiences of three to six million.[2] The public's appetite appeared insatiable.

The boom of the late 1990s fuelled Britain's obsession with home in ways that could not have been imagined even a few decades before. The consumer extravaganza that deluged the United States in the aftermath of the Second World War had arrived on Britain's shores in greatly reduced form. The austerity of the late 1940s and early 1950s – emblematized by the evangelical vegetarian Sir Stafford Cripps, Labour Chancellor of the Exchequer – did eventually give way by the mid-1950s to an era of comparative affluence.[3] However, this was still a relatively modest phenomenon. In 1965, less than a quarter of the nation's households had a telephone; 21.9 per cent still lacked a hot-water tap.[4] While sales of consumer durables drifted upwards in the 1960s and 1970s, they still lagged behind the gains posted in North America, Germany, and Japan.[5] Meanwhile, rates of home ownership had largely stalled. In 1980, just 55 per cent of Britons owned their own houses.

In the past two decades, by contrast, rates of home ownership have surged to 71 per cent.[6] Much of that gain came in the 1980s, as Mrs Thatcher, trumpeting the notion of a 'property-owning democracy', sought to consolidate the Conservative Party's base. The boomlet of the 1980s soon disappeared into the recession of the early 1990s. But the consumer extravaganza that followed in the last decade has been unprecedented both in size and in longevity. Between 1997 and 2004, consumer spending rose a whopping 27 per cent.[7] Items such as cars, washing machines, and personal computers – once undreamt-of luxuries – are today's necessities. Among the country's upper echelons, the rise in wealth has been especially notable. In 2003, 5.6 million Britons lived in detached houses, an increase of nearly a million on the previous decade.[8] Of new houses built today, 34 per cent have four or more bedrooms, as opposed to 7 per cent in 1971.[9] According to recent surveys, nearly 60 per cent of Britons now identify themselves as middle class.[10] This is the public who tunes in nightly to watch other people grapple with the burdens and glories of home ownership.

If any one person can be held responsible for the explosion in home programming, it is Ben Frow. A commissioning editor at Channel Four, now the head of features and entertainment at Channel Five, Frow has an uncanny sense of what the British public wants to watch in the evening. Unlike politicians or toothpaste manufacturers, who test the choppy waters of public opinion with market research and focus groups, Frow commissions only what he himself wants to see.[11] Within the trade, Frow's 'gut instinct', paired with his undeniable success, has made the forty-five-year old something of a mythical figure.[12] Frow can take credit for some of the biggest television hits of the past decade.[13] The domestic goddess Nigella Lawson owes her television career to him, and the bad-boy celebrity chef Jamie Oliver his rehabilitation. Frow made not only dirty houses (*How Clean is Your House?*), but also plastic surgery (*Cosmetic Surgery Live*) the stuff of prime-time viewing. Above all else, however, he is television's 'Mr Property', at the forefront of a tidal wave of property programming.[14] Working with a handful of independent television producers, Frow turned a hunch about Britons' obsession with their houses into a new television genre.

And yet, as Frow ruefully acknowledges, his instincts about taste extend only so far. He might know what the public wants, but when it comes to his own house, the man with an unerring eye for good television is prone to doubt and even a measure of self-loathing. The producer John Silver recalls an editing session with Frow for *Other People's Houses*, a programme that dissected British domestic taste. The subject was the choice of paint colour in the bathroom; Naomi Cleaver, the show's acerbic presenter, advised against cream. Frow, Silver remembers, put his head in his hands: 'Oh, God, I was up at six o'clock this morning painting my bathroom cream. I'm going to have go back and re-do it.'[15] Preoccupied by the house, Frow fears making a mistake. The 'world's biggest buyer of sofas', Frow always wants, by his own admission, 'what he doesn't have'.[16]

By commissioning on the basis of his own anxieties, Ben Frow caught the Zeitgeist. But what exactly was that Zeitgeist? In the late 1980s, a new generation of magazines had resuscitated the old idea that home was the place to express one's individuality. The barrage of competing television shows, one might logically assume, would have accelerated the trend towards self-differentiation by showcasing a wide variety of furnishing styles. But the explosion of property programming seems to have had precisely the opposite effect. In Britain today, houses are no longer just homes. They are property – in other words, investments. With the extraordinary inflation of the housing market and the decline in pension funds, houses have become the single most important asset that most Britons possess.[17] That fact alone might have encouraged conservative decorating choices. But by holding a mirror up to the nation's domestic landscape, television shows have instilled a new sort of self-consciousness in their viewers. Bombarded by programmes that depict cluttered dwellings and garishly coloured sitting-rooms decorated in the name of 'personality', viewers naturally begin to wonder how their own homes would measure up if viewed through television's unforgiving eye. As sales of neutral paint colours soar, it seems as if the British populace has opted for the same solution as the inter-war middle classes: safety first.

* * *

Before Frow and his cohort entered the picture, a television series that followed ordinary people as they attempted to sell a house would hardly have seemed promising subject-matter for prime-time viewing. Voyeurism was restricted to the homes of the rich and famous. *Through the Keyhole*, which toured the homes of second-rank celebrities, made its début in 1983.[18] With its jocular look at the properties of grandees, the show summed up the aspirational flavour of Mrs Thatcher's Britain. Home improvement was, with the exception of the pioneering Barry Bucknell, daytime television. Bucknell's *Do It Yourself*, which debuted in 1958, was Britain's first home renovation programme. It was practical, rather than fashionable. Bucknell's viewers were drawn from the very large numbers who wished to modernize their houses but could not afford the services of professionals.[19] Every week Bucknell offered tips about mending taps and hanging wallpaper, building bookshelves and managing dry rot. In 1962–3, Bucknell renovated for the cameras a dilapidated house in West Ealing; over the course of 39 weeks, *Bucknell's House* attracted a viewing audience of 5.5 million.[20]

By the 1990s, television had changed, but so, too, had the consumer landscape. What would affluence and a larger middle class mean for the nation's home owners?[21] The waning years of Thatcherism had produced two different answers.

In 1989 a new home magazine, *House Beautiful*, was launched into a market that had been stagnant since the inter-war period. A year earlier, there were just six titles, with the old standard-bearers of good taste, *Ideal Home* and *Homes and Gardens* at the head of the pack.[22] *House Beautiful* reflected a different idea; it harked back to the spirit of the lady art advisors. The magazine was 'designed for those intending to stamp their personality on their home but who need a helping hand'; according to its editor, Pat Roberts, it would show 'genuine empathy'.[23] At 90 pence, *House Beautiful* aimed for the mass market of suburban estate houses that the other periodicals had neglected. The homes it showcased were ordinary dwellings. Roberts' approach was 'democratic', notes Isobel McKenzie-Price, editorial director of the magazine giant IPC's home titles from 1999 to 2004: 'You don't have to look like a stately home or even a mini version of a stately home. . . . Just be yourself.'[24] Within two years, *House Beautiful* had become the best-selling home magazine in Britain.[25]

If *House Beautiful* stood for the proposition (as McKenzie-Price puts it) that 'You could be suburban and like it and that was fine', Martin Parr's *Signs of the Times* was much less sanguine. In 1990, Parr, a leading realist photographer, and Nicholas Barker, a BBC documentary producer, journeyed through Britain to document domestic taste. What they found was pathos. Self-delusion vied with fear and pomposity for the soul of Britain's home owners. Every suburban estate was full of people who thought that they had the best house in the neighbourhood.[26] Many – like the woman who deployed paper doilies around her relentlessly contemporary light switches in pursuit of a 'cottagey stately home kind of feel' – floundered in the grip of a misguided nostalgia.[27] Caught between the promise of upward mobility and the harsh realities of ordinariness, the British were beset by anxieties, eager to be 'a little bit different' but desperate, too, to fit in.[28] 'Taste,' Barker claimed, 'is all about embarrassment.'[29]

At the time, critics wondered whether *Signs of the Times* had not overplayed the pathos of its subjects' lives.[30] Parr and Barker – members of the upper middle class – surely found the taste of their subjects embarrassing, but did that mean that middle Britain was mired in a state of self-deception? After all, *House Beautiful*'s editor had struck a gold mine with a magazine that 'celebrated being ordinary'.[31] Roberts' insight was 'revolutionary', claims McKenzie-Price. By catering for its readers' taste rather than seeking to elevate it, *House Beautiful* reoriented the market. Magazines such as *Ideal Home* did not know what to make of the upstart: 'The big boys were really confused, but everyone else started pitching in and launching new magazines.'[32] Very quickly, the market segmented, based upon careful research into readers' desires. For those who liked the rustic look, there was *Country Living*; for those who wanted a more modern look, *Living, etc.* was born; readers with low budgets turned to *Homes and Ideas*. Whatever your preference, the

152 A stately light
switch from Martin
Parr and Nicholas
Barker, *Signs of the
Times*, 1992.

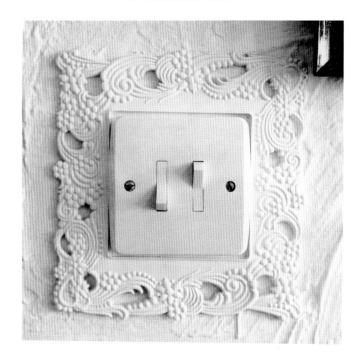

We wanted a cottagey
stately home kind of feel

message was similar: home was a place to express your personality. By the end of the
1990s, there were thirty-five home titles.[33]

The home television shows that began appearing in the 1990s adopted neither
Parr's grim view of British consumers nor the magazines' happy espousal of the
personality ideal. Rather, capitalizing on the fad for reality programming, they
made drama out of the dilemma of self-expression: the pain or pleasure of 'just
being yourself' before a viewing audience of millions.[34] *Changing Rooms*, the first
of a new breed of home programmes, débuted on BBC2 in 1994. Its premise was
simple. Each week, two couples – neighbours or friends – redecorated a room in
each other's homes. Based upon their knowledge of the other couple, and aided
by the show's own designers, they decided on a suitable scheme. It was a set-up
rife with the possibility of insult. Rather than quietly reading someone's personality from their home, you were supposed to create a room that you believed
they would appreciate, with all of the dangerous judgements that exercise
entailed. The personality optic had been reversed. Did your neighbours really
believe that your taste ran to a bright red living-room with zebra-patterned

panels? And if so, why did they think your home life would best be conducted (as one indignant owner complained) in a 'whore's palace'?[35] What had you done to convey that impression?

Three years later, *Changing Rooms* was garnering 6.9 million viewers weekly – beating both BBC1 News and ITV Drama.[36] Transferred the following year to BBC1, the programme regularly captured 30 per cent of the evening's viewers.[37] On Christmas Day 1998 it attracted an audience of 12 million.[38] Why the show succeeded was a subject of debate. Like other reality television shows, it offered titillating human spectacle, all the more spell-binding when the programme's participants departed from ordinary 'Mediterranean' schemes to embrace more daring makeovers.[39] Some people undoubtedly took away new decorating tips, learning how coffee-tables could be made from medium-density fibreboard, and unsightly walls rag-rolled into oblivion.[40] But lurking always below the surface was the possibility of disaster and raw emotion. There was more than a little *Schadenfreude* at work: 'Watching someone's snug corner of suburbia turn into some horrendous take on an airline toilet is totally compulsive.'[41]

When *Changing Rooms* first went on air, remembers Isobel McKenzie-Price, the editors of home magazines were thrilled. If interior decoration was prime-time television, that had to redound to the glossies' benefit. In the beginning, it seemed to be working that way. Makeover shows helped to propel consumers into the DIY stores, and, in the late 1990s, had boosted the sale of bright, strong colours.[42] And yet, the magazines' market research increasingly showed that *Changing Rooms*, and the makeover programmes that followed, were 'really turning consumers off'.[43] Those who had tried to replicate the quick fixes shown on *Changing Rooms* or BBC2's *Home Front* soon discovered that what looked good on television appeared shoddy under closer scrutiny.[44] Moreover, seeing other people's ludicrous schemes played out on television inhibited experimentation. The Chamber of Horrors was now on constant display in people's living-rooms. The indiscriminate use of MDF, the exotic colours, the kitschy ideas: eventually, notes McKenzie-Price, 'nobody wanted to be associated with it'.

Changing Rooms' flamboyant designer, Laurence Llewelyn-Bowen, came to personify everything that was wrong with makeover television.[45] Dressed in leather trousers, hunting jackets in shades of fuchsia velvet, and jewel-toned shirts with outsize cuffs, Llewelyn-Bowen was the small screen's Oscar Wilde. His schemes were outrageous, his sexuality was playfully indeterminate, and the papers could always count on him for a *bon mot*.[46] According to Llewelyn-Bowen, the Victorian 'design-o-saurs' – and especially John Ruskin '(boohiss, by the way)' – had discouraged the common man from expressing his individuality.[47] He, by contrast, advocated 'design democracy'. The encroachments of ghastly good taste threatened; the British eccentric needed preserving.[48] Llewelyn-Bowen lived in a 1920s suburban bungalow in Blackheath whose interior was 'inspired by Le Corbusier, with random holes in its walls', and filled with 'Peter Greenawayesque still lifes of apples and things': 'I want people to feel as though they might bump into Margaret Rutherford or Noel Coward at any minute'.[49]

As *Changing Rooms* entered its fifth season, Llewelyn-Bowen's optimism about the public's latent individualism looked increasingly misplaced.[50] Survey after survey revealed that the majority of householders would not allow the show's designers into their house.[51] Efforts to produce a book based on the series ran into difficulties, since many couples hastened to redecorate as soon as the cameras were out the door.[52] The BBC itself began to retreat from makeover shows. Compared with soaps or news programmes, series such as *Changing Rooms* were very cheap to produce; for the price of a single half-hour sitcom, the BBC could afford six episodes of *Changing Rooms*.[53] Still, the BBC's executives began to feel uneasy about the pride of place that makeover shows had in the broadcaster's schedules. On his appointment to the chairmanship of the BBC in 2001, Gavyn Davies promised an end to the reign of makeover television.[54]

As makeover television slowly declined (*Home Front* was finally axed in 2003, and *Changing Rooms* in 2004), a new genre – the property programme – was born. On the makeover shows, home owners were often overshadowed by the designers' antics. Property programming, by contrast, put the lives of ordinary people at the heart of the action.[55] Gone were the outlandish designers and their 'creative solutions' with MDF; enter a fleet of real-estate professionals with genuine expertise to offer a television audience. Property shows followed their 'contributors' in the process of buying, selling, or building houses. At the centre of the phenomenon were Channel Four and Ben Frow, who took advantage of the BBC's departure from the prime-time homes market. Between 2000 and 2002, Channel Four launched a raft of new shows: *Grand Designs* (people building their dream house); *Location, Location, Location* and *Relocation, Relocation* (buying one house and two houses, respectively); *From House to Home* (a gutted house remodelled on television); *Other People's Houses* (a programme about taste and renovation); and *Property Ladder* (how to make money from your property). Channel Five countered with *House Doctor*, a programme which featured an American real-estate agent who transformed hard-to-sell houses with a few tricks of the trade.

From the start, the impresarios of property programming were determined to set themselves apart from *Changing Room* and its ilk. 'Everything we did we did against that,' says John Silver of *Grand Designs*. 'We had Laurence Llewelyn-Bowen as our antichrist.'[56] Where *Changing Rooms* was 'like a kids' art programme', Hamish Barbour, producer of *Location, Location, Location*, describes his programmes as 'specifically bolted to the commercial reality'.[57] Authenticity is the key. At the heart of property programmes are narratives about real-life dilemmas and genuine people – as Silver puts it, 'you have to be able to see yourself in the central character'. The success of the shows hinges upon that identification. People who are too bland, Barbour has found, do not elicit strong emotions in the viewer. He urges his team to get guests 'who make them slightly nervous. You want people to be infuriating, to change their mind': 'If I'm not yelling at the screen, then there's something wrong.'

Though the property programmes play on some of the same sorts of emotions as *Changing Rooms* – Schadenfreude chief among them – they depend upon a more complex brand of voyeurism. They call upon the viewer to make constant judgements. You are to compare yourself with that week's guest, for better or for worse. Shows such as *Grand Designs*, Frow points out, provoke viewers to think 'if they can do it I can do it' or, 'All that money, all that architect, and they still built a horrible house. Eww, God, that kitchen is disgusting, isn't it? . . . God, I hate their sofa. Oh, I wouldn't have painted the front door that colour.' Either way, 'there's always a judgement'.[58] In this maelstrom of judgement, the show's presenters provide the ballast of expertise. At the end of each episode of *Grand Designs*, the show's genial presenter, Kevin McCloud, renders his own verdict on the house. Viewers, say Barbour and Silver, like to hear what the experts have to say. They might even adjust their own predispositions to harmonize with the presenter's opinions. According to John Silver, viewers often unconsciously echo McCloud's conclusions: 'They come up to you the next day . . . and say what Kevin has just said on the programme. But they own it, they like it. It's like that thing in a movie when you know more than a character knows about their situation.'

Property shows derive their drama from the gap between aspiration and realization: between what the guests hope to achieve and what the audience sees on the screen. This is the tension that drives the narrative. In spite of a stated desire to turn a profit, the people who appear on *Property Ladder* proceed with renovations that are unlikely to add value to their property. The contributors to *Location, Location, Location* often buy very different houses than they said they wanted. On *House Doctor*, hapless home owners explain their decorative rationale to the show's straight-talking estate agent, Ann Maurice, who swiftly pricks the bubble of their self-delusion. Videotaped segments, which feature potential buyers touring the house 'before' Maurice arrives on the scene, demonstrate just how appalling individual taste can be. Bedroom walls carpeted in pink shag, a flourish the house's owners find cosy, is anathema to would-be buyers.[59] A prized collection of Dresden dolls winking from every available surface is simply weird.

Personality, as it plays on property programmes, is a much more complicated matter than the home magazines acknowledge. A house decorated in the name of self-expression is more likely to be off-putting than appealing. Moreover, people who seek to express themselves often end up telling the world more than they intended. After watching a few property shows, it is difficult not to feel self-conscious about one's own decisions. Perhaps that tropical-themed sitting-room wasn't such a good idea after all. Ben Frow acknowledges that he has internalized the perspective of a vulnerable television viewer. His own house, he says, is 'all about what other people think': 'I'm not brave enough to have a house that reflects my personality. I have a house that reflects who I would like people to think I am.' Frow doesn't 'know any more' what he would do if he were braver. 'I always go back to Martha Stewart,' he says. 'I always go back to those greys and greens, and big windows and old furniture and scrubbed floors, and stuff, and lovely big bunches of flowers in jugs.' His own house, by contrast, is 'all white, white, white'.[60]

While Frow's décor is undoubtedly more refined than that of the vast majority of Britons, in his embrace of neutrals and streamlined furnishings he nonetheless resembles his fellow citizens. In 2003, bright colours lost 7 per cent of their market share, while magnolia paint strengthened its grip on the nation's dwellings; in 2005, sales of magnolia increased by 25 per cent from the previous year.[61] According to a host of critics, British homes are quickly becoming indistinguishable. Pale wood floors, furniture with clean lines: 'there is a dispiriting uniformity about it all'. The *Independent*'s Nick Foulkes claims to be 'one of the few people I know who lives amid old-fashioned clutter'.[62] In the *Sunday Times*, India Knight mourned the end of an era of 'swirls and flounces and nylony froufrou'. The owners of these things 'knew what they liked, and if they liked swirly carpet and salmon pink and ugly china figurines, then, really, so what? At least there was a bit of passion in their decorating choices.'[63] At least half of the houses for sale, claimed the *Mirror* in 2005, had been 'blanded over'.[64]

The 'blandification' of the British home is in part a consequence of the huge rise in property prices. Conceiving of your house as an investment discourages risk-taking. According to the *Daily Telegraph*, Ann Maurice of Channel 5's *House Doctor* has persuaded the 'nation to trade personality for profit by rebranding their homes an inoffensive shade of bland. . . .'[65] Even those who have no intention of selling have been converted to neutrals. The journalist Edel Morgan blames the property shows. 'There was a time when we were left to commit serial style misdemeanours and live with them in blissful oblivion'. Television has changed all that. As a parade of horribles marches across the small screen, home owners cling to the new buzz words, 'restraint and economy of style'. But now we 'are all so familiar with the "identikit look" that we could do it in our sleep'. What we need is 'a bit of glorious bad taste'.[66]

What critics view as dangerous homogenization the creators of property programming see as much-needed democratization. Daisy Goodwin, producer of *House Doctor* and *Grand Designs*, calls her shows 'educative', by which she means that they 'inform as well as entertain'.[67] Hamish Barbour says that he hopes his shows have 'armed people with the things they need to know': 'I like to think that we are empowering people.'[68] However self-serving such statements might at first seem, they gain credibility by comparison. A useful contrast is the radio series the BBC broadcast in 1971, *What's in a Room*. The series editors aimed to teach the 'principles of interior design'. But since 'rules alone are dull and lifeless without ideas to accompany them', they turned to 'our English country houses' for illumination.[69] The Elizabethan great hall of the Yorkshire manor house Burton Agnes highlighted the importance of a focal point, while Inigo Jones' magnificent double cube room at Wilton House demonstrated the virtues of a symmetrical scheme. To the listener who tuned in for guidance on the decoration of a suburban living-room, Wilton House's lessons were – to say the least – beside the point.

Implicit in the idea of democratization, of course, is the idea that viewers have something to learn. To some, that smacks of the same sort of condescension that underlay Martin Parr's *Signs of the Times*. And yet, the producers of the property programmes reject the idea they they followed in Parr's footsteps. *Signs of the Times* was 'very cold . . . and quite manipulative', says John Silver; Hamish Barbour thought the series 'unbelievably pompous'. By contrast, Silver and Barbour said, property shows address universal human needs and desires. Their goal is to reach the broadest audience possible. They are not aiming only for ABC1s (the non-manual working segment of the population), nor for the lucrative advertising market represented by eighteen- to thirty-four-year olds. Rather, as Silver points out, 'our business is hits, and hits mean lots of eyeballs'. Beyond a vague sense that their shows are 'aspirational', they hardly ever consider the class dimensions of property programming.

Still, it is surely relevant that many of the show's creators come from families who understood the meaning of ghastly good taste. Nearly all are the products of an upper middle-class background; some are the children of design professionals. Daisy Goodwin's mother is the noted interior decorator Jocasta Innes, while Zad Rogers, Barbour's business partner, is the son of the renowned architect Richard Rogers. This is not to say that they all necessarily agree as to what should be done. For instance, Silver views himself as a relativist on matters of taste, where Goodwin believes in 'absolute rules'.[70] They are not, at least not consciously, seeking to establish themselves as taste-makers. On the contrary, they are well aware of the arrogance of that role. 'You need to show people the best,' said *Grand Designs*' Kevin McCloud, but then added quickly, 'I sound very Reithian, don't I . . . ?'[71]

Given the massive viewership that the home programmes have attracted, it seems likely that they have at least in part fulfilled the edifying function that their producers intended. To some extent, mass entertainment has helped to reshuffle the old class deck.[72] As the numbers of first-time home buyers swell, the television programmes are there to help viewers navigate the financial perils of the property market. Styles that were formerly the exclusive property of a narrow segment of the British population have been projected into the homes of all who own a television. In a society still regulated by the intricate micropolitics of class behaviour – where the choice of 'settee' or 'sofa', 'lounge' or 'sitting-room', exposes a speaker as a member of the middle-middle or upper-middle class – television programmes have served to blur some distinctions among the broad swathe of people who can afford to spend money on their homes.[73] An investment banker might choose a vintage Conran sofa in white, while his secretary splurges on a white sofa from Ikea. To the untrained eye, the two sofas may not look all that different.[74] If homogenization is the result, perhaps that is the inevitable consequence of an expanded middle class.[75]

And yet one wonders, too, to what extent middle-class anxieties have been democratized alongside middle-class styles. If neither God nor Henry Cole today regulates what the British have in their houses, there is an arguably more effective force at work: the internalized glare of public scrutiny. Through the medium of television, attention to the judgements of one's friends and neighbours – the same standard of good taste which *Ideal Home* urged upon its readers in the 1920s and 1930s – has been magnified thousand-fold. When good taste is as important a means of claiming middle-class identity as occupation or heredity, mistakes carry a high price. 'Safety first', now as in the inter-war period, is the best precaution against getting it wrong.

The secret behind Ben Frow's success may be that he understands only too well how judgements about other people's taste have a tendency to come home to roost in one's own, heightened self-consciousness. Sometimes Frow wishes he were free of the inhibitions that have, in his career, served him so well. He thinks it a 'great shame' that he isn't bold enough to attempt his longed-for Martha Stewart interior. In the end, however, he cares too much about other people's opinions to take the risk. The irony, of course, is that hardly anyone ever sees his house. He doesn't really like to have people over, he says with a smile, 'because then they sit on the sofa and dent it'. While acknowledging that the self-consciousness that plagues him 'has become this big problem for people now', he nonetheless holds out hope for the dogged individualism of the British public: 'There are lots of houses where people are confident to let it reflect their personalities. Because you know what? They don't care that much about what other people think and more importantly, their property is not the most important thing to them in their lives. They've actually got decent lives.'[76]

LIST OF ABBREVIATIONS

AAD	Archive of Art and Design
ABRC	University of Glasgow Archives and Business Records Centre
DIA	Design and Industries Association
GRO	Glamorgan Record Office
HRO	Hampshire Record Office
MERL	Museum of English Rural Life – University of Reading
MODA	Museum of Domestic Architecture – Middlesex
NAL	National Art Library
PRO	National Archives: Public Record Office
RCAHMS	Royal Commission on the Ancient and Historical Monuments of Scotland
RIBA	Royal Institute of British Architects
WCA	Westminster City Archives
WYAS	West Yorkshire Archive Service

NOTES

INTRODUCTION: THE BRITISH AT HOME

1. Mark Ford, 'Religion of DIY Leaves Church Pews Empty', *Western Daily Press*, 9 March 2002, p. 3; 'DIY Taken Over From Religion Says Vicar', *Sunday Mercury*, 10 March 2002, p. 3.
2. In 2000, fewer than 8% of Britons attended church on Sunday in any week; fewer than 25% of the population belong to a church; and fewer than 10% of children go to Sunday school. See Callum Brown, *The Death of Christian Britain: Understanding Secularisation, 1800–2000* (London and New York, 2001), p. 3.
3. 'Vicar Attacks DIY Cult', *The Sentinel*, 10 March 2002, News, p. 3.
4. Ibid.
5. Christopher Berry, *The Idea of Luxury: A Conceptual and Historical Investigation* (Cambridge, 1994); Jules Lubbock, *The Tyranny of Taste: The Politics of Architecture and Design in Britain 1550–1960* (New Haven and London, 1995), esp. pp. 89–143. The luxury debates of the eighteenth century concerned not just the religious, but statesmen and intellectuals, who analysed the effects of luxury upon the nation's well-being. Maxine Berg and Elizabeth Eger, eds, *Luxury in the Eighteenth Century: Debates, Desires and Delectable Goods* (London, 2003); Istvan Hont and Michael Ignatieff, *Wealth and Virtue: The Shaping of Political Economy in the Scottish Enlightenment* (Cambridge, 1983); Maxine Berg and Helen Clifford, eds, *Consumers and Luxury: Consumer Culture in Europe, 1650–1850* (Manchester, 1999); John Crowley, *The Invention of Comfort: Sensibilities and Design in Early Modern Britain and Early America* (Baltimore, 2001), pp. 141–70; Nancy Cox, '"Beggary of the Nation": Moral, Economic and Political Attitudes to the Retail Sector in the Early Modern Period', in *A Nation of Shopkeepers: Five Centuries of British Retailing*, ed. John Benson and Laura Ugolini (London, 2003), pp. 26–51.
6. Office for National Statistics, Consumer Trends, 2005, Quarter 4; Office for National Statistics General Household Survey 2004; Office for National Statistics, Consumer Trends Datasets; Jane Bainbridge, 'Home Furnishings – Home Improvement', *Marketing*, 3 November 2004, Sector Insight, p. 30.
7. Charlotte Williamson, 'Design for the People', *Time Out*, 8 Oct. 2003, pp. 14–15.
8. Ford, 'Religion of DIY'; also 'DIY Taken Over From Religion'.
9. See, among others, Ralph Waldo Emerson, *English Traits* (Boston, 1856); Thomas Nicholas, *The Pedigree of the English People* (London, 1868); Robert Dohme, *Das englische Haus: Eine kultur- und baugeschichtliche Skizze* (Braunschweig, 1888); Hippolyte Taine, *Notes on England*, trans. with an introduction by Edward Hyams (London, 1995 [1860–70]), pp. 10, 14; on national character, Peter Mandler, *The English National Character: The History of an Idea from Edmund Burke to Tony Blair* (New Haven and London, 2006).
10. J.H. Goring, *The Ballad of Lake Laloo and Other Rhymes* (London, 1909).

11. Muthesius to the Grand Duke Carl Alexander of Saxe-Weimar, 1897. Quoted in Dennis Sharp, '"Introduction" to Hermann Muthesius', *The English House*, ed. Sharp, trans. Janet Seligman (London, 1979), p. xv. Sharp's edition is an abridged translation of Hermann Muthesius, *Das englische Haus: Entwicklung, Bedingungen, Anlage, Aufbau, Einrichtung und Innenraum* (Berlin, 2nd edn, 1908–11, 3 vols). On the English penchant for houses versus the continental acceptance of flats, see Sharon Marcus, *Apartment Stories: City and Home in Nineteenth-Century Paris and London* (Berkeley, 1999).

12. In 1866, the Society of Arts initiated the plaques scheme; the first plaque commemorated Lord Byron. In 1901, the London County Council took over responsibility for the plaques, which its successor body, the Greater London Council retained – until the Thatcher government abolished the GLC in 1986. Since then, English Heritage has managed the plaque scheme.

13. Neil McKendrick, John Brewer, and J.H. Plumb, *The Birth of a Consumer Society: The Commercialization of Eighteenth-Century England* (Bloomington, 1982); Maxine Berg, *Luxury and Pleasure in Eighteenth-Century Britain* (Oxford, 2005), esp. pp. 199–246; Charles Saumarez Smith, *Eighteenth-Century Decoration: Design and the Domestic Interior in England* (New York, 1993); Amanda Vickery, *The Gentleman's Daughter: Women's Lives in Georgian England* (New Haven and London, 1998), pp. 161–94; James Ayres, *Domestic Interiors: The British Tradition, 1500–1850* (New Haven and London, 2003); Carole Shammas, *The Pre-Industrial Consumer in England and America* (Oxford, 1990); Lorna Weatherill, *Consumer Behaviour and Material Culture in Britain, 1660–1760* (London and New York, 1988); Woodruff D. Smith, *Consumption and the Making of Respectability, 1600–1800* (London and New York, 2002), esp. pp. 105–38; John Styles, 'Manufacturing, Consumption and Design in Eighteenth-Century England', in *Consumption and the World of Goods*, ed. John Brewer and Roy Porter (London and New York, 1993), pp. 527–54; Nancy Cox, *The Complete Tradesman: A Study of Retailing, 1550–1820* (Aldershot, 2000).

14. John Benson, *The Rise of Consumer Society in Britain 1880–1980* (New York, 1994).

15. Philip Gilbert Hamerton, *Thoughts about Art* (Boston, 1871), pp. 346–68.

16. E.F. Benson, *As We Were: A Victorian Peep-Show* (New York, 1930), pp. 1–2; also Asa Briggs, *Victorian Things* (London, 1990 [1988]), esp. pp. 213–59; F. Gordon Roe, *Victorian Corners: The Style and Taste of an Era* (New York, 1968).

17. Lytton Strachey, *Queen Victoria* (New York, 1930 [1921]), p. 401.

18. W.E. Gladstone, *The Gladstone Diaries: vol. 9, January 1875–December 1880*, ed. H.C.G. Matthew (Oxford, 1986), p. 29.

19. Andrew Boyd, *The Recreations of a Country Parson*, 2nd Series (Boston, 1861), p. 390.

20. It has been estimated that in 1851, 2.6 million Britons counted as middle-class; by 1901, the middle class could claim 9.3 million members. Benson, *Rise of Consumer Society*, p. 25. On the middle classes, see especially Leonore Davidoff and Catherine Hall, *Family Fortunes: Men and Women of the English Middle Class 1780–1850* (London, 2002 [1987]); R.J. Morris, *Class, Sect and Party: The Making of the British Middle Class* (Manchester, 1990); R.J. Morris, *Men, Women, and Property in England, 1780–1870* (Cambridge, 2005); Simon Gunn, *The Public Culture of the Victorian Middle Class: Ritual and Authority and the English Industrial City, 1840–1914* (Manchester, 2000); Dror Wahrman, *Imagining the Middle Class: The Political Representation of Class in Britain, 1780–1840* (Cambridge, 1995); John Tosh, *A Man's Place: Masculinity and the Middle-Class Home in Victorian England* (New Haven and London, 1999); Christopher Breward, 'Fashionable Living', in *Design and the Decorative Arts, Britain 1500–1900*, ed. Michael Snodin and John Styles (London, 2001), pp. 401–29; Lori Loeb, *Consuming Angels: Advertising and Victorian Women* (New York and Oxford, 1994), p. 5; Simon Gunn, 'The Public Sphere, Modernity and Consumption: New Perspectives on the History of the English Middle Class', in *Gender, Civic Culture and Consumerism: Middle-Class Identity in Britain, 1800–1940*, ed. Alan Kidd and David Nicholls (Manchester, 1999), pp. 12–29; on genteel status, Brian Lewis, *The Middlemost and the Milltowns: Bourgeois Culture and Politics in Early Industrial England* (Stanford, 2001), pp. 357–64; Linda Young, *Middle-Class Culture in the Nineteenth Century: America, Australia and Britain* (London, 2003), esp. pp. 39–68, 153–88.

21. John Burnett, *A Social History of Housing, 1815–1985*, rev. edn (London, 1986); Stefan Muthesius, *The English Terraced House* (New Haven and London, 1982); for comparisons with working-class housing, Martin Daunton, *House and Home in the Victorian City: Working-Class Housing, 1850–1914* (London, 1983).
22. Rosamund Marriott Watson, *The Art of the House* (London, 1897), p. 97.
23. 'Some Odd Things at the Millais Sale', *The House: A Monthly for the Artistic Home*, June/July 1897, p. 181.
24. Vincent Sheean, *Personal History* (New York, 1934), pp. 312–13.
25. Lionel Lambourne, *The Aesthetic Movement* (London, 1996), p. 18.
26. On the Arts and Crafts, see especially, Peter Stansky, *Redesigning the World: William Morris, the 1880s, and the Arts and Crafts* (Princeton, 1985); Gillian Naylor, *The Arts and Crafts Movement* (Cambridge, MA, 1971); Stella Tillyard, *The Impact of Modernism, 1900–1920: Early Modernism and the Arts and Crafts Movement in Edwardian England* (London, 1988). On design more broadly, Nikolaus Pevsner, *Pioneers of Modern Design from William Morris to Walter Gropius* (New York, 1949, 2nd edn [1936]); John Gloag, *Victorian Comfort: A Social History of Design, 1830–1900* (New York, 1973 [1961]); Snodin and Styles, eds, *Design and the Decorative Arts*; David Brett, *On Decoration* (Cambridge, 1992). A notable exception to the rule is Thad Logan's *The Victorian Parlour* (Cambridge, 2001), which provides a refreshing portrait of Victorian taste.
27. In his *Travels in South Kensington*, Moncure Conway comments upon 'how little the principles thus explained by Mr. Ruskin are understood even among the learned'. Moncure Daniel Conway, *Travels in South Kensington with Notes on Decorative Art and Architecture in England* (New York, 1882), p. 213. See also Mrs E.T. Cook's satirical 'Ruskin Mania', *Good Words*, 35 (Aug. 1894): 538–40; and Arthur Lasenby Liberty's characterization of John Ruskin, *Proceedings of the Society of Arts*, 13 March 1900, *Journal of the Society of Arts*, 23 March 1900, p. 375. As Susan Lasdun demonstrates, George Scharf, the first director of the National Portrait Gallery, decorated in a manner that Henry Cole would have condemned. Susan Lasdun, *Victorians at Home* (New York, 1981), p. 99.
28. 'Decorative Art', *The Times*, 13 March 1877, V&A Newspaper Clippings, Jan. 1877–June 1878, vol. 1 (Misc.), AAD.
29. Books such as Peter Thornton's *Authentic Décor, The Domestic Interior, 1620–1920* (London, 1984), Charlotte Gere's *Nineteenth-Century Decoration: The Art of the Interior* (London, 1989), Alan and Ann Gore's *The History of English Interiors* (London, 1991), Nicholas Cooper's *The Opulent Eye: Late Victorian and Edwardian Taste in Interior Design* (London and New York, 1977) and James Chambers' *The English House* (London, 1985) have tended to focus upon the decorative schemes of the very wealthy or upon avant-garde developments such as the aesthetic movement or the Arts and Crafts.
30. On car-boot sales: Nicky Gregson and Louise Crewe, *Second-Hand Cultures* (Oxford and New York, 2003).
31. In many ways, as I learned, material culture transcended regional differences. Middle-class town-dwellers travelled to the nearest cities to buy furniture, or engaged the services of local furnishers, who in turn purchased from wholesalers. A good example of the latter is Maurice Hucker's home furnishings business in Taunton. Hucker kept illustrated catalogues of goods from major London wholesalers in his shop, and arranged for delivery directly to his customers' homes. See DD/XMSN/1 – Somerset Record Office. Furnishers in the north of England tended to procure their goods from local wholesalers. The Halifax furnishing firm of W.L. Dransfield dealt with a number of Halifax suppliers, as well as wholesalers in Leeds, Manchester, and Birmingham; they rarely bought from London. See Misc. 1008/1, WYAS – Calderdale. On catalogue businesses such as Kay's of Worcester, which by the turn of the century could claim 200,000 customers, see BA 5946/Ref. 970.5, Worcestershire Record Office. On material culture and regional variation more broadly: Alwyn Rees, *Life in a Welsh Countryside: A Social Study of Llanfihangel yng Ngwynfa* (Cardiff, 1951), p. 166; on Scottish interiors, Ian Gow, *The Scottish Interior: Georgian and Victorian Décor* (Edinburgh, 1992).

32. Benson, *Rise of Consumer Society*, p. 25.

33. On the US, especially Daniel Horowitz: *The Morality of Spending: Attitudes towards the Consumer Society in America, 1875–1940* (Chicago, 1985); T. Jackson Lears, *Fables of Abundance: A Cultural History of Advertising in America* (New York, 1994); T. Jackson Lears, *The Culture of Consumption: Critical Essays in American History, 1880–1980* (New York, 1983); Gwendolyn Wright, *Moralism and the Model Home: Domestic Architecture and Cultural Conflict in Chicago, 1873–1913* (Chicago, 1980); Richard L. Bushman, *The Refinement of America: Persons, Houses, Cities* (New York, 1992), esp. pp. 313–52; Karen Halttunen, 'From Parlor to Living Room, Domestic Space, Interior Decoration, and the Culture of Personality', in Simon J. Bronner, ed., *Consuming Visions: Accumulation and Display of Goods in America, 1880–1920* (New York, 1989), pp. 157–90.

34. On France: Leora Auslander, *Taste and Power: Furnishing Modern France* (Berkeley, 1996); Debora Silverman, *Art Nouveau in Fin-de-Siècle France: Politics, Psychology and Style* (Berkeley, 1989); Lisa Tiersten, *Marianne in the Market: Envisioning Consumer Society in Fin-de-Siècle France* (Berkeley, 2001); Marcus, *Apartment Stories*, esp. pp. 135–98; Rémy Saisselin, *The Bourgeois and the Bibelot* (New Brunswick, 1984); Rosalind Williams, *Dream Worlds: Mass Communication in Late Nineteenth-Century France* (Berkeley, 1982); Whitney Walton, *France at the Crystal Palace: Bourgeois Taste and Artisan Manufacture in the Nineteenth Century* (Berkeley, 1992); Nancy Troy, *Modernism and the Decorative Arts in France: Art Nouveau to Le Corbusier* (New Haven, 1991). On Germany: Sonja Günther, *Das deutsche Heim: Luxusinterieurs und Arbeitermöbel von der Gründerzeit bis zum '3. Reich'* (Berlin, 1984); Warren Breckman, 'Disciplining Consumption: The Debate on Luxury in Wilhelmine Germany', *Journal of Social History*, 24 (1991): 485–505.

35. Charles Harvey and Jon Press, *William Morris: Design and Enterprise in Victorian Britain* (Manchester, 1991).

36. Andrew R. Heinze, *Adapting to Abundance: Jewish Immigrants, Mass Consumption and the Search for American Identity* (New York, 1990).

37. Hamerton, *Thoughts*, p. 368.

1   MATERIAL GOOD: MORALITY AND THE WELL-TO-DO

1. On Syrie Maugham: Gerald McKnight, *The Scandal of Syrie Maugham* (London, 1980); Richard Fisher, *Syrie Maugham* (London, 1979). On the Barnardos: J. Wesley Bready, *Dr. Barnardo* (London, 1930); A.E. Williams, *Barnardo of Stepney* (London, 1943); Gillian Wagner, *Barnardo* (London, 1979); Mrs Barnardo and James Marchant, *Memoirs of the Late Dr. Barnardo* (London, 1907). On the scandals that threatened Barnardo's reputation: Seth Koven, *Slumming: Sexual and Social Politics in Victorian London* (Princeton, 2004), pp. 88–139.

2. Norman Wymer, *Dr. Barnardo* (London, 1962), p. 134.

3. W.S. Maugham, *Cakes & Ale* (London, 1963); Jeffrey Meyers, *Somerset Maugham: A Life* (New York, 2004), pp. 85–92; for Syrie's side, see Beverley Nichols, *A Case of Human Bondage* (London, 1966).

4. McKnight, *Scandal*, p. 85.

5. In Cecil Beaton's description, 'With the strength of a typhoon she blew all colour before her. For the next decade Syrie Maugham bleached, pickled or scraped every piece of furniture in sight.' Cecil Beaton, *Glass of Fashion* (New York, 1954), p. 247.

6. Drane to Mr Neale, 7 June 1909, D/DX 89/1/41, GRO – Cardiff.

7. Max Weber, *The Protestant Ethic and the 'Spirit' of Capitalism* (London, 2002 [1905]), p. 118; Colin Campbell, *The Romantic Ethic and the Spirit of Modern Consumerism* (Oxford, 1987), pp. 31–5, 102–37; Lewis, *The Middlemost and the Milltowns*, pp. 37–68; Peter Mandler, 'Issues Raised in *The Insatiability of Human Wants*', *Victorian Studies*, 44:4 (Nov. 2002): 658–9; Frank Trentmann, 'Beyond Consumerism: New Historical Perspectives on Consumption', *Journal of*

Contemporary History, 39 (3): 379; Margaret C. Jacob and Matthew Kadane, 'Missing, Now Found in the Eighteenth Century: Weber's Protestant Capitalist', *American Historical Review*, 108:1 (Feb. 2003): 20–49; W.D. Rubinstein, *Men of Property: The Very Wealthy in Britain since the Industrial Revolution* (New Brunswick, NJ, 1981); for an evaluation of the Weberian debate, which distinguishes between Quakers and Unitarians, on the one hand, and evangelical Nonconformists on the other, Michael R. Watts, *The Dissenters: The Expansion of Evangelical Nonconformity* (Oxford, 1995), pp. 330–46; on a similar phenomenon in early nineteenth-century America, Bushman, *The Refinement of America*, pp. 313–52.

8. Brown, *The Death of Christian Britain*, pp. 16–34, 170–98.

9. Vincent Miller, *Consuming Religion: Christian Faith and Practice in a Consumer Culture* (New York and London, 2003); T.J. Jackson Lears, 'From Salvation to Self-Realization: Advertising and the Therapeutic Roots of the Consumer Culture, 1880–1930', in *The Culture of Consumption*, pp. 3–38; John Harvey, 'Seen to be Remembered: Presentation, Representation and Recollection in British Evangelical Culture since the Late 1970s', *Journal of Design History*, 17 (June 2004): 177–92.

10. Boyd Hilton, *The Age of Atonement* (Oxford, 1986); Doreen Rosman, *Evangelicals and Culture* (London, 1984); Ian Bradley, *The Call to Seriousness: The Evangelical Impact on the Victorians* (New York, 1976); L.E. Elliott-Binns, *The Early Evangelicals: A Religious and Social Study* (London, 1953); Michael Hennell, 'Evangelicalism and Worldliness, 1770–1870', in *Popular Belief and Practice*, ed. G.J. Cuming and Derek Baker (Cambridge, 1972); G.R. Searle, *Morality and the Market in Victorian Britain* (Oxford, 1998). On the significance of evangelicalism to the making of the middle class, see Davidoff and Hall, *Family Fortunes*, esp. pp. 71–192; Tosh, *Man's Place*, pp. 36–42, 113–14.

11. John Walsh, Colin Haydon, and Stephen Taylor, *The Church of England c. 1689–c.1833: From Toleration to Tractarianism* (Cambridge, 1993); William Gibson, *The Church of England 1688–1832: Unity and Accord* (London and New York, 2001); Gordon Rupp, *Religion in England 1688–1791* (Oxford, 1986); Watts, *The Dissenters*.

12. John Beresford, ed., *The Diary of a Country Parson: The Reverend James Woodforde*, vol. 3: *1788–1792* (London, 1927), p. 310.

13. See especially Robert B. Shoemaker, *The London Mob: Violence and Disorder in Eighteenth-Century England* (London and New York, 2004); on illegitimacy, Michael Mason, *The Making of Victorian Sexuality* (Oxford, 1994), pp. 66–72.

14. Michael Curtin, 'A Question of Manners: Status and Gender in Etiquette and Courtesy', *Journal of Modern History*, 57: 3 (Sept. 1985): 395–423; Marjorie Morgan, *Manners, Morals and Class in England, 1774–1858* (New York, 1994), pp. 8–31; Lawrence Klein, 'Politeness for Plebes: Consumption and Social Identity in Early Eighteenth-Century England', in *The Consumption of Culture, 1600–1800*, ed. Ann Bermingham and John Brewer (London and New York, 1995), pp. 362–82.

15. Thomas Haweis, *Evangelical Principles and Practice* (1803) p. 30. Quoted in Arthur Skevington Wood, *Thomas Haweis 1734–1820* (London, 1957), p. 60.

16. See, for example, Joseph John Gurney's letter to his son J.H., 28 Feb. 1830, quoted in Joseph Bevan Braithwaite, *Memoirs of Joseph John Gurney*, vol. 1 (Philadelphia, 1854), pp. 406–8.

17. Grayson Carter, *Anglican Evangelicals: Protestant Secessions from the 'Via Media', c. 1800–1850* (Oxford, 2001); Kenneth Hylson-Smith, *Evangelicals in the Church of England, 1734–1984* (Edinburgh, 1988).

18. Dissenters had, since Puritan times, kept such 'spiritual diaries'. See Matthew Kadane, 'The Watchful Clothier: The Diary of an Eighteenth-Century Protestant Capitalist,' Ph.D. thesis, Brown University, 2005; Michael Mascuch, *Origins of the Individualist Self: Autobiography and Self Identity in England, 1591–1791* (Stanford, 1996), esp. pp. 55–70; Tom Webster, 'Writing to Redundancy: Approaches to Spiritual Journals and Early Modern Spirituality', *Historical Journal* 39: 1 (1996): 33–56.

19. John Leifchild, *Memoir of the Late Rev. Joseph Hughes, A.M. One of the Secretaries of the British and Foreign Bible Society* (London, 1835), p. 87. See also Benjamin Gregory, *The*

Thorough Business Man: Memoirs of Walter Powell (London, 1871), pp. 46–7; Christopher Tolley, *Domestic Biography: The Legacy of Evangelicalism in Four Nineteenth-Century Families* (Oxford, 1997), pp. 62–3.

20. J.P. Grant, ed., *Memoir and Correspondence of Mrs. Grant of Laggan* (Edinburgh, 1845), vol. 1, pp. 41–2; similarly, Eustace R. Conder, *Josiah Conder: A Memoir* (London, 1857), pp. 115, 121, 254.

21. Grant, *Memoir and Correspondence*, vol. 1, p. 43; also vol. 2, pp. 55–6.

22. Ibid., vol. 1, pp. 45–6.

23. Joseph John Gurney, Journal Entry for 8 July 1821 in Braithwaite, *Memoirs*, vol. 1, p. 212. On Gurney's moral struggles with wealth, see also David E. Swift, *Joseph John Gurney, Banker, Reformer and Quaker* (Middletown, CT, 1962); on the Gurneys, Augustus J.C. Hare, *The Gurneys of Earlham*, vol. 2 (New York, 1895), esp. pp. 326–7.

24. Braithwaite, *Memoirs*, vol. 1, p. 224.

25. See, for example, John Woolman, quoted in Gregory, *The Thorough Business Man*, p. 290.

26. John Barclay to Thomas Shillitoe, 30 June 1817 in *A Selection from the Letters and Papers of the Late John Barclay*, ed. A.R. Barclay (Philadelphia, 1847), p. 100.

27. Francis Wey, *A Frenchman Sees the English in the 'Fifties*, adapted by Valerie Pirie (London, 1935), p. 89.

28. Augustus Hare, *The Story of My Life* (London, 1896), vol. 1, p. 135; see also Charles J. Robinson, Review, *The Academy*, 3 Sept. 1893, Cutting Book no. 1, Mrs Talbot Coke Papers, Coke MSS., Trusley, NRA 4221, Private Collection.

29. George Macaulay Trevelyan, *The Life of John Bright* (Boston and New York, 1913), p. 173; also Edmund Yates, ed., *Celebrities at Home: Reprinted from 'The World'* (London, 1877), pp. 33–41.

30. Arnold Silver, ed., *The Family Letters of Samuel Butler 1841–86* (Stanford, 1962), pp. 89–90.

31. Samuel Butler, *The Note-Books of Samuel Butler*, ed. Henry Festing Jones (London, 1930), p. 213. On Butler, Steven Mintz, *A Prison of Expectations: The Family in Victorian Culture* (New York, 1983), pp. 172–87; Hugh Kingsmill, *After Puritanism* (London, 1929), pp. 57–110.

32. Discussed in Peter Raby, *Samuel Butler: A Biography* (Iowa City, 1991), p. 105; Philip Henderson, *Samuel Butler: The Incarnate Bachelor* (Bloomington, 1954), p. 60. Butler described the picture as 'certainly one of the funniest things I have seen outside Italian votive pictures'. Quoted in Henry Festing Jones, *Samuel Butler: A Memoir*, vol. 1 (London, 1919), p. 115.

33. On time, see Hilton, *Age of Atonement*, pp. 33–4.

34. A point made forcefully by Rosman, *Evangelicals and Culture*; see also Ford K. Brown, *Fathers of the Victorians: The Age of Wilberforce* (Cambridge, 1961), pp. 293, 408–14; Hennell, 'Evangelicalism and Worldliness'; Lasdun, *Victorians at Home*, pp. 34–44.

35. James Pope Hennessy, *Robert Louis Stevenson* (New York, 1974), p. 24; see, too, John Harvey, *The Art of Piety: The Visual Culture of Welsh Nonconformity* (Cardiff, 1995), pp. 27–37.

36. See Rosman, *Evangelicals and Culture*; Tolley, *Domestic Biography*, esp. pp. 11–55; Ernest Marshall Hose, *Saints in Politics: The 'Clapham Sect' and the Growth of Freedom* (London, 1953). For a Victorian critique of Clapham's embrace of comfort, George W.E. Russell, *Collections and Recollections by One Who Has Kept a Diary* (New York, 1899), pp. 90–1.

37. E.M. Forster, *Marianne Thornton: A Domestic Biography 1797–1887* (New York, 1956), p. 12.

38. Ibid., pp. 17–18. For Henry Thornton's attitude to self-denial, see Tolley, *Domestic Biography*, pp. 60–1.

39. Forster, *Marianne Thornton*, p. 5.

40. Ibid., p. 54.

41. On the Thornton family's attachment to Battersea Rise, see also Tolley, *Domestic Biography*, pp. 220–34; similarly, on the Gurney family's affection for Earlham, Hare, *Gurneys*, vol. 2, pp. 164, 184, 200, 255.

42. Forster, *Marianne Thornton*, p. 152.

43. Revd Isaac Taylor, ed., *The Family Pen: Memorials, Biographical and Literary of the Taylor Family of Ongar*, vol. 1 (London, 1867), p. 195.

44. Elizabeth Gurney's Journal for 17 May 1797, quoted in Swift, *Gurney*, pp. 24–5; Leifchild, *Memoir*, p. 252. My thanks to Abigail Newman for her observation on this point.

45. The Revd T. R. Birks, MA, Rector of Kelshall, Herts, *Memoir of the Rev. Edward Bickersteth, Late Rector of Watton, Herts*, vol. 1 (London, 1851), p. 98.

46. M.V. Hughes, *A London Child of the 1870s* (Oxford, 1977), p. 110.

47. See this point in Hilton, *Age of Atonement*, p. 268.

48. As John Brewer, among a host of other critics, has pointed out, Neil McKendrick's optimistic account of a late eighteenth-century 'consumer revolution' overstates the case. John Brewer, 'The Error of Our Ways: Historians and the Birth of Consumer Lecture', Public Lecture, Royal Society, 23 Sept. 2003 (Cultures of Consumption series). On the new commodities and their purchasers, McKendrick et al., *Birth of a Consumer Society*; Brewer and Porter, *Consumption and the World of Goods*; Berg, *Luxury and Pleasure*, pp. 199–246; Keith Wrightson, *Earthly Necessities: Economic Lives in Early Modern Britain* (New Haven and London, 2000), pp. 297–300; Berg, 'New Commodities', in *Consumers and Luxury*, ed. Berg and Clifford, pp. 63–85; Smith, *Consumption and the Making of Respectability*; Snodin and Styles, *Design and the Decorative Arts*, pp. 178–82, 235–9. On credit practices, Margot Finn, *The Character of Credit: Personal Debt in English Culture, 1740–1914* (Cambridge, 2003).

49. Stana Nenadic, 'Middle-Rank Consumers and Domestic Culture in Edinburgh and Glasgow, 1720–1840', *Past and Present*, 145 (Nov. 1994): 128–9, 145. See, too, Morris, *Men, Women and Property*, p. 361; Peter Guillery, *The Small House in Eighteenth-Century London* (New Haven and London, 2004).

50. Benson, *Rise of Consumer Society*, p. 13. Benson notes that the proportion of GNP devoted to consumer expenditure declined by more than 20% between 1880 and 1959, a statistic which, he notes, points to a problem with economic definitions of consumer society.

51. Benson, *Rise of Consumer Society*, p. 25.

52. Burnett, *Social History of Housing 1815–1985*. Burnett places the figure between an eighth and a tenth of income.

53. See John Plotz's work on portable property, 'Portable Properties: Objects on the Move in Victorian Greater Britain'. I am grateful to Plotz for sharing his unpublished work with me.

54. Taine, *Notes on England*, pp. 14, 26; John Field, 'Wealth, Styles of Life and Social Tone among Portsmouth's Middle Class, 1800–1875', in *Class, Power and Social Structure in British Nineteenth-Century Towns*, ed. R.J. Morris (Leicester, 1986), pp. 88–100.

55. On the furnishing of clerical homes more broadly, see Jane Hamlett, '"Ostentation is always unbecoming": Anglican and Wesleyan Methodist Clerical Homes', ms. chapter of her Royal Holloway Ph.D. thesis (2005), 'Materialising Gender: Identity and Middle-Class Domestic Interiors, 1850–1910'. I am grateful to Hamlett for sharing her unpublished work with me.

56. Wymer, *Dr. Barnardo*, p. 129.

57. On the evangelical influence upon the Victorians, among others: Hilton, *Age of Atonement*; Ian Bradley, *Call to Seriousness*; Ford K. Brown, *Fathers of the Victorians*; Noel Annan, *Leslie Stephen: The Godless Victorian* (New York, 1984); Melvin Richter, *The Politics of Conscience: T.H. Green and His Age* (Cambridge, MA, 1964), esp. pp. 13–51.

58. Davidoff and Hall, *Family Fortunes*, p. 360; Briggs, *Victorian Things*, p. 219; Jane Garnett, 'Nonconformists, Economic Ethics and Consumer Society in Mid-Victorian Britain', in *Culture and the Nonconformist Tradition*, ed. Alan Kreider and Jane Shaw (Cardiff, 1999); R.J. Helmstadter, 'The Nonconformist Conscience', in Peter Marsh, ed., *The Conscience of the Victorian State* (Syracuse, NY, 1979); Raphael Samuel, 'The Discovery of Puritanism, 1820–1914: A Preliminary Sketch', in *Island Stories: Unravelling Britain, Theatres of Memory, volume II*, ed. Alison Light, Sally Alexander, and Gareth Stedman Jones (London, 1998), pp. 276–323, esp. 294–313; H.L. Malchow, *Gentlemen Capitalists: The Social and Political World of the Victorian Businessman* (Stanford, 1992), pp. 160–257; Loeb, *Consuming Angels*, pp. 102–27.

59. Percy Russell, *Leaves from a Journalist's Note-Book* (London, 1874), p. 56.
60. R.W. Dale, *The Old Evangelicalism and the New* (London, 1889), p. 36. On the close relationship between hedonism and asceticism, Chandra Mukerji, *From Graven Images: Patterns of Modern Materialism* (New York, 1983). In the US: Vincent Scully, *The Shingle Style* (New Haven, 1965, 4th edn), p. 36; Katherine Grier, *Culture and Comfort: Parlor Making and Middle-Class Identity* (Washington, 1997), pp. 86–7.
61. Janet Minihan, *The Nationalization of Culture: The Development of State Subsidies to the Arts in Great Britain* (New York, 1977), p. 43.
62. On Cole, see Elizabeth Bonython and Anthony Burton, *The Great Exhibitor: The Life and Work of Henry Cole* (London, 2003).
63. The literature on the Crystal Palace is vast. See especially Jeffrey Auerbach, *The Great Exhibition of 1851: A Nation on Display* (New Haven and London, 1999); Thomas Richards, *The Commodity Culture of Victorian England: Advertising and Spectacle, 1851–1914* (Stanford, 1990), pp. 17–72; Briggs, *Victorian Things*, pp. 52–102; Louise Purbrick, ed., *The Great Exhibition of 1851: New Interdisciplinary Essays* (Manchester, 2001); Nikolaus Pevsner, *High Victorian Design: A Study of the Exhibits of 1851* (London, 1951); Paul Greenhalgh, *Ephemeral Vistas: The Expositions Universelles, Great Exhibitions and World's Fairs, 1851–1939* (Manchester, 1988); Hermione Hobhouse, *The Crystal Palace and the Great Exhibition: Art, Science and Productive Industry* (London, 2002).
64. Mrs E.M. Ward, *Memories of Ninety Years*, ed. Isabel McAllister (London, 1924), p. 66.
65. Ralph Wornum, 'The Exhibition as a Lesson in Taste', *Art Journal*, 1851, pp. i, vii, xxii, v–vi; Owen Jones, *On the True and the False in the Decorative Arts* (London, 1863 [lectures delivered in 1852]), esp. pp. 70–99; Lubbock, *Tyranny of Taste*, pp. 248–70.
66. Alan S. Cole, *Fifty Years of Public Work of Sir Henry Cole K.C.B. Accounted for in His Deeds, Speeches and Writings I and II* (London, 1884), p. 286.
67. 'Universal Infidelity in Principles of Design', *Journal of Design and Manufactures*, Aug. 1851, pp. 159–61.
68. As Lubbock notes, Pugin's influence upon design reform was hardly credited at the time. Lubbock, *Tyranny of Taste*, pp. 263–4. In the last decade, this dimension of his reputation has been resuscitated. See Paul Atterbury and Clive Wainwright, eds, *Pugin: A Gothic Passion* (New Haven and London, 1994), pp. 1–21, 105–16; Clive Wainwright, 'A.W.N. Pugin and the Progress of Design as Applied to Manufacture' and Paul Atterbury, 'Pugin and Interior Design', in *A.W.N. Pugin, Master of Gothic Revival*, ed. Paul Atterbury (New Haven and London, 1995), pp. 161–99; David Watkin, *Morality and Architecture Revisited* (Chicago, 2001), pp. 21–7.
69. Shirley F. Murphy, ed., *Our Homes and How to Make Them Healthy* (London and New York, 1883), p. 356.
70. 'The Kidderminster School of Art: Annual Meeting and Distribution of Prizes', *The Kidderminster Shuttle*, 15 Jan. 1881, Newspaper Clippings, Sept. 1880–Jan. 1882, vol. 1, f. 115, AAD; on the 'contagion of example' more broadly, Morgan, *Manners, Morals and Class*, pp. 58–62, 69.
71. On the links between the *Spectator*'s notions of virtuous consumption and the ideas of Ruskin and Morris, see Lubbock, *Tyranny of Taste*, pp. 112–13, 181–91.
72. Howard Caygill, *Art of Judgment* (London, 1989), pp. 38–102; John Brewer, *The Pleasures of the Imagination: English Culture in the Eighteenth Century* (New York, 1997), pp. xviii–xix, 87–98; Campbell, *Romantic Ethic*, pp. 154–9; Denise Gigante, *Taste: A Literary History* (New Haven and London, 2005), pp. 47–67, 72–6; David Kuchta, *The Three-Piece Suit and Modern Masculinity: England, 1550–1850* (Berkeley and Los Angeles, 2002), pp. 112–21; Smith, *Consumption*, pp. 81–3; Lawrence E. Klein, *Shaftesbury and the Culture of Politeness: Moral Discourse and Cultural Politics in Early Eighteenth-Century England* (Cambridge, 1994).
73. Brewer, *Pleasures of the Imagination*, pp. 82–4, 97–122; Caygill, *Art*, pp. 64–9; Kuchta, *The Three-Piece Suit*, pp. 95–112.

74. Joshua Reynolds, Discourse III: 'Delivered to the Students of the Royal Academy, on the Distribution of the Prizes, December 14, 1770', in *Discourses on Art*, ed. Robert R. Wark (New Haven and London, 1997), p. 44; Brewer, *Pleasures of the Imagination*, pp. 292–3.

75. 'The Diffusion of Taste among All Classes a National Necessity', *Blackwood's Edinburgh Magazine*, 87 (1860): 151–61; R.N. Wornum, 'Struggles of Taste', *Art Journal*, 2: 12 (1850): 301–4.

76. Jones, *On the True and the False*, p. 73; also, *The Builder*, 3 July 1852, in Newspaper Clippings, 1837–1852 (Misc.), AAD; 'South Kensington Museum', reprinted from *The Echo, The House-Furnisher and Decorators, Upholsterers & Cabinet Makers' Monthly*, April 1872, p. 40.

77. H.J.C., *The Art of Furnishing on Rational and Aesthetic Principles* (London, 1876), pp. 115–16; see, too, 'The Development of Taste by Education', *Dublin University Magazine*, 88 (1876): 754–58; 'Taste', *St. Paul's: A Monthly Magazine* (1867–8): 92–102.

78. G.L., *The Science of Taste: Being a Treatise on its Principles* (London, 1879), p. 246.

79. On Ruskin's objections to the hardening dictates of design reform: John Ruskin, 'Lecture III: Modern Manufacture and Design', in *The Two Paths: Being Lectures on Art and its Application to Decoration and Manufacture, Delivered in 1858–9* (London, 1859), pp. 94–5; Lubbock, *Tyranny of Taste*, pp. 280–90.

80. Karl Marx, *Capital*, vol. 1, ch. 1, section 4.

81. Bonython and Burton, *The Great Exhibitor*, pp. 18–19.

82. See for example, 'The "Fascination" Vase, Manufactured by Mintons', *Journal of Design and Manufactures*, Feb. 1850, p. 203; Alfred Jowers, 'On the Principles which Should Govern the Decoration of a Suite of Apartments in a First-Class Town Mansion, and On Those Applicable to the Same Purpose in a Country Seat', 1870, X (079) E 729.1.098, RIBA; *The Builder*, 3 July 1852, Newspaper Clippings, 1837–1852 (Misc.), AAD; Jones, *On the True and the False*, p. 98.

83. See Richard Payne Knight, *An Analytical Inquiry into the Principles of Taste* (London, 1805); discussed in the *Edinburgh Review*, 7 (Jan. 1806): 295–329.

84. Bonython and Burton, *The Great Exhibitor*, p. 157; on Pugin's views in this regard, Lubbock, *Tyranny of Taste*, pp. 246–7.

85. Department of Science and Art, *A Catalogue of the Museum of Ornamental Art at Marlborough House, Pall Mall. For the Use of Students and Manufacturers, and the Public*, 5th edn (London, 1853).

86. Anthony Burton, *Vision & Accident. The Story of the Victoria and Albert Museum* (London, 1999), pp. 38–9.

87. According to Cole, 'this room appears to excite far greater interest than many objects [of] high excellence', for 'every one is led at once to investigate the ornamental principle upon which his own carpet and furniture may be decorated'. Quoted in Burton, *Vision and Accident*, pp. 32–3. 'Instances of Bad Taste' from 'South Kensington Museum', reprinted from *The Echo, The House-Furnisher and Decorators, Upholsterers and Cabinet Makers' Monthly*, April 1872, p. 39. See also 'Fine-Arts: Reopening of the Museum of Ornamental Manufactures, Marlborough House', *Daily News*, 3 Sept. 1853, Newspaper Clippings, Nov. 1852–Oct. 1853, AAD.

88. 'Department of Practical Art, Marlborough House, Pall Mall', 6 Sept. 1852, Newspaper Clippings, 1837–53 (Misc.), AAD. On the Chamber of Horrors: Suga Yasuko, 'Designing the Morality of Consumption: "Chamber of Horrors" at the Museum of Ornamental Art, 1852–53', *Design Issues*, 20:4 (Autumn 2004): 43–56; Clive Wainwright, 'Principles True and False: Pugin and the Foundation of the Museum of Manufactures', *Burlington Magazine*, 135: 1095 (June 1994): 357–64.

89. *Catalogue of the Museum of Ornamental Art*, p. 21.

90. Ibid., p. 14; also Jowers, 'On the Principles', pp. 22; 'Lecture by Mr. Owen Jones on the Principles of Decorative Art', *People's Illustrated Journal*, 12 June 1852, Newspaper Clippings, 1837–1852 (Misc.), AAD.

91. Jones, *On the True and the False*, p. 84.

92. 'Which Direction is Ornamental Art Likely to Take in This Country, toward Elaboration or Simplicity', *Journal of Design and Manufactures*, Jan. 1852, p. 136.

93. 'The People at Marlborough House', *Observer*, 9 Jan. 1853, Newspaper Clippings, Nov. 1852–Oct. 1853 (Misc.), AAD.

94. On the *Household Words* article, 'Industrial Instruction', *Belfast Mercury*, 13 April 1852, Newspaper Clippings, Nov. 1852–Oct. 1853 (Misc.), AAD; see also K.J. Fielding, 'Dickens and the Department of Practical Art', *Modern Language Review*, 48 (1953): 270–7.

95. The judgement is that of H.T. Wood, the historian of the Royal Society of Arts. Quoted in Auerbach, *Great Exhibition*, p. 40.

96. Charles Dickens, *Hard Times* (New York and London, 2001 [1854]), p. 8. See, too, the scathing description of taste-making at Hampton Court, 'Please to Leave Your Umbrella' (1858): 'Taste proclaims to you what is the genteel thing; receive it and be genteel!' in *The Dent Uniform Edition of Dickens' Journalism*, vol. 3, ed. Michael Slater (Columbus, OH, 1999), pp. 483–8. My thanks to Peter Mandler for this reference.

97. 'The Schools of Design, Wilmington Square', *London Journal*, 25 June 1853, Newspaper Clippings, Nov. 1852–Oct. 1853 (Misc.), AAD.

98. Letter to the Editor by 'One of Them', *Morning Advertiser*, Newspaper Clippings, Nov. 1852–Oct. 1853 (Misc.), AAD.

99. Argus, 'A Mild Remonstrance against the Taste-Censorship at Marlborough House in Reference to Manufacturing Ornamentation and Decorative Design. To Manufacturers, Decorators, Designers, and the Public Generally' (London, 1853), p. 10. Gombrich identifies 'Argus' as F.J. Prouting, of Manchester. See Lubbock, *Tyranny of Taste*, pp. 273–7; E.H. Gombrich, *The Sense of Order: A Study in the Psychology of Decorative Art* (Oxford, 1979), p. 309.

100. Argus, 'A Mild Remonstrance', pt II, p. 33.

101. Ibid., pt. III, p. 16.

102. Ibid., p. 18.

103. Ibid., p. 17.

104. Letter to the Editor by 'One of Them', *Morning Advertiser*, Newspaper Clippings, Nov. 1852–Oct. 1853 (Misc.), AAD. See, too, the correspondence that followed Christopher Dresser's lecture, 'Ornamentation Considered as a High Art', given before the Society of Arts. Letters to the Editor, *House-Furnisher and Decorators, Upholsterers and Cabinet Makers' Monthly*, 1: 3 (1 April 1871) pp. 32–3.

105. *Morning Advertiser*, 24 Feb. 1853, Newspaper Clippings, Nov. 1852–Oct. 1853 (Misc.), AAD.

106. *Court Journal*, 19 Feb. 1853, Newspaper Clippings, Nov. 1852–Oct. 1853 (Misc.), AAD.

107. John Ruskin, 'Traffic', in *The Crown of Wild Olive and Sesame and Lilies* (New York, 1924), p. 46. 'Traffic' permitted Ruskin to 'fortify' one of his 'old dogmas', developed in *The Two Paths*, *The Stones of Venice*, and *The Seven Lamps of Architecture*: 'Taste is not only a part and an index of morality – it is the ONLY morality' (p. 44).

108. 'A Gossiping Editorial', *Furniture Gazette*, 13 Dec. 1873, p. 583.

109. Mr G.A. Audsley, 'What is the Influence upon Society of Decorative Art and Art-Workmanship in All Household Details?' *Transactions of the National Association for the Promotion of Social Science*, Liverpool Meeting, 1876, ed. Charles Wager Ryalls (London, 1877), p. 841. On the Social Science Association, see Lawrence Goldman, *Science, Reform and Politics in Victorian Britain: The Social Science Association, 1857–1886* (Cambridge, 2002).

110. Audsley, 'The True Principles of House Decoration', *Furniture Gazette*, Dec. 1876, p. 401.

111. Among many others: Angel Thompson, *Feng Shui: How to Achieve the Most Harmonious Arrangement of Your Home and Office* (New York, 1996), pp. xiv–vi.

112. See Hilton, *Age of Atonement*, pp. 255–339; Dale, *The Old Evangelicalism and the New*, pp. 44–7; Richter, *Politics of Conscience*, pp. 97–135; on *Lux Mundi*, Peter Hinchliff, *God and History: Aspects of British Theology 1875–1914* (Oxford, 1992), pp. 99–121.

113. Hilton, *Age of Atonement*, p. 276.

114. E. Luscombe Hull, *Sermons preached at Union Chapel, Kings Lynn, 1869*, 2nd series, p. 193. Quoted in Clyde Binfield, *So Down to Prayers: Studies in English Nonconformity 1780–1920* (London, 1977), p. 19; also see John Seed, 'Theologies of Power: Unitarianism and the Social Relations of Religious Discourse, 1800–1850', in *Class, Power and Social Structure*, ed. R.J. Morris, pp. 135–6.

115. Hilton, *Age of Atonement*, p. 283.

116. Andrew Kennedy Hutchinson Boyd, entry by T.B., *Dictionary of National Biography*, XXII Supplement (Oxford, 1937 [1921–22]), pp. 244–5; for Boyd's own self-description, Andrew Boyd, *St. Andrew's and Elsewhere* (London, 1894), p. 89; Andrew Boyd, *Lessons of Middle Age* (London, 1869), pp. 144–5.

117. Andrew Boyd, 'Concerning Disagreeable People', in *The Everyday Philosopher in Town and Country* (Boston, 1863), p. 154.

118. Boyd, *Recreations of a Country Parson, 1st Series*, pp. 175, 213.

119. Boyd, *Recreations*, p. 258. See also Boyd, *The Everyday Philosopher*, pp. 19–44.

120. Boyd, *Recreations*, p. 238.

121. Ibid., p. 239.

122. Ibid., p. 241. An image he re-used in *The Everyday Philosopher*, p. 30. For a late nineteenth-century echo, see J.R. Miller, DD, *Home-Making; or, The Ideal Family Life* (London, 1896), pp. 101–4.

123. W.J. Loftie to Macmillan, 11 March 1876, Add. Mss. 55075, British Library.

124. W.B.O., *Dictionary of National Biography, 1901–1911*, pp. 474–5. According to Garrett Anderson's *Hang Your Halo in the Hall: The Savile Club from 1868* (London, 1993) – quoting Max Beerbohm's account – Loftie was forcibly retired from the Church because he had debauched a parlour maid.

125. *Who Was Who, 1897–1916*, p. 436.

126. W.J. Loftie, *A Plea for Art in the House* (London, 1876), p. 89.

127. Ibid., p. 90. On Thomas Cook's reconciliation of tourism and devotion, Timothy Larsen, *Contested Christianity: The Political and Social Contexts of Victorian Theology* (Waco, TX, 2004), pp. 29–39.

128. Loftie, *A Plea*, p. 39.

129. *Brief Sketch of the Life of Elias Henry Davies, C.C.* (Pontypridd, 1900), p. 4. GRO – Cardiff, D/D X 305/8. See also the history of S. Aston & Son Ltd, established by zealous Nonconformists, who hired only teetotallers in their furnishing business. Samuel Aston, 'A Family Affair', TS history of S. Aston & Son Ltd 1870–1905, originally published in instalments in the *Astonian*, 1963, DD/DM/726/67, Denbighshire Record Office – Ruthin.

130. Alfred Gardiner, *John Benn and the Progressive Movement* (London, 1925), p. 51, 49. On the cross-over between the worlds of business and religion, R.J. Helmstadter, 'The Reverend Andrew Reed (1787–1862): Evangelical Pastor as Entrepreneur', in *Religion and Irreligion in Victorian Society: Essays in Honor of R.K. Webb*, ed. R.W. Davis and R.J. Helmstadter (London, 1992), pp. 7–28.

131. Gardiner, *John Benn*, p. 30.

132. Thomas Pratt, who ran the firm from 1880 with his father, Christopher, had laboured to improve Bradford's morals as chairman of the local Vigilance Committee and honorary treasurer of the Purity League; his brother Benjamin had retired from the family business to spread Methodism with the Reverend William Burgess' Wesleyan mission in Hyderabad, India. TS history of the firm, WYAS, pp. 1–5. Also interesting is the diary of J.B. Roberts of Masborough, a furnishing warehouseman whose spiritual diary is deposited at the Sheffield Archives, 34/F1/1.

133. Christopher Pratt & Son, Interiors, 1910 catalogue, p. 126.

134. TS history of the firm, WYAS, p. 6.

135. Annan, *Leslie Stephen*; more generally on secularization, Alan D. Gilbert, *Religion and Society in Industrial England: Church, Chapel and Social Change, 1740–1914* (London, 1976); Richard J. Helmstadter and Bernard Lightman, eds, *Victorian Faith in Crisis*

(Basingstoke, 1992); Jeffrey Cox, *English Churches in a Secular Society: Lambeth, 1870–1930* (Oxford, 1982); Gerald Parsons, ed., *Religion in Victorian Britain*, 5 vols (Manchester, 1988–97); Hugh McLeod, *Religion and Society in England, 1850–1914* (New York, 1996), pp. 169–224; on church attendance, K.D.M. Snell and Paul S. Ell, *Rival Jerusalems: The Geography of Victorian Religion* (Cambridge, 2000), esp. p. 17.

136. Quoted in Bea Howe, *Arbiter of Elegance* (London, 1967), p. 54. See also Gladstone's comment upon furniture shopping, 29 April 1840: 'more shopping: what coil of not merely worldly but material things. Yet beauty is beauty even in furniture.' *Gladstone Diaries*, ed. Matthew, vol. 3, p. 30.

137. 'The Moral Influence of Decoration', reprinted from the *Queen*, in *Furniture Gazette*, 21 Aug. 1875, p. 105; also Lucy Orrinsmith, *The Drawing-Room, its Decorations and Furniture* (London, 1877), p. 8.

138. Revd F. Barham Zincke, 'A Dishomed Nation', *Contemporary Review*, 38 (Aug. 1880): 179–80. On Zincke, see the *Oxford Dictionary of National Biography*, vol. 60, pp. 998–9.

139. Gwen Raverat, *Period Piece* (New York, 1953 [1952]), p. 197. Uncle Lenny was Leonard Darwin, president of the Eugenics Education Society, 1911–28.

140. 'Art in the House', *The Globe*, 8 Sept. 1880, p. 1, Newspaper Clippings, Sept. 1880–Jan. 1882, vol. 1, AAD.

141. 'Imitation as Applied to the Decorative Arts', *The Decorator: An Illustrated Practical Magazine and Advertiser for Cabinet Makers, Upholsterers, Carvers, Gilders, Paperhangers, House Painters and Glaziers*, April 1864, p. 21.

142. Rhoda and Agnes Garrett, *Suggestions for House Decoration in Painting, Woodwork and Furniture* (London, 1877), p. 54.

143. Frederick Litchfield, *Illustrated History of Furniture* (London, 1922, 7th edn [1892]), p. 403; Winifred Peck, *A Little Learning or a Victorian Childhood* (London, 1952), p. 61

144. Richard Church, *The Golden Sovereign* (London, 1957), p. 104.

145. H.G. Wells, *Marriage* (London, 1912), pp. 22–3. See, too, 'Silver and Its Reproduction', *House and Garden*, Nov. 1920, p. 14.

146. George Eliot, *Middlemarch* (London, 1965 [1872]), p. 302.

147. See D. Bruce Hindmarsh, *The Evangelical Conversion Narrative: Spiritual Autobiography in Early Modern England* (Oxford, 2005), esp. pp. 1–32, 344–9; Richter, *Politics of Conscience*, pp. 33–51; On the self, among others: Dror Wahrman, *The Making of the Modern Self: Identity and Culture in Eighteenth-Century England* (New Haven and London, 2004), esp. pp. 190–5, 265–321; Roy Porter, ed., *Rewriting the Self: Histories from the Renaissance to the Present* (London, 1997); Charles Taylor, *Sources of the Self: The Making of the Modern Identity* (Cambridge, MA, 1989); Alex Owen, *The Place of Enchantment: British Occultism and the Culture of the Modern* (Chicago and London, 2004), esp. pp. 114–47; Nikolas Rose, *Governing the Soul: The Shaping of the Private Self* (London, 1990); Ian Hacking, *Rewriting the Soul: Multiple Personality and the Sciences of Memory* (Princeton, 1995). On the connection between 'puritanism' and 'romanticism', see Campbell, *Romantic Ethic*, pp. 74–85, 134–7, 217–21.

148. Taine, *Notes on England*, p. 271.

149. Hare, *Story*, p. 295.

2   CATHEDRALS TO COMMERCE: SHOPPERS AND ENTREPRENEURS

1. On Benn's career, A.G. Gardiner, *John Benn and the Progressive Movement* (London, 1925).

2. Ernest Benn, *The Confessions of a Capitalist* (London, 1932 [1925]), p. 37; also John Andrews Benn, *Tradesman's Entrance* (London, 1935), pp. 94–9.

3. 'Our Raison D'Etre', *The House*, March 1897, p. 1.

4. 'In Search of the Latest', *The House*, Oct. 1898, p. 66.

5. 'In Search of the Latest', *The House*, June 1901, p. 153.

6. 'Illustrated Answers to Correspondents', *The House*, May 1899, p. 115.

7. On the department store, see Bill Lancaster, *The Department Store: A Social History* (London and New York, 1995); Geoffrey Crossick and Serge Jaumain, eds, *Cathedrals of Consumption: The European Department Store, 1850–1939* (Aldershot, 1999); Erika Rappaport, *Shopping for Pleasure: Women in the Making of London's West End* (Princeton, 2000); Kathryn A. Morrison, *English Shops and Shopping: An Architectural History* (New Haven and London, 2003), pp. 125–57. The term 'retail revolution' must be used cautiously. Claire Walsh's essay in *Cathedrals of Consumption* warns of overstating the 'newness' of the department store, while Nancy Cox demonstrates that many elements of modern retailing were already in place during the eighteenth century. Cox, *Complete Tradesman*; Berg, *Luxury and Pleasure*, pp. 247–78.

8. H.J. Jennings, *Our Homes and How to Beautify Them* (London, 1902), p. 122.

9. Sir William Hardman, *A Mid-Victorian Pepys: The Letters and Memoirs of Sir William Hardman, M.A., F.R.G.S.* (New York, 1923), p. 116.

10. *The Times*, 26 May 1887, Newspaper Clippings, March 1886–May 1887, AAD.

11. Penelope, Illustrated Answers to Correspondents, *The House*, June 1900, p. 158. For a selection of sale catalogues, see BA 8185/Ref. 705 185 – Worcestershire Record Office; DD/Mr 72, DP/COL 15 – Somerset Archive and Record Service, Taunton; D/DU 559/119 – Essex Record Office, Colchester.

12. E.J., 'Houses and How to Furnish Them', *Englishwoman's Domestic Magazine*, Sept. 1879, p. 289.

13. Maxine Berg, *The Age of Manufactures, 1700–1820* (Oxford, 1986); Berg, *Luxury and Pleasure*, pp. 85–110; W. Hamish Fraser, *The Coming of the Mass Market, 1850–1914* (Hamden, CT, 1981); J. Neville Bartlett, *Carpeting the Millions* (Edinburgh, 1978); Augustus Muir, *Nairn's of Kirkcaldy: A Short History of the Company* (Cambridge, 1956); W. Minchinton, *The British Tinplate Industry: A History* (Oxford, 1957); Lara Kriegel, 'Culture and the Copy: Calico, Capitalism and Design Copyright in Early Victorian Britain', *Journal of British Studies*, 43 (April 2004): 233–65; Edward Baines, *History of the Cotton Manufacture in Great Britain* (London, 1835).

14. On aniline dyes, Anthony Travis, *The Rainbow Makers: The Origins of the Synthetic Dyestuffs Industry in Western Europe* (Bethlehem, 1993); Simon Garfield, *Mauve: How One Man Invented a Color that Changed the World* (New York and London, 2000).

15. George Dodd, *The Textile Manufactures of Great Britain* (London, 1844), p. 70.

16. 'On the Multitude of New Patterns', *Journal of Design and Manufactures*, March 1849, p. 4; reprinted as 'New Patterns', *The Universal Decorator*, 3: 14 (1858): 4.

17. Paper duties were reduced in 1836, and again in 1846, before they were finally abolished by Gladstone in 1861. See Alan Victor Sugden and John Ludlam Edmondson, *A History of English Wallpaper, 1509–1914* (London, 1925), p. 139; Treve Rosoman, *London Wallpapers. Their Manufacture and Use, 1690–1840* (London, 1992).

18. Taine, *Notes on England*, p. 190.

19. 'On the Multitude of New Patterns', p. 4.

20. On the manufacture of papier mâché, see Samuel Timmins, ed., *The Resources, Products, and Industrial History of Birmingham and the Midland Hardware District: A Series of Reports* (London, 1866), pp. 566–73.

21. G.L., *The Science of Taste: Being a Treatise on Its Principles* (London, 1879), p. 99.

22. 'Leader', *The Decorator: An Illustrated Practical Magazine and Advertiser for Cabinet Makers, Upholsterers, Carvers, Gilders, Paperhangers, House Painters, and Glaziers*, Feb. 1864, p. 3.

23. 'Poetry in Art', *Furniture Gazette*, 4 Sept. 1880, p. 135. On the bath, 'Designer', Wolverhampton, Letter to the Editor, 'The Wolverhampton School of Art', *Midland Counties Express*, 10 Feb. 1872, Newspaper Clippings, July 1861–April 1862, vol. 1, AAD.

24. G.L., *The Science of Taste*, p. 90.

25. 'Messrs. Hoskins and Sewell', *Furniture Record*, 28 July 1899, p. 49. On this point, Loeb, *Consuming Angels*, p. 51.

26. 'A Glimpse at a Glasgow Furnishing House', *Cabinet Maker*, 1 March 1882.

27. 'Round the Trade: At Mr. H.L. Benjamin's', *Furnisher and Decorator*, 1 Nov. 1889, p. 14.

28. The standard works are Clive Edwards, *Victorian Furniture: Technology and Design* (Manchester, 1993); Pat Kirkham, *The London Furniture Trade, 1700–1870* (Leeds, 1988); on mass production more broadly, Charles F. Sabel and Jonathan Zeitlin, eds, *World of Possibilities: Flexibility and Mass Production in Western Industrialization* (Cambridge, 1997); George Dodd, *British Manufactures, Series IV* (London, 1845).

29. Guy Routh, *Occupations of the People of Great Britain* cited in Edwards, *Victorian Furniture*, p. 8. The expansion of the workforce was on a par with the expansion of the total labour force of the country. See P.G. Hall, *The Industries of London since 1861* (London, 1962), p. 71.

30. L.O.J. Boynton, 'High Victorian Furniture: The Example of Marsh and Jones of Leeds', *Furniture History*, 3 (1967): 55; Walther G. Hoffmann, *British Industry 1700–1950*, trans. W.O. Henderson and W.H. Chaloner (Oxford, 1955), pp. 79–80, 250.

31. Fraser, *Coming of the Mass Market*, p. 199.

32. Select Committee on the Sweating System, Minutes, Q. 2135, 2143, 2257–9, 6263–4; Royal Commission on Labour, Minutes, Q. 19753, P.P. 1892, XXXVI, part III.

33. Ernest Aves, 'The Furniture Trade', in Charles Booth, *Life and Labour of the People in London: The Trades of East London Connected with Poverty* (London, 1902 [1889]), pp. 157–218. On work conditions in the furniture trade, see Hew Reid, *The Furniture Makers: A History of Trade Unionism in the Furniture Trade, 1865–1972* (Oxford, 1986).

34. See Edwards, *Victorian Furniture*, pp. 7–9, 17.

35. 'A Glimpse at Whiteley's House Furnishing Department', *Cabinet Maker*, 1 Oct. 1881, p. 63.

36. On the firm William Scott Morton and machinery, Elspeth Hardie, 'William Scott Morton', *Antique Collector*, March 1988, pp. 70–7. See also undated, unattributed history of the firm William Birch, High Wycombe, D/GP/177, Buckinghamshire Record Office.

37. 'Quaint Sideboards', *Furniture Record*, June 1899, p. 6.

38. E. Gomme Ltd to Messrs C. & R. Light Ltd, Curtain Rd, London, n.d. [Nov. 1909], p. 255, D/GP/40, Buckinghamshire Record Office.

39. On innovation in the eighteenth century, Maxine Berg, 'From Imitation to Invention: Creating Commodities in Eighteenth-Century Britain', *Economic History Review* 55 (Feb. 2002): 1–30; Maxine Berg, 'New Commodities', in *Consumers and Luxury*, pp. 76–85.

40. Edwards, *Victorian Furniture*, pp. 145–6.

41. Amin Jaffer, *Furniture from British India and Ceylon: A Catalogue of the Collections in the Victoria and Albert Museum and the Peabody Essex Museum* (London, 2001).

42. 'Gutta Percha', *Littell's Living Age* [from *Chambers' Journal*], 14 (1847): 402.

43. Frederick Walton, 'On the Introduction and Use of Elastic Gums and Analogous Substances', *Journal of the Society of Arts*, 4 April 1862, pp. 329–30.

44. John Jackson, 'India-Rubber and Gutta-Percha, and their Sources', *Nature*, 55 (29 April 1897): 610–12.

45. 'Of Mechanical Processes for Producing Decorative Designs on Wood Surfaces', *Furniture Gazette*, 27 Dec. 1873, p. 629.

46. Jane Ellen Panton, *Homes of Taste: Economical Hints* (London, 1890), p. 46.

47. R. Davis Benn, 'Some New Suggestions for Sideboards', *Cabinet Maker and Art Furnisher*, Sept. 1898, p. 58.

48. Penelope, 'How to Furnish Tastefully for "Five Hundred"', *The House*, April 1899, pp. 52–5.

49. 'In Search of the Latest', *The House*, Nov. 1897, p. 133.

50. 'A Glimpse at Whiteley's House Furnishing Department', *Cabinet Maker*, 1 Oct. 1881, p. 63. On Whiteley's within the context of the Victorian retail landscape, Rappaport, *Shopping*, pp. 16–47.

51. See John Gregory Crace, Autobiography, 1881, JCG–21, AAD/1992/3. See also Megan Aldrich, *The Craces: Royal Decorators* (Brighton, 1990). For a list of the Craces' clients, List of

Patrons and Commissions, J.D. Crace & Son, JDC–29, AAD. Another such shop was the upholsterer George Seddon's elegant furniture showroom in Aldersgate. Lubbock, *Tyranny of Taste*, pp. 15–17.

52. Samuel Aston, 'A Family Affair', TS history of S. Aston & Son Ltd 1870–1905, originally published in instalments in the *Astonian*, 1963, DD/DM/726/67, Denbighshire Record Office – Ruthin.

53. James Hopkinson, *Victorian Cabinet Maker: The Memoirs of James Hopkinson, 1819–1894* (New York, 1968). Italics in the original.

54. *The House*, 1: 1 (27 Nov. 1875): 1. On household management: Kathryn Hughes, *The Short Life and Long Times of Mrs Beeton* (London, 2005).

55. Anthony Trollope, *Can You Forgive Her?* (London, 1986 [1864–5]), p. 46. On the high-end upholstery trade, Geoffrey Beard, *Upholsterers and Interior Furnishing in England 1530–1840* (New Haven and London, 1997).

56. Donald Shaw, *London in the Sixties (With a Few Digressions)* (London, 1909), pp. 194–5; Morrison, *English Shops*, pp. 93–123.

57. George Augustus Sala, *Gaslight and Daylight* (London, 1872 [1858]), p. 203.

58. Claire Walsh, 'Social Meaning and Social Space in the Shopping Galleries of Early Modern London', in *A Nation of Shopkeepers*, ed. Benson and Ugolini, pp. 52–79.

59. Morrison, *English Shops*, pp. 92–108, esp. p. 99.

60. George Clinch, 'The Arcades and Bazaars of London', *English Illustrated Magazine*, 14 (1895–6): 562–6.

61. Ward, *Memories of Ninety Years*, p. 30.

62. Clinch, 'Arcades and Bazaars', pp. 562, 565. In Leeds and Birmingham, arcades were more popular than department stores. Lancaster, *The Department Store*, p. 38.

63. 'Bazaars', *Chambers' Journal of Popular Literature*, 447 (26 July 1862): 49.

64. In smaller towns, these enterprises continued to be conducted at the same location, an arrangement that in some cases endured through the twentieth century. See 1906 Daldy, Colchester Recalled Project, Colchester Museum Resources Centre. Undertaking and estate agencies were also often combined. See Mrs Loftie, *Social Twitters* (London, 1879), p. 26.

65. See HF 57/6/1/2/1, University of Glasgow Archives and Business Records Centre.

66. Sir Ambrose Heal, 'Story of the Fourposter', Typescript, n.d. [1950s?], p. 9, AAD/1994/16/1496.

67. Anon., *House of Maple* (London, 1949). See also Charles Graves, 'Efficiency Plus was Sir Blundell's Secret', Great Shopkeepers, no. 13, *Evening News*, 2 Oct. 1957, AAD/2000/3/235, AAD.

68. Hugh Barty-King, *Maples Fine Furnishers: A Household Name for 150 Years* (London, 1992), p. 10.

69. On Blundell Maple, see the favourable appraisal of his former son-in-law, Hermann Freiherrn v. Eckardstein, *Lebenserinnerungen und politische Denkwürdigkeiten*, vol. 1 (Leipzig, 1920), p. 300.

70. Russell, *Leaves from a Journalist's Note-Book*, p. 57.

71. Ibid.

72. Barty-King, *Maples*, pp. 48, 55.

73. Ibid., p. 30.

74. On Holland & Sons, see Simon Jervis, 'Holland and Sons, and the Furnishing of the Athenaeum', *Furniture History*, 6 (1970).

75. James Jeffreys, *Retail Trading in Britain, 1850–1950* (Cambridge, 1954), pp. 16–18; Michael J. Winstanley, *The Shopkeeper's World, 1830–1914* (Manchester, 1983), pp. 37–8.

76. Nicholas A. Brawer, *British Campaign Furniture: Elegance under Canvas, 1740–1914* (New York, 2001), esp. pp. 163–4. Mrs Wigley, 'Where Shall I Buy – Shops or Stores', Domestic Puzzles, *The Leisure Hour*, 28 (1879): 331–4.

77. Whiteley's General Catalogue, 1885, p. 481, 726/14, WCA.

78. A.M.W. Stirling, *Victorian Sidelights: From the Papers of the Late Mrs. Adams-Acton* (London, 1954), p. 249.

79. William Whiteley, 'How to Succeed as a Shopkeeper', *Harmsworth Magazine*, 9 (Sept. 1902): 189–92.

80. On Shoolbred's new refreshment rooms, see 'Luxurious Shopping', *Lady's Pictorial*, 31 Dec. 1892, p. 1033; on this phenomenon, Rappaport, *Shopping*, pp. 74–107.

81. Hughes, *London Child*, p. 46.

82. Osbert Lancaster, *All Done from Memory* (Boston, 1953), p. 62.

83. 'Illustration of Furniture and Interior Design', *c.* 1900, HF 57/7/3/1/2, ABRC.

84. See, for instance, Wylie & Lochhead's report on the London furnishing houses. Directors' Minute Book no. 2, 19 Oct. 1915. HF 57/1/2/1/2, ABRC. Also Alison Adburgham, *Shopping in Style: London from the Restoration to Edwardian Elegance* (London, 1979); Morrison, *English Shops*, pp. 159–91.

85. Alison Adburgham, *Liberty's: A Biography of a Shop* (London, 1975).

86. Mrs Stuart Menzies, *Modern Men of Mark* (London, 1921), p. 68.

87. Tim Dale, *Harrods: the Store and the Legend* (London, 1981), p. 72.

88. Eric Newby, *A Traveller's Life* (Boston and Toronto, 1982), p. 37.

89. Reginald Pound, *Selfridge* (London, 1960); Rappaport, *Shopping*, pp. 142–77.

90. 'What Will the New Whiteley's Be Like?' *Paddington, Kensington and Bayswater Chronicle*, 29 Oct. 1910, P 137 Whiteley's, WCA.

91. 'Laying the Foundation Stone of the New Whiteleys' [1910], P 137 Whiteley's, WCA.

92. Leonard Henslowe, 'Representative British Industries: A Romance of Success', n.d. [1907/1908?], 'Told in an interview with Mr. S.J. Waring, chairman of Messrs. Waring and Gillow, Ltd.', 2233/33, WCA.

93. 'Art Furniture in Kensington', *The House*, May 1901, p. 111.

94. 'The Honours List, Sir Samuel J. Waring, Bart.', *Sidcup District Times*, 2 May 1919, 2233/33, WCA.

95. Office of the Deputy Prime Minister: Housing, Planning, Local Government and the Regions Memoranda, Memorandum by Ikea Property Investments Limited (PCP 15), prepared 9 Dec. 2002.

96. According to the *Connoisseur*, Waring's Rotunda was 'one of the sights of London'. 'The Connoisseur at Waring's', *Connoisseur* Aug. 1906 15 (60), John Johnson Collection, Furniture – Box 5, Bodleian Library, Oxford.

97. 'The Connoisseur at Waring's', Bodleian Library.

98. Ibid.

99. See 'The Kaiserin's Visit to Oxford Street', *Daily Telegraph*, 18 Nov. 1907, 2233/33, WCA.

100. 'Sir Samuel Waring, Bart., Honoured at Dinner, Scene of Remarkable Enthusiasm', *District Times*, 23 May 1919, 2233/33, WCA.

101. Ernest Benn, *Happier Days: Recollections and Reflections* (London, 1949), p. 99.

102. Cliftoniensis, 'Mr. Sam Waring: An Appreciation by One Who Knows Him', *The Magazine of Commerce*, n.d. [1907?], 2233/94, WCA.

103. 'The Honours List', WCA.

104. Cliftoniensis, 'Mr. Sam Waring', p. 219, WCA.

105. Mrs Jane Panton, *Most of the Game* (London, 1911), p. 12.

106. The advertisement duty was abolished in 1853, and the newspaper stamp in 1855. On advertising: Loeb, *Consuming Angels*; Richards, *Commodity Culture of Victorian England*; Henry Sampson, *A History of Advertising from the Earliest Times* (London, 1875).

107. T.R. Nevett, *Advertising in Britain: A History* (London, 1982), p. 93.

108. *Furniture and Decoration*, 1 April 1892, p. 61. The quote comes from Messrs Harrison & Jackson's advertisement. See 'The News of the Trade', *Cabinet Maker and Art Furnisher*, Oct. 1898, p. 110.

109. Agnes Gairdner, 1889 Diary [playbills tucked inside], DC 18/18/9, ABRC.

110. On the arrangement made by Scott Cuthbertson with *Hearth and Home*, see, for instance, T.H. Wynn to C.T.C. [Charlotte Talbot Coke], 30 Jan. 1904, Coke MSS.

111. Panton, *Homes of Taste*.

112. 'Toiletwares Old and New', July 1906, AAD/1978/2/281, AAD.
113. 'The Evolution of "Fouracres"', Heal & Son Ltd, p. 12, AAD/1978/2/287.
114. Unidentified newspaper clipping, 1937 pasted into Minute Book, S. Aston & Son, Ltd, 1931–56 [Minutes of Directors and Annual General Meetings], DD/DM/726/3, Denbighshire Record Office – Ruthin.
115. *The House*, Jan. 1902, p. iv.
116. On the Arts and Crafts splendours of Toynbee Hall, see Koven, *Slumming*, pp. 244–8. Samuel Barnett was Alice Hart's brother-in-law.
117. Letter from Alice Hart to the editor of *The House Beautiful*, Chicago, 8 Feb. 1905, *The House Beautiful and the Home*, 15 Feb. 1905, p. 86.
118. Mary Eliza Haweis, *The Art of Decoration* (London, 1881), p. 361.

3 ART AT HOME: HOW THE HOUSE BECAME ARTISTIC

1. On Haweis' colourful past, including a stint alongside Garibaldi at Capua, see the *Oxford Dictionary of National Biography*, vol. 25, pp. 873–5.
2. Amy Charlotte Bewicke Menzies, *Memories Discreet and Indiscreet by a Woman of No Importance* (London, 1917), p. 268.
3. E.W. Godwin, 'To Our Readers', *British Architect and Northern Engineer*, 9 (4 Jan. 1878): 1. Quoted in Juliet Kinchin, 'The Designer as Critic: E.W. Godwin and the Aesthetic Home', *Journal of Design History*, 18: 1 (2005): 21. Godwin's comment was a critical one; his point was that art was 'losing in individual force', and that the domestic interior had been colonized by amateurs.
4. Quoted in 'Art-Furniture and Bric-a-Brac', *Furniture Gazette*, 13 Oct. 1877, p. 274.
5. On the artistic home generally, Martha Crabill McClaugherty, 'Household Art: Creating the Artistic Home', *Winterthur Portfolio*, 18 (Spring 1983): 1–26; in France, Tiersten, *Marianne in the Market*, pp. 150–84 and Saisselin, *The Bourgeois and the Bibelot*, pp. 28–30.
6. Vestas, 'Notes and Queries on Artistic Home Decoration', *The Gentlewoman*, 12 July 1890, p. 34.
7. See, for example, Juliana Horatia Ewing, Diary Entry, 26 Nov. 1876, Sheffield Archives.
8. For a history of the 'art square', J.M. [James Morton], 'Notes Made in 1913 on some of my activities in A.M. & Co.', AAD 3/158–176/1991, p. 7; on Watts and Co., Michael Hall, '"Furniture of Artistic Character": Watts and Company as House Furnishers, 1874–1907', *Furniture History*, 32 (1996): 179–204; Tillyard, *Impact of Modernism*, p. 12.
9. For the Alma Tadema suite, on sale at Wallace's for £21, Mrs Talbot Coke, 'A Lovable House', *Hearth and Home*, 1 March 1894. Also Charlotte Gere with Lesley Hoskins, *The House Beautiful: Oscar Wilde and the Aesthetic Interior* (London, 2000), p.113.
10. 'Odds & Ends in Japanesque', *The House*, 1: 1 (March 1897): 46; on eclecticism, Logan, *Victorian Parlour*, pp. 72–5.
11. 'Odds & Ends in Japanesque', p. 46.
12. W. Macqueen-Pope, *Twenty Shillings in the Pound* (London, 1949 [1948]), p. 340; for an excellent discussion of women's handiwork, Logan, *Victorian Parlour*, pp. 163–82; Tillyard, *Impact of Modernism*, pp. 1–46; Roe, *Victorian Corners*, pp. 88–95.
13. Mrs C.S. Peel, *Life's Enchanted Cup* (London, 1933), p. 79; Zusanna Schonfield, *The Precariously Privileged: A Professional Family in Victorian London* (Oxford, 1987), pp. 87–8.
14. Panton, *Homes of Taste*, p. 33; on the fad for Japan, Anna Jackson, 'Imagining Japan: The Victorian Perception and Acquisition of Japanese Culture', *Journal of Design History*, 5 (1992): 245–56.
15. Panton, *Homes of Taste*, p. 75.
16. 'A Party of Taste', reprinted from *The Architect*, *Cabinet Maker*, 1 Nov. 1881.
17. Frank Thomas Bullen, *Confessions of a Tradesman* (London, 1908), p. 102. For reasons that had little to do with art, the shop was not a success.

18. V.S. Pritchett, *A Cab at the Door: A Memoir* (New York, 1968 [1967]), p. 143.

19. On Mrs Shaw's 'Art at Home' shop, see 'In Search of the Latest', *The House*, Dec. 1897, p. 178. Also 'A Criticism on Modern English Furniture', *Furniture Gazette*, 8 March 1879, p. 156.

20. *Hearth and Home*, 18 July 1895 [selected at random].

21. Advertisement, *Hearth and Home*, 13 Feb. 1902.

22. 'The Sinclair Galleries', *The House*, March 1900, p. 15; 'The Berkeley Galleries', *The House*, June 1901, pp. 154–6; advertisement for the Old Curiosity Shop, Inverness in *The Gentlewoman*, 3 Oct. 1908. As stores publicized their museum-like qualities, some museums sought to attract visitors with the sort of 'domestic amenities', such as tea rooms, which the nation's retailers had pioneered. See Jordanna Bailkin, *The Culture of Property: The Crisis of Liberalism in Modern Britain* (Chicago, 2004), pp. 132–3.

23. 'Warings' Antiques', *Connoisseur*, 5: 17 (Jan. 1903), Second Notice. See also 'Gillow's Furniture', March 1902 II:7 [no source recorded], John Johnson Collection, Furniture – Box 5, Bodleian Library.

24. Directors' Minute Books, Liberty & Co., WCA. Some West End furnishing houses had art directors, as 'Penelope' of *The House* noted. Penelope's Illustrated Answers, *The House*, June 1902, p. 196.

25. Until the post-Second World War rearrangement, the V& A's collection remained organized by material and technique, rather than in 'period rooms' (as was the practice in other countries). See Burton, *Vision and Accident*, pp. 156–66, 190–9. The South Kensington Museum did acquire and display a few historic rooms; it bought the Sérilly 'boudoir' (1869), the Sizergh Castle panelled room (1891), a room from the Old Palace at Bromley-by-Bow in 1894 and a panelled room from Clifford's Inn in 1903. Clive Wainwright, *The Romantic Interior: the British Collector at Home, 1750–1850* (New Haven, 1989), pp. 294–6.

26. 'At Heal and Son's', *Lady's Field*, 21 May 1904, n.p., AAD/1978/2/177, AAD.

27. 'The Sale of Pictures', *Furniture Record*, 13 Oct. 1899, p. 222.

28. This subscription volume included Reynolds' *Duchess of Devonshire and Her Daughter*, as well as Van Eyck's *Arnolfini Marriage*. See *The Hundred Best Pictures for Home Decoration*, ed. C. Hubert Letts (London, 1901), Acc. 726/288, WCA. For a memory of it, Hubert Nicholson, *Half My Days and Nights: Autobiography of a Reporter* (London, 1941), p. 4.

29. On Liberty, Adburgham, *Liberty's*; 'The Maker of "The House Beautiful," The Story of Liberty's', *Fortunes Made in Business: Life Struggles of Successful People*, 5 (1900): 210, 788/9, WCA.

30. 'Mr. Sam Waring: An Appreciation by One Who Knows Him', by Cliftoniensis, n.d., *Magazine of Commerce*, 2233/94, WCA.

31. Leonard Henslowe, 'Representative British Industries: A Romance of Success', [1907?], 'Told in an interview with Mr. S.J. Waring, chairman of Messrs. Waring and Gillow, Ltd.' 2233/33, WCA. See also 'Sir Samuel Waring, Bart., Honoured at Dinner, Scene of Remarkable Enthusiasm', *District Times*, 23 May 1919, 2233/33, WCA.

32. Denis Farr, *English Art, 1870–1940* (Oxford, 1978), pts 2 and 4; Stansky, *Redesigning the World*; on Omega, Christopher Reed, 'A Room of One's Own: The Bloomsbury Group's Creation of a Modernist Domesticity', in *Not at Home: The Suppression of Domesticity in Modern Art and Architecture*, ed. Christopher Reed (New York, 1996), pp. 154–60.

33. Christopher Reed, *Bloomsbury Rooms: Modernism, Subculture, and Domesticity* (New Haven and London, 2004), pp. 35–50, 87–90, 109–63, Tillyard, *Impact of Modernism*, pp. 60–9.

34. A point made by Lionel Lambourne, *The Aesthetic Movement*, p. 33. On the influence of *Japonisme* upon the Impressionists, see *Japonisme in Art: An International Symposium*, ed. Yamada Chisaburo (Tokyo, 1980); in French decorative arts, Silverman, *Art Nouveau*, pp. 126–32.

35. Mrs Haweis, *Beautiful Houses: Being a Description of Certain Well-Known Artistic Houses* (New York, 1882); Giles Walkley, *Artists' Houses in London, 1764–1914* (Brookfield, VT, 1994); Diane Sachko Macleod, *Art and the Victorian Middle Class: Money and the Making of Cultural Identity* (Cambridge, 1996), pp. 296–7; Caroline Dakers, *The Holland Park Circle: Artists and*

Victorian Society (New Haven and London, 1999). In the *Magazine of Art*, see, for instance the series 'The Homes of Our Artists', vol. 4 (1881). On domestic interiors as paradigmatic Bloomsbury artistic statements, Reed, *Bloomsbury Rooms*.

36. Macleod, *Art and the Victorian Middle Class*, p. 308.
37. Shonfield, *Precariously Privileged*, p. 88.
38. David Robertson, *Sir Charles Eastlake and the Victorian Art World* (Princeton, 1978), pp. 401–2.
39. 'Cosy Corner Chat', *The Gentlewoman*, 1 Nov. 1890, p. 601.
40. On Mrs Panton's novel *Having and Holding*, Bailkin, *Culture of Property*, pp. 137–9.
41. 'Treasure-Houses of Art – I', *Magazine of Art*, Jan. 1879, p. 143. See the *Art Journal's* series by Aymer Vallance on 'Furnishing and Decoration', which ran from January through to December of 1892. On house museums generally, see the work of Anne Higonnet, especially 'Private Museums, Public Leadership: Isabella Stewart Gardner and the Art of Cultural Authority', in *Cultural Leadership in America: Art Matronage and Patronage* (Boston, 1997), pp. 79–92.
42. On *The Artist*, which under the editorship of Charles Kains-Jackson from 1888 to 1894 became a centre of the 'Uranian' movement, see Laurel Brake, '"Gay Discourse" and *The Artist and Journal of Home Culture*', in *Nineteenth-Century Media and the Construction of Identities*, ed. Laurel Brake, Bill Bell, and David Finkelstein (New York, 2000), pp. 271–91.
43. 'From Month to Month', *The Artist*, 1 Jan. 1881, p. 17. On the artist as furnishing taste-maker, Hamerton, *Thoughts*, pp. 346–68.
44. See, for instance, 'Messrs. Twyford & Sons' Sanitary Works', *Furniture Gazette*, 1 May 1875, p. 533. On French decorative arts, Troy, *Modernism and the Decorative Arts*.
45. 'South Kensington Museum', reprinted from *The Echo* in *The House-Furnisher and Decorator*, April 1872, p. 40.
46. Lewis Day, 'The Place of Pictures in the Decoration of a Room', *Magazine of Art*, 4 (Nov. 1880–Oct. 1881) bound together, p. 322; also Mr Charles Eastlake, 'The Influence of Decorative Art', paper read at Social Science Congress on 'What is the Influence on Society of Decorative Art and Art-Workmanship in All Household Details?' *Furniture Gazette*, 28 Oct. 1876, p. 263.
47. 'Art Handicrafts for Women', *Furniture Gazette*, 18 Aug. 1883, p. 110.
48. Haweis, *Art of Decoration*, p. 378.
49. 'The China Mania', [reprinted, no source] *Furniture Gazette*, 13 Nov. 1875, p. 299; also, 'The Art of Furnishing', *Cornhill Magazine*, 31 (1875): 535–47.
50. James Whistler, *The Gentle Art of Making Enemies* (London, 1904 [1890]), p. 136.
51. See *Happy Home*, 30 March 1895, 6 April 1895, 20 April 1895; S. Martin Gaskell, 'Housing and the Lower Middle Class, 1870–1914', in Geoffrey Crossick, ed., *The Lower Middle Class in Britain, 1870–1914* (New York, 1977), pp. 159–83.
52. Mrs Talbot Coke, 'House Furnishing', *Woman at Home*, 1895 [bound vol. at Colindale gives no dates for individual issues], p. 74.
53. Exhibition of Design and Workmanship in Printing, Metropolitan School of Art, Dublin, 20 Nov. to 6 Dec. 1916, organized in conjunction with the Design and Industries Association, DIA/122, RIBA. On the DIA, Michael Saler, *The Avant-Garde in Interwar England: Medieval Modernism and the London Underground* (New York and Oxford, 1999).
54. See Mrs Talbot Coke, 'My Year Book for 1908', *Hearth and Home*, 5 March 1908.
55. Walter E. Downing, 'Furnishing on Established Lines', *Ideal Home*, Sept. 1920, p. 104.
56. Linda Slater, Bristol in Visitor's Book, Liberty's, n.d. [1920s], 788/27/1, WCA.
57. Haweis, *Art of Decoration*, p. 365. See, too, Hamerton, *Thoughts*, p. 348.
58. 'Chats with Celebrities: Mrs. Haweis', *Hearth and Home*, 11 Aug. 1892.
59. Howe, *Arbiter*, p. 78. Thus provoking consternation: A.C. Meynell, 'The Outer Colouring of Houses', *Magazine of Art*, 3 (Nov. 1879–Oct. 1880): 367.
60. Haweis, *Art of Decoration*, p. 369.
61. Howe, *Arbiter*, p. 175.

62. Among others, Lambourne, *Aesthetic Movement*; Elizabeth Aslin, *The Aesthetic Movement: Prelude to Art Nouveau* (London, 1969); Charlotte Gere with Lesley Hoskins, *The House Beautiful: Oscar Wilde and the Aesthetic Interior* (London, 2000), pp. 110, 113; William Gaunt, *The Aesthetic Adventure* (London, 1945); Macleod, *Art and the Victorian Middle Class*, pp. 267–335. The best account of the ideas behind the 'Queen Anne' style is Mark Girouard, *Sweetness and Light: The 'Queen Anne' Movement, 1860–1900* (New Haven, 1977).

63. See, for instance, 'Art at Home', *Saturday Review*, 20 Dec. 1873, pp. 777–8; 'Art in the Dining Room', *Saturday Review*, 12 Jan. 1878, Newspaper Clippings, Jan. 1877–June 1878 vol. II (Misc.), f. 205 AAD; 'A Party of Taste'; 'John Bull's New House', *All the Year Round*, 2nd series, 19 (1877–8): 5–10.

64. 'Art at Home', *Saturday Review*, p. 778.

65. 'The Furniture at Sir John Soane's Museum', *Cabinet Maker*, 1 Sept. 1880, p. 38; Visit in a lady's diary referring to an evening spent at the Soane Museum in the time of the curator James Wilde, Press Cuttings, Sir John Soane's Museum – Archive; see, too, attendance figures contained in Sir John Soane's Museum, Report for the Year Ending 1897, George H. Birch, Curator, Sir John Soane's Museum – Archive.

66. 'Mr. Oscar Wilde on House Decoration', *Furniture Gazette*, 10 Nov. 1883, p. 325.

67. Girouard, *Sweetness and Light*, p. 4.

68. Campbell, *Romantic Ethic*, pp. 180–95; Minihan, *Nationalization of Culture*, pp. 26–8, 161–2; Lyndel Saunders King, *The Industrialization of Taste: Victorian England and the Art Union of London* (Ann Arbor, 1985); Macleod, *Art and the Victorian Middle Class*, p. 104.

69. Lucy Crane, *Art and the Formation of Taste: Six Lectures* (Boston, 1887), p. 33. Similarly, Lewis Day, 'Decorative Art. – I', *Magazine of Art*, 3 (Nov. 1879–Oct. 1880): 104.

70. Herbert Byng Hall, *The Bric-à-Brac Hunter: Or, Chapters on Chinamania* (Philadelphia, 1875), p. 18.

71. 'Art of Furnishing', *London Society: An Illustrated Magazine*, 7 (1865): 503.

72. Michael Levey, *The Case of Walter Pater* (London, 1978), p. 95; A.C. Benson, *Walter Pater* (London, 1907), pp. 24–5.

73. See Benson, *Pater*, pp. 195–6; on his austerity, pp. 18–19.

74. Ellmann, *Oscar Wilde* (New York, 1988), p. 45.

75. Burgon's 'Some Remarks on Art', *New York Tribune*, 8 Jan. 1882, quoted in Ellmann, *Oscar Wilde*, p. 45.

76. George du Maurier, 'Six Mark Tea-Pot', *Punch*, 20 Oct. 1880.

77. 'The House Beautiful', *Furniture Gazette*, 8 Dec. 1883, p. 397.

78. Oscar Wilde, 'The Critic as Artist', in *Intentions* (London, 1913), p. 215. Wilde's statement was quickly ridiculed by *Punch* in 'Development', 99 (20 Sept. 1890): 135.

79. 'Art at Home', *Saturday Review*, pp. 777–8. As Whistler noted, the publication was otherwise known as the 'Saturday Reviler'. See Whistler, *Gentle Art*, p. 166; Dennis Denisoff, *Aestheticism and Sexual Parody* (Cambridge, 2001).

80. L.B. Walford, *Memories of Victorian London* (London, 1912), p. 149; on the horrors of an aesthetic daughter, 'John Bull's New House', pp. 5–10.

81. 'Art at Home', *Saturday Review*, p. 778.

82. 'A Party of Taste', reprinted from *The Architect*, *Cabinet Maker*, 1 Nov. 1881.

83. Lambourne, *Aesthetic Movement*, p. 124.

84. Frances Power Cobbe, 'Backward Ho!', *New Quarterly Magazine*, 5 (Oct. 1875–Jan. 1876): 231–62. On Cobbe, Sally Mitchell, *Frances Power Cobbe: Victorian Feminist, Journalist, Reformer* (Charlottesville, 2004), esp. pp. 186–266.

85. 'The Harm Aestheticism Has Done to Art', *Furniture Gazette*, 10 Feb. 1883, p. 104

86. 'The House of Liberty and Its Founder', *Daily Chronicle*, n.d. [1913?], 788/10, WCA.

87. Tony Joseph, *The D'Oyly Carte Opera Company, 1875–1982: An Unofficial History* (Bristol, 1994), esp. pp. 7–20.

88. Lambourne, *Aesthetic Movement*, p. 123.

89. Panton, *Homes of Taste*, p. 13.

90. Jane Ellen Panton, *Leaves from a Life* (New York, 1908), p. 304.
91. A point noted in Gere with Hoskins, *House Beautiful*, pp. 110, 113.
92. Kinchin, 'Designer as Critic', pp. 31–2; Susan Weber Soros, ed., *E.W. Godwin: Aesthetic Movement Architect and Designer* (New Haven and London, 1999); Susan Weber Soros, *The Secular Furniture of E.W. Godwin* (New Haven and London, 1999).
93. Quoted in H. Montogomery Hyde, ed., *The Three Trials of Oscar Wilde* (New York, 1956), p. 11.
94. Jennings, *Our Homes*, p. 55.
95. Haweis, *Art of Decoration*, p. 53.
96. Ibid., p. 30.
97. Ibid., p. 399.
98. John Marshall, Rector of the Royal High School, 'Amateur House Decoration', *Furniture Gazette*, 5 May 1883, p. 316.
99. Mrs Talbot Coke, 'A Furnished Flat', *Queen*, 1 Oct. 1887, p. 425. She described her improvised method of draping doorways in language that owed much to impressionism: 'it comes as it likes'. Mrs Talbot Coke, 'Drapery of Conservatory Door, &c.', *Queen*, 17 Dec. 1887, p. 823.
100. Halsey Ricardo, 'Art in the Home: The Principles of Modern Decoration', *The World: A Journal for Men and Women*, 30 June 1903, p. 1126.
101. On this point, see Rubinstein, *Men of Property*, esp. p. 61; Lewis, *Middlemost and the Milltowns*, pp. 346–50; on 'gentlemanly capitalism', P.J. Cain and A.G. Hopkins, *British Imperialism: Innovation and Expansion, 1688–1914* (London, 1993).
102. John Stuart Mill, *Principles of Political Economy*, quoted in Andrew Miles, *Social Mobility in Nineteenth- and Early Twentieth-Century England* (Basingstoke and London, 1999), p. 28.
103. Miles, *Social Mobility*, esp. pp. 21–65, 116–144. Lawrence Stone and Jeanne C. Fawtier Stone, *An Open Elite? England 1540–1880* (Oxford, 1984). Harold Perkin's assessment is considerably more negative than Miles': *Origins of Modern English Society* (London, 2002 [1969], pp. 423–34. See also Andrew Miles and David Vincent, eds, *Building European Society: Occupational Change and Social Mobility in Europe 1840–1940* (Manchester, 1993), esp. 18–39, 140–64.
104. Morgan, *Manners, Morals and Class*, p. 94.
105. Rubinstein, *Men of Property*, pp. 117–44; J. Mordaunt Crook, *The Rise of the Nouveaux Riches: Style and Status in Victorian and Edwardian Architecture* (London, 1999), esp. pp. 1–32, 153–87. Though *Who's Who* had been published since 1849, by the end of the century it was nearly defunct; the original *Who's Who* had consisted of lists of names of notables, without biographical details. In 1896, A. & C. Black acquired the rights to *Who's Who*, which they remodelled to include biographical entries (often penned by the entrants themselves). Unlike the existing reference books, limited to the titled and wealthy, *Who's Who* aimed to profile 'all the prominent persons in the United Kingdom'. Their first *Who's Who* included 5,000 names. J.D.N., *Adam & Charles Black, 1807–1957* (London, 1957), pp. 71–3.
106. H.G. Wells, *Kipps* (New York, 1927 [1905]), p. 326; also Guy Chapman, *Culture and Survival* (London, 1940), pp. 177–8.
107. Miles, *Social Mobility*, p. 32; Patricia Alden, *Social Mobility in the English Bildungsroman: Gissing, Hardy, Bennett, and Lawrence* (Ann Arbor, 1986 [1979]). For a contemporary satire on downward mobility, George W.E. Russell, *A Londoner's Log-Book 1901–2* (London, 1902), esp. pp. 76–85.
108. Morgan, *Manners, Morals and Class*, pp. 46–7; in the United States, Karen Halttunen, *Confidence Men and Painted Women: A Study of Middle-Class Culture in America, 1830–1870* (New Haven, 1982), esp. pp. 33–91.
109. 'Criminal Appeal', *Daily News*, 24 Aug. 1904, p. 12. On the contemporaneous success of 'disguises' in undercover investigative journalism, Koven, *Slumming*, pp. 25–69, 140–80. On such fears in the early modern city, Wahrman, *Making of the Modern Self*, pp. 202–7; Richard Sennett, *The Fall of Public Man* (New York, 1977).

110. Mrs Talbot Coke, *The Gentlewoman at Home* (London, 1892), p. 76. On this point: Christopher Breward, 'Fashionable Living', in *Design and the Decorative Arts*, ed. Snodin and Styles, p. 415; in France, Auslander, *Taste and Power*, pp. 264–305.
111. Howe, *Arbiter*, p. 174.
112. Ibid., pp. 224–70.
113. Ibid., p. 226.
114. Ibid., p. 236.
115. Mrs Haweis, 'Beautiful Homes', *Domestic Life*, 24 April 1897, p. 91.
116. Howe, *Arbiter*, p. 16.
117. Advertisement for cricket preceding 'Britain's Best Home' – 29 July 2003, Channel Four.

4 IN POSSESSION: MEN, WOMEN AND DECORATION

1. J.F. Winterbottom to Mr Edmonds, 27 Sept. 1867, 4M88W/A 1/6, HRO – Winchester.
2. Winterbottom to Edmonds, 16 Jan. 1868, 4M88W/A 1/6, HRO.
3. Logan, *Victorian Parlour*, pp. xii, 36–7.
4. On domesticity: especially Davidoff and Hall, *Family Fortunes*, pp. 149–92, 319–96; Nancy Armstrong, *Desire and Domestic Fiction: A Political History of the Novel* (New York and Oxford, 1987), pp. 59–95; Penny Sparke, *As Long As It's Pink: The Sexual Politics of Taste* (London, 1995), pp. 15–49. On Victorian women and shopping: Rappaport, *Shopping*; Judith Walkowitz, 'Going Public: Shopping, Street Walking, and Street Harassment in Late-Victorian London', *Representations*, 62 (Spring 1998): 1–30; Loeb, *Consuming Angels*, esp. pp. 16–45; Victoria de Grazia and Ellen Furlough, eds, *The Sex of Things: Gender and Consumption in Historical Perspective* (Berkeley and Los Angeles, 1996); Tiersten, *Marianne at the Market*.
5. Tosh, *Man's Place*, esp. pp. 1–142. On men and consumerism: Christopher Breward, *The Hidden Consumer: Masculinities, Fashion and City Life, 1860–1914* (Manchester, 1995); Margot Finn, 'Men's Things: Masculine Possession in the Consumer Revolution', *Social History*, 25:2 (May 2000): 133–55; Berg, *Luxury and Pleasure*, pp. 234–46; Frank Mort, *Cultures of Consumption: Masculinity and Social Space in Late-Twentieth-Century Britain* (London, 1996).
6. Speech in the House of Commons, 20 May 1867. Cited in J.A. and Olive Banks, *Feminism and Family Planning in Victorian England* (New York, 1964), p. 73.
7. See, for instance, Maple's Staff Record Book, 1894–1945. Until the First World War, Maple's employed only salesmen. AAD/2000/3/52.
8. On married women's property: Lee Holcombe, *Wives and Property: Reform of the Married Women's Property Law in Nineteenth-Century England* (Toronto, 1983); Susan Staves, *Married Women's Separate Property in England, 1660–1833* (Cambridge, MA, 1990); Mary Lyndon Shanley, *Feminism, Marriage and the Law in Victorian England, 1850–1895* (Princeton, 1989); in fiction, Tim Dolin, *Mistress of the House: Women of Property in the Victorian Novel* (Aldershot, 1997); Ben Griffin, 'Class, Gender, and Liberalism in Parliament, 1868–1882: The Case of the Married Women's Property Acts', *Historical Journal*, 46:1 (March 2003): 59–87. Margot Finn has warned of the danger of exaggerating the limitations on women's economic authority under coverture. See her 'Women, Consumption and Coverture in England, *c.* 1760–1860', *Historical Journal*, 39: 3 (1996): 703–22.
9. On the operation of trusts in practice: Morris, *Men, Women and Property*, pp. 233–63.
10. Finn, 'Women, Consumption'; Rappaport, *Shopping*, pp. 48–73.
11. Rappaport, *Shopping*, pp. 48–73.
12. Virginia Woolf, *Three Guineas* (London, 1938).
13. See John Robson, *Marriage or Celibacy: The Daily Telegraph on a Victorian Dilemma* (Toronto, 1995), pp. 126–7; Judith Flanders, *The Victorian House: Domestic Life from Childbirth to Deathbed* (London, 2003), p. 133.

14. L.O.J. Boynton, 'High Victorian Furniture: The Example of Marsh and Jones of Leeds', *Furniture History*, 3 (1967): 54–91. The theatre manager W.H.C. Nation furnished a mansion to receive his bride; on the day of the wedding, the woman changed her mind. Nation never occupied the house, nor did he sell it. Until the day he died, everything was left intact. George R. Sims, *My Life: Sixty Years' Recollections of Bohemian London* (London, 1917), p. 292.

15. *Matrimonial Times*, 15 Nov. 1875, p. 4.

16. Anthony Trollope, *Can You Forgive Her?* (London, 1986 [1864–5]), p. 168.

17. Robert Kerr, *The Gentleman's House; Or, How to Plan English Residences from the Parsonage to the Palace* (London, 1871 [1864]), p. 86.

18. William Mitford, 'Fashion and Furniture', *Furniture Gazette*, 14 March 1874; see, too, Lewis Day, 'The Woman's Part in Domestic Decoration', *Magazine of Art*, Nov. 1879–Oct. 1880, pp. 457–463; Sparke, *As Long as It's Pink*, pp. 50–69.

19. Dr Christopher Dresser, 'Good Taste in House Furnishing', *Furniture Gazette*, 3 Jan. 1874, p. 10. On Dresser: Stuart Durant, *Christopher Dresser* (London, 1993); Michael Whiteway, ed., *Shock of the Old: Christopher Dresser's Design Revolution* (London, 2004).

20. See, for instance, Charles Dance, Esq., 'Good News for the Ladies', *Lady's Newspaper and Pictorial Times*, 2 Jan. 1847. The *Lady's Newspaper* – sampled for the year 1862 – carried a work-table column, but no furnishing advertisements, articles, or regular columns on house furnishing. Even in the late 1870s, the *Englishwoman's Domestic Magazine* ran no articles on furniture or furnishing, in contrast to the very extensive coverage of Paris fashions, baby advice, needlework, and poetry. *Queen* was the trail-blazer here, commissioning Charles Eastlake's columns, later published as *Hints on Household Taste* and, as of 1887, Mrs Talbot Coke's regular feature. Margaret Beetham, *A Magazine of Her Own? Domesticity and Desire in the Woman's Magazine, 1800–1914* (London, 1996), pp. 96–8.

21. Loftie, *A Plea*, esp. pp. 21–2.

22. Garrett and Garrett, *Suggestions*, p. 21.

23. Ibid., p. 28. A similar assumption is made by Panton, *Homes of Taste*, p. 147. On the significance of the parlour, Logan, *Victorian Parlour*, pp. 23–35.

24. Quoted in Lawrence and Elisabeth Hanson, *Necessary Evil: The Life of Jane Welsh Carlyle* (London, 1952), p. 106. See also James Anthony Froude, ed., *Letters and Memorials of Jane Welsh Carlyle* (New York, 1883), vol. 1, pp. 408, 437; vol. 2, pp. 106, 294, 326, 335.

25. Ward, *Memories of Ninety Years*, p. 129; for a similarly harmonious account, Mary Marshall, *What I Remember* (Cambridge, 1947), p. 42.

26. Garrett and Garrett, *Suggestions*, p. 84.

27. 'New Styles in Furniture', *Cabinet and Upholstery Advertiser*, 9 Nov. 1878, p. 13. On men as presumed clients, Arthur Forbes, 'The Principles of Design in Furniture', *Furniture Gazette*, 3 Jan. 1874, p. 8; on men's control over large furniture purchases in the Georgian period, Vickery, *Gentleman's Daughter*, p. 167.

28. Basil Champneys, *Memoirs and Correspondence of Coventry Patmore* (London, 1900), vol. 1, p. 355.

29. Reprinted in *Building News*, 14 (12 April 1867): 260. On Arthur Munby's furnishing, see Derek Hudson, *Munby: A Man of Two Worlds: The Life and Diaries of Arthur J. Munby, 1828–1910* (London, 1972), pp. 329, 392.

30. Katharine Tynan, *Twenty-Five Years: Reminiscences* (London, 1913), pp. 178–83.

31. On Mr Anderson: W.S.M. to [illeg.], 8 Dec. 1881, f. 503; to Willie Leeper, 1 Sept. 1881, f. 209, Letter Book 1881–2, Acc. No. 1991/11, RCAHMS; W.S.M. to Robert Stewart, 8 Nov. 1881, f. 404; W.S.M. to C.E. Willet, Esq., 3 Dec. 1881, f. 494; W.S.M. to W.H. Henderson, Esq., 21 Jan. 1882, f. 579; W.S.M. to Mr Templeton, 5 June 1882, f. 882. Of course, it is possible that some of these men were merely acting as their wives' agents; because of the law of coverture, tradesmen trusted husbands more than they did wives. But these men were at the very least active parties to decisions; in other letters, men referred to their wives' desires where relevant, and some women also wrote to William Scott Morton directly.

32. Mrs Talbot Coke, 'Home Advice', *Hearth and Home*, 11 July 1895, p. 332; 10 April 1902, p. 1028.

33. Mrs Talbot Coke, 'Home Advice', *Hearth and Home*, 4 June 1896, p. 152.

34. Mrs Talbot Coke, 'Home Advice', *Hearth and Home*, 4 Aug. 1892, p. 293. It was, of course, telling that at the end of the century men's preferences found expression only through such circuitous routes. A few men did write in to decorating columnists themselves, and that in itself is perhaps surprising, given that the decorators on paper published principally in women's magazines.

35. On Dinah Craik's life, Sally Mitchell, *Dinah Mulock Craik* (Boston, 1983).

36. Walford, *Memories of Victorian London*, p. 201.

37. Rev. F. Barham Zincke, 'A Dishomed Nation', *Contemporary Review*, 38 (Aug. 1880): 179–80.

38. Tosh, *Man's Place*, pp. 24–5.

39. C. Dresser, Letter to the Editor, *Furniture Gazette*, 24 July 1875, p. 47.

40. John Galsworthy, *The Man of Property* in *The Forsyte Saga* (New York, 1933), p. 36. On the uniformity of men's dress, Kuchta, *The Three-Piece Suit*, pp. 162–78.

41. Among others: Robert Drane, Diary Entry, 9 May 1895, D/DXib 28/14, GRO; Ellaline Terriss, *Just a Little Bit of String* (London, 1955), p. 49. On the significance of houses to status, Morris, *Men, Women and Property*, esp. pp. 339–40.

42. Hardman, *Mid-Victorian Pepys*, p. 104.

43. Macleod, *Art and the Victorian Middle Class*, pp. 289–95. See also Arthur Forbes, 'The Principles of Design in Furniture', *Furniture Gazette*, 3 Jan. 1874, p. 8.

44. Frederick Locker-Lampson, *My Confidences: An Autobiographical Sketch Addressed to My Descendants* (New York, 1896), p. 246; see, too, Stewart Dawson, 'A Matter of Taste', *Belgravia: A London Magazine*, 86 (1895): 35–60.

45. G. Rivington, 'The Sales Department', *Furnishings*, April 1926, p. 15; Dennis Chapman, *The Home and Social Status* (London, 1955), pp. 31–2, 41; on inter-war male consumerism, Jill Greenfield, Sean O'Connell, and Chris Reid, 'Gender, Consumer Culture and the Middle-Class Male, 1918–1939', in *Gender, Civic Culture and Consumerism*, ed. Kidd and Nicholls, pp. 183–97.

46. Catalogue, PA 2084/20, leaflet illustrating bedroom furniture with dimensions, Berick trademark, 1938, Brookes Collection, Coventry Archives.

47. 'Furnishing Commentary – I: The West End', *Cabinet Maker and Complete House Furnisher*, 13 May 1939, p. 212.

48. Mary Gwynne Howell, 'House Husbandry', *Ideal Home*, Oct. 1925, pp. 312–14.

49. Women were considered especially susceptible to the aesthetic craze. See 'Art Training and Art Crazes', *Furniture Gazette*, 7 May 1881, p. 300.

50. 'The Saturday Review on Art at Home', *Furniture Gazette*, 7 Feb. 1874, p. 138.

51. Mrs Talbot Coke, 'A Man's Room', *Hearth and Home*, 1 Sept. 1892, p. 520. Of interest, too, are *Hearth and Home*'s leading articles for 30 March 1893 and 6 April 1893: 'Effeminate Men'.

52. Jeffrey Weeks, *Coming Out: Homosexual Politics in Britain from the Nineteenth Century to the Present* (London, 1977), pp. 4, 115–27, 162–3; Regenia Gagnier, *Idylls of the Marketplace: Oscar Wilde and the Victorian Public* (Stanford, 1986), pp. 140–3; Richard Dellamora, *Masculine Desire: The Sexual Politics of Victorian Aestheticism* (Chapel Hill, 1990); Alan Sinfield, *The Wilde Century: Effeminacy, Oscar Wilde and the Queer Moment* (New York, 1994), pp. vi, 1–21, 62–75; esp. pp. 84–105.

53. Reed, *Bloomsbury Rooms*, pp. 53–63.

54. Mrs Talbot Coke, 'Home Advice', *Hearth and Home*, 22 Oct. 1891, p. 737; also Eunice, 'Home Decoration', *The Lady*, 3 Oct. 1895, p. 460; 'On the Unaffected in Furnishing', *The House*, 5: 1 (July 1897): 219; Dellamora, *Masculine Desire*, pp. 193–217.

55. Tosh, *Man's Place*, pp. 170–94. A growing minority of middle-class men never married, or delayed marriage until they had reached their thirties.

56. Although the process of suburbanization was under way in the 1840s, with the building of austere Georgian terraces and later, fussier Italianate and Gothic houses on the city's

perimeter, the pace accelerated in the last two decades of the nineteenth century. From the earlier period, Thomas Morris, *A House for the Suburbs* (London, 1870). On suburbanization, Burnett, *Social History of Housing*, pp. 188–216; Helen C. Long, *The Edwardian House: The Middle-Class Home in Britain 1880–1914* (Manchester, 1993), pp. 49–61; Helena Barrett and John Phillips, *Suburban Style: The British Home, 1840–1960* (London, 1987); S. Martin Gaskell, 'Housing and the Lower Middle Class, 1870–1914', pp. 159–83; on the garden city movement, Standish Meacham, *Regaining Paradise: Englishness and the Early Garden City Movement* (New Haven and London, 1998).

57. C.F.G. Masterman, *The Condition of England* [1909], pp. 57–8, quoted in Burnett, *Social History of Housing*, p. 188.

58. Thomas Crosland, *The Suburbans* (London, 1905), p. 21. For an incisive analysis of Crosland, see A. James Hamerton, 'The English Weakness? Gender, Satire and "Moral Manliness" in the Lower Middle Class, 1870–1920', in *Gender, Civic Culture and Consumerism*, ed. Kidd and Nicholls, pp. 164–82; on suburban masculinity, Breward, *Hidden Consumer*, pp. 189–201.

59. Philip Gibbs, *The New Man: A Portrait Study of the Latest Type* (London, 1914), p. 187.

60. Ursula Bloom, *The Elegant Edwardian* (London, 1957), p. 130. See also Thomas Rohan, *Old Beautiful* (London, 1926) on doctors and parsons as antique collectors, pp. 25–6.

61. Bloom, *Elegant Edwardian*, p. 170. On clerical homes, Jane Hamlett, '"Ostentation is always unbecoming"'.

62. 'The Art of Upholstery', *Furniture Record*, 11 Aug. 1899, p. 73. For an angry reaction from the trade, 'A Counter Charge', *Furnishings*, Dec. 1926, p. 4.

63. Beryl Lee Booker, *Yesterday's Child, 1890–1909* (London, 1937), pp. 28–9. On the bachelor den, Breward, *Hidden Consumer*, pp. 180–1; on military men and material culture, Quintin Colville, 'The Role of the Interior in Constructing Notions of Class and Status: A Case-Study of Britannia Royal Naval College Dartmouth, 1905–1939', in *Interior Design and Identity*, ed. Susie McKellar and Penny Sparke (London, 2004).

64. Colonel Montague Cooke, *Clouds that Flee* (London, 1935), p. 32.

65. Elizabeth Montizambert, *London Discoveries in Shops & Restaurants* (London, 1924), pp. 52; 56. On military men as clients, see 'No. 1A Holland Park: The Residence of Vice-Admiral E.A. Taylor', *Antique Collector*, Jan. 1937, p. 352.

66. Trevor Royle, *The Kitchener Enigma* (London, 1985), p. 218. On Kitchener's tastes, see also Philip Magnus, *Kitchener: Portrait of an Imperialist* (London, 1958), pp. 200–1.

67. Royle, *The Kitchener Enigma*, p. 144.

68. P.W., 'The Late Lord Kitchener's Hobbies', n.d., *Country Life*, PRO 30/57/100. On Kitchener's 'work of great pleasure' in arranging his treasures at Broome Park, Menzies, *Memories Discreet*, p. 209.

69. Quoted in J.P. Blake, 'Chippendale Furniture for the Small Collector', *Old Furniture*, 2: 7 (15 Dec. 1927), John Johnson Collection, Furniture – Box 5, Bodleian Library, Oxford. On Grenfell, *Memoirs of Field-Marshal Lord Grenfell* (London, 1925); Thomas Rohan, *Confessions of an Antique Dealer* (New York, 1925), pp. 200–1.

70. Quoted in Holcombe, *Wives and Property*, p. 57.

71. Josephine Butler, ed., *Woman's Work and Woman's Culture: A Series of Essays* (London, 1869), p. xxv. This was a fear that even advocates of property reform shared; see Griffin, 'Class, Gender, and Liberalism in Parliament'.

72. On women's tendency to allocate particular items in their wills, Morris, *Men, Women and Property*, pp. 253, 264.

73. Frances Power Cobbe, *Duties of Women: A Course of Lectures* (London, 1881), p. 139.

74. Ibid., p. 148.

75. For Ngaio Marsh's description of her own inter-war venture in interior decoration, see Marsh, *Black Beech and Honeydew* (Auckland, 1981 [1966]), pp. 189–91.

76. Register of Members, Incorporated Institute of British Decorators, AAD/1988/20 PL5 & 6.

77. From 'Modern Upholstery', *Cabinet Maker and Art Furnisher*, July 1892, p. 20.

78. Mrs Panton's obituary describes her as 'a witty and outspoken conversationalist, with the courage of her opinions, and under a naturally impatient temperament there lay a fund of real kindness and wisdom. . . .' 'Mrs J.E. Panton', *The Times*, 21 May 1923, p. 11.

79. On the Garretts, see Elizabeth Crawford's *Enterprising Women: The Garretts and their Circle* (London, 2002), esp. pp. 169–217; also Emma Ferry, '"Decorators may be compared to doctors": An Analysis of Rhoda and Agnes Garrett's *Suggestions for House Decoration in Painting, Woodwork and Furniture (1876)*', *Journal of Design History*, 16: 1 (2003): 15–33.

80. Jo Manton, *Elizabeth Garrett Anderson* (New York, 1965), p. 221, fn. 3. On the difficulties architecture presented as a career for women, R. Weir Schulz, 'Architecture for Women', *Architectural Review*, 24 (1908): 153–4.

81. Rhoda had been raised in an evangelical household; her father John Fisher Garrett, was the rector of Elton, in Derbyshire. Although Elizabeth Garrett in 1861 characterized Rhoda as 'very Evangelical in creed', she added that 'this is the result of education, & has not done any serious harm'. Whether Rhoda remained a believer is not known. See Crawford, *Enterprising Women*, p. 25.

82. Ray Strachey, *Millicent Garrett Fawcett* (London, 1931), p. 58; 'Art Decoration', *The Furnisher and Decorator*, 1 March 1890, p. 117; Anthea Callan, *Angel in the Studio: Women in the Arts and Crafts Movement, 1870–1914* (London, 1979), pp. 171–2; Gerald Shaw, ed., *The Garrett Papers* (Cape Town, 1984); David Rubinstein, *A Different World for Women: The Life of Millicent Garrett Fawcett* (Columbus, 1991), p. 3.

83. Millicent Vince, 'Agnes Garrett: Pioneer of Women House Decorators', *The Woman's Leader*, 11 Sept. 1925, p. 259; Crawford, *Enterprising Women*, p. 172.

84. Moncure Conway, *Autobiography*, vol. 1 (Boston, 1904), p. 451.

85. Ethel Smyth, *Impressions that Remained* (London, 1923), vol. 2, p. 7; Rhoda Garrett, 'How to Improve the Interior of Modern Houses', *Transactions of the National Association for the Promotion of Social Science, Liverpool Meeting 1876*, ed. Charles Wager Ryalls (London, 1877).

86. Smyth, *Impressions*, vol. 2, p. 8.

87. 'Interview', *Women's Penny Paper*, 18 Jan. 1890, p. 145.

88. Ibid., p. 146.

89. Richard Pankhurst, *Sylvia Pankhurst: Artist and Crusader* (New York and London, 1979), pp. 13, 46; Patricia Romero, *E. Sylvia Pankhurst: Portrait of a Radical* (New Haven, 1987), pp. 9–10; Martin Pugh, *The Pankhursts* (London, 2001), pp. 44–5, 48–51, 82.

90. E. Sylvia Pankhurst, *The Life of Emmeline Pankhurst* (Boston and New York, 1936), p. 22; Christabel Pankhurst, *Unshackled: The Story of How We Won the Vote* (London, 1959), p. 38.

91. Pankhurst, *Unshackled*, pp. 25–6. According to Christabel, 'Mother's business efforts were all part of the experience that prepared her for the historic campaign of her later years' (pp. 27–8).

92. Pankhurst, *Life*, pp. 22–4, 30–1.

93. Quoted in Pugh, *Pankhursts*, p. 82.

94. 'House-Decorating as an Occupation', *The Young Woman*, April 1901, pp. 252–4; 'The World of Breadwinners – A Lady Decorator', *Woman*, 11 Jan. 1890; Agnes Garrett, 'Employment for Girls: House Decoration', *Atalanta*, 1 1887 p. 415. Mrs Loftie, writing in the 1870s on the subject of 'work for women', noted: 'The profession of house-decorating seems one likely to develop itself, and is apparently very well suited to ladies of taste and education.' Loftie, *Social Twitters*, p. 141.

95. Moncure D. Conway in *Scribner's Magazine*, reprinted in 'On Domestic Decoration', *Furniture Gazette*, 22 May 1875, p. 655. On Miss Cohen, 'Art in the Home', *The Expert*, May 1909, p. 176. Millicent Cohen – later Millicent Vince – published *Decoration and Care of the Home* (1923), *Furnishing and Decorating Do's and Don'ts* (1925), and *Practical House Decorating* (1932).

96. 'Art Decoration', *The Furnisher and Decorator*, 1 March 1890, p. 117. See also Crawford, *Enterprising Women*, p. 206; p. 319, n. 130.

97. 'The World of Breadwinners – a Lady Decorator', *Woman*, 11 Jan. 1890.

98. *The House*, 2: 9 (Nov. 1897): 139; Miss Crommelin and Mrs Barton wrote the survey of Furniture and Decoration for vol. 4 of the Woman's Library published by Chapman & Hall in 1903. In the 1901 census, Miss Helen Woollan (forty years of age) was living with her father, a chartered accountant, in Hampstead. On Miss Crommelin, Crawford, *Enterprising Women*, p. 206.

99. *The House*, 2: 9 (Nov. 1897): 138.

100. 'Women and Domestic Art', *The House*, 3: 17 (1 July 1898): 196.

101. On the women's press, Barbara Onslow, *Women of the Press in Nineteenth-Century Britain* (Basingstoke, 2000); Beetham, *Magazine of Her Own*.

102. 'Ubiquiteuse', *Woman*, 7 Dec. 1892; also *Lady's Pictorial*, 25 Nov. 1893, Cutting Book no. 1, Mrs Talbot Coke Papers, Coke MSS.

103. Mrs Talbot Coke, 'The Best Foot Foremost, pt. ii', *Hearth and Home*, 26 Sept. 1895, p. 684. Mrs Coke was the daughter of Major Henry Fitzgerald, 1st Life Guards. Although Irish by heritage, she was raised in Maperton House, Somerset. Her mother was the eldest daughter of the late Revd S. Wildman Yates, vicar of St Mary's Reading, and a distant relative of Sir Robert Peel. Charlotte Coke's husband, General John Talbot Coke was the heir to the Pinxton Collieries, whose profits helped to keep afloat the periodicals that Mrs Coke and her husband managed – *Hearth and Home* (the flagship publication and the most profitable), *Woman*, and *Myra's Journal* (the rump of the Beeton empire). On the financial situation of the three papers, see Second Bundle of H&H Correspondence, Mrs Talbot Coke Papers, esp. Mrs C.S. Peel to General Talbot Coke, 16 Oct. 1903, Coke MSS.

104. Mrs Talbot Coke, 'Home Advice', *Hearth and Home*, 11 July 1895, p. 332.

105. Heelas, Sons & Co. advertise their 'Rutland' wicker couch, suggested by Mrs Talbot Coke, as well as their cosy chair (ads in 21 Feb. 1895 number of *Hearth and Home*). Mrs Talbot Coke was commissioned to decorate a bedroom at Shoolbred's, and took part in the decoration of Messrs Wallace and Co.'s Oriental Showrooms. See 'Furnishing Lodgings', *Hearth and Home*, 19 May 1892 and 'An Oriental Hall', *Hearth and Home*, 9 March 1893. By 1893, the enamel manufacturer Aspinall had produced a boxed tin of Mrs Talbot Coke's favourite colours. Mrs Talbot Coke, 'Home Advice', *Hearth and Home*, 26 Jan. 1893, p. 314.

106. 'Other Folk's Rooms, Commented on by Mrs. Talbot Coke', *Hearth and Home*, 5 March 1908.

107. Mrs Talbot Coke, 'Artistic Hints for Home Decoration', *Queen*, 16 April 1887, p. 480.

108. Mrs Talbot Coke, 'Home Advice', *Hearth and Home*, 23 Jan. 1902, p. 518.

109. Torfrida, 'Home Decoration', *Lady's Companion*, 31 July 1897, pp. 208–9.

110. Torfrida, 'Our Diamond Jubilee Article on Home Decoration', *Lady's Companion*, 19 June 1897, p. 60.

111. 'Our Walls', *Hearth and Home*, 21 Dec. 1893, p. 201.

112. Answers to Correspondents, *St Stephen's Review* – Cutting Book no. 1, f. 11; Mrs Talbot Coke 'Individual Taste', no source, no date [*St Stephen's Review*?] – Cutting Book no. 1, Mrs Talbot Coke Papers, Coke MSS.

113. Mrs Talbot Coke, 'Home Advice', *Hearth and Home*, 14 March 1895, p. 648. See also Coke, 'Home Advice', *Hearth and Home*, 29 Oct. 1896, p. 924.

114. Peel, *Life's Enchanted Cup*, p. 64. Dorothy Peel was Mrs Talbot Coke's cousin, an editor at the Coke magazines, and an authority on home decoration in her own right (see Peel, *The New Home*, London, 1898).

115. Mrs Talbot Coke, 'Cosmopolitan Rooms', *Hearth and Home*, 20 Oct. 1892.

116. M.F. Billington, 'Leading Lady Journalists', *Pearson's Magazine*, n.d. – Cutting Book no. 1; also review of *The Gentlewoman at Home* in *Irish Society*, 18 June 1892 – Cutting Book no. 1, Mrs Talbot Coke Papers, Coke MSS.

117. 'Essarti', *Winter's Magazine*, 13 Aug. 1892 – Cutting Book no. 2, John Talbot and Charlotte Coke, Mrs Talbot Coke Papers, Coke MSS.

118. Review of *The Gentlewoman at Home* in *The Globe*, 4 June 1892 – Cutting Book no. 1, Mrs Talbot Coke Papers, Coke MSS.

119. *Winter's Weekly*, 16 June 1894 – Cutting Book no. 1, Mrs Talbot Coke Papers, Coke MSS.
120. For her critique of an Arts and Crafts bedroom set, see M.F. Billington, ed., *Marriage: Its Legal Preliminaries and Social Observances. Home Hints by Mrs. Talbot Coke* (London, 1900), p. 97.
121. See also J.S. Gibson, FRIBA, 'Artistic Houses', *Studio*, Sept. 1893, pp. 215–20. Mrs Talbot Coke's response is contained in 'Brave Words', no source, 12 Oct. 1893 – Cutting Book no. 1, Mrs Talbot Coke Papers, Coke MSS.
122. Lewis Day, 'Decoration by Correspondence', *Art Journal*, 1893, p. 86. See also 'A Lady's Library', *Furniture and Decoration*, 1 Sept. 1891, p. 113. For Day's views on decoration, see the *Magazine of Art* series, especially 'How To Decorate a Room', *Magazine of Art*, 4 (Nov. 1880–Oct. 1881): 182–6 and Lewis Day, 'The Woman's Part in Domestic Decoration', ibid., pp. 457–63.
123. Day, 'Decoration by Correspondence', p. 87.
124. On the women's press and consumerism: Rappaport, *Shopping*, pp. 108–41.
125. Mrs Talbot Coke, 'Different Opinions', *Hearth and Home*, 28 May 1896, p. 87.
126. Charlotte Coke's own mother was notably devout. See the obituary, *Western Gazette*, 5 Dec. 1884, Cutting Book no. 1 – John Talbot and Charlotte Coke, Mrs Talbot Coke Papers, Coke MSS.
127. The contrast in this regard with a nearly contemporaneous text, J.R. Miller's *Home-Making; or, The Ideal Family Life* (1896) is striking.
128. On Mrs Talbot Coke's 'moral support', see *Sala's Journal*, 25 June 1892 – Cutting Book no. 1, Mrs Talbot Coke Papers, Coke MSS.
129. *Hearth and Home*, 30 June 1892 – Cutting Book no. 1, Mrs Talbot Coke Papers, Coke MSS.
130. Mrs Talbot Coke, 'Little Pleasures', no source, no date – Cutting Book no. 1, f. 11, Mrs Talbot Coke Papers, Coke MSS.
131. There is a large literature on the New Woman. See especially Elaine Showalter, *Sexual Anarchy: Gender and Culture at the Fin de Siècle* (New York, 1990); Sally Ledger, *The New Woman: Fiction and Feminism at the Fin de Siècle* (Manchester, 1997); Angelique Richardson and Chris Willis, eds, *The New Woman in Fiction and in Fact: Fin de Siècle Feminisms* (Basingstoke, 2001); Ann Heilmann and Margaret Beetham, *New Woman Hybridities: Femininity, Feminism and International Consumer Culture, 1880–1930* (London, 2004); for France, Mary Louise Roberts, *Disruptive Acts: The New Woman in Fin-de-Siècle France* (Chicago and London, 2002).
132. Mrs Talbot Coke, 'A Useful Room', *Hearth and Home*, 7 Jan. 1892, p. 237. See, too, her criticisms of the 'mind-destroying "domestic virtue" era' and its 'virulently domestic women'. Charlotte Talbot Coke, Letter to the Editor, 15 Aug. 1898, *Daily Telegraph* – Cutting Book no. 2, Mrs Talbot Coke Papers, Coke MSS.
133. 'Pepper & Salt by the Cruet', *The Furnisher and Decorator*, 1 July 1890, p. 196.
134. 'Exhibition of Modern House Building and Furnishing at Gidea Park, Romford', *Votes for Women*, 29 Nov. 1911, AAD/1978/2/179, AAD.
135. Day, 'Decoration by Correspondence', p. 86; Mrs Talbot Coke, 'Home Advice', 19 Sept. 1895, p. 668; Mrs Talbot Coke, 'Home Advice', 14 Jan. 1897, Supplement, ii; Mrs Talbot Coke, 'Some Decorative Notions', *Hearth and Home*, 21 Feb. 1895, p. 530; 'Puck', 4 April 1895; 'Bachelor', 11 April 1895, *Hearth and Home*, Supplement, i.
136. Watson, *Art of the House*, p. 150. On Marriott Watson, Talia Schaffer, *The Forgotten Female Aesthetes* (Charlottesville and London, 2000), pp. 86–102.
137. 'Our Raison D'Etre', *The House*, 1: 1 (March 1897): 1.
138. Jenni Calder, *The Victorian Home* (London, 1977), p. 105.
139. On consumption and pleasure, Rappaport, *Shopping*, esp. pp. 159–69; Logan, *Victorian Parlour*, pp. 98–9, 104.
140. Mrs Talbot Coke, 'Home Advice', *Hearth and Home*, 17 Oct. 1895, p. 832.
141. Mrs Talbot Coke, 'Ups and Downs', *Hearth and Home*, 7 July 1892, p. 261.

142. Mrs Talbot Coke, 'Home Advice', *Hearth and Home*, 7 March 1895, p. 616; Mrs Talbot Coke, 'Little Economies', *The Gentlewoman*, 8 Nov. 1890 – Cutting Book no. 1, Mrs Talbot Coke Papers, Coke MSS.
143. Mrs Conyers Morrell, 'The Home', *Lady's Pictorial*, 12 Aug. 1899, p. 233.
144. Mrs Talbot Coke, 'Home Advice', *Hearth and Home*, 2 Jan. 1895, p. 314.
145. Torfrida, 'Home Decoration', *Cartwright's Lady's Companion*, 27 Feb. 1904, p. 342.
146. Mary Elizabeth Braddon, *Lady Audley's Secret* (Ware, 1997 [1862]), p. 184.
147. Mrs Talbot Coke, 'Home Advice', *Hearth and Home*, 2 July 1891, p. 209.
148. Shonfield, *Precariously Privileged*, pp. 195–206.
149. Miss Florence Mary Gardiner, *Furnishings and Fittings for Every Home* (London, 1894), p. 14.
150. Lady Duff Gordon, *Discretions and Indiscretions* (New York, 1932), p. 76.
151. Haweis, *Art of Decoration*, p. 269.
152. Horace Annesley Vachell, *The Homely Art* (London, 1928), p. 18. In remembering the early years of her life, Penelope Mortimer connected her mother 'only with rooms and with things; colors and furniture and food. She must have spoken, but my impression is that the sound of her voice didn't reach me'. Penelope Mortimer, *About Time: An Aspect of Autobiography* (New York, 1979), p. 59.
153. Chapman, *Home and Social Status*, pp. 24–5; on the immigrant metaphor, Pritchett, *Cab at the Door*, p. 56. For reflections on lower middle-class selfhood, Frank Mort, 'Social and Symbolic Fathers and Sons in Postwar Britain', *Journal of British Studies*, 38 (July 1999): 353–84.
154. Wells, *Marriage*, p. 283.
155. H.G. Wells, *Experiment in Autobiography: Discoveries and Conclusions of a Very Ordinary Brain, vol. II* (London, 1984 [1934]), p. 497
156. It was Rebecca West's scathing review of *Marriage* in *The Freewoman* that brought the fly into the old spider's web. West had a harsher opinion of Marjorie than did Wells. See 'Marriage' in Jane Marcus, ed., *The Young Rebecca: Writings of Rebecca West 1911–1917* (New York, 1982), pp. 64–70; also pp. 371–3.
157. Wells, *Marriage*, p. 281; see also W. Pett Ridge, *69 Birnam Road* (London, 1908), p. 332.
158. Wells, *Marriage*, p. 508.
159. Ibid., p. 498.
160. Ibid., p. 504.
161. Finn, 'Men's Things', esp. pp. 134–5.

5   HOME AS A STAGE: PERSONALITY AND POSSESSIONS

1. On 'personal journalism' and Yates' career, P.D. Edwards, *Dickens's 'Young Men': George Augustus Sala, Edmund Yates and the World of Victorian Journalism* (Aldershot, 1997), pp. 41–72.
2. Edmund Yates, *His Recollections and Experiences* (London, 1884), vol. 2, p. 330; on the founding of *The World*, Edwards, *Dickens's 'Young Men'*, pp. 138–49. E.W. Godwin led *The Architect*'s readers on a tour of his house in 1876. See Kinchin, 'The Designer as Critic', pp. 25–6.
3. The series débuted in August 1876 with a profile of Tennyson. In one year (1881), *The World*'s 'Celebrities at Home' included Mr Edwin Booth, Mr F.C. Burnand, Lord Randolph Churchill, the King of Bavaria, the King and Queen of Romania, the Earl of Denbigh, Lord Arthur Cecil, Professor Robertson Smith, Mr and Mrs Kendale and Mr Henry Labouchere, MP.
4. 'Celebrities at Home: Mr Wilkie Collins in Gloucester-Place', *The World*, 26 Dec. 1877, p. 4.
5. 'English Celebrities at Home, No. 1. Mr Tennyson at Haslemere', *The World*, 23 Aug. 1876, pp. 172–3.

6. 'Chats with Celebrities: Mrs Haweis', *Hearth and Home*, 11 Aug. 1892.

7. Auctions – often held on the deceased's premises – provided a posthumous corollary to the at-home profile. On Lord Beaconsfield's belongings, 'The Late Lord Beaconsfield', *The Times*, 23 April 1881, Newspaper Clippings, Sept. 1880–Jan. 1882, vol. II, AAD.

8. Where 'at-home' profiles of men tended to detail those rooms they could call their own, such as libraries or dens, women ranged widely through their domiciles.

9. Walter Benjamin, 'Louis-Philippe or the Interior', in *Illuminations*, trans. Harry Zohn (London, 1973), p. 169.

10. Apparent in his novel, Edmund Yates, *Broken to Harness: A Story of English Domestic Life* (London, 1865).

11. Stella Tillyard, *Aristocrats* (New York, 1994), pp. 132–5, 175–80; on the function of country houses, Stone and Stone, *An Open Elite?*, pp. 295–328. On the building and furnishing projects of the Protestant ascendancy, Toby Barnard, *Making the Grand Figure: Lives and Possessions in Ireland 1641–1770* (New Haven and London, 2004), pp. 21–187.

12. Wainwright, *Romantic Interior*, esp. pp. 71–207; Gillian Darley, *John Soane: An Accidental Romantic* (New Haven and London, 1999), pp. 97–116, 209–15. Thomas Hope's house on Duchess Street in London (chronicled in Hope's 1807 *Household Furniture and Interior Decoration Executed from Designs by Thomas Hope*), Horace Walpole's house at Strawberry Hill, and William Beckford's Fonthill Abbey were similarly distinctive residences. On Hope, David Watkin, *Thomas Hope 1769–1831 and the Neo-Classical Idea* (London, 1968). More generally, Geoffrey Beard, *Craftsmen and Interior Decoration in England 1660–1820* (Edinburgh, 1981).

13. Pro Patria, 'The Soanean Museum', *The Civil Engineer and Architect's Journal*, 1837, p. 44; Charles Knight's *Penny Cyclopaedia* cited in S.M. Ellis, 'Current Literature: Sir John Soane', *Fortnightly Review*, Jan. 1928; in defence, 'The House and Museum of Sir John Soane', *Monthly Supplement of the Penny Magazine*, 31 Oct.–30 Nov. 1837; 'The Museum of Sir John Soane', *Illustrated London News*, 25 June 1864, Press Cuttings, Sir John Soane Museum.

14. Report for the Year Ending 1897, George H. Birch, Curator, Sir John Soane Museum.

15. On character, Stefan Collini, *Public Moralists: Political Thought and Intellectual Life in Britain, 1850–1930* (Oxford, 1991); Morgan, *Manners, Morals and Class*, pp. 62–9; on notions of character within the context of credit, Finn, *Character of Credit*, pp. 18–21, 260–2, 320–1.

16. Warren Susman, '"Personality" and the Making of Twentieth-Century Culture', in *Culture as History: The Transformation of American Society in the Twentieth Century* (New York, 1984); also Raymond Williams, *Keywords* (New York, 1976), p. 194.

17. The point is Susman's, *Culture as History*, p. 277.

18. Marriott Watson, *Art of the House*, pp. 152–3.

19. E.F. Benson, *An Autumn Sowing* (London, 1987 [1917]), p. 14.

20. Ibid., p. 16.

21. Ibid., p. 15.

22. 'Drawing-Room Sundries', *The Furnisher and Decorator*, 2 Dec. 1889, p. 47.

23. 'Some Quaint Chairs', *Furniture and Decoration*, 1 March 1893, p. 34. See, too, Katie Arber, *Turn of the Century Style: Home Decoration and Furnishings between 1890 and 1910* (London, 2003); at the top end of the social scale, Cooper, *Opulent Eye*; on middle-class style, Long, *Edwardian House*; Helena Barrett and John Phillips, *Suburban Style: The British Home, 1840–1960* (London, 1987); on the Arts and Crafts, Roderick Gradidge, *Dream Houses: The Edwardian Ideal* (London, 1980).

24. *The House*, Aug. 1902, p. 254; Coke, *Gentlewoman at Home*, pp. 157–8.

25. See, for instance, 'An Indian "Gentleman's House"', *The Architect*, 15 Oct. 1881, pp. 247–8; 'A Real Japanese Drawing-Room', article by Sir Edward Arnold from the *Daily Telegraph* reprinted in *The Furnisher and Decorator*, 1 May 1890, p. 168. Christopher Dresser fitted out a Moorish house at the Alexandria Palace exhibition, *Furniture Gazette*, 30 Oct. 1875, p. 261. On such decoration as a reflection of imperial culture, Tim Barringer, 'Imperial Visions: Responses to India and Africa in Victorian Art and Design', in *The Victorian Vision: Inventing*

New Britain, ed. John MacKenzie (New York, 2001), pp. 315–33; Logan, *Victorian Parlour*, pp. 196–9. While the fad for pan-Asian decoration probably indicates a measure of popular imperialism, two cautions are in order here: (1) What characterized the Victorian interior was eclecticism, of which the 'oriental' was only one part. Rooms ranged well beyond the spoils of empire. Bona fide Indian-printed textiles were paired with fancy Japanese fans or London-confected 'Moorish' arches. (2) We should be wary of reading goods to signify particular attitudes. The Japanese fan did not necessarily betoken even cosmopolitanism; it may have been chosen because its colours harmonized with the existing decorative scheme, or because its purchaser took a fancy to a particular pattern.

26. 'Our Commissioner in the West of England', *The Furnisher and Decorator*, 1 Feb. 1890, p. 76.
27. 'Prunes and Prisms: Wall Designs', *Daily News & Leader*, 2 Jan. 1914, Newspaper Clippings, June 1913–Jan. 1914, vol. 1 (Misc.), AAD.
28. Thomas Wright, *The Life of John Payne* (London, 1919), pp. 140–1.
29. *The World and His Wife*, 1910 cited in Central Office of Information *At Home, 1900–1970* (London, 1995).
30. Cited in Christopher Hussey, *The Life of Sir Edwin Lutyens* (London, 1950), p. 159.
31. 'The Hall', *Myra's Journal*, 1 March 1891 – Cutting Book no. 1, Mrs Talbot Coke Papers, Coke MSS.
32. Mrs E.T. Cook, *Highways and Byways in London* (London, 1902), p. 301; on the furnishing of entrance halls, John Hudson Elder-Duncan, *The House Beautiful and Useful* (New York, 1907), p. 140.
33. In 1914, there were at least 900 synthetic dyes available to dyers and printers. See Johann Peter Murmann, *Knowledge and Competitive Advantage* (Cambridge, 2003), p. 25; Travis, *The Rainbow Makers*; Garfield, *Mauve*; Jacques Pouchepadass, *Champaran and Gandhi: Planters, Peasants and Gandhian Politics*, trans. James Walker (New Delhi and New York, 1999).
34. Mrs Talbot Coke, 'Colour in Cairo, &c', no source, no date – Cutting Book no. 1, Mrs Talbot Coke Papers, Coke MSS.
35. 'Prunes and Prisms' on the Silver Studio's 'very individual' designs, short description of the firm for the *Studio*, n.d. [1908?], SBR General, Box 4, Folder 3, MODA; Hestia, 'Other Folks' Houses', *The Gentlewoman*, 28 Jan. 1899, p. 120. For Omega's interpretations of emotional rooms, Reed, *Bloomsbury Rooms*, pp. 133–40.
36. Mrs Talbot Coke, 'Home Advice', *Hearth and Home*, 2 April 1896, p. 816.
37. 'Quaint Sideboards', *Furniture Record*, June 1899, p. 6; 'House Furnishing', *Woman at Home*, 1 (1894): 152.
38. 'Marion', 'Home Decoration', *Lady's Companion*, 28 Aug. 1897, p. 303.
39. Locker-Lampson, *My Confidences*, p. 194.
40. Thomas Charles Newman, *Many Parts* (London, 1935), p. 106; Peel, *Life's Enchanted Cup*, p. 149.
41. On the material divides within the middle classes, see the *Cornhill Magazine*'s series on how to live on various incomes, from £150 to £1,800 a year. The articles appeared in the May, June, July, and August 1901 issues, and were authored by G.S. Layard, G. Colmore, Mrs Earle, and Lady Agnew. See, too Harold Perkin, *Rise of Professional Society: England since 1880*, (London, 1989), pp. 78–101.
42. Gibbs, *New Man*, pp. 148–9.
43. Philip Gibbs, *The Pageant of the Years: An Autobiography* (London, 1946), esp. pp. 4–6.
44. Thorstein Veblen, *The Theory of the Leisure Class* (New York, 1994 [1899]), p. 17; similarly, R.H. Tawney, *The Acquisitive Society* (New York, 1920), pp. 34–7.
45. Among others, T.J. Lears, 'Beyond Veblen: Rethinking Consumer Culture in America', in *Consuming Visions*, ed. Simon Bronner, pp. 73–98; Loeb, *Consuming Angels*, pp. 158–79. For critiques of the idea of emulation for the eighteenth century, Colin Campbell, 'Understanding Traditional and Modern Patterns of Consumption in Eighteenth-Century England: A Character–Action Approach', in *Consumption and the World of Goods*, ed. Brewer

and Porter, pp. 40–57; Campbell, *Romantic Ethic*, pp. 17–57; Berg, *Luxury and Pleasure*, pp. 232–4, 251–2; Vickery, *Gentleman's Daughter*, pp. 162–4, 194; Weatherill, *Consumer Behaviour*, pp. 194–6.

46. 'Hestia', Answer to 'Madame Sans-Gene' and 'Other Folks' Houses', *The Gentlewoman*, 21 Jan. 1899, p. 88.

47. Among others, Davidoff and Hall, *Family Fortunes*, esp. pp. 149–92, 362. On the attitudes of Stuccovia, Russell, *Londoner's Log-Book*, pp. 76–7.

48. Amanda Girling-Budd, 'Comfort and Gentility: Furnishings by Gillows, Lancaster 1840–55', in *Interior Design and Identity*, ed. McKellar and Sparke, pp. 27–47; also Smith, *Consumption*, esp. pp. 105–38, 204–21; Mary Tew Douglas and Baron Isherwood, *The World of Goods* (New York, 1979), pp. 126–7.

49. Campbell, *Romantic Ethic*, p. 55.

50. Malchow, *Gentlemen Capitalists*. On the erosion of upper-class cultural authority in the inter-war period, Ross McKibbin, *Classes and Cultures, England 1918–1951* (Oxford, 1998), pp. 35–6, 42.

51. James Pope-Hennessy, *Queen Mary, 1867–1953* (New York, 1960), pp. 269–70, 289–90.

52. On white-collar workers, see Crossick, ed., *Lower Middle Class in Britain*, pp. 11–60; Geoffrey Crossick and Heinz-Gerhard Haupt, *The Petite Bourgeoisie in Europe 1780–1914: Enterprise, Family and Independence* (London and New York, 1995), esp. p. 85.

53. Guy Chapman, *Culture and Survival*, p. 174.

54. Frederick Willis, *101 Jubilee Road: A Book of London Yesterdays* (London, 1948), pp. 19–20. On the relationship between distinction and cultural authority: Pierre Bourdieu, *Distinction: A Social Critique of the Judgement of Taste* (London, 1984), pp. 260–317, esp. pp. 281–2. On the association of individuality with the working class, see Mike Savage, 'Individuality and Class: The Rise and Fall of the Gentlemanly Social Contract in Britain', in *Social Contracts under Stress: The Middle Classes of America, Europe, and Japan at the Turn of the Century*, ed. Olivier Zunz, Leonard Schoppa, and Nobuhiro Hiwatari (New York, 2002), pp. 47–65; on Bloomsbury and individualism, Reed, *Bloomsbury Rooms*, pp. 10–12, 15; on late eighteenth-century philosophical discussions of 'individual uniqueness', Wahrman, *Making of the Modern Self*, pp. 276–8; on the roots of individualism in Romanticism, Stana Nenadic, 'Romanticism and the Urge to Consume in the First Half of the Nineteenth Century', in *Consumers and Luxury*, ed. Berg and Clifford, pp. 208–27.

55. Charles Pooter, the hero of the Grossmith brothers' famed satire of lower middle-class life, resident in a six-roomed terrace in Holloway called The Laurels, was, according to his wife, Carrie, always carried off by 'some newfangled craze', whether it was the liberal use of enamel paint, or imitation stags' heads hung in the hallway to 'give it style'. George and Weedon Grossmith, *The Diary of a Nobody* (London, 1969 [1892]), pp. 30, 57.

56. 'Marion', 'A Drawing-Room in Oriental Style', *Lady's Companion*, 21 Aug. 1897, pp. 279–81.

57. W. Pett Ridge, *Outside the Radius* (New York, 1900 [1899]), p. 5.

58. C.S. Lewis, *Surprised by Joy* (London, 1955), p. 17.

59. P.N. Furbank, *E.M. Forster: A Life*, vol. 1 (London, 1977), p. 40.

60. J. Colmer, *E.M. Forster* (London, 1975), p. 3. Quoted in Reed, *Bloomsbury Rooms*, p. 6.

61. Mary Blanchard, *Oscar Wilde's America: Counterculture in the Gilded Age* (New Haven, 1998).

62. 'English Renaissance of Art', in *Complete Works of Oscar Wilde*, ed. and with introductions by Michael Monahan and W.F. Morse, vol. 11 (New York, 1927), p. 12.

63. Wahrman, *Making of the Modern Self*, p. 276.

64. Nikolas Rose, *The Psychological Complex: Psychology, Politics and Society in England, 1869–1939* (London, 1985); on popular understandings, Mathew Thomson, 'Psychology and the "Consciousness of Modernity" in Early Twentieth-Century Britain', in *Meanings of Modernity: Britain from the Late-Victorian Era to World War II*, ed. Martin Daunton and Bernhard Rieger (Oxford and New York, 2001), pp. 97–115; on Victorian psychology, Rick Rylance, *Victorian Psychology and British Culture* (Oxford, 2000).

65. Lady Duff Gordon, *Discretions and Indiscretions*, p. 83.

66. Clare Leighton, *Tempestuous Petticoat: The Story of an Invincible Edwardian* (New York, 1947), p. 101; Nicholson, *Half My Days*, p. 52; on John Buchan and the importance of a 'secure' personality, J.P. Parry, 'From the Thirty-Nine Articles to the Thirty-Nine Steps: Reflections on the Thought of John Buchan', in *Public and Private Doctrine: Essays in British History Presented to Maurice Cowling*, ed. Michael Bentley (Cambridge, 1993), pp. 209–35.

67. Peel, *Life's Enchanted Cup*, p. 256.

68. Review of R.G. Gordon, *Personality* in *Times Literary Supplement*, 4 March 1926, p. 156.

69. For an intriguing contrast with malleable early modern notions of selfhood, which Wahrman argues did not presuppose an inner core, see *Making of the Modern Self*, esp. pp. 166–71, 176–85.

70. Among others, R.C. Moberley, *Atonement and Personality* (New York, 1901); J.R. Illingworth, *Personality Human and Divine: Being the Bampton Lectures for the Year 1894* (London, 1894); G.H.S. Walpole, *Personality and Power: Or, The Secret of Real Influence*, 3rd edn (Milwaukee, WI, 1908); William Temple, *The Nature of Personality: A Course of Lectures* (London, 1915); Richard Wightman Fox, *Jesus in America: A History* (New York, 2004), pp. 307–50.

71. Coke, *Gentlewoman at Home*, p. 7.

72. William James, *The Principles of Psychology*, vol. 1 (New York, 1890), p. 291. James' formulation echoes a sentiment previously expressed by one of his brother's characters, Madame Merle. See Henry James, *Portrait of a Lady* (Oxford, 1995 [1881]), pp. 222–3.

73. Vachell, *Homely Art*, p. 7.

74. On this phenomenon in the United States, see especially Halttunen, 'From Parlor to Living Room', pp. 157–90; on self-realization, Lears, 'From Salvation to Self-Realization', pp. 3–38; in France, Silverman, *Art Nouveau*, esp. pp. 17–39, 229–69. In his book, *The English House* (1904–5), Hermann Muthesius observed: 'The Englishman sees the whole of life embodied in his house' (p. 7).

75. Mrs Talbot Coke, 'The House of My Pilgrimage', *Hearth and Home*, 30 Dec. 1909, p. 424.

76. Mrs Eustace Miles [Hallick Killick], *The Ideal Home and Its Problems* (London, 1911), p. 4.

77. 'A Day Nursery', *Queen*, 28 Jan. 1905, p. 145; *Sphere*, 24 Oct. 1908, n.p., Heal & Co., Press Cutting Book, AAD/1978/2/177.

78. Hamilton T. Smith, 'Nursery Furniture', *Cabinet Maker and Complete House Furnisher*, 5 Feb. 1921, p. 339. On nursery furniture more generally: *Sphere*, 24 Oct. 1908, n.p., AAD/1978/2/177; 'The Child and the Nursery', *Country Life*, 20 April 1912, AAD/1978/2/179.

79. The journalist Julia Cairns – who would become an authority on home furnishing – remembered how she had seasonally redecorated the six small rooms of her dolls' house, moving around the furniture 'to suit the mood of the moment'. Julia Cairns, *How I Became a Journalist* (London, 1960), p. 11. On the history of dolls' houses: Vivien Greene, *English Dolls' Houses of the Eighteenth and Nineteenth Centuries* (New York, 1979 [1955]).

80. See, for example, Martin Armstrong, *Victorian Peep-Show* (Plymouth, UK, 1938); Horace Collins, *My Best Riches: Story of a Stone Rolling Round the World and the Stage* (London, 1941), pp. 25–40. On childhood and the self, Carolyn Steedman, *Strange Dislocations: Childhood and the Idea of Human Interiority, 1780–1930* (Cambridge, MA, 1995); on the significance of home to Indian women in the late colonial period, Antoinette Burton, *Dwelling in the Archive: Women Writing House, Home, and History in Late Colonial India* (Oxford, 2003), esp. pp. 44–63.

81. Dorothy Pym, *Houses as Friends* (London, 1936); for a higher stratum, Sir Humphrey Noble, *Life in Noble Houses* (Newcastle-upon-Tyne, 1967).

82. Muriel St Clare Byrne, *Common or Garden Child: A Not Unfaithful Record* (London, 1942); Nicholson, *Half My Days*, p. 1.

83. Herbert Palmer, *The Mistletoe Child: An Autobiography of Childhood* (London, 1935), p. 25.

84. Lytton Strachey, 'Lancaster Gate', *Lytton Strachey by Himself*, 1994 quoted in Reed, *Bloomsbury Rooms*, p. 19.

85. Violet Trefusis, *Don't Look Round* (London, 1952), p. 42.

86. On her interiors, Philippe Jullian and John Phillips, *Violet Trefusis: Life and Letters* (London, 1976), pp. 32–3, 80–2.
87. Miles, *Ideal Home*, p. 231. On the intimate relationship between élite Edwardian women and their interiors, see Frederick Grisewood, *The World Goes By* (London, 1952), p. 196.
88. 'Penelope', Illustrated Answers to Correspondents, *The House*, 20: 4 (Oct. 1898): 80.
89. Miles, *Ideal Home*, p. 243.
90. Jennings, *Our Homes*, p. 130.
91. Coke, *Gentlewoman at Home*, p. 4.
92. Mrs Talbot Coke, 'Colour', *Hearth and Home*, 25 June 1891, p. 178.
93. Miles, *Ideal Home*, p. 20.
94. 'At Heal and Son's', *The Ladies' Field Supplement*, 27 Feb. 1904, p. 14, AAD/1978/2/177.
95. 'House Furnishing', *Woman at Home*, 2 (1894): 310.
96. Mrs Talbot Coke, 'Horrors', *Hearth and Home*, 19 Nov. 1891, p. 864; see also 'Eunice', 'Home Decoration [Answers]', *The Lady*, 18 July 1895, p. 97.
97. Mrs Talbot Coke, 'Home Advice', *Hearth and Home*, 11 June 1891, p. 113; Mrs Talbot Coke, 'How Not to Do It', *Hearth and Home*, 20 July 1893, p. 340.
98. See Jean-Christophe Agnew, 'A House of Fiction: Domestic Interiors and the Commodity Aesthetic', in *Consuming Visions*, ed. Bronner, p. 136; on 'insatiability', Campbell, *Romantic Ethic*, esp. pp. 86–8; Regenia Gagnier, *The Insatiability of Human Wants: Economics and Aesthetics in Market Society* (Chicago, 2000).
99. Vachell, *Homely Art*, p. 6.
100. Aymer Vallance, 'The Furnishing and Decoration of the House – IV. Furniture', *Art Journal*, April 1892, pp. 112–18; Joseph Crouch and Edmund Butler, *The Apartments of the House: Their Arrangement, Furnishing and Decoration* (London, 1900), p. 130.
101. Elder-Duncan, *House Beautiful*, p. 26.
102. Peel, *Life's Enchanted Cup*, p. 79.
103. See Susman, *Culture as History*, pp. 277–8; Adrian Forty, *Objects of Desire: Design and Society, 1750–1980* (New York, 1986), pp. 106–7.
104. Mrs Talbot Coke to 'Green Sleeves', 'Home Advice', *Hearth and Home*, 25 March 1897, p. 812.
105. For example, Mrs Talbot Coke, 'On Building Up', *Hearth and Home*, n.d., p. 358 – Cutting Book no. 2 – Mrs Talbot Coke Papers.
106. For his part, Tawney believed that the comfortable middle classes had been 'punished by the attainment of their desires', and were destined, as a consequence, never to be contented. Tawney, *Acquisitive Society*, p. 36.
107. Gibbs, *New Man*, p. 247.
108. Ibid., p. 244.
109. Ibid., p. 251.
110. 'Mr Desmond F. Talbot Coke', Isis Idols, *The Isis*, 24 Oct. 1903 – Cutting Book no. 2 – John Talbot and Charlotte Coke, Mrs Talbot Coke Papers, Coke MSS.
111. Desmond Coke, *Confessions of an Incurable Collector* (London, 1928), p. 4.
112. Ibid., pp. 247–8.
113. Ibid., pp. 6–7. Not that Coke bore his mother any animus; to the contrary, he dedicated his *Art of the Silhouette* to her: 'In Love to My Mother Who Gave Me – Among Much Else – the Fierce Joy of Collecting'.
114. Coke, *Confessions*, p. 95.
115. 'The Home of Art at Heal and Son's', *Tatler*, Supplement, no. 75, 3 Dec. 1902, p. 6.

6   DESIGNS ON THE PAST: ANTIQUES AS A FAITH

1. Diary Entry, 22 Dec. 1898, D/DXib 28/17, GRO.
2. Diary Entry, 1 Jan. 1898 D/DXib 28/17, GRO.

3. The best scholarly account of the antiques trade is Stefan Muthesius, 'Why Do We Buy Old Furniture? Aspects of the Authentic Antique in Britain 1870–1910', *Art History*, 11: 2 (June 1988): 231–54; also Ronald Pearsall and Graham Webb, *Inside the Antique Trade* (Shaldon, UK, 1974). On pre-1850 antiquarianism, the authoritative text is Wainwright, *Romantic Interior*. For an antique dealer's memoirs, see Rohan, *Confessions of an Antique Dealer* and *Old Beautiful*; Thomas Rohan, *In Search of the Antique* (London, 1927).

4. Alfred North Whitehead, *Dialogues of Alfred North Whitehead* (Boston, 1954), p. 3.

5. Litchfield, *Illustrated History*, pp. 376–7.

6. Muthesius, 'Why Do We Buy Old Furniture', p. 231. On auctions in early eighteenth-century Ireland, Barnard, *Making the Grand Figure*, pp. 96–7. The interiors of antiquarians are the exception here: Wainwright, *Romantic Interior*. On the modernity of the idea of 'age-value', Alois Riegl, 'The Modern Cult of Monuments: Its Character and Its Origins' [1903], *Oppositions*, 25 (Fall 1982): 21–51.

7. On Shaw, see Roy Strong, *And When Did You Last See Your Father? The Victorian Painter and British History* (London, 1978), pp. 64–5.

8. On antiquarians, see Philippa Levine, *The Amateur and the Professional: Antiquarians, Historians, Archaeologists in Victorian England, 1838–1886* (Cambridge, 1986); Martin Myrone and Lucy Peltz, *Producing the Past: Aspects of Antiquarian Culture and Practice, 1700–1850* (Aldershot, 1999). On Strawberry Hill, Fonthill Abbey, and Abbotsford, see Wainwright, *Romantic Interior*.

9. Henry Treffry Dunn, Rossetti's assistant, described the Cheyne Walk house as 'a sort of miniature South Kensington Museum and Zoo combined'. Henry Treffry Dunn, *Recollections of Dante Gabriel Rossetti and His Circle*, ed. Gale Pedrick (New York, 1904), pp. 38, 17–21, 38–42. Among others, Charles Edward Jerningham [Marmaduke] and Lewis Bettany, *The Bargain Book* (London, 1911), pp. 113–14. For a contemporary description, Hudson, *Munby*, p. 160.

10. As Frederick Litchfield observes, picture sales of 1830–40 were printed in quarto volumes, with extensive descriptions, while furniture catalogues provided one-line summaries. See Litchfield, *Illustrated History*, p. 377.

11. George Augustus Sala, *Twice Round the Clock* (New York, 1971 [1858/9]), p. 171.

12. Ibid., pp. 173, 172.

13. Lady Charlotte, the widow of the Welsh ironmaster Sir John Guest, was a woman of accomplishments, fluent in French, German, and Italian. As a young woman, she had studied Greek, Latin, Hebrew, and Persian, and taught herself to etch upon copperplate. After her husband died, she managed the Dowlais Ironworks, mastering double-entry bookkeeping. Montague J. Guest, ed., *Lady Charlotte Schreiber's Journals: Confidences of a Collector of Ceramics and Antiques throughout Britain, France, Holland, Belgium, Spain, Portugal, Turkey , Austria and Germany from the Year 1869 to 1885,* 2 vols (London, 1911); Revel Guest and Angela V. John, *Lady Charlotte: A Biography of the Nineteenth Century* (London, 1989); Ann Eatwell, 'Private Pleasure, Public Beneficence: Lady Charlotte Schreiber and Ceramic Collecting', in *Women in the Victorian Art World*, ed. Clarissa Campbell Orr (Manchester, 1995), pp. 125–45. As used in the 1720s and 1730s, the term 'chinamania' described the fad for Chinese porcelain imports (mostly new wares), which were of finer quality than British products. On china-collecting in the eighteenth and early nineteenth centuries, Charles Lamb, 'Old China', *London Magazine*, March 1823, pp. 269–72; Berg, *Luxury and Pleasure*, pp. 46–84; Jenny Uglow, 'Vase Mania', in *Luxury in the Eighteenth Century*, ed. Berg and Eger, pp. 151–62; Karen Fang, 'Empire, Coleridge, and Charles Lamb's Consumer Imagination', *Studies in English Literature*, 43 (Autumn 2003): 815–43.

14. Entry for 17 June 1874 in *Gladstone Diaries*, ed. H.C.G. Matthew, vol. 8, p. 501. On Gladstone's art collecting, Marcia Pointon, 'W.E. Gladstone as an Art Patron and Collector', *Victorian Studies*, 19 (1975): 73–98; Jonathan Conlin, 'Gladstone and Christian Art, 1832–1854', *Historical Journal*, 46: 2 (2003): 341–74.

15. On the trade in antiquities before 1850, Wainwright, *Romantic Interior*, pp. 26–53. Until the early nineteenth century, curiosity dealers were also known as 'nicknackitarians'. Before Soho (and especially Wardour Street) became the centre of the trade, Moorfields boasted a number of antiquities brokers.

16. Henry James, *The Spoils of Poynton*, Preface to the New York edition (London, 1987 [1897]), p. 26.

17. *The Spoils of Poynton* tells the story of Mrs Gereth, forced to choose between harmonious relations with her son, Owen, and the objects to which she has devoted her life. Mrs Gereth's husband had left Owen the house, Poynton, and its meticulously assembled antique furnishings; he provided Mrs Gereth with a dower house – a disposition of assets common among propertied families. However, when Owen chooses the vulgar Mona Brigstock, daughter of the hideously appointed Waterbath, as his bride, Mrs Gereth refuses to leave her house; she cannot bear the idea that Poynton will be sullied by Mona's depredations. The assault upon Mrs Gereth's treasures establishes the drama of the novel. To stave off the despoliation of Poynton, Mrs Gereth first tries to match Owen with Fleda Vetch, a penniless young woman of superior taste whom she has befriended. Forced to leave Poynton, Mrs Gereth retaliates by taking her choicest possessions with her. On *The Spoils of Poynton*, Virginia Llewellyn Smith, *Henry James and the Real Thing: A Modern Reader's Guide* (Basingstoke, 1994), pp. 107–39; Sandra Kumamoto Stanley, 'Female Acquisition in *The Spoils of Poynton*', in *Keeping the Victorian House*, ed. Vanessa Dickerson (New York, 1995), pp. 131–48.

18. Alongside the 'antique furniture dealers' there were 34 curiosity shops. Post Office London Trades' Directory for 1870, p. 1390; p. 1520. For 1890, see Post Office London Trades Directory for 1890, p. 1488. There were 35 curiosity dealers in 1890. Muthesius, 'Why Do We Buy Old Furniture', p. 243.

19. Post-Office London Trades' Directory for 1910, p. 1347.

20. 'The Sinclair Galleries', *The House*, 37 (March 1900): 15. See also the case of Mr J. Rochelle Thomas, proprietor of the Georgian Galleries, whose father owned a shop in Birmingham from 1859 to 1910: 'Personalities of the World of Art and Antiques', *Antique Collector*, Feb. 1935, p. 2. On the early antiques trade, Rohan, *Old Beautiful*, pp. 151–88; Rohan, *In Search of the Antique*.

21. Spawning cinemas and skating rings, private car hire and a garage along the way. See D/D A/B (Solomon Andrews & Son) in the Glamorgan Record Office, Cardiff.

22. On Marshall and the Hereford Antique Furniture Company, K 38/Cb, Herefordshire Record Office. Marshall's diaries are contained in K38/Cc13–18.

23. Charles Edward Jerningham and Lewis Bettany, *The Bargain Book* (London, 1911), p. 32.

24. See, for instance, J.H. Ewing, Diary entries for 17 July 1877, HAS 41/20; 7 Feb. 1878, HAS 41/21, Sheffield Archives.

25. 'The Sinclair Galleries', p. 15.

26. Letter to the Editor, *Antique Collector*, 8 Aug. 1931, p. 277.

27. 'Yarns of Collecting', *Antique Collector*, 15 Aug. 1931, p. 293.

28. Montizambert, *London Discoveries*, p. 46.

29. Ibid., pp. 48–56.

30. Rollo Charles, 'Robert Drane and the Ceramics Collection', *Amgueddfa* [*Bulletin of the National Museum of Wales*], Summer/Autumn 1974, p. 17.

31. C.H.B. Quennell, 'Modern Furniture II', *Country Life*, 14 May 1918, pp. lviii–x.

32. Rosamund Marriott Watson, *The Art of the House* (London, 1897), p. 85.

33. Patrick Wright, *On Living in An Old Country: The National Past in Contemporary Britain* (London, 1985).

34. Stephen Kern, *The Culture of Time and Space, 1880–1918* (Cambridge, MA, 1983).

35. Panton, *Homes of Taste*, p. 145; also Gibbs, *Pageant of the Years*, pp. 1–2.

36. Among her other decorative enthusiasms, Mrs Talbot Coke, too, had a fondness for old things. However, she did not advocate antiques in place of new objects. See Coke, *Gentlewoman at Home*, pp. 54–5, 63–74.

37. Coke, *Confessions*, p. 244.
38. W. Carew Hazlitt, 'The Bourgeois Collector', *Connoisseur*, 1: 4 (Dec. 1901): 233.
39. Among many others, W. Twopeny, *Old English Metalwork* (London, 1904); John Starkie Gardner, *Old Silver-Work Chiefly English from the XVth to the XVIIIth Centuries* (London, 1903); Margaret Jourdain, *Old Lace: A Handbook for Collectors* (London, 1908); C.H.B. Quennell and Marjorie Quennell, *A History of Everyday Things in England* (London, 1918–31); Gertrude Jekyll, *Old English Household Life: Some Account of Cottage Objects and Country Folk* (London, 1925).
40. 'The Art of Furnishing', *Cornhill Magazine*, 31 (1875), reprinted in the *Furniture Gazette*, 5 June 1875, p. 719.
41. 'The Renascence of Domestic Comfort and Distinction', *Lady's Pictorial*, 21 Oct. 1905, p. 692.
42. G.W.W., 'Wesley's House and Its Antiques', *Antique Collector*, June 1935, p. 147.
43. 'Modern v. Antique: A Plea for Present-Day Work', *Cabinet Maker and Art Furnisher*, 12 March 1910, p. 345.
44. Michael Jopling's remark, as recorded by Alan Clark, *Diaries* (London, 1993), p. 192.
45. 'A Reader Speaks Out', *Antique Collector*, Nov. 1933, p. 662.
46. Frederick William Burgess, *Chats on Household Curios* (New York, 1914), p. 21; see, too, 'The Effects of Time', *House and Garden*, Aug. 1921, p. 24.
47. Robert Drane to F.C. Andrews, n.d., rec'd 24 May 1906, D/D A/B 31/5/61, GRO.
48. W.H. Helm, 'The Making of "Antique" Furniture', *Nineteenth Century*, Dec. 1921, pp. 1031–7. See also Margaret Vivian, *Antique Collecting* (London, 1937), pp. 6–10.
49. See Herbert Cescinsky, *The Gentle Art of Faking Furniture* (New York, 1967 [1931]), p. 152; Jerningham and Bettany, *Bargain Book*, p. 276; Richard Aldington, *Life for Life's Sake* (New York, 1941), p. 27.
50. The Curator of the Cardiff Museum was a 'perfect fraud and cunning humbug, an ignorant pretender'. Drane Diary Entry for 23 Dec. 1898, D/DXib 28/17; Diary Entry for 21 June 1901, D/DXib 28/26, GRO.
51. Panton, *Homes of Taste*, p. 47.
52. Frederick Litchfield, *How to Collect Old Furniture* (London, 1904), p. 137; Ethel Deane, *Byways of Collecting* (London, 1908), pp. 191–2.
53. 'Hints to Collectors', *Collectors' Circular*, 4 July 1903, p. 41.
54. Herbert R. Dear, 'Why Not Collect Old Drinking Glasses?' *Antique Collector*, Oct. 1935, p. 291; James Henry Duveen, *Collections and Recollections* (London, 1934), p. 15; Deane, *Byways*, p. 2.
55. Rohan, *Confessions of an Antique Dealer*, pp. 11–12.
56. Hazlitt, 'The Bourgeois Collector', p. 233; William Carew Hazlitt, *The Confessions of a Collector* (London, 1897); also, Grisewood, *The World Goes By*, p. 29. On bourgeois collectors more generally, Saisselin, *Bourgeois and the Bibelot*, pp. 119–68.
57. John Downes, 'Antique Auctions' [Letter to the Editor], *Antique Collector*, 7 Nov. 1931.
58. James and William Tweed, Ledger, 1912–15, 57D93/1, WYAS, Bradford. On the association of collecting with men: Bailkin, *Culture of Property*, p. 120; in France, Auslander, *Taste and Power*, pp. 296–305.
59. Coke, *Confessions*, pp. 241, 18–21.
60. George W.E. Russell, *Social Silhouettes* (New York, 1906), p. 268.
61. For example, Deane, *Byways*, p. 134. On antiques as cure for materialism, Rohan, *Old Beautiful*, p. 54. However, temptation could, on occasion, short-circuit moral scruples. Rohan, *Confessions of an Antique Dealer*, pp. 56–7.
62. Elder-Duncan, *House Beautiful*, p. 103. As Margaret Vivian counselled, 'Avarice is a trap for the unwary'. Vivian, *Antique Collecting*, p. 3.
63. Litchfield, *How to Collect*, p. 119.
64. Robert Drane to Mr T. Cooke, Jr, 12 March 1843, D 147/1/1, GRO.
65. Horace Annesley Vachell, *Quinneys': A Comedy in Four Acts* (New York, 1916 [first performed at the Haymarket Theatre, 1915]), p. 16. See also *Quinney's Adventures* (London, 1924);

Quinneys for Quality (London, 1938). Also Horace Annesley Vachell, *Quests: The Adventures and Misadventures of a Collector* (London, 1954), p. 64.

66. Vachell, *Quinneys'*, p. 16.
67. Ibid., pp. 97, 61.
68. 'My Special Page', *Queen Street Pictorial Monthly*, April 1892.
69. Diary Entry, 14 May 1894, D/DXib 28/13, GRO.
70. See, among others, Diary Entries, 27 Feb. 1897 and 25 July 1897, D/DXib 28/16; 7 Dec. 1898, D/DXib 28/17, GRO.
71. Diary Entry, 17 June 1897, D/DXib 28/16, GRO.
72. Diary Entry, 7 Dec. 1898, D/DXib 28/17, GRO.
73. Among others, Diary Entries, 27 July 1898, D/DXib 28/17; 24 Oct. 1898, D/DXib 28/17, GRO.
74. 'To Our Readers', *The Connoisseur and Collector's Journal*, 1: 1 (Jan. 1895): 5.
75. 'In the Sale Room', *Connoisseur*, 1:4 (Dec. 1901): 272; A.E. Reveirs-Hopkins, 'Hepplewhite Furniture for the Small Collector', *Old Furniture* iii:ix (15 Feb. 1928), John Johnson Collection, Furniture – Box 5, Bodleian Library. On 'proselytizing', see the antique dealer Rohan's *Old Beautiful*, p. 46.
76. Marriott Watson, *Art of the House*, p. 104.
77. On these movements: Owen, *Place of Enchantment*; Alex Owen, *The Darkened Room: Women, Power and Spiritualism in Late Victorian England* (London, 1989); Alison Winter, *Mesmerized: Powers of Mind in Victorian Britain* (Chicago, 1998); Janet Oppenheim, *The Other World: Spiritualism and Psychical Research in England, 1850–1914* (Cambridge, 1985); Michael Saler, 'Clap if You Believe in Sherlock Holmes', *Historical Journal*, 46:3 (Sept., 2003): 599–622.
78. Rohan, *Confessions of an Antique Dealer*, p. 12.
79. Ethel Deane, '*None So Blind*' (Boston, MA, 1910).
80. Alfred Docker, *Religion: What It Really Is* (London, 1919), pp. vii–viii.
81. Ibid., pp. 24, 1.
82. Ibid., p. 106.
83. In her *roman-à-clef*, Vivian described the mother of her heroine, Aurelia, as 'a devotee of the cold, dull religion of the period . . . not lenient to sinners'. Margaret Vivian, *Dr. Jaz: The Adventures of a Woman Doctor* (London, 1933), p. 11.
84. Margaret Vivian, *Do We Survive Death? A Psychic Booklet* (London, 1946).
85. Rohan, *Confessions of an Antique Dealer*, p. 213.
86. Margaret Vivian, *The Doorway* (London, 1941) pp. 27–8.
87. Ibid., pp. 58, 76.
88. Coke, *Confessions of an Antique Dealer*, p. 245.
89. Vivian, *Antique Collecting*, p. 64; see also Rohan, *Confessions of an Antique Dealer*, pp. 143–5, p. 208; in France, Silverman, *Art Nouveau*, p. 241.
90. Hugh Conway, 'A Cabinet Secret', in *Bound Together Tales* (New York, 1884), p. 55.
91. See, for instance, Drane's correspondent Percy H. Bate, who referred to his drinking glasses as his 'first love'. Percy H. Bate to Robert Drane, 15 Feb. 1898, D/DXib 28/17, GRO. Similarly, Desmond Coke referred to silhouettes as 'my first love'. Coke, *Confessions of an Antique Dealer*, p. 180.
92. Carew, *Confessions of an Antique Dealer*, p. 352.
93. 'Old Furniture: The Art of Collecting Oak', *Connoisseur*, 1:1 (Sept. 1901): 29.
94. Vachell, *Quests*, p. 56.
95. 'The Place of Antiques in Flat Life' [Editor's Column], *Antique Collector*, Sept. 1935, p. 233.
96. Riegl, 'Modern Cult', pp. 28–9.
97. Marriott Watson, *Art of the House*, p. 78. Her second husband, the author H.B. Marriott Watson, wrote a number of ghost stories, many collected in his *Heart of Miranda* (London, 1898).
98. Hall, *Bric à Brac Hunter*, p. 22.
99. Thomas Rohan, *Billy Ditt: the Romance of a Chippendale Chair, 1760–1925* (London, 1932).

100. 'An Old Bureau', reprinted by permission of the Star Newspaper Company, *The House*, 12:2 (Feb. 1898): 248–9; similarly, C.H.B. Kitchin, 'The Chelsea Cat', in *Second Ghost Book*, ed. Cynthia Asquith (London, 1952), pp. 71–92; Roger Pater, 'De Profundis', *The Supernatural Omnibus*, ed. with an introduction by Montague Summers (Garden City, NY, 1932), pp. 383–96.
101. Armstrong, *Victorian Peep-Show*, pp. 24–5.
102. Elliott O'Donnell, *Scottish Ghost Stories* (London, 1911), p. 201; Mary Wylde, *A Housewife in Kensington* (New York and London, 1937), p. 194; Sir Oliver Lodge, *Christopher: A Study in Human Personality* (London, 1918), pp. 97–8.
103. Stirling, *Life's Little Day*, p. 54.
104. Cook, *Highways and Byways*, p. 225.
105. Pym, *Houses*, pp. 174–5.
106. Ibid., pp. 136–7.
107. Virginia Woolf, 'A Haunted House', in *Monday or Tuesday* (Richmond, 1921).
108. M.R. James, *Ghost-Stories of an Antiquary* (London, 2nd imp., 1905); *More Ghost Stories of an Antiquary* (London, 1920). On James, Richard William Pfaff, *Montague Rhodes James* (London, 1980).
109. Summers, ed., *The Supernatural Omnibus*, p. xxi. On the Victorian haunted house: Marcus, *Apartment Stories*, pp. 116–27; Julia Briggs, *Night Visitors: The Rise and Fall of the English Ghost Story* (London, 1977); Julian Wolfreys, *Victorian Hauntings: Spectrality, Gothic, the Uncanny and Literature* (Basingstoke, 2002); Jack Sullivan, *Elegant Nightmares: The English Ghost Story from Le Fanu to Blackwood* (Athens, OH, 1978); Neil Wilson, *Shadows in the Attic: A Guide to British Supernatural Fiction, 1820–1950* (Boston Spa and London, 2000).
110. Elizabeth Bowen, 'Introduction', in *Second Ghost Book*, ed. Asquith, p. vii.
111. M.R. James, *More Ghost Stories of an Antiquary*, p. v.
112. Marcus, *Apartment Stories*, pp. 116–27.
113. M.R. James, 'The Diary of Mr Poynter', *A Thin Ghost and Others* (London, 1919), p. 66. My thanks to Tom Gleason for introducing me to James.
114. See Sir Ernest Bennett, *Apparitions and Haunted Houses: A Survey of the Evidence* (London, 1939) for incidents of haunted houses elicited by Bennett's 1934 Society for Psychical Research BBC broadcast. Terriss, *Just a Little Bit of String*, p. 147.
115. Hugh Walpole, 'Mrs Porter and Miss Allen', in *The Oxford Book of Twentieth-Century Ghost Stories*, ed. Michael Cox (Oxford, 1996), pp. 57–8.
116. Review of Emily Post, *The Personality of a House* in *Times Literary Supplement*, 29 May 1930, p. 459.
117. See, for instance, Collin Brooks, 'Possession on Completion', in *Second Ghost Book*, ed. Asquith, pp. 179–90.
118. On family heirlooms in a Welsh farming village, Rees, *Life in a Welsh Countryside*, p. 44.
119. Jennifer Wayne, *Growing Up in the Thirties* (London, 1979), pp. 124–5.
120. 'Cardiff Collector's Antiques', *The Times*, 4 July 1916, p. 10. This was only part of Drane's collection. Some of it went to the Cardiff Museum; the rest was auctioned off at Christie's in 1922. See *The Times*, 13 Dec. 1922, p. 7.
121. D 197/1/41b, GRO.

7   MODERN LIVING: THE TRIUMPH OF SAFETY FIRST

1. Christopher Hussey, 'The Queen's Dolls' House', *Country Life*, 16 Feb. 1924, pp. 242–51. The house was intended to represent the sort of mansion in which the King and Queen of England might live in the year 1924. A.C. Benson and Sir Lawrence Weaver, eds., *Everybody's Book of the Queen's Dolls' House* (London, 1924). Queen Mary's dolls' house is displayed at Windsor Castle.

2. See Daunton and Rieger, eds, *Meanings of Modernity*. On this paradox in the pre-war period, see Gabriel Mourey, *Across the Channel: Life and Art in London*, trans. Georgina Latimer (London, 1896), p. 2.

3. Paul Greenhalgh, 'The English Compromise: Modern Design and National Consciousness 1870–1940', in *Designing Modernity: The Arts of Reform and Persuasion 1885–1945*, ed. Wendy Kaplan (London, 1995), esp. pp. 126–7.

4. Bloomsbury is an exception that proves the norm. In an important reinterpretation, Chris Reed argues that Bloomsbury pioneered a distinct brand of 'domestic modernism', which has been overshadowed by art history's obsession with the industrial modernism represented by Le Corbusier. Fry and his friends began from the premise that modern life required new interiors. Reed, *Bloomsbury Rooms*, pp. 210–11, p. 224–7. On taste and the modern in inter-war architecture, Lubbock, *Tyranny of Taste*, pp. 299–332.

5. Hamilton Smith, '"George V" Furniture', *Furnishing Trades' Organiser*, May 1935, AAD/1994/16/1759, AAD.

6. Serge Chermayeff, 'A New Spirit and Idealism', *Architects' Journal*, 4 Nov. 1931, pp. 619–20. Extracts from a paper read at Heal and Son's. On Chermayeff, Alan Powers, *Serge Chermayeff: Designer, Architect, Teacher* (London, 2001).

7. Saler, *Avant-Garde*; Fiona Macarthy, *A History of British Design 1830–1979* (London, 1979); Design and Industry, A Proposal for the Foundation of a Design and Industries Association, n.d. [1915?], DIA/122, RIBA. Also, Frank Pick, 'An Edinburgh Address on Design & Industry', one of a series delivered in the Royal Scottish Academy Galleries, Edinburgh, during the Exhibition of Design and Workmanship in Printing, Oct. 1916, first published 1917, DIA/123, RIBA; 'Membership: Its Privileges and Responsibilities', n.d. [1918?], PeH/3/2–6/22, RIBA.

8. These directions corresponded to the inclinations of its two guiding lights – Peach and Brewer. See Hamilton Smith, 'Design and Industries Association – the Early Years', *Design for Today*, May 1935, AAD/1994/16/1759 Box 1 of 2. On the Board of Trade proposal, see the correspondence contained in PeH/3/2–6/22, RIBA. On the exhibition, Catalogue of an Exhibition of Household Things, designed primarily to serve their purpose, Whitechapel Art Gallery, Oct.–Dec. 1920, DIA/122, RIBA. Also 'What is the D.I.A.?' The 'Ideal Home' Exhibition, Olympia, PeH/3/2–6/22, RIBA.

9. Peach to Brewer, 22 Dec. 1915, PeH/3/2–6/22, RIBA; Brewer to Peach, 30 June 1916, PeH/3/2–6/22, RIBA.

10. 'Empire Art at Wembley', *The Times*, 28 May 1924, AAD/1978/2/179, AAD.

11. P.A. Best, 'What the Modernist Exhibition Has Proved', *Furnishing Trades' Organiser*, April 1928, p. 264.

12. Joseph Emberton, FRIBA, 'Our Obsolete Housing', *Furnishing Trades' Organiser*, March 1933, p. 129.

13. J. Ronald Fleming, 'The New and Old in Decoration', 16 June 1932, TS published as 'The Answer – "I Like It": A Plea and Some Argument in Favour of Modernity', *Harper's Bazaar*, 1933, AAD 1/3–1981.

14. Chermayeff, 'A New Spirit and Idealism'.

15. 'Extraordinary Savings on Furniture', *Northern Echo*, 8 May 1936, AAD/1994/16/1817, PRO.

16. Obituary of Sir Ambrose Heal, *Daily Telegraph*, 17 Nov. 1956, AAD/1994/16/219, AAD. On the history of Heal's, see Susanna Goodden, *At the Sign of the Fourposter: A History of Heal's* (London, 1984).

17. Mrs Maufe and Arthur Greenwood quoted in Tim Benton, 'Up and Down at Heal's: 1929–1935', *Architectural Review*, Feb. 1978, p. 110.

18. Robert Harling, 'The Master Craftsman', *Sunday Times*, 22 Nov. 1956, AAD/1994/16/219, AAD. See also Dodie Smith's description of Ambrose Heal in the second volume of her autobiography, *Look Back with Mixed Feelings* (London, 1978), pp. 272–5. He gave the 'impression of conscious superiority' (p. 272).

19. On Dodie Smith's life, see her four autobiographies, as well as Valerie Grove's biography, *Dear Dodie: The Life of Dodie Smith* (London, 1996).

20. 'The Flat of Dodie Smith', *Town and Country Homes*, Jan. 1932, AAD/1994/16/1633, AAD.

21. Grove, *Dear Dodie*, p. 78.

22. M. Dane, 'A Dramatic Author's Flat', *Homes and Gardens*, Jan. 1933, AAD/1994/16/1649, AAD; see, too, Dodie Smith, *Look Back with Astonishment* (London, 1979), pp. 110–11.

23. M. Dane, 'A Dramatic Author's Flat'.

24. See especially the sales and attendance figures for the Metal and Glass Furniture Exhibition, 1933. Minutes of Board Meetings – 8, 1932–34, AAD/1978/2/7.

25. Mrs Greene to Messrs Frederick Tibbenham, 22 June 1934, HiO/17/1, RIBA. Mrs Greene and her husband had commissioned Oliver Hill to build them a house, Joldwynds, in the art deco style.

26. 'Modernistic Furniture: Passing Phase or New Era', *Furnishings*, Dec. 1928, p. 22; 'A Dip into the Future', *House and Home*, Nov. 1933, p. 2; Leslie Lewis, 'The New Lacquered Style', *Ideal Home*, May 1928, p. 407; Cecil Hunt, *Author-Biography* (London, 1935), pp. 281–2; 'A Modern Nursery', *Star*, 25 March 1933, AAD 1/100–1981, AAD; 'Art Exhibitions', *The Times*, 22 Sept. 1930, AAD/1978/2/445, AAD; N.L.C., 'Steel in the Home', *Country Life*, 17 Oct. 1931, AAD/1978/2/445; John de la Valette, 'The Dorland Hall Exhibition and Some of its Lessons', AAD 1978/2/444, AAD; Mr Shapland, '"The Home Is Not a Machine for Living"', *Furnishing Trades' Organiser*, Dec. 1934, AAD/1994/16/1759 Box 1 of 2, AAD.

27. Saler, *Avant-Garde*, pp. 92–121.

28. 'Margaret', 'Modern Furnishing', *House and Home*, Nov. 1933, p. 23.

29. The Exhibition of British Industrial Art in Relation to the Home, staged at Dorland Hall in June–July 1933, was largely captured by modernists; Ambrose Heal designed the dining-room, Wells Coates designed a minimum flat; Oliver Hill furnished a dining-room, and Serge Chermayeff displayed a weekend house. See David Jeremiah, *Architecture and Design for the Family in Britain, 1900–70* (Manchester, 2000), pp. 92–7.

30. See, for example, 'Why the Furnisher Dare Not "Go Modern"', *Furnishing Trades' Organiser*, July 1933, p. 22; James Morton to George Walton, 14 Dec. 1930, AAD 4/510–1978, AAD.

31. Cairns, *How I Became*, p. 17; Architectural Editor, 'Modern Homes for Moderate Means', *Ideal Home*, March 1928, pp. 60–4; 'House of the Month', *Modern Home*, Aug. 1938, p. 36.

32. A.J. Ayer, *Part of My Life* (Oxford, 1977), p. 139. Ayer's London flat that he took in 1947 was furnished 'almost wholly upon Renee's advice', though the couple had divorced in 1941. She had become enamoured of the off-white, spare style in the 1930s. Ayer, *More of My Life* (London, 1984), p. 34.

33. 'Gomme Upholstery Contributes a Brilliant New Chapter to the Records of Contemporary Furniture Design', n.d. [1930s], p. 8, D/GP 80, Buckinghamshire Record Office; on modern furniture as it played in the *Daily Mail*'s Ideal Home exhibitions, Deborah Ryan, *The Ideal Home through the 20th Century* (London, 1997), pp. 61–85.

34. See *Architectural Review*, March 1935, AAD/1994/16/1759 Box 1 of 2, AAD; Leslie Lewis, 'Restraint in Modern Furnishing', *Ideal Home*, April 1928, p. 299.

35. Heal's advertisement – 'Contemporary Furniture', *Daily Telegraph*, 8 July 1933, AAD/1994/16/1649, AAD.

36. Sir Ambrose Heal, 'Modernism Only Just Beginning', *Furnishing Trades' Organiser*, Feb. 1933, p. 81.

37. 'Modern Living by Whiteley's', undated catalogue, 1930s, 726/59, WCA.

38. 'Drawing Room in Green and Ivory', *Modern Home*, Aug. 1938, p. 37; Chapman, *Home and Social Status*, pp. 44–5; Anon., *Furnishing and Re-Furnishing* (London, 1938), pp. 44–51; on neo-Georgianism and Margaret Jourdain, Alison Light, *Forever England: Femininity, Literature and Conservatism between the Wars* (London and New York, 1991), pp. 34–6; Peter Mandler, *The Fall and Rise of the Stately Home* (New Haven and London, 1997), pp. 278–81.

39. 'Ideas in Modern Furnishing', *Cabinet Maker and Complete House Furnisher*, 10 Oct. 1936, p. 31; Chapman, *Home and Social Status*, p. 99; see, too, Maurice S.R. Adams, *Modern Decorative Art* (London, 1930).

40. 'Gomme Upholstery Contributes a Brilliant New Chapter'; PA 2084/4, PA 2084/19, PA 2084/36, PA 2084/42/1, Brookes Collection, Coventry City Archive; Volume of Advertisements, Astons, DD/DM/726/185 – Denbighshire Record Office, Ruthin. Also Paul Oliver, 'A Lighthouse on the Mantlepiece: Symbolism in the Home', in Paul Oliver, Ian Davis, and Ian Bentley, *Dunroamin: The Suburban Semi and its Enemies* (London, 1981), pp. 173–92.

41. 'Hastings' New Headquarters', *Cabinet Maker and Complete House Furnisher*, 5 Dec. 1936, p. 359.

42. 'Return to Traditional Themes', *Cabinet Maker and Complete House Furnisher*, 26 Dec. 1936, p. 479.

43. Silent Salesmen catalogue pages, E.G. Ltd H.W., n.d. [1930s], PA 2084/42/1 and PA 2084/42/2, Brookes Collection, Coventry City Archive.

44. Cecil Harcourt-Smith, Letter to the Editor, 'The Victorian Home', *The Times*, 4 July 1931; 'The Victorian Cult', *Birmingham Post*, 29 June 1931, AAD/1978/2/445, AAD; 'Antiques not Luxuries', [editor's column], *Antique Collector*, 18 July 1931, p. 165.

45. 'Bright Victorianism', *Evening Standard*, 13 June 1931; P.L.M., 'Victorian Art', *Illustrated Carpenter & Builder*, 26 June 1931, AAD/1978/2/445, AAD; 'Mansard Gallery', *The Times*, 26 June 1931; *Daily Telegraph*, 18 April 1931, AAD/1978/2/445.

46. *Country Life*, 2 May 1931, AAD/1978/2/445, AAD. 'Amusing', *The Lady*, 8 March 1928, p. 257. Osbert Sitwell's rooms represented the 'amusing style'. Reed interprets 'amusing' as a form of modernism, overshadowed in the 1930s and now forgotten. Reed, *Bloomsbury Rooms*, esp. pp. 236–8, 247–54, 261–8.

47. Among others, 'The Victorian Cult', *Birmingham Post*, 29 June 1931; G.S.M., 'Victorian Objects Valued High', *Bazaar*, 20 June 1931, AAD/1978/2/445, AAD.

48. *Country Life*, 2 May 1931, AAD/1978/2/445, AAD.

49. On the 1935 Exhibition, Saler, *Avant-Garde*, pp. 133–4.

50. 'The Design in Industry Exhibition', *Cabinet Maker*, 5 Jan. 1935, AAD/1994/16/1759, Box 1 of 2.

51. 'Olympia and Burlington House: Where Do They Make Contact?' *Cabinet Maker*, 12 Jan. 1935, p. 37; Raymond Mortimer, 'Decorative Art', *New Statesman*, 14 Jan. 1935; Philip Hendy, 'Art in Industry', *London Mercury and Bookman*, Feb. 1935; Our Art Critic, 'British Art in Industry', *The Times*, 5 Jan. 1935, AAD/1994/16/1759, Box 1 of 2.

52. *Architect and Building News*, 11 Jan. 1935, AAD/1994/16/1759, Box 1 of 2.

53. Joseph Thorp, 'Art in Industry', *Architects' Journal*, 10 Jan. 1935, AAD/1994/16/1759, Box 1 of 2.

54. *Architect and Building News*, 11 Jan. 1935, AAD/1994/16/1759, Box 1 of 2.

55. 'Small Classical Houses', *House and Garden*, March 1921, p. 43. On the eclipse of the 'amusing style', Reed, *Bloomsbury Rooms*, pp. 251–77; on inter-war conservative domesticity more broadly, Light, *Forever England*; Sparke, *As Long as It's Pink*, pp. 15–49, 140–62.

56. Davide C. Minter, *The Book of the Home: A Practical Guide for the Modern Household*, vol. 1 with an Introduction by Lady Jekyll, DBE (London, 1927), pp. 44–5. Although Fry is not mentioned, this was probably intended as a critique of post-impressionist rooms as well as Edwardian experimentation.

57. 'Furnishing the House of Character for £175: The Living Room', *Woman's Life*, 28 Feb. 1931, AAD/1994/16/1633, AAD.

58. 'When Buying Furniture Insist on Seeing the "Majority" Lines', *Home Furnisher*, Jan. 1924, p. 263.

59. S.P.B. Mais, 'Letters of a Schoolmaster in Khaki: The House Beautiful', *Evening News*, 10 Nov. 1916, AAD/1978/2/355.

60. Wylde, *Housewife in Kensington*, pp. 57–9.

61. 'Fitness for Purpose: The Essential Quality in Furniture', *Our Homes and Gardens*, Jan. 1920, pp. 226–8, AAD/1978/2/179, AAD; 'Small Homes Simplify Decoration', *Home Furnisher*, Aug. 1923, p. 142. On home-making in the inter-war period, Ryan, *Ideal Home*, pp. 33–85; Jeremiah, *Architecture*, pp. 39–122.

62. A partial list includes *Homes and Gardens* (1919), *Ideal Home* (1920), *House and Garden* (1920), *Home Furnisher* (1923), *Town and Country Homes* (1926), *Home Mirror* (1926), *Woman and Home* (1926), *Modern Home* (1928), *My Home* (1928), *House and Home* (1933), *The Home Journal* (1934), *The New House* (1935), *Vogue House & Garden Book* (1936).

63. 'A Survey of London's Dormitories', *The New House*, Sept. 1935, pp. 27, 44.

64. 'A Notable Modern House on Campden Hill', *House and Garden*, Aug. 1921, p. 19. 'The immediate thrill was sought at the expense of abiding satisfaction, by the deliberate misuse of material, by the upsetting of the established order, by the eccentric perversion of detail.'

65. 'Outstanding Features of the Decoration and Furnishing Section', *Ideal Home*, April 1939, p. 327; 'The Selection of Draperies', *Home Furnisher*, April 1924, p. 35; Josephine Hawkes, 'Fabrics – Some Things We Can Do', *Ideal Home*, March 1928, pp. 174–5; 'Practical Points concerning Curtains', *The New House*, July 1935.

66. Dorothy Stote, 'Your Own Little Home', *Modern Home*, Dec. 1928, p. 18.

67. Ibid., p. 18.

68. Marquis d'Oisy, 'New Ideas in Furnishing the Dining Room', *Ideal Home*, Jan. 1928, p. 14.

69. Lulie M. James, 'The Cottage Bedroom', *Ideal Home*, Jan. 1923, p. 13; also Anon., *Furnishing and Re-furnishing*, pp. 37–42.

70. 'Your Problem, Please!', *Modern Home*, Aug. 1934, pp. 28–9; 'Just Ask *Modern Home*', *Modern Home*, Nov. 1934; 'Your Problems and Other Peoples', *Modern Home*, Dec. 1934; 'Your Home Problems', *Modern Home*, Oct. 1938, p. 99; 'Jack Dare's Home Problem Pages', *Modern Home*, Jan. 1938, p. 70; more generally, G. Maltby Clark, 'Harmonising Ancient and Modern', *The New House*, Oct. 1936, p. 15.

71. For example, 'Straight from the Horse's Mouth', *Vogue House and Garden Book*, 5 Oct. 1938, pp. 26–7; 'Some Furnishing Schemes', *Home Furnisher*, Jan. 1924, p. 243; Edward Newman, FIBD, 'A Short Guide to Successful Colour Scheming', *Ideal Home*, March 1939, pp. 171–2.

72. On Sybil Colefax, a 'gallant old snob' in Beverley Nichols' description. See Beverley Nichols, *A Case of Human Bondage* (London, 1966), p. 53; Kirsty McLeod, *A Passion for Friendship: Sibyl Colefax and Her Circle* (London, 1991); Penny Sparke, *Elsie de Wolfe: The Birth of Modern Interior Decoration* (New York, 2005).

73. Typescript introduction for the book by Fleming, signed G.H.B., *c.* 1968, AAD 1/7–1981.

74. J. Ronald Fleming, TS on interior design, p. 55, AAD 1/6–1981, AAD.

75. Louise Ward, 'Chintz, Swags and Bows: The Myth of English Country-House Style, 1930–1990', in *Interior Design and Identity*, ed. McKellar and Sparke, pp. 92–113.

76. 'Taste in Furnishing, From a Talk by Ronald Fleming', *Radio Times*, n.d. [1930s?], p. 576, AAD 1/167–1981; J. Ronald Fleming, 'A Talk on Decoration', 1931, TS, AAD 1/1–1981. On the BBC's interest in interior design, Reed, *Bloomsbury Rooms*, pp. 260–1; Julian Holder, '"Design in Everyday Things": Promoting Modernism in Britain, 1912–1944', in *Modernism in Design*, ed. Paul Greenhalgh (London, 1990), pp. 123–43.

77. 'Furnishing Commentary – I: The West End', *Cabinet Maker and Complete House Furnisher*, 13 May 1939, p. 212.

78. Basil Ionides, *Colour in Everyday Rooms: With Remarks on Sundry Aspects of Decoration* (London, 1934), p. 85. See, too, Millicent Vince, *Furnishing and Decorating Do's and Donts* (London, 1925).

79. Basil Ionides, *Colour and Interior Decoration* (London, 1926). For a similar such chart, 'Furnishing at a Glance', *Modern Home*, Jan. 1938, p. 33.

80. Ionides, *Colour in Everyday Rooms*, p. vii.

81. See John Cornforth, *London Interiors from the Archives of Country Life* (London, 2000).

82. Oswald Milne, Lecture, n.d. [1921?], MiO 1/1, RIBA.

83. Edward Maufe, 'Modern Influences on London Architecture: The Home', TS text of public lecture given at RIBA, 21 Feb. 1934, MaE/136/2, RIBA.

84. See, for instance, the records of Edward Hughes, DD/G/344, Denbighshire Record Office – Ruthin.

85. Letter from angry shareholder to Chairman Maple, received in office 4 Feb. 1930, AAD/2000/3/235, AAD; Raymond Rice Byrne to H.S. Warton, Esq., 26 May 1933, AAD/2000/3/251.

86. Benn, *Happier Days*, p. 101.

87. J.B. Jeffreys, *Retail Trading in Britain 1850–1950* (Cambridge, 1954), cited in Clive Edwards, *Twentieth-Century Furniture: Materials, Manufacture, and Markets* (Manchester, 1994), p. 160; Janice Winship, 'Culture of Restraint: The British Chain Store 1920–1939', in *Commercial Cultures: Economies, Practices, Spaces*, ed. Peter Jackson, Michelle Lowe, Daniel Miller, and Frank Mort (Oxford and New York, 2000), pp. 15–34; Andrew Alexander, John Benson, and Gareth Shaw, 'Action and Reaction: Competition and the Multiple Retailer in 1930s Britain', *International Review of Retail, Distribution and Consumer Research* 9: 3 (1999): 245–59; Morrison, *English Shops*, pp. 193–249.

88. Annual Reports and Statements of Accounts, DD/DM/726/7, Denbighshire Record Office – Ruthin; 'History of the Business of S. Aston & Son Limited', DD/DM/726/67, Denbighshire Record Office – Ruthin.

89. My account derives from Ross McKibbin's excellent overview in *Classes and Cultures*, pp. 46–8; see also Perkin, *Rise of Professional Society*, pp. 266–73; Barrett and Phillips, *Suburban Style*, pp. 125–53.

90. Chapman, *Home and Social Status*, esp. pp. 26–7; also Burnett, *Social History of Housing*, p. 251. On middle-class expenditure in the late 1930s, see Philip Massey, 'The Expenditure of 1,360 British Middle-Class Households in 1938–9', *Journal of the Royal Statistical Society*, 105: 3 (1942): 159–96. In all of Massey's income brackets, average expenditure on furniture exceeded the amount spent on men's clothing (p. 183).

91. This figure includes outright ownership as well as mortgaged houses.

92. Oliver et al., *Dunroamin*, pp. 13–14.

93. McKibbin, *Classes and Cultures*, p. 97; on fears about strangers, Light, *Forever England*, pp. 78–100.

94. 'Josephine Hawkes Tells You How to Renovate Your Tired Rooms', *Modern Home*, Oct. 1928, p. 36; Oliver et al., *Dunroamin*, p. 88.

95. 'A Dining-Room Lounge', *Modern Home*, Feb. 1934, p. 30; Marquis d'Oisy, 'Wall Hangings of Today', *Ideal Home*, Feb. 1928, p. 84; Vivian Thompson, MA, 'Peculiarities of Colour', *Ideal Home*, Feb. 1928, p. 93; Paul Vaughan, *Something in Linoleum* (London, 1994), pp. 62–3.

96. Fredda, 'Spring Repairs: How's Your House Looking?', *Modern Home*, Jan. 1938, p. 34.

97. 'Joan Has Such Good Taste', Sanderson wallpaper advertisement, *Ideal Home*, Feb. 1928, p. 125; another variant, 'Do come in . . . !' The Medici Society advertisement, *House and Garden*, Oct. 1923, p. i.

98. Subtle was the operative word. Mrs Leslie Menzies, 'A Little House Over Your Garage', *Modern Home*, Oct. 1928, p. 12.

99. Sidney R. Campion, *Sunlight on the Foothills* (London, 1941), pp. 160–1.

100. M.H.S., 'The Art of Salesmanship', *Furnishings*, Dec. 1928, pp. 26–7.

101. 'Straight Talks to Salesmen', *Furnishing Trades' Organiser*, May 1933, p. 260.

102. Nicholson, *Half My Days*, pp. 130–1. O'Niel was the stage name of Lady Constance Malleson. Her autobiography is *After Ten Years: A Personal Record* (London, 1931).

103. 'The Use and Misuse of Black in Decoration', *House and Garden*, Aug. 1921, p. 43.

104. Lancaster, *All Done*, p. 13. One post-Second World War account began with the half-serious declaration that the inter-war 'middle classes were composed of all those who used napkin rings'. Roy Lewis and Angus Maude, *The English Middle Classes* (London, 1949), p. 13.

105. On Bulley, Alan Powers, 'Margaret Bulley', *Crafts*, Jan./Feb. 2005, pp. 24–5.

106. Binfield, *So Down to Prayers*, p. 183.
107. Clutton-Brock 'Experiments in Taste', *Times Literary Supplement*, 12 Oct. 1933, p. 685.
108. For efforts to improve working-class taste, see the Council for Art and Industry's efforts to equip a model working-class flat, BT 57/11, PRO; on post-Second World War decorative choices, Chapman, *Home and Social Status*, esp. pp. 16–17, 20, 22.
109. Rose, *Psychological Complex*, pp. 90–1, 138–42, 194–5.
110. Julia Cairns, 'The Home Decorative', *Eve*, 21 Oct. 1925, AAD/1978/2/179. On the idea of a 'basic personality type', which fuses class, nation, and personality, see B.M. Spinley, *The Deprived and the Privileged: Personality Development in English Society* (London, 1953), pp. 5, 14–5, 100–1.
111. Noel Carrington, *Design in the Home* (London, 1933), p. 44. On attitudes towards housing during the war, Mass-Observation, *An Enquiry into People's Homes* (London, 1943).
112. Aubrey Noakes, *Charles Spencelayh and His Paintings* (London, 1978), p. 58.
113. Edward Newman, 'War-Time Windows', *Ideal Home*, Nov. 1939, pp. 324–5. The well-appointed bomb shelter capitalized upon advancements in built-in furniture to offer 'luxurious sleeping for two' in a 'handsome oak version of the bunk-bed'. 'Dug-Out Comfort', *Ideal Home*, Nov. 1939, p. 322.
114. Elizabeth Bowen, *The Mulberry Tree: Writings of Elizabeth Bowen*, selected and introduced by Hermione Lee (London, 1986), p. 97.
115. Nichols, *Case*, p. 151.
116. Coke, *Confessions*, p. 35.

EPILOGUE: YOUR NEIGHBOUR'S HOUSE

1. On the limited role of ethics in shopping today, Daniel Miller, *The Dialectics of Shopping* (Chicago and London, 2001), pp. 111–34.
2. 'The Top Five Property Shows', *Independent on Sunday*, 13 April 2003, News, p. 13. At three million viewers, a show captured approximately 12% of a weekday evening's viewers; at six million, approximately 25%.
3. Ina Zweiniger-Bargieloswka, *Austerity in Britain: Rationing, Controls, and Consumption 1939–1955* (Oxford, 2000); Claire Langhamer, 'The Meanings of Home in Postwar Britain', *Journal of Contemporary History*, 40: 2 (2005): 341–62; for a contemporary analysis of homes, see, too, Chapman, *Home and Social Status*.
4. Only 38% had a refrigerator/freezer. *Abstract of Regional Statistics*, 3 (London, 1967); Douglas and Isherwood, *The World of Goods*, pp. 100, 127; Matthew Hilton, *Consumerism in Twentieth-Century Britain: The Search for a Historical Movement* (Cambridge, 2003); F. Graham Pyatt, *Priority Patterns and the Demand for Household Durable Goods* (Cambridge, 1966); A.H. Halsey, *British Social Trends since 1900: A Guide to the Changing Social Structure of Britain* (London, 1988 [1972]), p. 374.
5. In 1971, 64% of UK citizens had a washing machine; 69% had a refrigerator; 91% had a television; 38% had a telephone; 44% had one car; 7% had two or more cars. *Social Trends*, 3, 1972, ed. Muriel Nissel (London, 1972), p. 103. J.F. Pickering, *The Acquisition of Consumer Durables: A Cross-Sectional Investigation* (New York, 1977). On household resources, Peter Townshend, *Poverty in the United Kingdom* (Berkeley, 1979). On Japan, Patricia L. Maclachlan, *Consumer Politics in Postwar Japan* (New York, 2002); on the US, Lizabeth Cohen, *A Consumer's Republic: The Politics of Mass Consumption in Post-War America* (New York, 2003); Susan Strasser, Charles McGovern, and Matthias Judt, eds, *Getting and Spending: European and American Consumer Societies in the Twentieth Century* (Cambridge, 1998); on Europe, Heinz-Gerhard Haupt, *Konsum und Handel: Europa im 19. und 20. Jahrhundert* (Göttingen, 2002); on Americanization, Victoria de Grazia, *Irresistible Empire: America's Advance through Twentieth-Century Europe* (Cambridge, 2005), pp. 336–75; on

post-war class mobility in Britain, John Goldthorpe, *Social Mobility and Class Structure in Modern Britain* (Oxford, 1987 [1980]).

6. Kate Barker, *Review of Housing Supply*, Interim Report (London, 2003), p. 7. Andrew Adonis and Stephen Pollard caution against fetishizing home ownership, observing that because most home owners are heavily indebted with huge mortgages, they have simply 'exchanged one form of landlord for another: the building society' (p. 192). Andrew Adonis and Stephen Pollard, *A Class Act: The Myth of Britain's Classless Society* (London, 1997), pp. 191–5.

7. This figure is adjusted for inflation. Stephen King, 'Consumers May At Last Be Recognising their Apparent Riches Were an Illusion', *Independent*, 23 May 2005, Business, p. 56; Hamish McRae, 'Higher Interest Rates Won't Stop Us Splashing Out Yet', *Independent*, Business, p. 11; Samuel Brittan, 'An Economic Miracle Revisited', *Financial Times*, 23 May 2003, Comment, p. 21; Edward Russell-Walling, 'View from London: Consumption Boom May Be Coming to an End', *Financial Times*, 19 Nov. 2001. Not all of that spending was dedicated to commodities, though goods far outweighed services in the total. Between 1996 and 2005, insurance premiums also rose by 67%, car repair costs by 63%, council tax bills by 70% and education by 62%. David Smith, 'If Britain Is Doing So Well, Why Doesn't It Feel Like It?' *Sunday Times*, 27 Feb. 2005, Business, p. 4. On the gap between consumer spending and GDP: 'Fasten Your Seatbelts', *The Economist*, 4 Sept. 2004; on shopping, Peter K. Lunt and Sonia M. Livingstone, *Mass Consumption and Personal Identity* (Milton Keynes, 1992), pp. 86–100.

8. Jamie Doward, Tom Reilly, and Mary Graham, 'Great Divide as Census Reveals Two Nations Growing Far Apart', *Observer*, 23 Nov. 2003, News, p. 7.

9. *Social Trends*, 34: 2004 edition, p. 151, Table 10:4.

10. Tristram Hunt, 'Victory of the Middle Class, *Guardian*, 10 May 2002, Leader pages, p. 17. By contrast, the MORI survey (2002) showed that 68 per cent of the 1,895 people interviewed believed themselves working-class, up from 51% in 1994. Jeremy Watson, 'Now We Are All Working Class', *Scotland on Sunday*, 25 Aug. 2002, p. 14. Stephen Aldridge, 'Life Chances and Social Mobility: An Overview of the Evidence' (Prime Minister's Strategy Unit) places the proportion of the middle-class population at 42% (p. 23). The National Readership Survey (2001) revealed that 50.6% of the population could be classified as ABC1s – those who work in professional, managerial, or other white-collar jobs.

11. Interview with Ben Frow, Controller of Features and Entertainment, Channel Five, London, 8 June 2005.

12. 'Interview: Ben Frow', *Televisual*, 1 Nov. 2002, p. 22; interview with Hamish Barbour, Glasgow, 17 June 2005: 'He has an amazing ability to put his finger right on the button. He's terribly unusual in that respect. . . . And because he trusts his own taste and judgement, he's made some great calls.' Interview with Paul Welling, London, 10 June 2005.

13. David Rowan, 'Five's New Fixer', *Evening Standard*, 19 Nov. 2003, A, p. 53; David Rowan, 'The Demons That Drive Miss Daisy', *Evening Standard*, 22 Dec. 2004, A, p. 44; Nick Powell on Frow, *Broadcast News* by Produxion.com, 14 Oct. 2002; John Plunkett, 'How Now Ben Frow' *Guardian*, 26 April 2004, Media p. 4; Ciar Byrne, 'Vocation, Vocation, Vocation', *Independent*, 31 Jan. 2005, n.p.

14. Maggie Brown, 'The Hit Man', *Guardian*, 31 March 2003, Media, p. 8.

15. Interview with John Silver, London, 10 June 2005.

16. Nick Powell on Frow, *Broadcast News* by Produxion.com, 14 Oct. 2002. Interview with Frow.

17. Between 1996 and 2002, housing prices rose an estimated 9% per annum. Kate Barker, *Review of Housing Supply: Securing Our Future Housing Needs*, Interim Report: Analysis (HMSO, Dec. 2003), p. 6. On the idea of 'housing careers', Mike Savage, James Barlow, Peter Dickens, and Tony Fielding, *Property, Bureaucracy and Culture: Middle-Class Formation in Contemporary Britain* (London and New York, 1992), pp. 80–98.

18. *Through the Keyhole* started in 1983 as a short segment on ITV's morning show; it became a fully fledged programme in 1987. Hosted by David Frost and the American-born Loyd Grossman (until 2003), *Through the Keyhole* is part game show, part at-home profile. Each week, two houses are shown. The audience at home is told to whom they belong; meanwhile, a panel of celebrities attempts to guess who lives in the house. The programme's tagline is: 'Who'd live in a house like this?'

19. 'Glue It Yourself with Barry Bucknell', *Yorkshire Post*, 3 March 2003; on middle-class, post-war standards of living, Lewis and Maude, *English Middle Classes*, pp. 203–17; on housing, with a focus on modernism, Jeremiah, *Architecture*, pp. 164–208; on DIY and house-centredness, Peter Willmott and Michael Young, *Family and Class in a London Suburb* (London, 1960), pp. 15–27.

20. Bucknell began his career on Joan Gilbert's *About the Home* (1956–7). Anthony Hayward, 'Obituary: Barry Bucknell', *Independent*, 22 Feb. 2003; 'Obituary, Barry Bucknell', *Daily Telegraph*, 22 Feb. 2003, p. 25. Dennis Barker, 'Obituary: Barry Bucknell: DIY Hero to Postwar Women', *Guardian*, 27 Feb. 2003, p. 24. On DIY more broadly, Jeremiah, *Architecture*, pp. 164–5.

21. Richard Woods and Cherry Norton, 'Cloning the Middle Classes', *The Times*, 17 Jan. 1999, Features; Richard Reeves, 'The Belief That More Education Will Create More Equal Opportunities Has Been Proved Wrong', *New Statesman*, 24 May 2004; Savage et al., *Property, Bureaucracy and Culture*, pp. 132–58.

22. *Ideal Home* posted a circulation of 286,809 in 1988; *Homes and Gardens* followed with 231,145; *House and Garden*, 148,721; *Country Homes & Interiors*, 93,685; *World of Interiors*, 70,983; *Traditional Homes*, 32,331. David Reed, 'Media: Will Home Stay So Sweet for Glossies?' *Marketing*, 23 Feb. 1989; interview with Giles Kime, London, Deputy Editor, *Homes and Gardens*, London, 16 Sept. 2005.

23. 'Launchpad', *Campaign*, 27 Jan. 1989, n.p.

24. Interview with Isobel McKenzie-Price, New York, 27 July 2005; interview with Kime.

25. Belinda Archer, 'Special Report on Top Consumer Magazines', *Campaign*, 1 Nov. 1991.

26. A humorous take was offered by the series, *Keeping Up Appearances* (1990–5) starring that indomitable snob, Hyacinth Bucket (pronounced Bouquet).

27. On the country-house ideal, Ward, 'Chintz, Swags and Bows', in *Interior Design and Identity*, ed. McKellar and Sparke, pp. 92–113; Mandler, *Fall and Rise*, pp. 412–13.

28. Martin Parr and Nicholas Barker, *Signs of the Times: A Portrait of the Nation's Tastes* (Manchester, 1992), foreword.

29. Lauris Morgan Griffiths, 'Life is Suite', *Evening Standard*, 3 Jan. 1992, p. 43; 'The Eye of the Beholder', *Art Review*, 1 Feb. 2002, pp. 54–5; Richard McClure, 'What's Wrong with the Way We Live Now?' *Financial Times*, 9 Feb. 2002, Arts, p. 6; 'Nation of Aspirations', *Time Out*, 20 Feb. 2002, p. 50. More broadly, Stephen Bayley, *Taste: The Secret Meaning of Things* (New York, 1991).

30. Val Williams, 'Ordinary People', *Independent*, 1 Dec. 1991, Sunday Review, p. 10.

31. Interview with McKenzie-Price.

32. Andy Fry, 'The Décor Decade', *Marketing*, 17 Dec. 1998.

33. Interview with Suzanne Imre, Editor-in-Chief, *Living etc.*, London, 22 June 2005; interview with Kime.

34. On reality programming (and specifically *Big Brother*), see Peter Bazalgette, *Billion Dollar Game: How Three Men Risked It All and Changed the Face of TV* (New York, 2005). Bazalgette's company produced *Changing Rooms*. On prosperity, the unequal distribution bears remembering. Between 1979 and 2001, the percentage of households with children in relative poverty increased by 18% – from 14% to 32%. Wendy Piatt, 'From Rags to Rags', *New Statesman*, 18 Aug. 2003.

35. 'You Changed My Room into a Tart's Palace', *Daily Record* [Scotland], 5 March 1998, p. 25.

36. 'TV DIY Programmes Leap in Popularity with Viewers', *DIY Week*, 12 Dec. 1997, p. 22.

37. Georgina Pattinson, 'Design of the Times', *The Sentinel*, 24 Dec. 1998, Television, p. 31.

38. Ibid.

39. Interview with Linda Clifford, London, 8 Nov. 2005; Chris Bray, 'Last Night's View', *Mirror*, 14 Aug. 1998, Features, p. 32; Stuart Jeffries, 'House of Pain', *Guardian*, 1 Aug. 1998, Features, p. 5; Ann Treneman, 'Phew. Give That Woman a Decoration', *Independent*, 7 Nov. 1997, Features, p. 19.

40. 'Consume Property', *Time Out*, 21 May 2003, p. 41.

41. 'Pen in a Gimmick too Far', *Hull Daily Mail*, 26 Jan. 1999, p. 2; Emma Cook, 'Taste: the Final Frontier', *Independent*, 28 Dec. 1997, Features, p. 12

42. 'TV DIY Programmes Leap in Popularity with Viewers', *DIY Week*, 12 Dec. 1997, p. 22; Georgette McCready, 'Everyone's Changing Rooms', *Bath Chronicle*, 20 Oct. 1998, p. 2. David Smith, 'Booming Britain Paints the Town Red', *Express*, 11 April 2000.

43. Interview with McKenzie-Price.

44. Ian Parker, 'Tired and Emulsional', *Observer*, 16 Aug. 1998, Review, p. 10; Simon Worthington, 'DIY Duffers Count Cost of Copying Makeover Shows', *Evening Standard*, 27 June 2001, p. 16.

45. Margaret Morrison, 'This Man Can Seriously Damage Your Living Room', *Scotland on Sunday*, 9 Jan. 2000, Spectrum, p. 14. Jeffries, 'House of Pain', p. 5; Brian Viner, 'The Blonde Arm of the Law', *Mail on Sunday*, 13 Sept. 1998, p. 46.

46. Deborah Ross, 'The Wild Man of DIY', *Independent*, 3 Aug. 1998, Features, pp. 1, 9; Kate Watson-Smyth, 'The Objects of Our Affections', *Independent*, 26 March 2003, Features, p. 10; Lina Das, 'Changing Names', *Mail on Sunday*, 11 July 1999, pp. 12–13.

47. Laurence Llewelyn-Bowen, 'A Quiet Riot in the Home', *Financial Times*, 1 March 2003, FT Weekend House and Garden, p. 12.

48. Laurence Llewelyn-Bowen, 'Please Wales, Don't Copy', *Western Mail*, 1 May 2004, Features, p. 4.

49. Rachel Cooke, 'A Question of Taste,' *Sunday Times*, 2 Aug. 1998, Features.

50. On this point, Miller, *The Dialectics of Shopping*, p. 55.

51. 'Back to Basics for DIY', *Aberdeen Evening Express*, 6 Feb. 2004, Features, p. 8.

52. Julia Fisher, 'Room for Improvement', *Daily Mail*, 15 Nov. 1999, pp. 44–5.

53. John Plunkett, 'TV Finds Real Winner in Property Market', *Observer*, 16 Feb. 2003, p. 7.

54. In 2000, Jane Root, the Controller of BBC2 suggested changes to the format of home programming. Jane Robins, 'BBC Decides That What Tired Old Makeover Programmes Need is a Completely New Look', *Independent*, 21 April 2000, News, p. 9. On Davies, John Plunkett, 'Auntie Decides What Not to Wear', *Observer*, 4 May 2003, Business, p. 7.

55. On this shift, Rupert Smith, 'Reality – the Next Stage', *Guardian*, 1 Dec. 2003, Features, p. 17.

56. Interview with Silver.

57. Interview with Barbour.

58. Interview with Frow.

59. David McIntosh, 'What Do You Mean, Nasty Pink?' *Evening News* (Edinburgh), 25 May 2000, p. 32.

60. Interview with Frow.

61. Richard Moriarty, 'We're All Mad on Magnolia', *Express*, 6 May 2004, News, p. 18; Arifa Akbar and Helen McCormack, 'DIY by Numbers', *Independent*, 28 March 2005, pp. 12–13.

62. Nick Foulkes, 'Whose Taste Is It Anyway?' *Independent*, 23 Feb. 2005.

63. India Knight, 'Fighting the Thin Culture', *Sunday Times*, 29 Aug. 2004, Features, p. 4.

64. Flic Everett, 'TV is Awash with Know-Alls Telling Us How to Live', *Mirror*, 3 May 2005, Features, p. 25.

65. Angela Pertusini, 'M is for Mindlessness', *Daily Telegraph*, 16 April 2005, Property, p. 2. Everett, 'TV is Awash with Know-Alls', p. 25.

66. Edel Morgan, 'Death to Minimalism! Long Live Bad Taste!', *Irish Times*, 13 May 2004, City Edition, Residential Property, p. 55.

67. Rowan, 'The Demons'.

68. Interview with Barbour.

69. Elaine Denby, *What's in a Room: Some Aspects of Interior Design* (London, 1971), p. 1.
70. Interview with Silver.
71. Gerard Gilbert, 'From Here to Modernity', *Independent*, 13 Sept. 2004, Features, pp. 2–3
72. While emphasizing that class is alive and well, Adonis and Pollard acknowledge the 'rise of a unified consumer and popular culture', Adonis and Pollard, *Class Act*, p. 33.
73. On these sorts of distinctions, Kate Fox, *Watching the English: The Hidden Rules of English Behaviour* (London, 2004), esp. pp. 73–83. Earlier in the century, T.H. Pear, *English Social Differences* (London, 1955), esp. pp. 85–118. On class in Britain today more broadly: Adonis and Pollard, *Class Act*; Ivan Reid, *Class in Britain* (Cambridge, 1998); David Cannadine, *The Rise and Fall of Class in Britain* (New York, 1999), esp. pp. 167–94; by way of comparison, Gerry Pratt, 'The House as an Expression of Social Worlds', in *Housing and Identity*, ed. James Duncan (New York, 1982), pp. 135–80.
74. This inability to draw fine distinctions (underestimated in my opinion) serves – at least to some degree – to confound Bourdieu's famous argument. For an amusing analysis of the proliferation of snobberies in the face of apparent homogenization, see Euan Ferguson, 'We're All Snobs Now', *Observer*, 30 Sept. 2001, Review, p. 1; Savage et al., *Property, Bureaucracy and Culture*, pp. 99–131.
75. Jasper Gerard, 'Laurence of Suburbia', *Sunday Times*, 10 March 2002, Features.
76. Interview with Frow.

SELECTED BIBLIOGRAPHY

ARCHIVES

Archive of Art and Design – London
Bedfordshire and Luton Archives and Records Service
Birmingham City Archives
Birmingham University Information Services, Special Collections
Bodleian Library, University of Oxford – John Johnston Collection
Buckinghamshire Records and Local Studies Service
Coke MSS., Trusley, NRA 4221, Private Collection
Colchester Museum Resources Centre
Coventry Archives
Cumbria Record Office – Carlisle
Denbighshire Record Office, Ruthin (Clwyd Record Office)
Duke University Special Collections – North Carolina
East Sussex Record Office – Lewes
Edward Barnsley Archive – Petersfield
Essex Record Office – Chelmsford
Essex Record Office – Colchester
Geffrye Museum – London
Glamorgan Record Office – Cardiff
Glasgow City Archives
Greater Manchester Record Office
Hampshire Record Office – Winchester
Herefordshire Record Office – Hereford
Lancashire Record Office – Preston
London Metropolitan Archive
Museum of Domestic Design and Architecture – Middlesex University
Museum of English Rural Life – University of Reading
National Archives: Public Record Office – London

National Art Library
National Monuments Record Office – Swindon
Oxfordshire Record Office
Portsmouth Museums and Records Service
Royal Commission on the Ancient and Historical Monuments of Scotland
Royal Institute of British Architects
Sheffield Archives
Sir John Soane's Museum – London
Somerset Archive and Record Service – Taunton
Tyne and Wear Archives Service – Newcastle
University of Glasgow Archives and Business Records Centre
Westminster City Archives
West Yorkshire Archive Service – Bradford
West Yorkshire Archive Service – Calderdale
Worcestershire Record Office – Worcester

PRIMARY SOURCES

Adams, William Scovell. *Edwardian Portraits.* London: Secker & Warburg, 1957.
Aldington, Richard. *Life for Life's Sake.* New York: Viking Press, 1941.
Anon. *Furnishing and Re-Furnishing.* London: Country Life, 1938.
Anon. *House of Maple.* London: Maple, 1949.
Argus. *A Mild Remonstrance against the Taste-Censorship at Marlborough House in Reference to Manufacturing Ornamentation and Decorative Design. To Manufacturers, Decorators, Designers, and the Public Generally.* London: Houlston & Stoneman, 1853.
Armstrong, Martin. *Victorian Peep-Show.* Plymouth, UK: Michael Joseph, 1938.
Ayer, A.J. *Part of My Life.* Oxford: Oxford University Press, 1977.
Barclay, A.R., ed. *A Selection from the Letters and Papers of the Late John Barclay.* Philadelphia: Henry Longstreth, 1847.
Barker, Lady [Mary Anne Broome]. *The Bedroom and the Boudoir.* London: Macmillan, 1878.
Beaton, Cecil. *Glass of Fashion.* New York: Doubleday, 1954.
Begg, W. Proudfoot. *The Development of Taste, and Other Studies in Aesthetics.* Glasgow: James Maclehose, 1887.
Benn, Ernest. *The Confessions of a Capitalist.* London: Ernest Benn, 1932 [1925].
—— *Happier Days: Recollections and Reflections.* London: Ernest Benn, 1949.
Bennett, Sir Ernest. *Apparitions and Haunted Houses: A Survey of the Evidence.* London: Faber & Faber, 1939.

Benson, A.C. and Sir Lawrence Weaver, eds. *Everybody's Book of the Queen's Dolls' House.* London: The Daily Telegraph/Methuen, 1924.

Benson, E.F. *Our Family Affairs, 1867–1896.* London: Cassell, 1920.

—— *As We Were: A Victorian Peep-Show.* New York: Blue Ribbon Books, 1930.

—— *An Autumn Sowing.* London: Hogarth Press, 1987 [1917].

Beresford, John, ed. *The Diary of a Country Parson: The Reverend James Woodforde.* 5 vols. London: Oxford University Press, 1927.

Betjeman, John. *Ghastly Good Taste: Or, A Depressing Story of the Rise and Fall of English Architecture.* London: Chapman & Hall, 1933.

Billington, Mary Frances, ed. *Marriage: Its Legal Preliminaries and Social Observances. Home Hints by Mrs. Talbot Coke.* London: F.W. Sears, 1900.

Birks, T.R. *Memoir of the Rev. Edward Bickersteth, Late Rector of Watton, Herts.* London: Beeleys, 1851.

Bloom, Ursula. *Victorian Vinaigrette.* London: Hutchinson, 1956.

—— *The Elegant Edwardian.* London: Hutchinson, 1957.

Booker, Beryl Lee. *Yesterday's Child, 1890–1909.* London: John Long, 1937.

Boyd, Andrew. *The Recreations of a Country Parson,* 2nd series. Boston: Ticknor & Fields, 1861.

—— *St. Andrew's and Elsewhere.* London: Longmans, 1894.

Braithwaite, Joseph Bevan. *Memoirs of Joseph John Gurney.* 2 vols. Philadelphia: Lippincott, Grambo, 1854.

Bullen, Frank Thomas. *Confessions of a Tradesman.* London: Hodder & Stoughton, 1908.

Bulley, Margaret Hattersley. *Have You Good Taste? A Guide to the Appreciation of the Lesser Arts.* London: Methuen, 1933.

Burgess, Frederick William. *Chats on Household Curios.* New York: Frederick A. Stokes, 1914.

Burke, Edmund. *Philosophical Enquiry into the Origin of Our Ideas of the Sublime and Beautiful, with an Introductory Discourse concerning Taste.* Gloucester: Bryant & Jefferies, 1841 [1757].

Butler, Josephine, ed. *Woman's Work and Woman's Culture: A Series of Essays.* London: Macmillan, 1869.

Byrne, Muriel St Clare. *Common or Garden Child: A Not Unfaithful Record.* London: Faber & Faber, 1942.

Cairns, Julia. *How I Became a Journalist.* London: Thomas Nelson, 1960.

Campion, Sidney. *Sunlight on the Foothills.* London: Rich & Cowan, 1941.

Carrington, Noel. *Design in the Home.* London: Country Life, 1933.

Cescinsky, Herbert. *The Gentle Art of Faking Furniture.* New York: Dover Publications, 1967 [1931].

Champneys, Basil. *Memoirs and Correspondence of Coventry Patmore.* 2 vols. London: George Bell, 1900.

Chapman, Dennis. *The Home and Social Status.* London: Routledge & Kegan Paul, 1955.

Chapman, Guy. *Culture and Survival.* London: Jonathan Cape, 1940.

Church, Richard. *Over the Bridge: An Essay in Autobiography.* London: Heinemann, 1955.

—— *The Golden Sovereign.* London: Heinemann, 1957.

Cobbe, Frances Power. *The Life of Frances Power Cobbe.* London: R. Bentley, 1894.

Coke, Desmond. *Confessions of an Incurable Collector.* London: Chapman & Hall, 1928.

Coke, Mrs Talbot. *The Gentlewoman at Home.* London: Henry, 1892.

Cole, Alan S. *Fifty Years of Public Work of Sir Henry Cole K.C.B. Accounted for in His Deeds, Speeches and Writings.* London: George Bell, 1884.

Collins, Horace. *My Best Riches: Story of a Stone Rolling Round the World and the Stage.* London: Eyre & Spottiswoode, 1941.

Conder, Eustace R. *Josiah Conder: A Memoir.* London: John Snow, 1857.

Conway, Moncure. *Travels in South Kensington with Notes on Decorative Art and Architecture in England.* New York: Harper & Brothers, 1882.

Cook, Mrs E.T. *Highways and Byways in London.* London: Macmillan, 1902.

Cooke, Colonel Montague. *Clouds that Flee.* London: Hutchinson, 1935.

Courtney, Janet Elizabeth. *Recollected in Tranquillity.* London: Heinemann, 1926.

Crane, Lucy. *Art and the Formation of Taste: Six Lectures.* Boston: Chautauqua Press, 1887.

Crosland, Thomas. *The Suburbans.* London: John Long, 1905.

Crouch, Joseph and Edmund Butler. *The Apartments of the House: Their Arrangement, Furnishing and Decoration.* London: At the Sign of the Unicorn, 1900.

Dale, R.W. *The Old Evangelicalism and the New.* London: Hodder & Stoughton, 1889.

Deane, Ethel. *Byways of Collecting.* London: Cassell, 1908.

—— 'None So Blind'. Boston, MA: Reid Publishing, 1910.

Decorator. *The Paper Hanger, Painter, Grainer and Decorator's Assistant.* London: Kent, 1879.

Denby, Elaine. *What's in a Room: Some Aspects of Interior Design.* London: BBC Publications, 1971.

Department of Science and Art. *A Catalogue of the Museum of Ornamental Art at Marlborough House, Pall Mall. For the Use of Students and Manufacturers, and the Public.* London: Eyre & Spottiswoode, 1853 [fifth edn].

Docker, Alfred. *Religion: What It Really Is.* London: Cursitor Publishing, 1919.

Dodd, George. *The Textile Manufactures of Great Britain.* London: Charles Knight, 1844.

Dohme, Robert. *Das englische Haus: eine kultur- und baugeschichtliche Skizze*. Braunschweig: Westermann, 1888.

Duff Gordon, Lady [Lucy Wallace Sutherland]. *Discretions and Indiscretions*. New York: Frederick A. Stokes, 1932.

Dunn, Henry Treffry. *Recollections of Dante Gabriel Rossetti and His Circle*, ed. Gale Pedrick. New York: James Pott, 1904.

Duveen, James Henry. *Collections and Recollections*. London: Jerrolds, 1934.

Eastlake, Charles Lock. *Hints on Household Taste in Furniture, Upholstery and Other Details*. London: Longmans, Green, 1868.

Edis, Robert William. *Decoration and Furniture of Town Houses*. London: Kegan Paul, 1881.

Elder-Duncan, John Hudson. *The House Beautiful and Useful*. New York: John Lane, 1907.

Emerson, Ralph Waldo. *English Traits*. Boston: Phillips, Sampson, 1856.

Festing Jones, Henry. *Samuel Butler: A Memoir*. London: Macmillan, 1919.

Fletcher, Margaret. *O, Call Back Yesterday*. Oxford: Basil Blackwell, 1939.

Fortescue, Lady Winifred. *Beauty for Ashes*. Edinburgh and London: William Blackwood, 1948.

Froude, James Anthony, ed. *Letters and Memorials of Jane Welsh Carlyle*. New York: Charles Scribner's Sons, 1883.

G. L. *The Science of Taste: Being a Treatise on Its Principles*. London: Edward Stanford, 1879.

Galsworthy, John. *The Forsyte Saga*. New York: Charles Scribner's Sons, 1933.

Gardiner, Miss Florence Mary. *Furnishings and Fittings for Every Home*. London: Record Press, 1894.

Garrett, Rhoda and Agnes Garrett. *Suggestions for House Decoration in Painting, Woodwork and Furniture*. London: Macmillan, 1877.

Gibbs, Philip. *The New Man: A Portrait Study of the Latest Type*. London: Isaac Pitman, 1914.

—— *The Pageant of the Years: An Autobiography*. London: Heinemann, 1946.

Gladstone, W.E. *The Gladstone Diaries*, ed. H.C.G. Matthew. Oxford: Clarendon Press, 14 vols, 1968–94.

Goring, J.H. *The Ballad of Lake Laloo and Other Rhymes*. London: Utopia, 1909.

Grant, J.P. Grant, ed. *Memoir and Correspondence of Mrs. Grant of Laggan*. 3 vols. Edinburgh: Thomas Allan, 1845.

Gregory, Benjamin. *The Thorough Business Man: Memoirs of Walter Powell*. London: Strahan, 1871.

Grisewood, Frederick. *The World Goes By*. London: Secker & Warburg, 1952.

Grossmith, George and Weedon Grossmith. *The Diary of a Nobody*. London: Folio Society, 1969 [1892].

H.J.C. [H.J. Cooper]. *The Art of Furnishing on Rational and Aesthetic Principles.* London: Henry S. King, 1876.

Hall, Herbert Byng. *The Bric-à-Brac Hunter: Or, Chapters on Chinamania.* Philadelphia: J.B. Lippincott, 1875.

Hamerton, Philip Gilbert. *Thoughts about Art.* Boston: Roberts Brothers, 1871.

Hamilton, Cicely Mary. *Life Errant.* London: J.M. Dent, 1935.

Hardman, Sir William. *A Mid-Victorian Pepys: The Letters and Memoirs of Sir William Hardman, M.A., F.R.G.S.* New York: George Doran, 1923.

Hare, Augustus. *The Gurneys of Earlham.* 2 vols. New York: Dodd, Mead, 1895.

—— *The Story of My Life.* London: George Allen, 1896.

Haweis, Hugolin. *Four to Fourteen by a Victorian Child.* London: Robert Hale, 1939.

Haweis, Mary Eliza. *The Art of Decoration.* London: Chatto & Windus, 1881.

—— *Beautiful Houses: Being a Description of Certain Well-Known Artistic Houses.* New York: Scribner & Welford, 1882.

Hazlitt, William Carew. *The Confessions of a Collector.* London: Ward & Downey, 1897.

Hope, Thomas. *Household Furniture and Interior Decoration Executed from Designs by Thomas Hope.* London: John Tiranti, 1946 [1807].

Hopkinson, James. *Victorian Cabinet Maker: The Memoirs of James Hopkinson, 1819–1894.* New York: Augustus M. Kelley, 1968.

Hudson, Derek. *Munby: A Man of Two Worlds. The Life and Diaries of Arthur J. Munby, 1828–1910.* London: John Murray, 1972.

Hughes, M.V. *A London Child of the 1870s.* Oxford: Oxford University Press, 1977 [1934].

—— *A London Girl of the 1880s.* Oxford: Oxford University Press, 1978.

—— *A London Home in the 1890s.* Oxford: Oxford University Press, 1978.

Hunt, Cecil. *Author-Biography.* London: Hutchinson, 1935.

Illingworth, J.R. *Personality Human and Divine: Being the Bampton Lectures for the Year 1894.* London: Macmillan, 1894.

Ionides, Basil. *Colour and Interior Decoration.* London: Country Life, 1926.

—— *Colour in Everyday Rooms: With Remarks on Sundry Aspects of Decoration.* London: Country Life, 1934.

James, Henry. *The Spoils of Poynton.* Harmondsworth: Penguin, 1987 [1897].

James, M.R. *Ghost-Stories of an Antiquary.* London: Edward Arnold, 2nd imp., 1905.

—— *More Ghost-Stories of an Antiquary.* London: Edward Arnold, 1920.

James, William. *The Principles of Psychology*, vol. 1. New York: Henry Holt, 1890.

Jennings, H.J. *Our Homes and How to Beautify Them.* London: Harrison, 1902.

Jerningham, Charles Edward [Marmaduke] and Lewis Bettany. *The Bargain Book.* London: Chatto & Windus, 1911.

Jones, Owen. *On the True and False in the Decorative Arts.* London: Strangeways & Walden, 1863. (Lectures delivered in 1852.)

Kenward, James. *The Suburban Child*. Cambridge: Cambridge University Press, 1955.

Kerr, Robert. *The Gentleman's House: Or, How to Plan English Residences from the Parsonage to the Palace*. London: John Murray, 1871 [1864].

Lancaster, Osbert. *Homes Sweet Homes*. London: John Murray, 1939.

—— *All Done from Memory*. Boston: Houghton Mifflin, 1953.

Leifchild, John. *Memoir of the Late Rev. Joseph Hughes, A.M. One of the Secretaries of the British and Foreign Bible Society*. London: T. Ward, 1835.

Leighton, Clare. *Tempestuous Petticoat: The Story of an Invincible Edwardian*. New York: Rinehart, 1947.

Letts, C. Hubert, ed. *The Hundred Best Pictures for Home Decoration*. London: Charles Letts for William Whiteley, 1901.

Lewis, C.S. *Surprised by Joy*. London: Geoffrey Bles, 1955.

Lewis, Lesley. *The Private Life of a Country House (1912–1939)*. Newton Abbot and London: David & Charles, 1980.

Lewis, Roy and Angus Maude. *The English Middle Classes*. London: Phoenix House, 1949.

Litchfield, Frederick. *How to Collect Old Furniture*. London: Bell, 1904.

—— *Illustrated History of Furniture*. London: Truslove & Hanson, 1922 [1892].

—— *Antiques Genuine and Spurious, An Art Expert's Recollections and Cautions*. London: Bell, 1924 [1921].

Locker-Lampson, Frederick. *My Confidences: An Autobiographical Sketch Addressed to My Descendants*. New York: Charles Scribner's Sons, 1896.

Loftie, Mrs M.J. *The Dining Room*. London, Macmillan, 1876.

—— *Social Twitters*. London: Macmillan, 1879.

Loftie, W.J. *A Plea for Art in the House, With Special Reference to the Economy of Collecting Works of Art, and the Importance of Taste in Education and Morals*. London: Macmillan, 1876.

Loudon, J.C. *An Encyclopaedia of Cottage, Farm, and Villa Architecture*. London: Longman, 1833.

Macqueen-Pope, W. *Twenty Shillings in the Pound*. London: Hutchinson, 1949 [1948].

Marriott Watson, Rosamund. *The Art of the House*. London: George Bell, 1897.

Marsh, Ngaio. *Black Beech and Honeydew*. Auckland: Collins, 1981 [1966].

Marshall, Mary. *What I Remember*. Cambridge: Cambridge University Press, 1947.

Menzies, Amy Charlotte Bewicke. *Memories Discreet and Indiscreet by a Woman of No Importance*. London: Herbert Jenkins, 1917.

Miller, J.R. *Home-Making; or, The Ideal Family Life*. London: Sunday School Union, 1896.

Moberley, R.C. *Atonement and Personality*. New York: Longmans, Green, 1901.

Montizambert, Elizabeth. *London Discoveries in Shops & Restaurants*. London: Women Publishers, 1924.

Morris, Thomas. *A House for the Suburbs.* London: Simpkin, Marshall, 1870.

Morris, William. *The Collected Works of William Morris.* London: Longmans, Green, 24 vols, 1910–15.

Mortimer, Penelope. *About Time: An Aspect of Autobiography.* New York: Doubleday, 1979.

Muthesius, Hermann. *Das englische Haus: Entwicklung, Bedingungen, Anlage, Aufbau, Einrichtung und Innenraum.* Berlin: E. Wasmuth, second edn, 3 vols, 1908–11 [1904].

—— *The English House.* Ed. with an introduction by Dennis Sharp; trans. Janet Seligman. London: Crosby Lockwood Staples, 1979.

Newby, Eric. *A Traveller's Life.* Boston and Toronto: Little, Brown, 1982.

Newman, Thomas Charles. *Many Parts.* London: Hutchinson, 1935.

Nicholas, Thomas. *The Pedigree of the English People.* London: Longmans, Green, Reader, 1868.

Nichols, Beverley. *A Case of Human Bondage.* London: Secker & Warburg, 1966.

Nicholson, Hubert. *Half My Days and Nights: Autobiography of a Reporter.* London: William Heinemann, 1941.

Orrinsmith, Lucy. *The Drawing-Room, its Decorations and Furniture.* London: Macmillan, 1877.

Palmer, Herbert. *The Mistletoe Child: An Autobiography of Childhood.* London: J.M. Dent, 1935.

Panton, Jane Ellen. *Homes of Taste: Economical Hints.* London: Sampson Low, Marston, Searle & Rivington, 1890.

—— *Leaves from a Life.* New York: Brentanos, 1908.

—— *Most of the Game.* London: Eveleigh Nash, 1911.

Parr, Martin and Nicholas Barker. *Signs of the Times: A Portrait of the Nation's Tastes.* Manchester: Cornerhouse Publications, 1992.

Peck, Winifred. *A Little Learning or a Victorian Childhood.* London: Faber & Faber, 1952.

Peel, Mrs C.S. *Life's Enchanted Cup.* London: John Lane, The Bodley Head, 1933.

Pritchett, V.S. *A Cab at the Door: A Memoir.* New York: Random House, 1968 [1967].

Pugin, Augustus W.N. *Contrasts: or a Parallel between the Noble Edifices of the Fourteenth and Fifteenth Centuries and Similar Buildings of the Present Day.* London: C. Dolman, 1841 [1836].

Pym, Dorothy. *Houses as Friends.* London: Jonathan Cape, 1936.

Quennell, C.H.B. and Marjorie Quennell. *A History of Everyday Things in England.* London: B.T. Batsford, 1918–31.

Raverat, Gwen. *Period Piece.* New York: Norton, 1953 [1952].

Rees, Alwyn. *Life in a Welsh Countryside: A Social Study of Llanfihangel yng Ngwynfa.* Cardiff: University of Wales Press, 1951.

Ridge, W. Pett. *Outside the Radius.* New York: Dodd, Mead, 1900 [1899].

Rohan, Thomas. *Confessions of an Antique Dealer.* New York: Frederick A. Stokes, 1925.

—— *Old Beautiful.* London: Mills & Boon, 1926.

—— *In Search of the Antique.* London: Mills & Boon, 1927.

—— *Billy Ditt: The Romance of a Chippendale Chair, 1760–1925.* London: Mills & Boon, 1932.

Ruskin, John. *The Two Paths: Being Lectures on Art and Its Application to Decoration and Manufacture, Delivered in 1858–9.* London: Smith, Elder, 1859.

—— *The Crown of Wild Olive and Sesame and Lilies.* New York: A.L. Burt, 1924.

Russell, George W.E. *Collections and Recollections by One Who Has Kept a Diary.* New York: Harper & Brothers, 1899.

—— *A Londoner's Log-Book, 1901–2.* London: Smith, Elder, 1902.

Russell, Percy. *Leaves from a Journalist's Note-Book.* London: Wyman, 1874.

Sala, George Augustus. *Gaslight and Daylight.* London: Tinsley Brothers, 1872 [1858].

—— *Twice Round the Clock.* New York: Humanities Press, 1971 [1858/9].

Shaw, Donald. *London in the Sixties (With a Few Digressions).* London: Everett, 1909.

Shaw, Henry. *Specimens of Ancient Furniture Drawn from Existing Authorities.* London: Henry G. Bohn, 1866 [1836].

Sheean, Vincent. *Personal History.* New York: Literary Guild, 1934.

Silver, Arnold, ed. *The Family Letters of Samuel Butler, 1841–86.* Stanford: Stanford University Press, 1962.

Sims, George R. *My Life: Sixty Years' Recollections of Bohemian London.* London: Eveleigh Nash, 1917.

Smith, Dodie. *Look Back with Mixed Feelings.* London: W.H. Allen, 1978.

Smyth, Ethel. *Impressions that Remained.* 2 vols. London: Longmans, Green, 1923.

Sparrow, W.S., ed. *The Modern Home: A Book of British Domestic Architecture.* London: Hodder & Stoughton, 1905.

Stirling, A.M.W. *Life's Little Day: Some Tales and Other Reminiscences.* New York: Dodd, Mead, 1924.

—— *Victorian Sidelights: From the Papers of the Late Mrs. Adams-Acton.* London: Ernest Benn, 1954.

Strachey, Lytton. *Queen Victoria.* New York: Harcourt Brace, 1930 [1921].

Taine, Hippolyte. *Notes on England.* Trans. with an introduction by Edward Hyams. London: Caliban Books, 1995 [1860–70].

Tawney, R.H. *The Acquisitive Society.* New York: Harcourt, Brace & Howe, 1920.

Taylor, Isaac., ed. *The Family Pen: Memorials, Biographical and Literary of the Taylor Family of Ongar.* 2 vols. London: Jackson, Walford & Hodder, 1867.

Temple, William. *The Nature of Personality: A Course of Lectures.* London: Macmillan, 1915.

Terriss, Ellaline. *Just a Little Bit of String.* London: Hutchinson, 1955.

Thirkell, Angela. *Three Houses*. London: Oxford University Press, 1931.

Trefusis, Violet. *Don't Look Round*. London: Hutchinson, 1952.

Trevelyan, George Macaulay. *The Life of John Bright*. Boston and New York: Houghton Mifflin, 1913.

Tynan, Katharine. *Twenty-Five Years: Reminiscences*. London: John Murray, 1913.

Vachell, Horace Annesley. *Quinneys': A Comedy in Four Acts*. New York: George Doran Co., 1916.

—— *Quinney's Adventures*. London: John Murray, 1924.

—— *The Homely Art*. London: Shoolbred & Co., 1928.

—— *Quests: The Adventures and Misadventures of a Collector*. London: Seeley Service & Co., 1954.

Veblen, Thorstein. *The Theory of the Leisure Class*. New York: Dover Publications, 1994 [1899].

Vivian, Margaret. *Dr. Jaz: The Adventures of a Woman Doctor*. London: Arthur H. Stockwell, 1933.

—— *Antique Collecting*. London: Isaac Pitman, 1937.

—— *The Doorway*. London: The Psychic Press, 1941.

—— *Do We Survive Death? A Psychic Booklet*. London: Spiritualist Press, 1946.

Walford, Lucy. *Memories of Victorian London*. London: Edward Arnold, 1912.

Walpole, G.H.S. *Personality and Power: Or, The Secret of Real Influence*. Milwaukee, WI: Young Churchman, 1908.

Walsh, J.H. *A Manual of Domestic Economy Suited to Families Spending from £100 to £1000 a year*. London: G. Routledge, 1857.

Ward, Mrs E.M. *Memories of Ninety Years*, ed. Isabel McAllister. London: Hutchinson, 1924.

Ward, Mrs Humphry. *A Writer's Recollections*. London: Collins, 1918.

Wayne, Jennifer. *Growing Up in the Thirties*. London: Victor Gollancz, 1979.

Weber, Max. *The Protestant Ethic and the 'Spirit' of Capitalism*. London: Penguin, 2002 [1905].

Wells, H.G. *Marriage*. London: Macmillan, 1912.

—— *Experiment in Autobiography: Discoveries and Conclusions of a Very Ordinary Brain, vol. II*. London: Faber & Faber, 1984 [1934].

Wey, Francis. *A Frenchman Sees the English in the 'Fifties*. Adapted by Valerie Pirie. London: Sidgwick & Jackson, 1935.

Whitehead, Alfred North. *Dialogues of Alfred North Whitehead*. Boston: Little Brown, 1954.

Wilde, Oscar. *The Complete Works of Oscar Wilde*, ed. and with introductions by Michael Monahan and W.F. Morse. New York: Wm. H. Wise, 1927.

Williamson, G.C. *Murray Marks and His Friends: A Tribute of Regard*. London: John Lane, the Bodley Head, 1919.

Willis, Frederick. *101 Jubilee Road: A Book of London Yesterdays.* London: Phoenix House, 1948.

Wilmott, Peter and Michael Young. *Family and Class in a London Suburb.* London: Routledge & Kegan Paul, 1960.

Wright, Thomas. *The Life of John Payne.* London: T. Fisher Unwin, 1919.

Wylde, Mary. *A Housewife in Kensington.* New York and London: Longmans, Green, 1937.

Yates, Edmund. *His Recollections and Experiences.* London: Richard Bentley, 1884.

——, ed. *Celebrities at Home: Reprinted from 'The World'.* London: Office of 'The World', 1877.

SECONDARY SOURCES

Adburgham, Alison. *Liberty's: A Biography of a Shop.* London: Allen & Unwin, 1975.

Adonis, Andrew and Stephen Pollard. *A Class Act: The Myth of Britain's Classless Society.* London: Hamish Hamilton, 1997.

Alexander, David. *Retailing in England during the Industrial Revolution.* London: Athlone Press, 1970.

Annan, Noel. *Leslie Stephen: The Godless Victorian.* New York: Random House, 1984.

Appadurai, Arjun, ed. *The Social Life of Things: Commodities in Cultural Perspective.* Cambridge: Cambridge University Press, 1986.

Arber, Katie. *Turn of the Century Style: Home Decoration and Furnishings between 1890 and 1910.* London: Middlesex University Press, 2003.

Atterbury, Paul and Clive Wainwright, eds. *Pugin: A Gothic Passion.* New Haven and London: Yale University Press, 1994.

Auerbach, Jeffrey. *The Great Exhibition of 1851: A Nation on Display.* New Haven and London: Yale University Press, 1999.

Auslander, Leora. *Taste and Power: Furnishing Modern France.* Berkeley and Los Angeles: University of California Press, 1996.

Ayres, James. *Domestic Interiors: The British Tradition, 1500–1850.* New Haven and London: Yale University Press, 2003.

Bailkin, Jordanna. *The Culture of Property: The Crisis of Liberalism in Modern Britain.* Chicago: University of Chicago Press, 2004.

Banham, Reyner. *Theory and Design in the First Machine Age.* London: Architectural Press, 1960.

Barnard, Toby. *Making the Grand Figure: Lives and Possessions in Ireland, 1641–1770.* New Haven and London: Yale University Press, 2004.

Barrett, Helena and John Phillips. *Suburban Style: The British Home, 1840–1960.* London: Macdonald, 1987.

Barty-King, Hugh. *Maples: Fine Furnishers: A Household Name for 150 Years.* London: Quiller Press, 1992.

Bayley, Stephen. *Taste: The Secret Meaning of Things*. New York: Pantheon, 1991.

Beetham, Margaret. *A Magazine of Her Own? Domesticity and Desire in the Woman's Magazine, 1800–1914*. London: Routledge, 1996.

Benson, John. *The Rise of Consumer Society in Britain, 1880–1980*. New York: Longman, 1994.

Benson, John and Laura Ugolini, eds. *A Nation of Shopkeepers: Five Centuries of British Retailing*. London: I.B. Tauris, 2003.

Berg, Maxine. *The Age of Manufactures, 1700–1820*. Oxford: Oxford University Press, 1986.

—— *Luxury and Pleasure in Eighteenth-Century Britain*. Oxford: Oxford University Press, 2005.

Berg, Maxine and Helen Clifford, eds. *Consumers and Luxury: Consumer Culture in Europe, 1650–1850*. Manchester: Manchester University Press, 1999.

Berg, Maxine and Elizabeth Eger, eds. *Luxury in the Eighteenth Century: Debates, Desires and Delectable Goods*. London: Macmillan, 2003.

Bermingham, Ann and John Brewer, eds. *The Consumption of Culture, 1600–1800*. London and New York: Routledge, 1995.

Berry, Christopher. *The Idea of Luxury: A Conceptual and Historical Investigation*. Cambridge: Cambridge University Press, 1994.

Binfield, Clyde. *So Down to Prayers: Studies in English Nonconformity, 1780–1920*. London: J.M. Dent, 1977.

Bonython, Elizabeth and Anthony Burton. *The Great Exhibitor: The Life and Work of Henry Cole*. London: V&A Publications, 2003.

Bourdieu, Pierre. *Distinction: A Social Critique of the Judgement of Taste*. Trans. by R. Nice. London: Routledge & Kegan Paul, 1984.

Bradley, Ian. *The Call to Seriousness: The Evangelical Impact on the Victorians*. New York: Macmillan, 1976.

Brawer, Nicholas. *British Campaign Furniture: Elegance under Canvas, 1740–1914*. New York: Harry Abrams, 2001.

Brett, David. *On Decoration*. Cambridge: Lutterworth Press, 1992.

Breward, Christopher. *The Hidden Consumer: Masculinities, Fashion and City Life, 1860–1914*. Manchester: Manchester University Press, 1995.

Brewer, John. *The Pleasures of the Imagination: English Culture in the Eighteenth Century*. New York: Farrar, Straus, Giroux, 1997.

Brewer, John and Roy Porter. *Consumption and the World of Goods*. London and New York: Routledge, 1993.

Briggs, Asa. *Victorian Things*. London: Penguin, 1990 [1988].

Bronner, Simon J., ed. *Consuming Visions: Accumulation and Display of Goods in America, 1880–1920*. New York: W.W. Norton, 1989.

Brown, Callum. *The Death of Christian Britain: Understanding Secularisation, 1800–2000*. London and New York: Routledge, 2001.

Brown, Ford K. *Fathers of the Victorians: The Age of Wilberforce.* Cambridge: Cambridge University Press, 1961.

Burnett, John. *A Social History of Housing, 1815–1985* [rev. edn]. London: Methuen, 1986.

Burton, Anthony. *Vision and Accident: The Story of the Victoria & Albert Museum.* London: V&A Publications, 1999.

Burton, Antoinette. *Dwelling in the Archive: Women Writing House, Home, and History in Late Colonial India.* Oxford: Oxford University Press, 2003.

Bushman, Richard L. *The Refinement of America: Persons, Houses, Cities.* New York: Knopf, 1992.

Calder, Jenni. *The Victorian Home.* London: Batsford, 1977.

Calloway, Stephen. *Twentieth-Century Decoration: The Domestic Interior from 1900 to the Present Day.* London: Weidenfeld & Nicolson, 1988.

Campbell, Colin. *The Romantic Ethic and the Spirit of Modern Consumerism.* Oxford: Basil Blackwell, 1987.

Chambers, James. *The English House.* London and New York: W.W. Norton, 1985.

Chapman, Tony and Jenny Hockey, eds. *Ideal Homes? Social Change and the Experience of the Home.* London and New York: Routledge, 1999.

Collini, Stefan. *Public Moralists: Political Thought and Intellectual Life in Britain, 1850–1930.* Oxford: Clarendon Press, 1991.

Conrad, Peter. *The Victorian Treasure House.* London: Collins, 1973.

Cooper, Nicholas. *The Opulent Eye: Late Victorian and Edwardian Taste in Interior Design.* London: Architectural Press, 1977.

Cornforth, John. *English Interiors, 1790–1848: The Quest for Comfort.* London: Barrie & Jenkins, 1978.

Cox, Nancy. *The Complete Tradesman: A Study of Retailing, 1550–1820.* Aldershot: Ashgate, 2000.

Crawford, Elizabeth. *Enterprising Women: The Garretts and their Circle.* London: Francis Boutle Publishers, 2002.

Crook, J. Mordaunt. *The Rise of the Nouveaux Riches: Style and Status in Victorian and Edwardian Architecture.* London: John Murray, 1999.

Crossick, Geoffrey, ed. *The Lower Middle Class in Britain, 1870–1914.* New York: St Martin's Press, 1977.

Crossick, Geoffrey and Serge Jaumain, eds. *Cathedrals of Consumption: The European Department Store, 1850–1939.* Aldershot: Ashgate Press, 1999.

Crowley, John. *The Invention of Comfort: Sensibilities and Design in Early Modern Britain and Early America.* Baltimore: Johns Hopkins University Press, 2001.

Czikszentmihalyi, Mihaly and Eugene Rochberg-Halton. *The Meaning of Things: Domestic Symbols and the Self.* Cambridge: Cambridge University Press, 1981.

Dakers, Caroline. *The Holland Park Circle: Artists and Victorian Society.* New Haven and London: Yale University Press, 1999.

Dale, Tim. *Harrods: the Store and the Legend*. London: Pan Original, 1981.

Daunton, Martin. *House and Home in the Victorian City: Working-Class Housing, 1850–1914*. London: Edward Arnold, 1983.

Daunton, Martin and Bernhard Rieger, eds. *Meanings of Modernity: Britain from the Late Victorian Era to World War II*. Oxford and New York: Berg, 2001.

Davidoff, Leonore and Catherine Hall. *Family Fortunes: Men and Women of the English Middle Class, 1780–1850*. London: Hutchinson, second edn 2002 [1987].

DeGrazia, Victoria. *Irresistible Empire: America's Advance through Twentieth-Century Europe*. Cambridge, MA: Harvard University Press, 2005.

DeGrazia, Victoria and Ellen Furlough, eds. *The Sex of Things: Gender and Consumption in Historical Perspective*. Berkeley and Los Angeles: University of California Press, 1996.

Dellamora, Richard. *Masculine Desire: The Sexual Politics of Victorian Aestheticism*. Chapel Hill: University of North Carolina Press, 1990.

Denvir, Bernard. *The Late Victorians: Art, Design and Society, 1852–1910*. London: Longman, 1986.

Dickerson, Vanessa, ed. *Keeping the Victorian House*. New York: Garland, 1995.

Douglas, Mary Tew and Baron Isherwood. *The World of Goods*. New York: Basic Books, 1979.

Dutton, Ralph. *The Victorian Home*. London: Bracken Books, 1984 [1954].

Edwards, Clive. *Victorian Furniture: Technology and Design*. Manchester: Manchester University Press, 1993.

—— *Twentieth-Century Furniture: Materials, Manufacture, and Markets*. Manchester: Manchester University Press, 1994.

Fine, Ben. *The World of Consumption: The Material and Cultural Revisited*. London and New York: Routledge, 2002, second edn.

Finn, Margot. *The Character of Credit: Personal Debt in English Culture, 1740–1914*. Cambridge: Cambridge University Press, 2003.

Flanders, Judith. *The Victorian House: Domestic Life from Childbirth to Deathbed*. London: HarperCollins, 2003.

Forster, E.M. *Marianne Thornton: A Domestic Biography, 1797–1887*. New York: Harcourt, Brace, 1956.

Forty, Adrian. *Objects of Desire: Design and Society, 1750–1980*. New York: Pantheon Books, 1986.

Fox, Kate. *Watching the English: The Hidden Rules of English Behaviour*. London: Hodder & Stoughton, 2004.

Fraser, W. Hamish. *The Coming of the Mass Market, 1850–1914*. Hamden, CT: Archon Books, 1981.

Fuss, Diana. *The Sense of an Interior: Four Rooms and the Writers that Shaped Them*. London: Taylor & Francis, 2004.

Gagnier, Regenia. *Idylls of the Marketplace: Oscar Wilde and the Victorian Public.* Stanford: Stanford University Press, 1986.

—— *The Insatiability of Human Wants: Economics and Aesthetics in Market Society.* Chicago: University of Chicago Press, 2000.

Garfield, Simon. *Mauve: How One Man Invented a Color that Changed the World.* London: Faber and Faber, 2000.

Gere, Charlotte. *Nineteenth-Century Decoration: The Art of the Interior.* London: Weidenfeld & Nicolson, 1989.

Gere, Charlotte with Lesley Hoskins. *The House Beautiful: Oscar Wilde and the Aesthetic Interior.* London: Lund Humphries, 2000.

Gigante, Denise. *Taste: A Literary History.* New Haven and London: Yale University Press, 2005.

Girouard, Mark. *Sweetness and Light: The 'Queen Anne' Movement, 1860–1900.* New Haven: Yale University Press, 1977.

Gloag, John. *Victorian Comfort: A Social History of Design, 1830–1900.* New York: St Martin's Press, 1973 [1961].

Goldthorpe, John. *Social Mobility and Class Structure in Modern Britain.* Oxford: Clarendon Press, 1987 [1980].

Goodden, Susanna. *At the Sign of the Fourposter, A History of Heal's.* London: Lund Humphries, 1984.

Gore, Alan and Ann Gore. *The History of English Interiors.* London: Phaidon, 1991.

Gow, Ian. *The Scottish Interior: Georgian and Victorian Décor.* Edinburgh: Edinburgh University Press, 1992.

Gregson, Nicky and Louise Crewe. *Second-Hand Cultures.* Oxford and New York: Berg, 2003.

Grier, Katherine. *Culture and Comfort: Parlor-Making and Middle-Class Identity.* Washington: Smithsonian Institute Press, 1997.

Guillery, Peter. *The Small House in Eighteenth-Century London.* New Haven and London: Yale University Press, 2004.

Gunn, Simon. *The Public Culture of the Victorian Middle Class: Ritual and Authority and the English Industrial City, 1840–1914.* Manchester: Manchester University Press, 2000.

Günther, Sonja. *Das deutsche Heim: Luxusinterieurs und Arbeitermöbel von der Gründerzeit bis zum '3. Reich'.* Berlin: Werkbund Archiv, 1984.

Hamlett, Jane. 'Materialising Gender: Identity and Middle-Class Domestic Interiors, 1850–1910'. Unpublished Ph.D. thesis, Royal Holloway College, 2005.

Hardyment, Christina. *Home Comfort: A History of Domestic Arrangements.* London: Viking, 1992.

Harvey, Charles and Jon Press. *William Morris: Design and Enterprise in Victorian Britain.* Manchester: Manchester University Press, 1991.

Harvey, John. *The Art of Piety: The Visual Culture of Welsh Nonconformity.* Cardiff: University of Wales Press, 1995.

Haupt, Heinz-Gerhard. *Konsum und Handel: Europa im 19. und 20. Jahrhundert.* Göttingen: Vandenhoeck & Ruprecht, 2002.

Hilton, Boyd. *The Age of Atonement.* Oxford: Clarendon Press, 1986.

Hilton, Matthew. *Consumerism in Twentieth-Century Britain: The Search for a Historical Movement.* Cambridge: Cambridge University Press, 2003.

Hobhouse, Hermione. *The Crystal Palace and the Great Exhibition: Art, Science and Productive Industry.* London: Athlone Press, 2002.

Holcombe, Lee. *Wives and Property: Reform of the Married Women's Property Law in Nineteenth-Century England.* Toronto: University of Toronto Press, 1983.

Hont, Istvan and Michael Ignatieff. *Wealth and Virtue: The Shaping of Political Economy in the Scottish Enlightenment.* Cambridge: Cambridge University Press, 1983.

Horowitz, Daniel. *The Morality of Spending: Attitudes towards the Consumer Society in America, 1875–1940.* Chicago: Ivan R. Dee, 1985.

Howe, Bea. *Arbiter of Elegance.* London: Harvill Press, 1967.

Hughes, Kathryn. *The Short Life and Long Times of Mrs. Beeton.* London: Fourth Estate, 2005.

Hylson-Smith, Kenneth. *Evangelicals in the Church of England, 1734–1984.* Edinburgh: T. & T. Clark, 1988.

Jackson, Alan. *Semi-Detached London: Suburban Development, Life and Transport 1900–39.* Didcot: Wild Swan, 1991 [1973].

Jeremiah, David. *Architecture and Design for the Family in Britain, 1900–70.* Manchester: Manchester University Press, 2000.

Kaplan, Wendy. *Designing Modernity: The Arts of Reform and Persuasion, 1885–1945.* London: Thames & Hudson, 1995.

Kern, Stephen. *The Culture of Time and Space, 1880–1918.* Cambridge, MA: Harvard University Press, 1983.

Kidd, Alan and David Nicholls, eds. *Gender, Civic Culture and Consumerism: Middle-Class Identity in Britain, 1800–1940.* Manchester: Manchester University Press, 1999.

King, Lyndel Saunders. *The Industrialization of Taste: Victorian England and the Art Union of London.* Ann Arbor: UMI Research Press, 1985.

Kingsmill, Hugh. *After Puritanism.* London: Duckworth, 1929.

Kirkham, Pat. *The London Furniture Trade, 1700–1870.* Leeds: Furniture History Society, 1988.

—— Rodney Mace and Julia Porter. *Furnishing the World: The East London Furniture Trade, 1830–1980.* London: Journeyman, 1987.

Klein, Lawrence E. *Shaftesbury and the Culture of Politeness: Moral Discourse and*

Cultural Politics in Early Eighteenth-Century England. Cambridge: Cambridge University Press, 1994.

Kocka, Jürgen and Allen Mitchell. *Bourgeois Society in Nineteenth-Century Europe.* Oxford and Providence: Berg, 1993.

Koven, Seth. *Slumming: Sexual and Social Politics in Victorian London.* Princeton: Princeton University Press, 2004.

Kreider, Alan and Jane Shaw, eds. *Culture and the Nonconformist Tradition.* Cardiff: University of Wales Press, 1999.

Kuchta, David. *The Three-Piece Suit and Modern Masculinity: England, 1550–1850.* Berkeley and Los Angeles: University of California Press, 2002.

Kwint, Marius, Christopher Breward and Jeremy Aynsley, eds. *Material Memories.* Oxford: Berg, 1999.

Lambourne, Lionel. *The Aesthetic Movement.* London: Phaidon, 1996.

Lancaster, Bill. *The Department Store: A Social History.* London and New York: Leicester University Press, 1995.

Larsen, Timothy. *Contested Christianity: The Political and Social Contexts of Victorian Theology.* Waco, TX: Baylor University Press, 2004.

Lasdun, Susan. *Victorians at Home.* New York: Viking, 1981.

Lears, T. Jackson. *The Culture of Consumption: Critical Essays in American History, 1880–1980.* New York: Pantheon, 1983.

——*Fables of Abundance: A Cultural History of Advertising in America.* New York: Basic Books, 1994.

Levine, Philippa. *The Amateur and the Professional: Antiquarians, Historians, Archaeologists in Victorian England, 1838–1886.* Cambridge: Cambridge University Press, 1986.

Lewis, Brian. *The Middlemost and the Milltowns: Bourgeois Culture and Politics in Early Industrial England.* Stanford: Stanford University Press, 2001.

Light, Alison. *Forever England: Femininity, Literature and Conservatism between the Wars.* London and New York: Routledge, 1991.

Loeb, Lori. *Consuming Angels: Advertising and Victorian Women.* New York and Oxford: Oxford University Press, 1994.

Logan, Thad. *The Victorian Parlour.* Cambridge: Cambridge University Press, 2001.

Long, Helen. *The Edwardian House: The Middle-Class Home in Britain, 1880–1914.* Manchester: Manchester University Press, 1993.

Lubbock, Jules. *The Tyranny of Taste: The Politics of Architecture and Design in Britain, 1550–1960.* New Haven and London: Yale University Press, 1995.

Macarthy, Fiona. *A History of British Design, 1830–1979.* London: Allen & Unwin, 1979.

McKellar, Susie and Penny Sparke, eds. *Interior Design and Identity.* London: Palgrave Macmillan, 2004.

McKendrick, Neil, John Brewer and J.H. Plumb. *The Birth of a Consumer Society: The Commercialization of Eighteenth-Century England.* Bloomington: Indiana University Press, 1982.

Mackenzie, John, ed. *The Victorian Vision: Inventing New Britain.* New York: Harry Abrams, 2001.

McKibbin, Ross. *Classes and Cultures, England 1918–1951.* Oxford: Oxford University Press, 1998.

Macleod, Dianne Sachko. *Art and the Victorian Middle Class: Money and the Making of Cultural Identity.* Cambridge: Cambridge University Press, 1996.

McLeod, Hugh. *Religion and Society in England, 1850–1914.* New York: St Martin's Press, 1996.

Malchow, H.L. *Gentlemen Capitalists: The Social and Political World of the Victorian Businessman.* Stanford: Stanford University Press, 1992.

Mandler, Peter. *The Fall and Rise of the Stately Home.* New Haven and London: Yale University Press, 1997.

Marcus, Sharon. *Apartment Stories: City and Home in Nineteenth-Century Paris and London.* Berkeley and Los Angeles: University of California Press, 1999.

Mascuch, Michael. *Origins of the Individualist Self: Autobiography and Self Identity in England, 1591–1791.* Stanford: Stanford University Press, 1996.

Meacham, Standish. *Regaining Paradise: Englishness and the Early Garden City Movement.* New Haven and London: Yale University Press, 1998.

Miles, Andrew and David Vincent, eds. *Building European Society: Occupational Change and Social Mobility in Europe, 1840–1940.* Manchester: Manchester University Press, 1993.

Miller, Daniel. *The Dialectics of Shopping.* Chicago and London: University of Chicago Press, 2001.

—— ed. *Acknowledging Consumption: A Review of New Studies.* London and New York: Routledge, 1995.

Minihan, Janet. *The Nationalization of Culture: The Development of State Subsidies to the Arts in Great Britain.* New York: New York University Press, 1977.

Mintz, Steven. *A Prison of Expectations: The Family in Victorian Culture.* New York: New York University Press, 1983.

Morgan, Marjorie. *Manners, Morals and Class in England, 1744–1858.* New York: St Martin's Press, 1994.

Morley, John. *The History of Furniture.* Boston and London: Little, Brown, 1999.

Morris, R.J. *Class, Sect and Party: The Making of the British Middle Class.* Manchester: Manchester University Press, 1990.

—— *Men, Women and Property in England, 1780–1870.* Cambridge: Cambridge University Press, 2005.

——, ed. *Class, Power and Social Structure in British Nineteenth-Century Towns.* Leicester: Leicester University Press, 1986.

Morrison, Kathryn A. *English Shops and Shopping: An Architectural History*. New Haven and London: Yale University Press, 2003.

Mort, Frank. *Cultures of Consumption: Masculinity and Social Space in Late-Twentieth-Century Britain*. London: Routledge, 1996.

Mukerji, Chandra. *From Graven Images: Patterns of Modern Materialism*. New York: Columbia University Press, 1983.

Muthesius, Stefan. *The English Terraced House*. New Haven and London: Yale University Press, 1982.

Naylor, Gillian. *The Arts and Crafts Movement*. Cambridge, MA: MIT Press, 1971.

Oliver, Paul, Ian Davis, and Ian Bentley. *Dunroamin: The Suburban Semi and Its Enemies*. London: Barrie & Jenkins, 1981.

Owen, Alex. *The Place of Enchantment: British Occultism and the Culture of the Modern*. Chicago and London: University of Chicago Press, 2004.

Pearsall, Ronald and Graham Webb. *Inside the Antique Trade*. Shaldon, Devon: Keith Reid, 1974.

Pevsner, Nikolaus. *Pioneers of Modern Design from William Morris to Walter Gropius*. New York: Simon & Schuster, 1949, second edn [1936].

—— *High Victorian Design: A Study of the Exhibits of 1851*. London: Architectural Press, 1951.

Purbrick, Louise, ed. *The Great Exhibition of 1851: New Interdisciplinary Essays*. Manchester: Manchester University Press, 2001.

Rappaport, Erika. *Shopping for Pleasure: Women in the Making of London's West End*. Princeton: Princeton University Press, 2000.

Reed, Christopher. *Bloomsbury Rooms: Modernism, Subculture, and Domesticity*. New Haven and London: Yale University Press, 2004.

——, ed. *Not At Home: The Suppression of Domesticity in Modern Art and Architecture*. New York: Thames & Hudson, 1996.

Reid, Hew. *The Furniture Makers: A History of Trade Unionism in the Furniture Trade, 1865–1972*. Oxford: Malthouse Press, 1986.

Richards, Thomas. *The Commodity Culture of Victorian England: Advertising and Spectacle, 1851–1914*. Stanford: Stanford University Press, 1990.

Roe, F. Gordon. *Victorian Corners: The Style and Taste of an Era*. New York: Praeger, 1968.

Rose, Nikolas. *The Psychological Complex: Psychology, Politics and Society in England, 1869–1939*. London: Routledge & Kegan Paul, 1985.

—— *Governing the Soul: The Shaping of the Private Self*. London: Routledge, 1990.

Rosman, Doreen. *Evangelicals and Culture*. London: Croom Helm, 1984.

Rubinstein, W.D. *Men of Property: The Very Wealthy in Britain since the Industrial Revolution*. New Brunswick: Rutgers University Press, 1981.

Ryan, Deborah. *The Ideal Home through the 20th Century*. London: Hazar Publishing, 1997.

Saisselin, Rémy. *The Bourgeois and the Bibelot.* New Brunswick: Rutgers University Press, 1984.

Saler, Michael. *The Avant-Garde in Interwar England: Medieval Modernism and the London Underground.* New York and Oxford: Oxford University Press, 1999.

Saumarez Smith, Charles. *Eighteenth-Century Decoration: Design and the Domestic Interior in England.* New York: H.N. Abrams, 1993.

Saunders, Peter. *A Nation of Home Owners.* London: Unwin Hyman, 1990.

Saunders King, Lyndel. *The Industrialization of Taste.* Ann Arbor: UMI Research Press, 1985.

Savage, Mike, James Barlow, Peter Dickens and Tony Fielding. *Property, Bureaucracy and Culture: Middle-Class Formation in Contemporary Britain.* London and New York: Routledge, 1992.

Schaffer, Talia. *The Forgotten Female Aesthetes.* Charlottesville, VA and London: University Press of Virginia, 2000.

Searle, G.R. *Morality and the Market in Victorian Britain.* Oxford: Clarendon Press, 1998.

Seigel, Jerrold. *The Idea of the Self: Thought and Experience in Western Europe since the Seventeenth Century.* Cambridge: Cambridge University Press, 2005.

Shammas, Carole. *The Pre-Industrial Consumer in England and America.* Oxford: Oxford University Press, 1990.

Shonfield, Zusanna. *The Precariously Privileged: A Professional Family in Victorian London.* Oxford: Oxford University Press, 1987.

Silverman, Debora. *Art Nouveau in Fin-de-Siècle France: Politics, Psychology and Style.* Berkeley and Los Angeles: University of California Press, 1996.

Snodin, Michael and John Styles, eds. *Design and the Decorative Arts, Britain 1500–1900.* London: V&A Publications, 2001.

Soros, Susan Weber. *The Secular Furniture of E.W. Godwin.* New Haven and London: Yale University Press, 1999.

—— ed. *E.W. Godwin: Aesthetic Movement Architect and Designer.* New Haven and London: Yale University Press, 1999.

Sparke, Penny. *As Long as It's Pink: The Sexual Politics of Taste.* London: HarperCollins, 1995.

—— *Elsie de Wolfe: The Birth of Modern Interior Decoration.* New York: Acanthus Press, 2005.

Stansky, Peter. *Redesigning the World: William Morris, the 1880s and the Arts and Crafts.* Princeton: Princeton University Press, 1985.

Staves, Susan. *Married Women's Separate Property in England, 1660–1833.* Cambridge, MA: Harvard University Press, 1990.

Steedman, Carolyn. *Strange Dislocations: Childhood and the Idea of Human Interiority, 1780–1930.* Cambridge, MA: Harvard University Press, 1995.

Steegman, John. *Victorian Taste: A Study of the Arts and Architecture from 1830 to 1870*. London: Nelson's University Paperbacks, 1970 [1950].

Stone, Lawrence and Jeanne C. Fawtier Stone. *An Open Elite? England, 1540–1880*. Oxford: Clarendon Press, 1984.

Sugden, Alan Victor and John Ludlam Edmondson. *A History of English Wallpaper, 1509–1914*. London: B.T. Batsford, 1925.

Susman, Warren. *Culture as History: The Transformation of American Society in the Twentieth Century*. New York: Pantheon, 1984.

Swift, David E. *Joseph John Gurney: Banker, Reformer and Quaker*. Middletown, CT: Wesleyan University Press, 1962.

Taylor, Charles. *Sources of the Self: The Making of the Modern Identity*. Cambridge, MA: Harvard University Press, 1989.

Thornton, Peter. *Authentic Décor: The Domestic Interior 1620–1920*. London: Weidenfeld & Nicolson, 1984.

Tiersten, Lisa. *Marianne in the Market: Envisioning Consumer Society in Fin-de-Siècle France*. Berkeley and Los Angeles: University of California Press, 2001.

Tillyard, Stella. *The Impact of Modernism, 1900–1920: Early Modernism and the Arts and Crafts Movement in Edwardian England*. London: Routledge, 1988.

—— *Aristocrats*. New York: Farrar, Straus, Giroux, 1994.

Tolley, Christopher. *Domestic Biography: The Legacy of Evangelicalism in Four Nineteenth-Century Families*. Oxford: Clarendon Press, 1997.

Tosh, John. *A Man's Place: Masculinity and the Middle-Class Home in Victorian England*. New Haven and London: Yale University Press, 1999.

Troy, Nancy. *Modernism and the Decorative Arts in France: Art Nouveau to Le Corbusier*. New Haven: Yale University Press, 1991.

Vickery, Amanda. *The Gentleman's Daughter: Women's Lives in Georgian England*. New Haven and London: Yale University Press, 1998.

Wahrman, Dror. *Imagining the Middle Class: The Political Representation of Class in Britain, 1780–1840*. Cambridge: Cambridge University Press, 1995.

—— *The Making of the Modern Self: Identity and Culture in Eighteenth-Century England*. New Haven and London: Yale University Press, 2004.

Wainwright, Clive. *The Romantic Interior. The British Collector at Home, 1750–1850*. New Haven: Yale University Press, 1989.

Walkley, Giles. *Artists' Houses in London, 1764–1914*. Brookfield, VT: Ashgate Publishing, 1994.

Walton, Whitney. *France at the Crystal Palace: Bourgeois Taste and Artisan Manufacture in the Nineteenth Century*. Berkeley and Los Angeles: University of California Press, 1992.

Watts, Michael R. *The Dissenters: The Expansion of Evangelical Nonconformity*. Oxford: Clarendon Press, 1995.

Weatherill, Lorna. *Consumer Behaviour and Material Culture in Britain, 1660–1760.* London and New York: Routledge, 1988.

Williams, Raymond. *Keywords.* New York: Oxford University Press, 1976.

Williams, Rosalind. *Dream Worlds: Mass Communication in Late Nineteenth-Century France.* Berkeley and Los Angeles: University of California Press, 1982.

Winstanley, Michael J. *The Shopkeeper's World, 1830–1914.* Manchester: Manchester University Press, 1983.

Wolff, Janet and John Seed. *The Culture of Capital: Art, Power and the Nineteenth-Century Middle Class.* Manchester: Manchester University Press, 1988.

Wright, Gwendolyn. *Moralism and the Model Home: Domestic Architecture and Cultural Conflict in Chicago, 1873–1913.* Chicago: University of Chicago Press, 1980.

Wright, Patrick. *On Living in an Old Country: The National Past in Contemporary Britain.* London: Verso, 1985.

Wrightson, Keith. *Earthly Necessities: Economic Lives in Early Modern Britain.* New Haven and London: Yale University Press, 2000.

Young, Linda. *Middle-Class Culture in the Nineteenth Century: America, Australia and Britain.* London: Palgrave Macmillan, 2003.

INDEX

Page references in italics indicate illustrations.

ILLUSTRATION CREDITS